VIVA - FACTS ON FILE

# GUIDE TO GOOD WRITING

D-9

VIVA - FACTS ON FILE

# GUIDE TO GOOD WRITING

**MARTIN H. MANSER**

DAVID H. PICKERING AND STEPHEN CURTIS
Associate Editors

Viva Books

New Delhi | Mumbai | Chennai | Kolkata | Bangalore | Hyderabad | Kochi | Guwahati

**First Indian Edition 2007**
**Reprinted 2010**

**VIVA BOOKS PRIVATE LIMITED**

- 4737/23 Ansari Road, Daryaganj, New Delhi 110 002
  E-mail: vivadelhi@vivagroupindia.net, Tel. 42242200
- 76, Service Industries, Shirvane, Sector 1, Nerul, Navi Mumbai 400 706
  E-mail: vivamumbai@vivagroupindia.net, Tel. 27721273, 27721274
- Jamals Fazal Chambers, 26 Greams Road, Chennai 600 006
  E-mail: vivachennai@vivagroupindia.net, Tel. 28290304, 28294241
- B-103, Jindal Towers, 21/1A/3 Darga Road, Kolkata 700 017
  E-mail: vivakolkata@vivagroupindia.net, Tel. 22836381, 22816713
- 7, Sovereign Park Apartments, 56-58, K. R. Road, Basavanagudi, Bangalore 560 004
  E-mail: vivabangalore@vivagroupindia.net, Tel. 26607409, 26607410
- 101-102 Mughal Marc Apartments, 3-4-637 to 641, Narayanguda, Hyderabad 500 029
  E-mail: vivahyderabad@vivagroupindia.net, Tel. 27564481, 27564482
- Beevi Towers, First Floor, SRM Road, Kaloor, Kochi 682 018, Kerala
  E-mail: vivakochi@vivagroupindia.net, Tel: 0484-2403055, 2403056
- 232, GNB Road, Beside UCO Bank, Silpukhuri, Guwahati 781 003
  E-mail: vivaguwahati@vivagroupindia.net, Tel: 0361-2666386

***www.vivagroupindia.com***

*Published by arrangement with*

Facts on File, Inc.
132 West 31st Street
New York 10001
USA



ISBN: 978-81-309-1514-2

Published by Vinod Vasishtha for Viva Books Private Limited, 4737/23, Ansari Road, Daryaganj, New Delhi-110 002. Printed and bound by Anand Sons, Delhi - 110092.

# CONTENTS

## PART II WRITING FUNDAMENTALS

# INTRODUCTION

Everywhere in the modern world the emphasis is on speed, and nowhere have things moved faster than in communications. Messages travel at the speed of light, and we humans seem to feel that we have to imitate the wonderful machines that flash our words around the globe in fractions of a second. We have become a race of scribblers, jotting memos, punching in text messages, rushing off e-mails, and dashing off quick "Happy Birthday" or "Thank You" cards, often not worrying much whether what we write gets our message across or even makes sense. Fewer and fewer of us, it seems, take the time to write properly. Fewer and fewer of us perhaps *know* how to write properly. Fashions in the teaching of English have changed over the years, and we can easily find that we have finished our education but have never grasped the principles of correct English. Then the day comes when we have to write an important letter, prepare a speech or presentation, or hand in an essay or assignment, and suddenly we are at a loss.

Are you unsure about how to write good, clear English? If you are, this book has been specifically designed to help you. It comes in two major sections: Chapters 1 to 3, of Part I, deal with the writing process itself; chapters 4 to 9, which make up Part II, deal with grammar, spelling, usage, and punctuation. Some writing manuals begin with grammar and then move on to discuss writing. The authors of this book believe, however, that it is better to get something down on paper in draft form first and to polish up the grammar afterward, hence the placement of the "Preparing to Write," "Writing Your Document," and "Revising Your Document" chapters at the beginning. These chapters treat writing as a task that can be divided into manageable parts: thinking, researching, and planning; writing; and revising. Each of these activities is explained in detail with the help of examples.

In order to write good English, however, we also need to be aware of the rules that govern the use of words and the construction of sentences. The later chapters therefore contain a review of grammar, a discussion of how words are formed and used in practice, advice on sensitive language issues, a list of words that are often confused ("Is it *continual* or *continuous*?"), and a guide to punctuation ("Where do I put a comma?"). The book concludes with information about additional reference tools to help with problems of grammar and vocabulary and a glossary of grammatical terms.

There are two ways of finding what you need within the pages of this book. If you want help with a general topic (for example, planning, summarizing, verbs, spelling, or commas), you can find your way to the relevant section either through the Table of Contents or the Index. If you are unsure about how to use a particular word, for example, whether you should use *affect* or *effect,* then you can look up either of these words in the Index, where you will be directed to the page where the usage of the word or words in question is discussed.

So, if you are faced with a particular task, such as writing a formal letter, a report, or an assignment, then you will find help here. If you need to develop your understanding of the basic rules of English grammar, punctuation, spelling, or usage, all the information and guidance you need is provided. The authors hope that you will find this book a useful, practical—and at times perhaps even inspiring—guide to writing good English.

Martin H. Manser
David H. Pickering
Stephen Curtis

*Part I*

# THE WRITING PROCESS

# INTRODUCTION

The purpose of this section is to guide you through the process of producing a written document that will say what you want it to say and achieve the purpose that you want it to achieve.

This book starts from the assumption that writing belongs in the category of basic tasks—that it is on a similar level to, say, cooking or driving. Just as most people ought to be able to drive a car or cook an egg, because ordinary living is a lot more complicated if they cannot perform these simple tasks for themselves, so most people ought to take the time to acquire the rudiments of writing. There are, of course, people who are born with a natural talent for writing and people who write for a living. When we call someone "a writer," we usually mean that he or she is a journalist or an author. But there are a great many people, too, who are natural-born cooks or who earn their daily bread baking bread for others, and there are just as many who support their families by driving trucks, limousines, or even racing cars. The existence of experts and professionals does not exempt the rest of us from learning the basic skills that they have developed to a particularly high degree. This is as true of writing as it is of any similar activity. Writing skills can be learned. There are well-established procedures that can be followed when you are preparing or composing a document. This part of the book will familiarize you with those skills and procedures and help you to undertake this basic process with more than merely basic equipment.

When we analyze any process from beginning to end, breaking it down into its different stages and discussing each of those stages in some detail, the analysis is likely to make the process seem more extended and elaborate than it generally is in real life. That does not mean that the process is in itself especially complicated, mysterious, or intimidating. Explaining even the most basic task usually takes longer than actually performing it.

Furthermore, not all the procedures outlined in the following pages will be relevant to every writing task you face. Common sense will tell you—if the clock and your schedule do not—how much time and effort you should expend on a particular writing task. Common sense will likewise tell you which procedures are relevant to even the most minor compositional duties and which will be most useful to you personally. Your own habits, strengths, and weaknesses will probably make you want to concentrate on some aspects of the writing process more than others. Everything dealt with in this section of the book, however, is worth looking into for the day when you are suddenly confronted with the job of composing that vital letter, report, or assignment that presents far more of a challenge to your authorial know-how than an everyday memo or set of notes. It is worth considering the writing process as a whole, in case you can pick up any tips that will lighten your particular burden, or in case something stated here points out a bad writing habit that could be replaced by a better one.

If the talk of tasks and burdens suggests that writing is all labor and no reward, then let it be said that there is as much satisfaction and pleasure to be gained from writing as from the exercise of any other skill. Cooks who produce perfect omelets or drivers who take hairpin turns smoothly and without unnerving their passengers have a right to feel pleased with themselves. So do people who write well. And their efforts are just as likely to be appreciated.

## THE FOUR STAGES OF THE WRITING PROCESS

The task of writing is like many other tasks: What we tend to think of as the whole is in fact only a part. Just as building a wall involves more than laying bricks in rows and cementing them together with mortar, so writing involves more than filling a screen or a sheet of paper with words. That is the main part, the crucial part, perhaps, but we neglect the other parts at our peril.

As with so many other jobs, the before and the after in writing are as important as the central act. An old saying states that composition is 10 percent inspiration and 90 percent perspiration. This is distressingly true, but there are more useful and relevant ways of working out the percentages. The average writing task can be broken down roughly as follows: 50 percent preparation, 25 percent creation, and 25 percent revision. On that basis, we may even have to change our view of what constitutes the main part of the task.

However small the job, time spent thinking, planning, and researching before you sit down at your desk to begin your text is anything but wasted time. The better prepared you are, the easier it will be to find the right words to put across your point. This is an obvious fact, but so often disregarded. Likewise, when you write "The end" for the first time or come to the point where you would normally add your signature, the task is still not finished. Since Greek and Roman times, experienced creative writers have urged their disciples to "polish"—that is, to revise and perfect—everything they write. "*Polissez-le sans cesse, et le repolissez,*" said the French classical poet Nicolas Boileau. We might freely translate his advice as "Polish your work nonstop, and then sit right down and polish it again." Even if you are not aiming at classical perfection, you will need to look over your work carefully and revise it. Word-processing spell-check programs only check your spelling; they do not edit your work. They cannot tell you that your work would benefit from a little shortening here and a little filling out there. If you can persuade a candid (and literate) friend to look over what you have written, so much the better, because fresh eyes often spot what familiarized eyes slide over. But even if you have such a friend, and he or she has time available, the final responsibility is yours. It would be a pity if the 75 percent (of preparation and creation) were spoiled because you omitted to pay sufficient attention to the final 25 percent (revision).

In a nutshell, then, the four stages of the writing process are

- Thinking and researching
- Planning

- Writing
- Revising

These four stages do not always separate so neatly in practice. While you are thinking, researching, or planning, a way of formulating a point may occur to you, and instead of writing a note, you may find yourself writing a paragraph that you will incorporate, unchanged, into your final version. Many people revise as they go along or find that they have to get a particular section just right before they can continue confidently with the rest of a piece of work. Some people are terrified by a blank screen or a blank piece of paper and have to be fully prepared before they can make the first stroke. Other people are deterred not by the blankness of a screen or paper but by a mental blankness that afflicts them if they try to think about a task in the abstract. Such people may need to start writing before they can start thinking. Common sense and experience will soon show you what works best for you. There is no substitute, in the end, for learning by doing. This book calls itself a *Guide to Good Writing*, and you should use this section as a guide rather than as an inflexible set of rules.

The order presented above, however, is the logical order—the order in which an organized person would set about the task. And the more organized you are, the better, especially if you are facing a deadline. Allow yourself as much time as you can, and divide the time you have appropriately, remembering especially to leave yourself sufficient time to revise and correct your work at the end. In the next three chapters, we will look at these four stages in more detail.

# 1

# Preparing to Write

## THINKING AND RESEARCHING

The writing process starts in your head. It may seem a little pedantic to elevate thinking into a separate stage of the process, but how can you start writing until you know what you want to write? Besides, the great advantage of writing as a means of communication is that you have time to consider carefully what you are going to communicate. When you communicate in conversation, generally speaking, you have to make things up as you go along. There are several disadvantages to writing something as opposed to saying it, and we shall consider these later, but one distinct advantage is you do not have to put down on paper the first thing that comes to mind. Use that advantage. Remember also that the first virtue in writing of any kind is clarity. Clear writing comes first and foremost from clear thinking.

### Thinking

There are three questions that you have to think about. You must answer these for yourself before you go any further.

- What kind of document am I writing?
- What am I writing about?
- Whom am I writing to or for?

The nature of the piece of work you have in hand—school assignment, letter, report—will affect the way you style what you write. The status of the reader you have in mind—instructor, friend, child, boss—will also partly determine the style you choose. The nature of the text and the identity of the reader also have a bearing on the type of information that you put into your writing and may have to be assembled beforehand. Statistics may be useful for some purposes, for example. Detailed descriptions of objects, scenes, or processes may be required. You may be expected to quote from literary or scientific works, and if you use quotations, then you will also be expected to provide some kind of referencing system. The clearer you are about the kind of task you are engaged in, the easier it will be to prepare for it and accomplish it.

In many instances somebody else will have set you a particular writing task. If so, this person will probably have defined the task for you. In many cases, however, you will be writing on your own initiative, so you must define the task for yourself. Consider carefully the three questions listed above. When you have found answers to them, you should be in a position to produce a concise statement of what you intend to do, what we might call, adopting business terminology, a "mission statement."

## THE TASK DEFINED: THE MISSION STATEMENT

Your "mission statement" should be no more than a brief note that sums up your purpose in writing. Whether you write it down or keep it in your head will depend on your personal preferences and your power of memory, but it is generally safer to jot down thoughts and ideas and have them as a visual aid. For example,

> *Talk to be given to members of Ultraville Rotary Club on chairman and treasurer's visit to Rotary Club of Infraham, VA, and arrangements for return visit of Infraham R.C. officers*

or,

> *Short story for Ladyfriend magazine based on incident at bowling alley last Saturday night: main character, Lucia, 40s, 3 kids, meets younger man*

or,

> *Brief explanatory statement for department colleagues about reasons for opposing proposed relocation from downtown premises to new greenfield site*

Your mission statement is for your eyes only. So long as it is clear to you what kind of piece you intend to produce, what it is about, and what kind of readership you are targeting, it does not matter at this stage if an outsider would understand it or not. For example, you know what happened at the bowling alley and what kind of person Lucia is; the rest of the world will find out in due course.

The purpose of the mission statement, whether mental or written down, is twofold. First, it provides you with your initial impetus: You have defined your task, so now you can set about doing it. Second, as you proceed, or when you reach the end, it enables you to check that you are doing, or have done, what you set out to do. Once you have established the basic nature of your undertaking, it is time to begin assembling your material.

## MORE THINKING

Everything you write—whatever it is, whatever it is about, whomever it is intended for—should contain something that comes uniquely and individually from you. If you are intending to write something fairly brief, there is a good chance that your own knowledge, experiences, and ideas will provide you all the material that you need. You simply have to set your memory to work and use your reason and your imagination to put the material into a proper order. The document will, as a consequence, bear your personal stamp.

Even if your task is to write something more extensive, and even if you realize from the outset that your existing personal resources will not be sufficient to provide everything you require, your personal input in the form of your individual approach to the topic is still going to be the freshest and most valuable element in the piece. If you are starting from scratch and have undertaken to write on a subject you know little or nothing about, you will need to establish a connection with that subject or else your work will be very heavy going, both for you and for your reader. Whatever the situation, therefore, in order to supply the vital personal touch you will need to do some creative thinking before you begin any research.

The process of creative thinking is not easy to describe and cannot really be done to order. At this point you will have to use up some of your allotted 10 percent of inspiration. A certain amount of free association is called for. What does the topic mean to you? What sort of ideas or images does it call up for you? What do you immediately and naturally connect with it? If someone said X to you, what would your first thought or your first reaction be?

Remember, too, that ideas do not have to come in the form of statements. If they come in the form of questions, they can be equally, if not more, useful. List the basic question words—*who, why, how, what, when, where,* and *which*—and apply them to your topic. If you know little or nothing about a subject, ask yourself what you would like to know. If you are already familiar with it, ask yourself what it is that particularly interests you. Consider why something happened, or if the time and place at which it happened were significant. Think whether you know precisely how something happened or how something is done, and whether it is worth finding out. Do not be afraid to ask yourself apparently obvious or stupid questions. The answers may be less obvious, self-evident, or irrelevant than you think. In posing these questions you may come across an entirely new angle on the subject that nobody else has thought of because the answer was assumed to be a foregone conclusion. Why did the dog not bark in the night? wondered Sherlock Holmes, and the answer provided the key to the mystery. Why are there subtle differences between the finches on the various islands in the Galapagos? asked Charles Darwin; working out the answer was a milestone in the development of his theory of evolution. How many children had Lady Macbeth? queried the literary critic F. R. Leavis, not intending to throw new light on the play so much as to deride a previous school of critics whose method was to treat Shakespeare's characters as if they were real people. Any student of *Macbeth* might nevertheless find it interesting to consider Leavis's "stupid" question, for Lady Macbeth says, "I have given suck and know / How tender 'tis to love the babe that milks me," yet in the play there is no sign that children feature in the home life of the Macbeths. Does this tell us something about the characters and situation of the Macbeth couple, or is it an inconsistency on Shakespeare's part that tells us more about his priorities when devising a play? Wrestling with—or simply letting your mind play with—questions such as these can often arouse your interest and set your creativity to work.

In order to illustrate this stage of proceedings, let us now turn to a concrete example. Let us assume that you have been asked, or have decided, to write something about the British writer Charles Dickens and America. It might be a school or college assignment; it might be a talk you are giving to a local society or an article you are writing for a newspaper or magazine.

If you are unfamiliar with the subject, then, as has been said, your first jottings are likely to be in question form. For example,

*Did Charles Dickens visit America? If so, when and why?*
*Did he write about America? If so, what?*
*What did he think of America?*
*What did Americans think of him?*
*Were his novels popular in America?*

You may already be familiar with the basic facts. Dickens did visit America; in fact, he came twice, in 1842 and in 1867–68. He wrote a book describing his first trip called *American Notes,* and a central episode of his novel *Martin Chuzzlewit,* written shortly after that first visit, is set in the United States. He had great expectations of American society, believing it would be a great improvement on the class-ridden, inegalitarian societies of Europe. His first trip began promisingly, but when he left New England for the then less developed states of the interior, his views changed radically. The picture he painted of 1840s America in *American Notes* and *Martin Chuzzlewit* was a largely unfavorable one. Americans were, understandably, less than pleased by the way in which Dickens depicted them. His early novels had been immensely popular in the United States; his later novels were still avidly read, but his personal reputation was less high. However, by the time of his second visit, which took place shortly before his death, there had been a good deal of forgiving and forgetting on both sides. On that occasion, Dickens came mainly to give readings from his own works. People flocked to hear him, and the tour was an unqualified success.

It is a substantial topic. If you were set to write about it, you might well wish to select some particular aspect on which to focus. But our business at the moment is not to discuss the topic as such (*see* DEFINING THE TOPIC, page 38) but to use it simply as a model to show how you might organize your thoughts on any subject. Simply producing ideas or questions is not enough; you have to find ways of linking them together—to think connectedly as well as creatively.

A simple list of points is not the only way, or necessarily the best way, of marshaling your first thoughts. You might prefer to put them down in columns:

| *Places* | *Dickens's attitude* | *Reasons* |
|---|---|---|
| *New England* | *positive* | *public adulation*<br>*like Europe* |
| *Missouri* | *negative* | *too wild*<br>*pestered by press*<br>*did 't like the people* |

Some people find that a graphic presentation enables them to see the links between different aspects of the subject more clearly. They set out their thoughts in the form of a diagram, for example, in what is usually known as a web chart or spider chart. To create such a chart, first put down the main ideas or themes and circle them. Then use straight lines to connect them with subsidiary points or with each other:

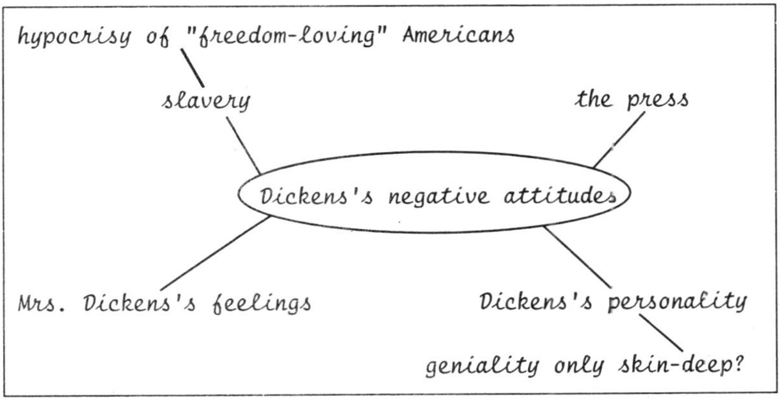


If it suits you better, it is possible to produce a similar effect over a larger surface than a sheet of paper. You might, for example, write out your main ideas or points on separate cards or pieces of paper and pin them to a board, linking them by pieces of tape or ribbon. This may make it easier to move things around as you spot new connections. Note that questions can figure in columns or diagrams along with statements.

The probability is that as you start noting down your ideas, in whatever form, they will suggest other ideas. Your list will grow longer, or your web, more complex. It is important to try to keep things under control so that a rough shape begins to emerge. At the very least, you need to know by the end of this stage where your main areas of interest—and where your main areas of ignorance—are so that you can direct your research accordingly. Your interest, you must remember, is specific to you and is going to give this piece of writing its all-important personal signature.

## CARD INDEXES

The sooner you begin to organize your ideas the better. One-tried-and-true method is the use of a card index. Once you know where your main areas of interest lie and what the main topics are that you are likely to be covering, you can make out an index card for each particular subject, with a key word as a heading, and then arrange the cards alphabetically by their headings in a box. As your research proceeds, you can add to the material on a card or add more cards from any sources you consult—always making a note of where a particular item comes from. It takes considerable self-discipline to maintain a card index, or a similar electronic index, and it is probably only worth doing when you are undertaking a large-scale piece of writing, such as a dissertation or long report. The index can, however, save a lot of time at the planning stage if your material from all sources is already at least partially organized.

## Researching

The starting point for your research may well be fairly obvious. If you are a student, you will probably have been provided with a reading list. If you were working on the Dickens project, you would want to read, or reread, *American Notes* and the relevant sections of *Martin Chuzzlewit,* before you read anything else. From there you might branch out to a biography of Dickens or books or articles by scholars on Dickens generally or on Dickens's relations with America in particular.

The research materials that writers and scholars use are traditionally divided into **primary sources** and **secondary sources**. A primary source is a text that forms part of the subject matter that you are writing about. In the Dickens case, the two books mentioned in the previous paragraph would be primary sources, as would any contemporary accounts of what Dickens did in America, such as a diary or journal entry or any articles from newspapers or magazines of the time that show firsthand the reaction of the American public to the novelist's visit or to any opinions he expressed then or later. Mark Twain, for instance, wrote a report on a reading by Dickens that he attended at the Steinway Hall in New York City in January 1868, which can be accessed on the Internet.

Material that is written about a subject by consulting primary sources and that discusses the subject or gives someone else's opinion on it is a secondary source. From the point of view of our example, books or articles written by literary critics or other scholars about Dickens and his travels in America are secondary sources.

If you were writing about an entirely different subject such as wine making in California, your primary sources would be any material published by actual winemakers, statistics compiled by the wine-making industry or the federal or state government, and so on. Your secondary sources would be books or articles by enologists (people who study wine making scientifically), economists, or journalists about the Californian wine trade. If you write something that discusses a topic rather than describing something that you have actually experienced, your book, article, or report has the potential to be a secondary source for somebody else.

In the final analysis, primary sources are more valuable than secondary sources, and any academic work that does not show evidence of consultation of primary sources is likely to be criticized for that very reason. This does not mean that secondary sources have no value, however—far from it. You might equally be criticized for knowing nothing at all of what secondary sources have had to say on the subject in question. Likewise, as anyone who has tried to write an academic essay knows, other people's ideas can stimulate your own, and other people's judgments can support your own or, if you disagree with them or find them wanting, help you to form your own. The important thing at any level of writing is to resist the temptation to let secondary sources do your work for you. Nobody wants to read somebody else's ideas copied out or warmed up by you. Have confidence that your own ideas are worthwhile. Use secondary sources as a stimulus, not as a crutch.

One final note about secondary sources is that they frequently quote from primary ones. It is perfectly proper for you to use primary material from a secondary source, especially if it is difficult for you to consult the primary source yourself, providing that you give a proper reference for it (*see* REFERENCES, page 89).

## COLLECTING MATERIAL

The first place to look for possible research material is in your own home among the books you own, magazines you subscribe to, pieces you have previously written, or notes you have made that have a bearing on the topic at hand. Do not forget to consult general reference books, such as encyclopedias, dictionaries, atlases, and almanacs. They lie idle in many homes when they ought to be making a positive contribution, and they usually contain a great deal of useful material.

Once you have exhausted resources at home, your probable first port of call will be a public library. If you are new to this kind of work, you may be aware of your local library only as a place from which you can borrow books to read for entertainment or instruction at home. Many libraries have a reference section that is almost as extensive as the lending section, the only difference being that you have to study these books on the premises and cannot take them home. In addition to such general works as encyclopedias, dictionaries, atlases, and almanacs, your library's reference section may contain books on the specific topic you are interested in, such as standard editions of works by major authors, technical manuals, or official government publications. It will also subscribe to a large number of periodicals and keep on file previous issues so that you can consult them.

The facilities available at any particular library will depend on the size of the community it serves and the demands that community makes on it. Your own library's card catalog or computerized catalog will enable you to see what it has available and to search for what you want by its title, its author, or its subject. If you are looking for something that is not in its own collection, your library may be able to get it for you on loan from another library or at least tell you where to find it. Remember that a library's best resource is often its knowledgeable staff. Librarians are there to help you, and if you have problems locating something on your own, they will usually be able to help.

So far, this discussion has taken a very traditional, not to say old-fashioned, line, speaking of research as if all sources were to be found in print. This is, of course, emphatically not the case. It is probably no longer even the case that people reach first of all for a book or a magazine when they require additional information. Modern technology has vastly increased the resources available to anyone who has access to a computer, especially a computer connected to a modem and a phone line. A great deal of information is now available on CD-ROM or, in some cases, on DVD. It is often easier (though not always cheaper) to search a dictionary or encyclopedia, say, on CD-ROM, using a computer, than to thumb through the same work in its printed form.

The Internet provides information on almost any subject that you can mention. It too can offer searchable versions of basic texts (for instance Dickens's *American Notes*). The fact that these texts are searchable by electronic means is probably their most valuable asset. It is much easier and quicker to do a computer search than to thumb backward and forward to a printed index. It is also possible to look for topics that might not be covered in an ordinary index. Anyone who has research to do and is still unable to use a search engine to look for information should learn this basic modern-age skill as soon as possible.

There is an art to searching the Internet. If you type, for example, the words *Charles Dickens America* into the search engine Google, you are given almost a half million options (if you type in *wine making California,* you are offered more than 2 million). There is a great deal of material on the Internet that either proves to be irrelevant to the specific topic or, frankly, is dross. Nonetheless, an enormous amount of it is extremely valuable and can be accessed from the comfort of your own home. If you can refine your search and make your search criteria (the words that you type into the search engine) as specific as possible, the results can be very useful. Very often you can find a Web site that has links to other sites containing similar or related material. There are several Internet hub sites, for example, devoted to Charles Dickens that provide links to other sites on specific aspects of his life and works or that can put you in touch with individuals or organizations whose main concern is to study them.

In some respects, searching the Internet seems to represent an advance on consulting books and other written material, but research does not have to be modern, state-of-the-art, and electronic to be effective. There is a method of research that is in a sense more "primitive" than reading books but can often produce the most valuable information of all: asking other people.

Your immediate family and friends may be able to give you useful information and pointers. A straw vote conducted among your circle of friends and relations—or among people in the street, if you feel confident enough to approach them—may provide a useful guide to prevailing opinions on an issue or current preferences. A formal or informal interview with somebody can provide much valuable primary material on a subject. If, for example, you were intending to write a piece for a local newspaper on a topic of interest for people in your locality, the obvious course would be to go and speak to the people most closely involved and record their experiences or views. A pocket tape recorder is vital for this kind of work unless you have a very retentive memory or know shorthand. If you wish to collect the views of a number of different people on the same issue, then it is usually best to draw up a questionnaire. It is much easier to compare the responses of different people if you are sure that you have asked them all precisely the same question. If you want your work to have any scientific credentials, in the broadest sense, then it is essential to use a questionnaire to ensure that you have not affected the responses by perhaps phrasing your questions in slightly different ways to different people. You should also, usually, reproduce the questionnaire you used either in the text or in an appendix or footnote.

Any research you do, however, of whatever kind, is only as valuable as the records you make of it. Research that is not recorded well can be a complete waste of time. Those who do not learn from history are compelled to repeat it, we are told. Those who do not take clear, usable, and relevant notes are compelled to do the same with their research.

## TAKING NOTES

The most important aspect about taking notes is that you should be able to understand them later when you want to use them to plan or compose the piece you are writing. Most people who have attended a lecture or presentation and tried to take notes of what the speaker was saying have had the galling experience of looking at those notes later and finding that they cannot make head or tails of what they scribbled down, or that what they assumed to be a major point worth noting turned out to be a relatively minor issue in the context of the lecture as a whole.

Mishaps of this kind are excusable in a lecture, where information is being fed in a continuous stream and where a lot depends on the skill of the lecturer or presenter. A good speaker will proceed at a moderate pace to allow the audience to take in what he or she is saying, will repeat essential points or information for emphasis, and will also give reference points along the way (*firstly, secondly, finally,* and so on) that should benefit note takers.

When note taking from written sources, however, always read the passage from beginning to end before you start jotting down notes so that you get the writer's overall drift. You might miss something valuable if you do not see where it fits into the overall argument. Likewise, always have your mission statement and your sense of what your own work is to be about at the forefront of your mind when you are taking notes and extracts. The source writer was probably not writing simply to suit the purposes of someone with your particular interest and will have included a lot of material that, while it may be interesting, is not relevant to the task you have in hand. Research is not simply about finding material. It is also about sifting through the material that you do find. Always write clear notes; check your notes again when you have finished to make sure everything is still comprehensible. If you make rough notes in the course of a lecture or talk, go back over them as soon as you have a spare moment and rewrite them in a clear form while the speaker's words and arguments are still fresh in your mind. Always note down precisely where you found the information in the book, journal, or Web site you are studying so that you can find it again if something remains unclear or you want to follow up the material. Always, finally, make sure you note down any bibliographic information you may need for your references: the full title, the name(s) of the author(s), the publisher's name, and the place and date of publication, or the title and author of a Web site, the Web address, and the date on which you accessed the site. (*See also* REFERENCES, page 89; REFERENCE RESOURCES, page 360.)

Let us assume that you are writing about wine making, in California or elsewhere, and you decide that you had better begin by checking out some of the basics. You might look up an entry on wine in an encyclopedia and find something like this:

> The wine that is produced from grapes in temperate regions throughout the world falls into three main categories: table wines, sparkling wines, and fortified wines.
>
> Table wines, as their name suggests, are drunk primarily as accompaniments to meals. They are further distinguished by their color, as red, white, or rosé (pink). Red wines are made from purple grapes, the skins

> of which are left in the vats with the juice during the early stages of the fermentation process. White wines are made either from green grapes or from purple grapes. In the latter case, the grape skins are removed before the fermentation process commences. Rosé wines are sometimes produced by mixing red and white wine, but a true rosé is made like a red wine, from purple grapes, except that the skins are left in the vats for a much shorter period and only until the required pink coloring has been achieved.
>
> Sparkling wines are distinguished by the fact that they are bubbly and need to be kept in special bottles. Carbon dioxide gas is either introduced artificially into the wine after it is made or produced by a secondary fermentation process. Sparkling wines are drunk mainly to celebrate festive occasions, and the most famous varieties are produced in the Champagne region of France.
>
> Fortified wines are so called because a quantity of stronger liquor—usually grape brandy—is added during fermentation. This increases the alcoholic content of the wine from the 9 to 14 percent of standard table wines to between 15 and 22 percent. Some fortified wines, such as sherry and vermouth, are drunk mainly as appetizers before a meal, while others, such as port, are usually drunk after a meal as digestives.

If your principal interest is in wine making, there are certain things in this passage that might or might not be relevant. The passage, for instance, remarks on the occasions when the different types of wine are generally drunk. That is quite a handy way of defining their differences but is not necessarily of major importance—not, at least, of equal importance to the fact that there are three basic categories of wine. You need to be able to distinguish between major and minor pieces of information. The easiest method is to emphasize the more important facts by underlining them or highlighting them with a fluorescent marker. With this in mind, your first note might be

---

XYZ ENCYCLOPEDIA ENTRY "WINE" (PAGE XXX)

---

*3 types of wine*

---

*-Table wine (drunk with meals)*
*-Sparkling wine (dr. at celebrations)*
*-Fortified wine (dr. before/after meals)*

Using a certain amount of abbreviation or personal shorthand speeds things up considerably. Just make sure that everything is reexpandable afterward. Safety first suggests that you write out a key word in full the first time before abbreviating it and that you should not be too cryptic; if you reduced *(dr. at celebrations)* to *(dr. celebs)*, for example, you might find yourself wondering if you had "drunken celebrities" in mind rather than "drunk at celebrations." Omitting all or almost all the vowels in a word is a fairly standard trick, so you might reduce *(dr. at celebrations)* to, say, *(dr. @ celbratns)* without forfeiting too much in the way of clarity. People who are used to sending text messages between cell phones are likely to be better at this than people who are not.

The other most substantial piece of information in the passage has to do with the different colors of table wine, and color appears to be mainly related to the use or nonuse of grape skins. A note to this effect might read

3 TYPES TABLE WINE—DISTINGUISHED BY COLOR

Red—made from purple grapes—skins in
White—md. fr. white grapes—or fr. purp. grapes (skins out)
Rosé—md. fr. purp. grapes—skins in till pink/sometimes md. by mixing red & white wine

It is often clearer to take your notes in the form of a list rather than to write discursive notes that attempt to follow the style of the source writer (*see* PARAPHRASING, page 22). This is especially the case when you are extracting basic factual information. Note again, these jottings are for your eyes only. They do not have to be grammatically perfect (even in shorthand). If you can follow them, that is enough.

There are other aspects in this passage that you might want to note, depending on your particular interest at the time. It is also often important to make a note of things that are *not* covered in a particular passage but that you may wish to find out about later. This passage, for instance, mentions "fermentation" and the "fermentation process" several times but does not describe the process. If you are not clear what fermentation is—it is obviously something essential to wine making—then you should look it up in the same encyclopedia there and then. If you do not have time to do that right away, then leave a message to yourself in your notes—or, better, on a special sheet, pad, or computer file for personal memoranda—to remind yourself to sort out the issue in your next work session.

## CRITICAL THINKING

If you are obtaining simple basic facts from an encyclopedia, then you can be fairly certain that the information it contains is accurate. Research would be a lot simpler if you could have the same degree of trust in every source in print or on the Web as you can in the text of a respectable encyclopedia.

Unfortunately, this is not the case. Consequently, the writing process involves a good deal of critical thinking, in addition to creative thinking, and from a very early stage. The ability to think critically is vital when you are revising your own work, but critical thinking also ought to come into play while you are doing your research, firstly so that you can distinguish between what is useful and valuable for your own purposes in your sources and what is not, and secondly so that you do not necessarily take everything as absolutely true and accurate because it happens to appear on paper or the Web.

Perhaps we should first clear up a common misapprehension. Critical thinking is not the same thing as negative thinking or censorious thinking. Assessing a piece of writing critically does not mean that you deliberately set out to try to find fault with it or prove it to be worthless. A good literary critic picks out and praises what is good in something at the same time that he or she recognizes and, if appropriate, censures anything that is inaccurate, carelessly thought out, or poorly expressed. The main work of criticism is to analyze and evaluate things as to their nature and their quality. Critical thinking, to put it another way, is all about making distinctions: distinguishing the good from the bad, the useful from the useless, the accurate from the inaccurate, and so on. You may or may not be called on to pass judgment on the intrinsic literary merits of a piece of writing, but you will certainly need to be able to decide whether a source is valuable and/or trustworthy.

The first distinction that we usually need to make is between fact and opinion. A fact is something that is objectively and demonstratively true or something that actually happened and can be proved to have happened. An opinion is what someone believes to be the case. There is nothing wrong with having opinions or with having beliefs or preferences, but what one person believes, another person may dispute, and as the proverb says, "One man's meat is another man's poison." Opinion is always debatable and does not have the same credibility as fact.

This much is obvious. Problems arise, however, from the fact that people are naturally comfortable with their own opinions and generally believe that other people ought to share them. Consequently, they may present them as if they were facts. People also sometimes present opinion—or allegations—as fact because they are not conscientious enough about distinguishing the two or because they deliberately set out to mislead others. Whatever the motives, it is important for us as readers and researchers not to be misled. We should apply our minds critically to what is presented to us and retain a degree of skepticism until convinced.

Let us examine the distinction between fact and opinion a little further on the basis of a few examples. The statement "Charles Dickens was born in 1812" is a statement of fact. No normal person would want to go to the bother of checking through the official records to verify a date given in thousands of reliable sources. That is something we can take on trust. The statement "Charles Dickens was a great writer" is not a statement of fact, however. Millions of readers over a period of more than 150 years may have believed Dickens to be a great writer, but that does not make it an indisputable fact. Some people—a small minority, admittedly—dispute his greatness. The precise meaning of the word *great* when applied to a creative artist is also sometimes a matter of debate. In any event, the word *great* implies a judgment, and judgments are always open to question. This does not mean that we cannot venture to make such statements, simply that when we make them we should be aware that we may be called upon to justify them. Likewise, when we read them, we should expect the persons who wrote them to be able to back them up.

The statement "Red wines are made from purple grapes, the skins of which are left in the vats with the juice during the early stages of the fermentation process" is another statement of fact. The statement "Red wine is the perfect accompaniment to a steak," on the other hand, is a statement of opinion. It sounds rather similar to what was said in the passage quoted in the previous section, but the encyclopedia-type article was more guarded. It put forward a more general proposition: "Table wines, as their name suggests, are drunk primarily as accompaniments to meals." Not only is it speaking of table wines in general, but it adds the important qualifying word *primarily,* precisely because the author knows that people often drink ordinary red or white wine on its own. Similar qualifying words, *mainly* and *usually*, are also used in the passage with respect to the circumstances under which the other types of wine mentioned are normally drunk.

Since they contain these qualifications, we can accept these statements as generally true, that is as having more or less an equivalent status to fact. If we formulate the statement in a more specific way, however, and say, as above, "Red wine is the perfect accompaniment to a steak," then we are on less factual ground. Plenty of people might argue that a steak tastes better if you drink beer with it, or plain water, or nothing at all. Again, the use of the judgmental adjective *perfect* is an indicator that we are dealing with an opinion, as was the use of *great* in the statement about Dickens. If we were determined not to stray from strict fact, we should have to say something like "Red wine is often drunk with a steak" or add a phrase to show that we recognize that what we are saying represents a commonly held belief: "Many people think that red wine is the perfect accompaniment to a steak."

In the examples given above, the distinction between fact and opinion is pretty clear, and the issues being discussed are relatively minor insofar as the question of whether red wine goes well with steak is not a matter of life and death. But if in the course of researching a piece on the subject of wine you came across the statement "Drinking red wine can prevent heart disease," how ought you to treat it? Is it a fact or an opinion?

You will notice that statement says "can prevent," not "prevents," so the writer is exercising some caution. Does that make it safe to present this slightly qualified assertion as a fact? Unless you are a medical specialist, you are unlikely to have at your fingertips the knowledge that would enable you to answer that question. So you have to think critically. You might first want to investigate the credentials of the publication in which you found the information. If it appeared, for example, in something published or sponsored by the wine industry, you might feel that it would be in the industry's interests to suggest that drinking one of its products had important health benefits and treat the information with caution. If you discovered it in a reputable scientific journal, you might be more inclined to believe it, especially if it were to be supported by a battery of statistics. Even so, you might well be aware from experience that even experts disagree. What one scientist claims to have proved today, another scientist will often claim to have disproved tomorrow. If you are able to consider the evidence and weigh it and decide definitely in favor of one side or the other, then all well and good. But if you do not have the knowledge or cannot do the necessary research to reach clarity on the issue, then you ought not to suggest to your reader that you know the true facts. The safest rule is to treat everything that you do not know for certain to be fact as opinion, and to word what you write in such a way as to make it clear to your reader where facts end and opinions start.

To summarize this subsection,

- critical thinking is the art of making distinctions;
- critical thinking should be used first and foremost to ascertain what is valuable and useful for your project and what is not;
- the distinction between fact and opinion is of primary importance;
- if in doubt, be skeptical.

## EVALUATING SOURCES

Let us now look at another piece of prose—with the remarks made in the previous paragraphs in mind—and see how we can apply critical principles to the task of producing valuable notes.

> **One Hundred Fiftieth Anniversary of First Recorded Flight**
>
> The Chinese, Marco Polo reported, were able to build kites large and strong enough to be able to lift a full-grown man into the air at a time when Western aviators were still covering themselves with feathers and trying to imitate the birds. It was only when Western aviation went counterintuitive and started to rely on science that it finally got off the ground. The first person ever to fly in a heavier-than-air machine was probably the coachman of British baronet and engineer, Sir George Cayley. Today marks the 150th anniversary of the day the anonymous charioteer took to the air, and some experts regard it as a more important occasion than the 100th anniversary of the Wright brothers' much shorter hop later this year.
>
> Cayley, who lived from 1773 to 1857, is generally known as the father of aerodynamics. His identification of the four forces that act on bodies moving through the air—lift, thrust, drag, and weight—revolutionized thinking on the subject. It was based on the work of Swiss physicist Daniel Bernoulli on the behavior of fluids in motion. But Cayley was no mere theoretician. He was a prolific inventor. To him we owe the invention of artificial limbs, the caterpillar tractor, a new type of telescope, and an internal-combustion engine powered by gunpowder. He was also interested, as were most men of his time, in railroad engineering. Naturally, then, his interest in flight led him to spend a large part of his time designing, constructing, and flying model and full-sized gliders, and his crowning achievement came in 1853, when the man who was usually drawn by four white horses along the Queen's highway was hauled up into the air by teams of workers from Cayley's estate and flew a total distance of 900 feet.
>
> When he came down again, the first thing the coachman did was to quit his job. "I was hired to drive, not to fly," he said. Some people have no sense of occasion.

In assessing this passage, we have to perform a fairly complex sifting operation. There appears to be a good deal of useful information in it, but it is not presented in what we might call an "encyclopedic" style. There is very little in it that is presented as opinion, but that does not necessarily mean that it is all true-blue fact. There is also a certain amount of what we might, perhaps unkindly, call "decoration" in it, and most of that is likely to be dispensable.

The tone and style of the passage mark it as essentially journalistic. The reader has the sense that the author is trying to "write up" a story, making the material more interesting and entertaining for the reader than it would be if presented in plain terms. The clearest evidence for this is at the beginning, where the writer provides information that, although picturesque, is only loosely related to the remainder of the passage, and in the jokiness of certain sections, such as the references to the coachman or the "anonymous charioteer." The writer also does not seem to be quite sure whether this really is a momentous anniversary. How does Cayley's feat compare with that of the Wright brothers? An expert in aviation history would probably have an opinion on the subject that would be worth listening to. To be told that "some experts regard it" as a more important anniversary is of no great value, and we should be wary of simply repeating a comment like that without finding out the opinion of at least one genuine expert or authoritative source. Furthermore, in what sense do we "owe" a gunpowder-fueled internal-combustion engine to Sir George, when very few of us nowadays are filling up our tanks with saltpeter? Finally, did the coachman really say the words he is quoted as saying—it is an extremely quotable quote—or did some journalist then or now invent them because they make such a neat ending to the story?

In other words, we ought not to trust this passage too far. It does not carry the same weight as an entry in an encyclopedia. On the other hand, we ought not to dismiss it out of hand. The fact that it is journalistic and not scholarly and that it contains a few attempts at humor does not mean that it is of no interest at all. Someone who was intending to write about the history of aviation, someone who was interested in technological progress in the 19th century in general, or even someone who wanted to write about relations between the upper classes in 19th-century England and their servants might find this passage useful or stimulating. Most people have heard about Orville and Wilbur Wright; the name George Cayley is far less well known. He seems to have done enough to merit some attention, however, with or without a journalist's help.

With all this in mind, how should we go about taking notes? Probably the best course in this instance, given the fact that we have some doubts about the total reliability of the passage is to jot down points to be followed up and verified. Assuming that our major interest was in the aeronautical angle, we might note the following:

---

*Cayley, Sir George (1773–1857)*

---

*<u>Check out:</u>*
*Coachman made first heavier-than-air flight in 1853 (?)*
*What kind of machine?*
*Is there a picture?*
*Other gliders designed by Cayley?*
*More important than Wright brothers?*

If we were interested in Cayley's general contribution to 19th-century technology, we might make a rather different set of notes:

---

*Cayley, Sir George (1773–1857)*
*aviator, scientist, inventor*

---

*Chiefly known for building machine in which <u>first heavier-than-air flight</u> was made in 1853*

*Check out:*
*How did he apply Bernoulli's theory?*
*"Father of aerodynamics"?*
*Other inventions*
*Artificial limbs, caterpillar tractor, telescope, internal-combustion engine powered by gunpowder*
*Value of these inventions, relation to present-day forms?*
*Nature of interest in railroad engineering?*

In both cases, the next step is to consult a weightier volume or do a Web search. You should continue to delve into the questions until you feel confident that you have established the facts and can take notes without queries.

In summing up, therefore, we might say that valuable and interesting information may be found in almost any source. We must, however, be careful to evaluate sources critically and if we have any doubts about their accuracy seek corroboration elsewhere.

## PARAPHRASING AND SUMMARIZING

In the two previous subsections the notes that have resulted from our reading of the sources have been brief, sketchy, and abstract. They have not attempted to follow the line of argument presented by the original author; rather, they have simply picked out pieces of useful information or lines of inquiry to be followed and recorded them in the briefest possible form. Most notes are taken in this way.

There are occasions, however, when it is useful or necessary to stick more closely to the original and to preserve something of the progression of the argument from the source. The process of reproducing another writer's text in your own words without attempting to reduce the length of the passage substantially is known as paraphrasing. If you set out to reproduce another writer's ideas and arguments but at considerably less length and in less detail, then you are summarizing it.

Producing a paraphrase or a summary sometimes constitutes a writing task in its own right, but the skills involved in making an effective paraphrase or summary are closely related to those required for taking notes. As mentioned in the previous paragraph, when you are assembling your materials prior to beginning, you may well want to have available a closer approximation to the structure source author's own text than is provided by ordinary notes. We shall therefore deal with these processes here.

### Paraphrasing

The art of paraphrasing consists of re-creating an original text in its entirety using your own words, not those of the author. It can be particularly useful if your reader might have difficulty in following the original text or if the style of the original text is markedly different from the style you are employing for your own piece and you want to make it fit in. When paraphrasing, you should, as much as possible, avoid quoting from the original. If the author uses a particularly distinctive word or phrase that you wish to retain, then you should put it in quotation marks. At the same time, you should remember that because you are going to be using different words, you may inadvertently alter the original author's meaning if you are not careful.

Paraphrasing is distinct from quoting insofar as you do not use the source author's own words. Nonetheless, paraphrased material needs to be attributed to the person who first produced it, otherwise, even though you are using your own words, you are effectively plagiarizing someone else's work (*see* PLAGIARISM, page 35). The easiest way to avoid this pitfall is to treat a paraphrase as if it were a piece of reported speech (in other words, *X says/states that* . . .). (*See* REPORTING SPEECH, page 167.)

The need to utilize a **reporting verb** (for example, *to say, confirm, express, report,* and so on) plus *that* is something that you can use to your advantage. You can and should try to suggest the tone of the passage you are paraphrasing or the author's attitude toward the information he or she is presenting through your choice of verb. To begin by writing "X says/states that . . ." tells us very little about X's tone. This is perfectly acceptable if the material is neutral in tone or does not represent a particular stage in an argument. If the passage has an emotional quality, however, you can help to convey this by beginning "X complains that . . .," "X insists that . . .," "X gleefully asserts that . . .," or whatever fits the context. Similarly, if the author is presenting an argument or responding to arguments put forward by someone else, you can register that fact by saying "X argues that . . .," "X admits that . . .," "X counters this argument by suggesting that . . ."

Following as an example of a text that you might want to paraphrase, is a passage from a letter written by Charles Dickens to his biographer, John Forster, and reproduced in the latter's *The Life of Charles Dickens*. Dickens is describing and commenting on a banquet he attended in Boston:

> It was a most superb affair; and the speaking *admirable*. Indeed, the general talent for public speaking here, is one of the most striking of the things that force themselves upon an Englishman's notice. As every man looks on to being a member of Congress, every man prepares himself for it; and the result is quite surprising. You will observe one odd custom—the drinking of sentiments. It is quite extinct with us, but here everybody is expected to be prepared with an epigram as a matter of course (Forster, n.d., 427).

The letter was written in 1842. The style is therefore old-fashioned, but Dickens records his impressions with characteristic vigor. In paraphrasing, we should attempt to keep the vigor, if possible, but remove the old-fashioned feel. We also need to ensure that we understand exactly what Dickens is talking about. He mentions a custom, "the drinking of sentiments," that was "extinct" in Britain even then and is so far out of fashion nowadays in the United States that *Merriam-Webster's Collegiate Dictionary* does not even record this sense of the word *sentiment*. A *sentiment,* to quote the *Shorter Oxford English Dictionary,* was "an epigrammatical expression of some striking or agreeable thought or wish announced in the manner of a toast." The *Shorter Oxford* illustrates its definition by quoting from the Irish dramatist R. B. Sheridan's comedy *School for Scandal,* (1777), in which the rakish

Charles Surface says to a moneylender of his acquaintance: "Come, Mr. Premium, I'll give you a sentiment: here's *Success to usury!*" However, "the drinking of sentiments" is probably just the kind of distinctive phrase that, as has been said, could be quoted directly.

This is a weak paraphrase that borrows from the original. In this instance then, we should avoid anything such as the following:

> Dickens says that the dinner was a superb affair and notes that the speaking was "admirable," commenting particularly on the fact that Americans, unlike Englishmen, have a talent for public speaking.

The word *admirable* has been put in quotation marks presumably because Dickens (or Forster) italicized it in the original. Italics were used, however, not to highlight a particular quality of the speaking, but to emphasize how much Dickens enjoyed and appreciated the speeches that were given. *Admirable* is not in itself a distinctive term. It does not really merit quotation, especially since so much has been lifted from the original ("a [most] superb affair," "talent for public speaking") that, for consistency's sake and honesty's sake, quotation marks should have been used far more widely. In addition, Dickens does not say that Americans are good at public speaking and Englishmen are not. He says that he, as an Englishman, is impressed by how widespread the capacity for public speaking is among Americans, which is a somewhat different thing.

A better paraphrase might read something like this:

> Dickens enthused to Forster about the dinner. He was particularly impressed by the ordinary American's ability to stand up and make a speech in public. He attributed this talent to the fact that every American aspired to become a member of Congress and took care to acquire the skills necessary for public office. In this context, he called Forster's attention to the custom of "the drinking of sentiments" (making a witty or epigrammatic toast), which had been preserved in America whereas it had died out in England. Every diner, he observed, had an appropriate epigram ready.

This example employs the simple method of distancing the paraphrase from the original through the use of the past tense. The tense you adopt for a paraphrase depends mainly on the tense you are using for the rest of your text. It would be perfectly possible to put the above passage into the present tense or to make an equally effective but different paraphrase using the present. However, the fact that the bulk of Dickens's original is in the present tense increases the temptation to borrow his words. Shifting the tense makes you think twice before succumbing to that temptation.

When you have completed a paraphrase, you should always check it against the original to ensure that you have not omitted anything important. In this case, everything seems to have been covered, but you might feel that underlying Dickens's appreciation of the general talent for public speaking and his comment that "every man looks on to being a member of Congress" is an awareness of the democratic nature of American society (compared to

19th-century Britain) that enables every man (not yet every person!) to harbor political ambitions. It would not, perhaps, be stretching things too far to make that explicit in the paraphrase.

## Summarizing

The art of summarizing is slightly more complicated than that of paraphrasing, simply because it involves reducing the length of the source passage considerably. The length of a summary will vary depending on particular requirements, but generally speaking, a summary should be between a quarter and a third of the length of the original. To put that perhaps more cogently, you will need to dispense with between two-thirds and three-quarters of the bulk of your source passage. Under these conditions, there is seldom any reason to keep the wording of the original. You must have the confidence to use your own words, just as when paraphrasing.

The ability to compose a good summary is a useful skill for a writer, not merely in the preparatory stages of the writing process, which we are mainly concerned with here, but also in the latter stages. You may very well have to reduce the bulk of your own work when revising it. Book and newspaper publishers frequently stipulate the maximum number of words they require, and you can easily find yourself in the position of having to pare down, if not boil down, your text to fit the space available. Similarly, business reports often have to fit in a very few pages. It is also often useful to provide a summary of your argument at the end of a longer piece of writing; indeed, a summarizing conclusion is a favorite way of winding up a lecture, report, or dissertation.

The standard method for making a summary involves identifying the main points in a passage, writing them down in note form, then making a plan and drafting a brief text on the basis of those notes. In some respects, therefore, it constitutes a condensed version of several aspects of the writing process as a whole, particularly those we have been dealing with in the present section. To illustrate the technique, let us take the passage below, currently consisting of 284 words, and reduce it to a summary of not more than 100 words.

> The transcontinental railroads constructed after the Civil War did more than open up the West for further settlement and for the commercial exploitation of its vast natural resources. They also established it as a tourist destination.
>
> Easterners already familiar with stories of the heroic struggles of the pioneers and of the sublime, empty landscapes in which they lived out their rugged and exciting lives were now to be given the chance to experience the adventure for themselves. As early as 1871, the Northern Pacific Railroad commissioned the painter Thomas Moran and the photographer William Henry Harvey to accompany a surveying expedition to the Yellowstone region. The images they brought back were reproduced in guidebooks and brochures available from railroad stations and offices in the East. Other railroad companies were not slow to follow Northern Pacific's lead and publicize the dramatic scenery to be enjoyed along their own routes.

> Not content with supplying evocative imagery of the West, the railroad companies, often in collaboration with other entrepreneurs, created a complete tourist infrastructure that linked railroads with hotels and local transportation to major sites. They were also at pains to ensure that the environments the tourists found when they reached their destinations were fully in keeping with their preconceived notions of the West. They frequently themed the buildings they erected and the services they set up. The Santa Fe Railway and the Fred Harvey Company built the Hopi House at the Grand Canyon, modeled on a traditional Native American dwelling. Travelers en route to Yellowstone with Northern Pacific were met at Gardiner station by yellow stagecoaches. The accommodations provided by Great Northern to visitors of Glacier National Park took the form of Swiss-style chalets or log cabins.

The first task, as always, is to read through the whole passage carefully and make sure that we have understood it. We then identify and note down its main points, the essential ideas or pieces of information that the writer wishes to convey to the reader. In this instance we might take them to be the following:

1. *The railroads opened up the West for tourism*
2. *They had pictures made of the West to be used for marketing purposes*
3. *Railroad and other companies created a tourist infrastructure*
4. *Their aim was to preserve the popular image of the West*
5. *They shaped buildings, etc., to fit in with this image*

As always, we should try to express these main points in our own words. The original text, for example, does not use the word *marketing,* but it would seem to be a word that accurately describes what was going on. Nor does the text use the term *tourist infrastructure,* but it is very difficult to think of an alternative that expresses the same idea with equal economy. We do not have many words at our disposal, so we have to generalize and boil down the text to its essentials. A phrase such as "the popular image of the West" will have to suffice for all the various things that the passage says or implies about the way Easterners thought about the West. When taking notes on the main points, we are already beginning to condense the passage.

Once we have established the main points in the passage and noted them as concisely as possible, we next have to flesh them out with some key details. To say that, however, immediately poses the question, what constitutes a key detail? What distinguishes a detail that you ought to retain from one that you ought to discard?

In this particular case, we can leave out most of the names. The passage does not center itself on any one particular instance of the phenomenon it is telling us about; it is concerned with the phenomenon as such and uses specific examples to illustrate its points. Though the writer specifically mentions various railroad companies, the passage is not about one company's activities, but about an activity that all the transcontinental railroads engaged in. In our summary, therefore, we can generalize by referring simply to "the railroads" or "the railroad companies," without doing violence to the passage's basic meaning. And we shall also, probably, have to find some way of making reference to the tourist sites in general terms for the same reason. Obviously, too, "the painter Thomas Moran and the photographer William Henry Harvey" will have to become "a painter and a photographer," if they merit a mention in our summary.

So much for the kind of thing we might leave out. What do we put in? Take the first main point as an example: "The railroads opened up the West for tourism." That is fair enough as a restatement of the author's theme, but it is a very bald restatement. It needs some context. It might sound as if the main purpose of the railroads' westward drive was to develop the tourist trade, which it self-evidently was not. Tourist business was an important and valuable business but subsidiary to the principal commercial purpose. The author acknowledges as much, and our summary ought to find space to do the same. Likewise, this process took place at a specific time in history. The passage uses the phrase "after the Civil War" and mentions one specific date, 1871. These dates, however, give the starting point for the process, which must have extended over a good many years. It is probably better, then, to think of these developments happening during a particular period rather than at a precise time in history and to choose as our key detail a phrase that suggests as much—perhaps "during the later years of the 19th century" or "during the final decades of the 19th century."

An extended plan of main points plus key details might therefore look something like the example that follows:

1. The railroads opened up the West for tourism
   - not simply for settlement and trade
   - during later years of the 19th century
2. They had pictures made of the West to be used for marketing purposes
   - painter and photographer sent to Yellowstone
   - brochures and guidebooks sold in the East
3. Railroad and other companies created a tourist infrastructure
   - stations linked to hotels, transportation
4. Their aim was to preserve the popular image of the West
   - heroic frontier life, unspoiled wilderness, scenic grandeur
5. They shaped buildings, etc., to fit in with this image
   - Native American-style buildings, stagecoaches, etc.

Our second set of notes contains as many words as we were going to allow ourselves for the whole summary. Fortunately, setting material out as a list of notes is not usually the most compact way of presenting it. Writing it out in proper sentences can take fewer words.

At this point we need to check our notes against the original passage to make sure that we have, in fact, covered all the essential points. Once we have made that check, however, the standard advice is to set the original passage aside and to write the summary on the basis of the notes and of the general sense of the material that we retain in our head.

When free of the original, it is always worth checking that the order of main points is the most effective order. In this particular case, point 4 contains an idea that is really relevant to the passage as a whole. If there had not been a "popular image of the West," if Easterners had not been attracted by the idea of the frontier life, the railroad companies might never have had the idea of promoting tourism in the first place. The "popular image" is not simply linked to the provision of Western-style facilities around scenic sites. We might slip this information in at a different point, consequently—perhaps when the idea of tourism is mentioned.

A summary of the passage in under 100 words might take this form:

> Railroad companies opened up the West not only for settlement and commerce, but also for tourism, exploiting Easterners' desire to experience the unspoiled scenic grandeur of the West and the exciting life of pioneers. These companies marketed the West through paintings and photographs published in brochures and guidebooks, and, often in partnership with other companies, created an infrastructure of hotels and transportation to service the main sites. They helped preserve the popular view of the West by, for example, constructing buildings modeled on Native American dwellings or log cabins and by using stagecoaches to transport visitors.

This reproduces the essence of the original passage. We may, nevertheless, have the feeling that a good deal has been lost. It is easier to condense a piece of poor writing than a piece of good writing, because poor writing is often loosely structured and padded out with largely irrelevant material or simple verbiage. Tightening up the structure and removing the padding can only improve a passage. A well-organized piece that is succinctly written and where the ideas are illustrated by well-chosen examples will suffer more when filleted.

It is worth noting that when we have to try to fit a large amount of information into a relatively small number of words, we often, of necessity, have to resort to longer and more formal words and more complex grammatical constructions than we might normally use. The phrase "exploiting Easterners' desire to experience" in our summary might be considered an example of compacting that is approaching the limits of what the ordinary reader might be comfortable with. If you are not constrained to a fixed number of words, then it is best to keep things simple, but it is also useful to be able to use complex words and constructions with confidence and clarity.

To summarize, finally, the essential points in summarizing,

- select the main points from the passage;
- add to these the key details needed to put the main points in context;
- check your notes against the original passage, then put the original aside;
- write your summary on the basis of your notes and your general impression of the passage;
- check your summary for clarity.

# QUOTATIONS

There are two important aspects to the use of quotations. The first is selecting the best word, phrase, or passage to quote; the second is incorporating the words you have chosen to quote into your own text. The second of these is a matter that will be dealt with later (*see* INCORPORATING QUOTATIONS INTO TEXT, page 33).

## Rules for Quoting

We may be inclined to think of quotations as belonging primarily to academic writing, particularly literary essays. There is a virtual obligation to quote if you are discussing a play, a novel, or the work of other scholars, but a well-chosen quotation can enhance any type of writing. Words taken directly from a source document can be used to support your own arguments and to give them greater authority by showing that others think the same way that you do (or, alternatively, to give you something to argue against) or to illustrate a point you are making. In the preparatory stages of writing, too, you will frequently find that the easiest way of writing a note is to put down exactly what is said in the source material rather than putting the idea into your own words.

There are certain rules for quotation, however, that should be observed even if you are only quickly jotting down something for use primarily as a note:

1. You must quote accurately
2. You should quote a meaningful section of text
3. You should make a note of where your quotation comes from

These are the essential rules. There are also additional rules that will mainly apply to people writing academic assignments:

4. You should always quote for a purpose
5. You should not quote too often
6. You should not make your quotations too long
7. You should not always rely on your quotations to speak for themselves

The reason for the first rule is obvious. There is no point in appealing to another writer for assistance in assembling your text—which is essentially what you are doing when you quote—and then carelessly distorting that other author's meaning. When you jot down a quotation as a note, you may believe at the time that it is unlikely to form part of your final text, but you may very well change your mind later, so always follow the exact wording of the original.

The phrase "a meaningful section of text" in the second rule is deliberately all inclusive. It may often be sufficient for your purposes to quote a single word from a text if you want to call attention to the particular term that an author uses to describe or explain something. When you are taking notes, however, it is usually better to put down a longer piece of text, because you will probably need a certain amount of context to remind yourself of why you selected those words to quote. Alternatively, or in addition, it is often useful to jot down immediately some indication of what you intend to use the quotation for, as in the following example:

> ". . . Bring forth men-children only, / For thy undaunted mettle should compose / Nothing but males." (Macbeth 1.7, 72–74) Shows that Macbeth is thinking in terms of having a family

"A meaningful section of text" also implies a piece of text that can stand alone and convey meaning. As the above lines from *Macbeth* indicate, a single line of poetry, while it may look complete in itself, does not always convey any meaning unless it is attached to what comes before or after.

The third rule has been mentioned before. A quotation is like any other note. You may want to check later whether there is more useful material where you found the first piece. And if you use the quotation in the text, you will need to give a reference for it.

It is also worth adding here that if you are taking notes and you jot down a quotation, you should put it in quotation marks. It is unlikely that you will confuse Shakespearean verse with your own comments, but a piece of ordinary prose might be indistinguishable from one of your own paraphrases if you do not mark it at the time.

The first of the additional rules, number 4, stems from the general injunction that all the material you assemble in the preparatory stages of the writing process should be oriented toward the task set by yourself in your original mission statement. Over and above this, however, when you come to write your text, you should avoid quoting simply for the sake of it. The essential element in anything you write is your own input. This applies as much to an essay on an author or a literary topic as to any other piece of work. Do not quote merely to show that you have read the text. You can show your familiarity with it much better by making informed and intelligent comments on it than by reproducing large chunks in every paragraph. Do quote, however, to back up or illustrate a specific point.

It is irritating to find the flow of an argument continually broken up by contributions from other authors, especially when the bibliographical references have to be included: "What Jones terms 'a complete waste of time' (1987, 111) and Smith castigates as 'a willful squandering of public money' (2002, 67), Robinson applauds as 'a highly successful experiment in social engineering' (1999, 533)." We do not necessarily need the exact words of Smith, Jones, and Robinson to get the point. Be selective when quoting. One apposite quotation is better than four or five that do not add anything substantial to the text. The familiar adage "Less is more" applies to quotations, as it does to many aspects of the writing process.

A further justification for rule 5 is the limit established by law to the amount that you can quote from a copyrighted work if your own work is published. A few relatively brief quotations will normally count as **fair use**, meaning that your citations taken from another publication are permitted without obtaining the express permission of the copyright holder (though it may still be courteous to obtain permission). Lengthy and frequent quotation from a particular published work will involve obtaining such permission.

The longer the passage you quote, the greater the justification needed for including it. While it is impossible to prescribe a maximum length for a quotation, the point of rule 6 is that you should think carefully before suspending the flow of your own ideas to interrupt with a lengthy exposition of someone else's ideas.

Rule 7 is intended as a reminder that you will usually need to show, directly or indirectly, why you have chosen to insert a quotation. A quotation should work for you in the sense that it should advance or strengthen your argument. It is up to you, however, to make sure that it does its job by providing an appropriate context for it, which means indicating how it contributes. The following, for example, is insufficient:

> Macbeth has Macduff's children murdered out of jealousy: "Upon my head they placed a fruitless crown / And put a barren scepter in my grip" (3.1.62–63).

The quotation is not inappropriate, if you are discussing the role of children in the play, but you are expecting the reader to make a mental leap or to fill in the gaps you have left by not explaining that, in your view, the fact that Macbeth has given up any hope of passing on his crown to a son of his own sharpens his hatred of any man with children (and, in any event, Macbeth's immediate target in act 3 scene 1 is Banquo's son, Fleance).

## Selecting Quotations

The principles that should govern the selection of quotations are implicit in the rules suggested in the previous subsection. Quotations should be selected because they make a point better than you could make it in your own words, or because it is particularly important to include the testimony of the particular person in your argument in his or her own words. The words you quote should be clear, should constitute "a meaningful section of text" (rule 2), and should, if possible, be striking. It is seldom worth quoting someone saying something that anyone could have said.

It is difficult to illustrate the process of selecting quotations, because each source text is different and each writer will have a different purpose in view. Nevertheless, readers who have reached this point in the present text should have acquired some familiarity with the relations between Charles Dickens and the 19th-century American public. Let us return to the example of a writing project proposed earlier. Here is a section from John Forster's biography of Dickens in which Forster puts forward an explanation for the particular enthusiasm with which Dickens was received at the beginning of his first visit to the United States. Let us see what we might extract from it.

> Unmistakably to be seen, in this the earliest of his letters, is the quite fresh and unalloyed impression first received by him at this memorable visit; and it is due, as well to himself as to the country which welcomed him, that this should be considered independently of any modification or change it afterwards underwent. Of the fervency and the universality of the welcome there could be no doubt, and as little that it sprang from feelings honourable both to giver and receiver. The sources of

> Dickens's popularity in England were in truth multiplied many-fold in America. The hearty, cordial, and humane side of his genius had fascinated them quite as much; but there was also something beyond this. . . . I do not say it either to lessen or increase the value of the tribute, but to express simply what it was; and there cannot be a question that the young English author, whom by his language the Americans claimed equally for their own, was almost universally regarded by them as a kind of embodied protest against what was believed to be worst in the institutions of England, depressing and overshadowing in a social sense, and adverse to purely intellectual influences. In all their newspapers of every grade of the time, the feeling of triumph over the Mother Country in this particular is predominant. You worship titles, they said, and military heroes, and millionaires, and we of the New World want to show you, by extending the kind of homage that the Old World reserves for kings and conquerors to a young man with nothing to distinguish him but his heart and his genius, what it we think in these parts worthier of honour than birth or wealth, a title or a sword (Forster, n.d., 425).

Great writers such as William Shakespeare or Dickens, Ralph Waldo Emerson, Robert Frost, or Oscar Wilde sometimes seem to write in quotations. There are gold nuggets on every page, memorable lines in plenty. Forster was not a great writer. He is important insofar as he was a personal friend of Dickens, knew him intimately for most of his adult life, wrote the first biography after consulting Dickens about the project during the latter's lifetime and drawing extensively on personal letters he had received from him, and published the work within four years of Dickens's death. He is consequently a very valuable source of information, but his words are not particularly striking. That deficiency, however, gives him more in common with the average kind of author you might be using as a source. Quotations do not choose themselves but have to be chosen. There is always, incidentally, the option of paraphrasing material that is not particularly quotable.

Probably the most striking aspect of this passage is its ending, a fine, rolling, 19th-century sentence full of noble sentiment and high-sounding words. Forster is attempting to speak as the voice of America and adopts a suitably grand style. Unfortunately, what the voice of America has to say is not really reducible into conveniently sized material suitable for quotation. You might want to extract from it the description of Dickens as "a young man with nothing to distinguish him but his heart or his genius," but otherwise you really have to quote the sentence as a whole—and it is a rather long sentence—or set it aside. Moreover, an American voice speaking for itself would probably be of more interest than that of an Englishman draping himself in the Stars and Stripes.

The criterion of "strikingness," then, is not particularly useful in this instance. What other criteria might we apply? The most useful are those that were used in the process of summarizing (*see* SUMMARIZING, page 25). If we can distinguish the main points and the key details of the passage, we will get to the heart of what the author is trying to say. That is where we should find the most quotable elements.

Forster seems to be saying four things essentially:

- At first, Dickens was genuinely glad to be in America, and Americans were genuinely glad to welcome him.
- Americans appreciated Dickens's novels for the same reasons that the English did, but they also had additional reasons for appreciating them.
- Democratic Americans felt that Dickens shared their distaste for repressive, class-ridden English institutions.
- Consequently, Americans felt that they, rather than the English, were the people who could truly honor his genius.

If we could find phrases or sentences relating to some or all of these points (the quotations do not necessarily have to encapsulate them), we should come away with a useful haul.

The phrase "the fervency and universality of his welcome" seems to capture the essence of the first point. It is not perhaps a form of words that would occur at once to a modern writer, but it would not be difficult to fit it into a modern sentence: "Dickens's earliest letter home shows that he was amazed and delighted by what Forster calls 'the fervency and universality of his welcome.' " Continuing on, Forster's sentence "The sources of Dickens's popularity were multiplied many-fold in America" could be retained to exemplify the second point—with the option of extracting the core of it, "were multiplied many-fold," if that fits in more conveniently.

There is quite a striking phrase in the passage that sums up the third point. Dickens was seen as an "embodied protest against what was believed to be worst in the institutions of England." Here we have arrived at the center of interest in this passage. Forster's formulation of the point is strong and neat. The rest of that sentence, however, is not particularly easy to follow, and if we need to expand on the point, we could probably do better by explaining it in our own words. This statement is definitely worth keeping.

The final point takes us into Forster's grand conclusion, but the sentence preceding it might be worth noting down: "In all their newspapers of every grade at the time, the feeling of triumph over the Mother Country in this particular is predominant." It is not a very neat sentence but could be made more suitable for reuse, perhaps, by the omission of some words and the insertion of ellipses (*see* INCORPORATING QUOTATIONS INTO TEXT immediately below): "In all their newspapers . . ., the feeling of triumph over the Mother Country . . . is predominant." (On the basis of the rule that quotations should not be relied on to speak for themselves, we might need to remind a reader that at that time, 1842, many British people, and perhaps some Americans, still thought of Britain as the mother country of the United States, despite the lapse of nearly 70 years from the Declaration of Independence.)

## Incorporating Quotations into Text

It is very likely that at some point in your work, you will want to include the exact words said or written by another person. There are rules governing the way in which quotations should be presented in text. These are dealt with briefly here.

The first rule to remember is that you should always quote accurately. When you are taking notes, be very careful that you copy out the extract that you need *exactly* as it is written in the source. The same applies if you write down words spoken by somebody, although in this case you will have to add your own punctuation.

The second rule stems from the first: Do not quote from memory. Even if you think you have a crystal-clear recollection of what was written or said, always check the source to confirm that your memory is correct. If you cannot find the source, it is usually safer to offer a paraphrase in your own words than to risk misquoting the original. Memory does play tricks. Some misquotations become almost better known than originals. Shakespeare is often credited with writing "We are such stuff as dreams are made of," when he actually wrote, "We are such stuff / As dreams are made on" (*The Tempest* 4.1.156–157). Similarly, the saying "Money is the root of all evil" is in fact a misquotation from the Bible; the actual quotation is "The love of money is the root of all evil" (1 Timothy 6:10, King James Version). Always check.

The third rule also stems from the first. If you need to alter anything in the passage you are quoting, you must make it plain to the reader that you have done so. For instance, if you omit part of the passage because it is irrelevant to the point you are making or because the quotation as it stands is uncomfortably long, you should represent the omitted words by an ellipsis (. . .). Forster, in the passage previously quoted from his biography of Dickens, writes, "In all their newspapers of every grade of the time, the feeling of triumph over the Mother Country in this particular is predominant." If you feel that the phrases "of every grade of the time" and "in this particular" do not add greatly to the essential meaning of the sentence, you may omit them and write instead: "In all their newspapers . . ., the feeling of triumph over the Mother Country . . . is predominant."

The fourth rule is that you should always be careful to ensure that the words you quote fit grammatically into the framework you provide for them and that the framework and the quotation together make good sense. For instance, suppose the person you are quoting says, "I woke and found myself alone." You could write "Belinda said, 'I woke and found myself alone.' " The use of a verb such as *say* without a conjunction such as *that* enables you to put down the exact words the person uses. But you cannot write "Belinda said that 'I woke and found myself alone,' " or "Belinda described how 'I woke and found myself alone.' " Both of these are ungrammatical according to the rules for reported speech. If you were reporting what Belinda said without actually quoting it, you would have to write "Belinda said that she woke and found herself alone." You must follow the same pattern even if you use quotation marks to show that you are using the same words that she used.

There is a problem here that we can solve only by referring to rule three. You must indicate any departures from the wording of the original. If you change a word in the original in order to make it fit inside your sentence, you must put the replacement word into brackets ([]). So, continuing with the example used in the previous paragraph, you could write "Belinda described how '[she] woke and found [herself] alone,' " though it would be neater to write "Belinda described how she 'woke and found [herself] alone.' "

The elements you will most likely need to change to fit a quotation into text are the personal and reflexive pronouns, the tense of verbs, and the capital letters at the beginnings of sentences. Here are examples of each of these three.

*Original:* We must cultivate our garden.
*Altered to fit context:* You should follow Voltaire's advice and "cultivate [your] garden."

*Original:* A nightingale sang in Berkeley Square.
*Altered to fit context:* "If ever the day should come when a "nightingale [sings] in Berkeley Square," . . .

*Original:* The country is obviously in terminal decline. Economic prospects are worse than they have ever been.
*Altered to fit context:* The country's "[e]conomic prospects are worse than they have ever been," according to the *Wall Street Journal.*

For further discussion on the use of brackets, see BRACKETS (page 353). For further discussion on the use of ellipsis, see ELLIPSIS (page 348). For the correct punctuation to use with quotation marks, see chapter 4, page 167, and chapter 7, page 356.

## Plagiarism

Plagiarism is the offense of passing off another person's written work or ideas as your own. To avoid charges of plagiarism, all quotations should be shown in quotation marks and attributed to their original author by means of a reference (*see* REFERENCES, page 89). When you are paraphrasing or generally presenting ideas that are identifiable as coming from another person's works—that is, usually another person's particular opinions as opposed to facts that are available from a variety of sources—you should indicate where the ideas came from. For example, referring to the passage used as a source of quotations in the previous subsection, you should not borrow Forster's insight that, in honoring Dickens, Americans felt that they were showing the superiority of their values to those of the "Mother Country," without indicating that it comes from Forster, even if you use your own words rather than a direct quotation. Simply adding a phrase such as "as Forster suggests" or "according to Forster" is sufficient to keep things straight.

### PHOTOCOPYING

Throughout this section there has been an implicit assumption that all the material collected in preparation for a writing project is written down by hand or by machine. It has probably occurred to many readers that it would be much simpler to make a photocopy of anything required. If you cannot, for example, borrow a book from the library because it belongs in the reference section, then you can simply photocopy the relevant pages.

The only problems with photocopying are the following. First, there are legal restrictions on the photocopying of copyrighted works. The staff at your library should be able to advise on the extent to which it is permissible to make photocopies, or you can seek guidance from a book such as *The Chicago Manual of Style,* but photocopying limits lie in a legal gray area. Second, assembling material means, first and foremost, selecting it. It may be convenient to have some photocopied pages, but you still have to go through them and pick out the passages that relate to your project. Admittedly, it may be easier to do this by highlighting the relevant passages with a fluorescent marker, but the work still has to be done.

# THINKING AND RESEARCHING: AN OVERVIEW

- The writing process begins in your head. Before you start, consider carefully what kind of document you are writing, what you are writing about, and whom you are writing for. Work out a mental or written "mission statement."
- Your own input is the most valuable element in any piece of writing. Before you begin, generate your own ideas by thinking creatively around the topic and asking productive questions. Organize your ideas.
- Decide whether your own mental resources are sufficient or you need to do additional research. If research is required, use your own books, visit a library, and search the Internet.
- Assemble the material you need to carry out your writing task in the form of clear notes. Supplement your notes with paraphrases, summaries, and quotations, as appropriate.
- Make a plan.

# PLANNING

## Why Make a Plan?

There are few pieces of writing that do not benefit from being planned, at least informally, in advance. The more complex the writing task you have in hand, the more useful it is to have a plan and the more detailed that plan is likely to be. But even if you simply have to write a letter—a business or official letter, in particular—then a plan will help ensure that you have covered all the necessary points Planning will help you as a writer. It will give shape to your task; it will break it down into separate stages so that you do not feel you are setting out toward some impossibly distant final goal; it will enable you to measure your progress. Planning will also help your reader. If your piece has a planned and coherent structure, in which one point leads logically to the next, it will be much easier for your reader to follow. Indeed, in any piece of writing that involves your reader in following an argument, it is often advisable to let your plan be a visible, rather than invisible, structure—a set of explicit pointers to show the reader where you intend to take him or her next.

It is true that by planning you are likely to forfeit a certain amount of spontaneity. But spontaneity in writing is not perhaps as desirable a quality as it might seem. It might be wonderfully exciting and invigorating for a writer at the desk to be seized suddenly by a brilliant idea and to feel impelled to follow it wherever it leads. But the reader may not share the excitement of the chase. The reader may simply think "What's this all about?" or "Where is the author leading me?" or "What has all this got do with what the author was saying on the previous page?" A brilliant idea is a wonderful thing, but it is usually a more effective element if it does not appear out of nowhere but rather seems to arise naturally from what preceded it.

Paradoxically, the effect of naturalness is more often than not achieved by careful planning. Think of the dramatic appearance or reappearance of a character in a play or movie. Did it suddenly come into the writer's head to bring in that character at that particular moment? Possibly, but it is more likely that the writer had been planning from the outset to give the audience a pleasant or unpleasant surprise. Novelists, dramatists, and screenwriters plan. Poets probably plan long poems. Planning is a creative activity. When you plan, you are, among other things, organizing your material for the best aesthetic effect.

Spontaneity, to take this point further, is not necessarily the same thing as liveliness. Liveliness is always a welcome quality, but it will come more from your own mind and personality as these are expressed in the way you write. Spontaneity, the sense that something is done on the spur of the moment, is fine in a personal letter or e-mail, for the best personal communications give the impression that the writer is speaking to you via the paper or screen. But even some personal letters would benefit from planning. We have probably all at some time received a lengthy "Dear Friends" letter at Christmas or the New Year, in which the writer proceeds to tell us—and the rest of his or her acquaintances—everything that has happened to the family in the course of the previous 12 months with little regard for logic or chronology or for whether we are familiar with all the *dramatis personae*. A little organization, and a little empathy with the reader, would often not go amiss. Not planning more often results in rambling and repetition than in a "fine careless rapture."

Finally, when you make a plan, you are not forging a set of manacles that you will have to wear for the duration of your writing task. A plan can be altered at any time to accommodate new insights that emerge in the course of composition. As soon as you have a brilliant new idea, it is probably best to record it in written form, as notes or text, and then go back and adjust your plan. Do not chance it, hoping that everything will magically come together. You will get to your directions sooner and with fewer detours if you have an accurate map updated to take account of the newest circumstances.

## Preparing a Plan

When you have completed your thinking and research, you will probably have accumulated a mass of data. Unless you have been meticulously operating a card file system or some computer-based equivalent, the chances are that your material will be spread over a number of sheets of paper or a number of computer files. You now need to bring all that material together and begin seriously to organize it.

In theory, it may seem difficult to organize your data if you do not have a plan and difficult to make a plan if you have not organized your data. In practice, we multitask. You may have conducted your research on the basis of a rough plan that you sketched out when you first identified your main areas of interest in the topic, in which case you can adapt that plan in light of any new insights you have gained. It may be that you prefer to draw a line under the first stage in the process and start afresh. In either case, your first requirement is a precise statement of the topic you are going to write about —a title, if what you are writing happens to be an academic assignment, a journal article, or a report—followed by a list of the main points you intend to address—a list that could possibly become a list of main headings in a formal piece.

## DEFINING THE TOPIC

Defining, redefining, or reaffirming the precise nature of the task ahead of you is important at this stage. Several of the topics that were used for example purposes in the previous section were very large scale. You could easily write a book about Charles Dickens and America or about wine making in California. In the course of investigating such a subject, you will probably have realized how much there is to write about and that if you endeavor to cover the whole of it when you have only limited time and space available, the results will inevitably be superficial. Do not bite off more than you can chew. Be realistic about what you can achieve, and if necessary, scale down your ambitions.

It may be that in the course of doing your research, you have realized that your main interest lies in—or that the most interesting material that you have been able to collect relates to—a particular area of the subject. If that happens to be the case, consider defining your topic around that particular area. You might, for example, concentrate on the history of wine making in California, the economics of California wine making, or a typical day at a California winery. If you are writing on a broad topic, it is possible and desirable to deal with some specific instances, but it is just as possible, if you are writing on a more narrowly defined subject, to include a section that covers broader issues. If, say, you choose to write about Charles Dickens in Boston—where he enjoyed himself most and where the impressions on both sides were most positive—nothing prevents you from alluding to the fact that relations were less rosy elsewhere, for instance, by comparing what made Boston congenial to Dickens with what was lacking when he visited other parts of the country in 1842.

## ORGANIZING THE MATERIAL

To illustrate the planning of a writing task, from the point at which the topic is finally defined onward, we shall use a fresh example.

Let us assume that you have decided to write on the subject of tourism. Let us further assume that while collecting material on this vast topic you have become aware that while tourism provides a vital source of revenue in many areas of the world, the attitude of local people toward tourists is often ambivalent. You have also come across a comment by, let's say, a local hotelier or politician at some prime tourist destination who is on record as saying "Here, the tourist is always a welcome guest." You are struck by this comment and decide to take it as your title. How do you set about planning a piece of writing on this subject under this heading?

The usual method is similar to the one adopted when making a summary (*see* SUMMARIZING, page 25). First make a list of your main points. If, as was suggested above, you are inclined to think that there are two sides to this particular issue and that an influx of tourists has both advantages and disadvantages to local residents, then these points are likely to fall into two distinct categories:

*Advantages*

*Tourists bring money into the area*
*Jobs are created for the local community*
*New facilities are built that also benefit the local community*
*Locals benefit from contact with people from other countries*
*The area is "put on the map"*

*Disadvantages*

*The needs of local people become subordinate to those of the visitors*
*Local industries or agriculture may suffer as funds are diverted to setting up a tourist industry*
*Tourism can damage the environment*
*The tourist trade is subject to outside influences*
*Local residents can become "a human zoo"*

If your main points are outlined as above, the next stage is to list subpoints under each of them with the eventual aim of producing a plan that will correspond roughly to the order of paragraphs in your full version, each subpoint indicating an amount of material that will fill one paragraph, or possibly more than one. But you should also be beginning to think about the overall scheme of your piece. Are you going to deal with all the advantageous aspects as a block and then deal with all the disadvantageous ones? Or are you going to mingle the two, perhaps citing an advantage, but then showing that there is also a downside to it?

Assuming for the moment that you adopt the first alternative, keeping advantages and disadvantages separate, a more detailed plan might look like the following:

*Advantages*

*Tourists bring money into the area*
*-Scenically attractive areas are often poor areas*
*-The country may need hard currency*

*Jobs are created for the local community*
*-In hotels*
*-In transportation*
*-Existing industries expand to supply goods and services to visitors*

New facilities are built that also benefit the local community
-Roads, airports, and other transportation links
-Utilities
-Entertainments

Locals benefit from contact with people from other countries
-Learning languages
-Finding out how other people live

The area is "put on the map"
-All sorts of benefits can flow from the fact that people from outside the area get to know it and like it

---

Disadvantages

---

The needs of local people become subordinate to those of the visitors
-First-world needs are not the same as third-world needs
-"He who pays the piper calls the tune"

Local industries or agriculture may suffer as funds are diverted to setting up a tourist industry
-Land used for building hotels, etc.
Tourism can damage the environment
-Specific examples

The tourist trade is subject to outside influences
-Different areas compete with one another
-Fashions change
-Terrorist threat, etc.

Local residents can become "a human zoo"
-Local culture becomes tourist entertainment and loses meaning

A further level of detail would introduce examples to illustrate particular points, which you would perhaps expect to deal with in less than a paragraph, always depending on the scale of the piece and the material you have available. Let's use the following point, listed under disadvantages, to go into greater detail:

Tourism can damage the environment
- Natural features are eroded or polluted
  - The Great Barrier Reef
  - The Dolomites
  - Trails in national parks
- Historic towns suffer increased traffic and air pollution
  - Bath, England
  - Salzburg, Austria

If you feel that it might not work to present the whole case for one side and follow it with the whole case for the other side, you could try the second option of interspersing advantages and disadvantages. You might need to select slightly different material in this instance, so that you provided an appropriate negative aspect for each positive aspect you put forward. If the piece were planned in this way, the resulting outline might look something like this:

---

Tourists bring money into the area

---

Scenically attractive areas are often poor areas
The country may need hard currency

But: Does the money go to local people or mainly to, e.g., large, possibly multinational hotel chains?
Tourist money cannot be solely relied on for area's economic well-being

---

Jobs are created for the local community

---

In, e.g., hotels and transportation

But: These are mainly low-level service jobs
Existing industries may expand to supply goods and services to visitors

But: If there are no existing industries, will they be set up locally or will materials and labor be shipped in from elsewhere?

---

New facilities are built that also benefit the local community

---

Roads, airports and other transportation links
Utilities
Entertainments

*But: Do local communities really benefit, as is often claimed?*

*Example—Olympic Games in Atlanta, Barcelona*
*Former Olympic Villages become luxury housing too expensive for local residents*

---

*Locals benefit from contact with people from other countries*

---

*Learning languages*
*Finding out how other people live*

*But: Their customs and culture can become curiosities for patronizing tourists*

---

*The area is "put on the map"*

---

*All sorts of benefits can flow from the fact that people from outside the area get to know it and like it*

*But: The way of life of local people may be changed forever; there is no going back*

For the purposes of this particular example, neither of the two plans is superior to the other. What is important is that the plan should embody all the material you have chosen to write about and that it is organized according to the principles that suit you and your intended purpose best.

## FORMAL PLANS

What we have been drawing up is an informal plan insofar as it is intended for your own use and guidance. There may be occasions when you have to submit a formal plan or outline. In such a case, the basic principle remains the same, but each level of detail has to be marked by a different rank in a notation. One common hierarchy of symbols is as follows:

- First level—Roman numerals followed by a period—I.
- Second level—capital letters followed by a period—A.
- Third level—Arabic numerals followed by a period—1.
- Fourth level—lowercase letters followed by a period—a.
- Fifth level—Arabic numerals in parentheses—(1)
- Sixth level—lowercase letters in parentheses—(a)

If we were to set out the original informal plan for the tourism project in this way, the formal outline would look like this:

I. Advantages
    A. Tourists bring money into the area
        1. Scenically attractive areas are often poor areas
        2. The country may need hard currency

- B. Jobs are created for the local community
  1. In hotels
  2. In transportation
  3. Existing industries expand to supply goods and services to visitors
- C. New facilities are built that also benefit the local community
  1. Roads, airports, and other transportation links
  2. Utilities
  3. Entertainments
- D. Locals benefit from contact with people from other countries
  1. Learning languages
  2. Finding out how other people live
- E. The area is "put on the map"
  1. A. All sorts of benefits can flow from the fact that people from outside the area get to know it and like it

II. Disadvantages
- A. The needs of local people become subordinate to those of the visitors
  1. First-world needs are not the same as third-world needs
  2. "He who pays the piper calls the tune"
- B. Local industries or agriculture may suffer as funds are diverted to setting up a tourist industry
  1. Land used for building hotels, etc.
- C. Tourism can damage the environment
  1. Natural features are eroded or polluted
     - a. The Great Barrier Reef
     - b. The Dolomites
     - c. Trails in national parks
  2. Historic towns suffer increased traffic and air pollution
     - a. Bath, England
     - b. Salzburg, Austria
- D. The tourist trade is subject to outside influences
  1. Different areas compete with one another
  2. Fashions change
  3. Terrorist threat, etc.
- E. Local residents can become "a human zoo"
  1. Local culture becomes tourist entertainment and loses meaning

Only comparatively rarely will you need to use all six levels in a plan.

One different style that is becoming increasingly used is 1., 1.1, 1.1.1, etc., for the different levels:

1. Advantages
   - 1.1 Tourists bring money into the area
     - 1.1.1 Scenically attractive areas are often poor areas
     - 1.1.2 The country may need hard currency
   - 1.2 Jobs are created for the local community
     - 1.2.1 In hotels
     - 1.2.2 In transportation
     - 1.2.3 Existing industries expand to supply goods and services to visitors

- 1.3 New facilities are built that also benefit the local community
  - 1.3.1 Roads, airports, and other transportation links
  - 1.3.2 Utilities
  - 1.3.3 Entertainments
- 1.4 Locals benefit from contact with people from other countries
  - 1.4.1 Learning languages
  - 1.4.2 Finding out how other people live
- 1.5 The area is "put on the map"
  - 1.5.1 All sorts of benefits can flow from the fact that people from outside the area get to know it and like it

2. Disadvantages
   - 2.1 The needs of local people become subordinate to those of the visitors
     - 2.1.1 First-world needs are not the same as third-world needs
     - 2.1.2 "He who pays the piper calls the tune"
   - 2.2 Local industries or agriculture may suffer as funds are diverted to setting up a tourist industry
     - 2.2.1 Land used for building hotels, etc.
   - 2.3 Tourism can damage the environment and so on.
     - 2.3.1 Natural features are eroded or polluted
       - 2.3.1.1 The Great Barrier Reef
       - 2.3.1.2 The Dolomites
       - 2.3.1.3 Trails in national parks

## DIALOGUING WITH THE READER

In the discussion of the preparatory and planning processes so far, the reader has been left on the sidelines somewhat, but being aware of whom you are writing for is just as important as being aware of what you are writing and what you are writing about. As the writer, you are the prime mover in any writing task—you are saying what you want to say—but saying it has little purpose if your message is not understood by and does not resonate with the reader.

An awareness of the reader can be particularly helpful when making a plan, especially if what you are writing is aimed at a very specific audience. If you are unsure of the most effective way to arrange your material, it may assist you to enter into an imaginary dialogue or question-and-answer session with the sort of person to whom you are addressing your remarks.

If you are arguing a case, for instance, this method can be especially useful.

> If I said *this,* what would you naturally say in reply?
> If you made *that* objection, how would I counter it?
> I say *this,* but you remain unconvinced. What further evidence can I offer to help change your mind?

You do not, however, have to imagine the reader as an adversary.

> I know that you are interested in *this.* I want to call your attention to *that.* What can I say about *that,* which will link it to your main area of interest?

You could, if it is helpful, draw up a rough plan in dialogue form:

> I say: Tourism creates jobs. The X hotel in Y employs 400 people.
> You say: Waiting tables and changing bedclothes, what kind of a job is that?
> I say: A good job, if the alternative is living in a shantytown and begging.

Continue the dialogue until it reaches a logical conclusion, then by removing the speech prefixes and tidying up the wording, you will have a workable plan.

## INTRODUCTION AND CONCLUSION

The plans that have been drawn up by way of example so far cover only the body of the piece; the introduction and the conclusion have been left out of the account. The plan is not complete until you have decided how you are going to begin and end. In some respects, the beginning and the ending are the most important parts of the piece, especially the beginning. When starting, you have to arouse the reader's interest and persuade him or her that what follows is worth reading. When finishing, you have to repay the reader's attention by showing that everything that he or she has read has been to some purpose and has led to a valuable conclusion. All this said, it is easier to plan an introduction and conclusion once you have a firm idea of what you are going to say and in what order, so it often helps to plan these last.

There is a simple and traditional model for a speech to an audience that runs as follows:

- Say what you're going to say
- Say it
- Say that you've said it

If you are writing something that you intend to read aloud, then you should beware of straying too far from these guidelines. Listeners, especially note-taking listeners, require a certain amount of repetition if they are to receive and understand your message.

Even if you are writing to be read rather than heard, there is a good deal of merit in this prescription. Readers generally appreciate being told what to expect and then being led to a more or less predetermined goal along a clear route. The standard introduction, then, provides a concise statement of what your intention is, how the piece is to be structured, what the main points are to be, and what the conclusion is to be. For a comparatively brief piece of writing, there may be no need to draw up a plan for a standard introduction, because it is unlikely to be more than a paragraph in length and in planning it you will more or less have written it, as shown in the example below.

> **Here the Tourist Is Always a Welcome Guest**
>
> Many areas of the world now depend on tourism for a substantial part of their income. My aim in this essay is to discuss both the immediate financial gains and the other benefits that tourism can bring to such an area and its local community. But creating the large-scale infrastructure necessary to cater to tourists' needs can bring enormous changes to the

> area and its people. Not all these changes are likely to be welcome to the inhabitants, and I shall also be discussing the disadvantages that tourism brings with it. Nonetheless, on balance, I conclude that the disadvantages are outweighed by the advantages and that, consequently, in most parts of the world the tourist is, indeed, always a welcome guest.

This example is an exceedingly safe and straightforward way of beginning a piece of writing. It may "arouse the reader's interest"—assuming that the reader is predisposed to be interested in matters relating to the tourist trade—but it will not capture his or her attention. There must be more striking and imaginative ways of starting.

Indeed there are. You could begin with some more dramatic fact, if you have one at your disposal, such as, "The world over, some 500 million people now make their living directly or indirectly from the tourist trade." You could begin with a significant question: "Have you ever considered, as you lie by the pool in a swanky hotel in some exotic location, precisely what the person you have just sent off to bring you a glass of iced tea thinks of tourists like you?" You could begin with a little piece of action or dialogue (this is a journalistic favorite): "Mr. Schwenk, the hotel manager, was having a busy day. The lady from Michigan was having problems with her dog; the gentleman from Munich had just dropped his cell phone in the pool; the bus had broken down on the way to collect a party of visitors from the airport. Was Mr. Schwenk troubled? Not at all, it seemed. He handed me my key with his usual gleaming smile. 'Here,' he said, 'the tourist is always a welcome guest.' "

Any such introduction would work if it suited your purpose, your material, and your reader. Nevertheless, whatever kind of sentence or paragraph you use as a launchpad, it will have implications for the way you treat your material, and you may have to adjust your plan accordingly. Bringing in Mr. Schwenk may seem like a brilliant idea, but you then have to decide whether to use him further or dismiss him. In any event, you would be well advised to ensure that the basic material that is included in the standard introduction features in your more imaginative introduction as well. The reader needs to know pretty soon that Mr. Schwenk has only a minor role in a larger-scale production.

It is possible to construct an "imaginative" conclusion, too. Experienced writers know, however, that if it is sometimes difficult to find a beginning, finding an ending is often the hardest part of all. The simplest type of conclusion is usually the best. Sum up your argument as briefly as possible and state as clearly as you can the idea or impression that you wish to leave with your reader.

> No one could argue that tourism is an unalloyed blessing for the host community. There are costs, above all environmental and cultural costs. But for most areas and most communities, as I have shown, the economic benefits are undeniable, and opening themselves up to the tourist trade can mean the difference between survival and inevitable decline. In my view, then, the tourist ought to be treated as a valued customer and encouraged to come again.

# PLANNING: AN OVERVIEW

- Organize your material if you have not already organized it.
- Use creative thinking techniques or an imaginary dialogue with the reader to assist you.
- Draw up a plan, first identifying the main points you have to make and using them as headings.
- List subpoints under the main headings.
- Check that the plan is complete and logically ordered.
- Consider your introduction and conclusion.
- Begin to write.

# 2

# Writing Your Document

## GETTING STARTED

There seems no good reason why ordinary, businesslike, sensible people should not be able to sit down and begin the work of composition that they have spent a lot of time and effort preparing for. Writing, as has been said before, is just a task, similar to many other tasks. It would be nice to think that if you sat down and applied your mind to the material, composition would then prove to be relatively easy. You researched diligently, planned carefully, now you reap your reward as the words start to flow out onto the paper or screen.

Unfortunately, it does not always happen like that. The work you did beforehand will undoubtedly make things much easier for you in the long run, but there is no guarantee that good preparation will automatically result in effortless performance. Writing can be hard work. Getting started on a piece of writing can be particularly hard. Far from flowing, words seem to get stuck somewhere—either between your brain and your fingertips or in some back area of your brain where your consciousness cannot find them. Meanwhile, the page or the screen remains resolutely blank.

Do not take this gentle warning to imply that there are always problems when you begin a piece of writing or that if you sit down and words do start to flow, you must be doing something wrong. Far from it. Most writers have good days and bad days. Most writers find some pieces virtually write themselves, while others have to be hammered out word by word and sentence by sentence. If your fingers are flying over the buttons from the outset, be thankful and press on. You can then skip ahead in this chapter to the section on DRAFTING (page 51).

The keynote of this subsection, however, is that making a start can prove difficult. If the next paragraph describes your experiences, then stay with the text. The difficulties can be overcome.

At some time or other almost everyone experiences difficulties in getting started: You sit down at your desk, feeling rather tense and conscious that you have a fairly long and possibly arduous task ahead of you. You check your notes and your plan. You pause to gather your thoughts before launching out. You find that the pause prolongs itself as you stare at the blank page or screen. The words that you hoped would spill forth obstinately refuse to come. In order to break the spell, you force yourself to write something down, but you do so without conviction. The few words or sentences you have squeezed out look clumsy and inadequate and seem not to be at all what you wanted to say. You erase them and are back to square one. You try again, and the same thing happens. All the while, the little confidence and resolve you began with are ebbing away, and the magnitude of the task seems to be increasing. The dreaded words *writer's block* come to mind.

## Writer's Block

Let us try to get this particular distraction out of the way at the very beginning. You may ask why, if writing is a task and skill comparable to many others, there is no such thing as "chef's block" or "driver's block." There are, no doubt, psychological factors that can cause a practitioner of any skill to lose suddenly the ability to practice it. Writers seem particularly vulnerable to them. Instances of celebrated and successful literary figures finding themselves apparently unable to begin new work or complete work already begun have been well publicized. If you find yourself staring at a blank screen or a blank sheet of paper and you cannot nerve yourself to begin writing, despite the fact that all your material has been neatly organized and your plan is laid out in full beside you, are you then suffering from writer's block?

No, it is far more likely that you are having an attack of writer's cold feet. It is not at all uncommon to be intimidated by a blank page or screen. Even the most humdrum writing task involves some use of the creative imagination, enabling us to string words together deliberately in order to communicate, yet the creative imagination seems to be a rather delicate function of the mind and easily intimidated. In addition, everyone starts with an image of what the final text ought to look like and gets frustrated when early attempts do not live up to this image. But you can and you must get around these problems. Otherwise all your preparatory work will be wasted.

Forget writer's block, think positively, do not lose heart, and make it as easy as you can for yourself. If you do have problems starting, try the suggested procedures immediately following.

## Breaking the Spell

There are certain practical steps that you can take in order to make it easier to write.

- Find yourself a quiet place where there are no distractions. We hear of great books being written on the kitchen table. It is unlikely that they were written while the kids were in the kitchen with the author or while the author was trying to cook a meal. If necessary, take the phone off the hook and ignore the doorbell. You need to be able to concentrate.
- Divide up the work into finite and achievable tasks. Try to complete a particular task—for example, writing one section or a certain number of words—within the time you have allowed for a writing session. If, for any reason, you are unable to finish, do not waste time feeling guilty; concentrate instead on what you have achieved this session and tell yourself that, having got this far, you will surely be able to get further next time.
- Set aside a specific amount of time to write. Deadlines are bracing. If you allow yourself an open-ended session, you may well find that, as

Parkinson's law states, your work will simply expand to fill the time available—in other words, you write no more in three hours than you would have written in two if you had set yourself a cutoff point and worked toward it. Furthermore, idleness and distraction activities have the ability to expand toward infinity as well. If you have real problems or cannot concentrate, take a short break away from your desk, make yourself a coffee, and think about something else. But do not give up. Go back and work out the rest of the session.

- Use any means you can to strengthen your self-discipline. Give yourself pep talks, listen to a favorite piece of music, promise yourself a reward when you complete a task. Warn yourself that the task will not go away.
- If you are stuck, try discussing the problem with other people. They may have a good idea, or their encouragement may help to overcome your lack of confidence.
- Be realistic. Do not set yourself too big a task or to work for too long. Above all, do not expect to produce a final version at the first attempt.
- Do not necessarily start at the beginning. Start at any point where you find an easy way in. Write first about whichever part of the topic is freshest in your mind or most engages your interest. You can write the introduction later.
- Get started. If you really can't think of anything sensible to say—which is highly unlikely if you are well prepared—write the first thing that comes into your head. But do not get too critical. Do not get into the write-erase-despair routine. Try to keep on writing. Reassure yourself: This is not the final version; there is plenty of time available to get it right. This is just the first draft.

Let us consider the two final points in a little more detail.

It was suggested at the end of the previous chapter that the introduction can be compiled, along with the conclusion, after you have planned the body of the text. It can also be written, however, after all other writing is complete for the simple reason that you can write an introduction more confidently when you know precisely what it introduces. This applies especially to pieces of writing that require an introduction of a relatively straightforward "say what you're going to say" kind. If you have in mind a more dramatic scene-setting introduction that sets the tone for the rest of the piece, or from which the rest of the piece is intended to grow organically, then it obviously makes sense to start with it if you can, but do not become fixated on writing the introduction at the beginning, particularly if it is causing you problems. You will be able to fill in even important gaps later. If necessary, move on.

If you move on, choose a section in which you have plenty to say, where there is a substantial amount of information to be communicated or a substantial argument to be put forward. This section may very well be at your first main point, but if you have made a detailed plan, there is nothing to stop you from beginning at any point along the way. It can easily happen that you have recently been researching, or thinking about, one particular aspect of your topic, and you are, as a result, bursting with ideas about it. If you have some creative steam, exploit it to get yourself started rather than letting it dissipate. Perhaps when you have completed this particular section, you will feel more confident to go back to the beginning and write the rest of the text in sequence, but there is no necessity to do this. You can deal with the sections in any order, perhaps tackling what seem to you the easiest or most difficult first. You can then allocate the pieces you have written to their proper places in the overall scheme as a separate exercise. One word of warning, however: If you write sections out of order, it is particularly important to apply rigorous consistency checks (*see* CHECKING FOR CONSISTENCY, page 86) when you make your final revisions.

The last of the points listed above may seem like a counsel of despair, but it is not entirely so. In order to achieve something, we often have to ignore temporarily considerations that are undoubtedly relevant to the task but that we cannot cope with at the particular moment. Trying to keep everything in mind can be inhibiting when the most urgent need is simply to make some progress. That is frequently the case for writers.

Even experienced writers have to find their way into each new writing task and may start tentatively. Only gradually do they become fully aware of the demands imposed by the undertaking and of the methods they will use to meet them. You will know when you sit down to begin what kind of thing you are writing and what you are writing about. You may not know precisely *how* you are going to write. And that is a question that is difficult to decide in the abstract. Even if, on the basis of the kind of piece you are writing and the kind of reader you envisage for it, you have already decided to adopt a particular style and tone, making the decision is not quite the same as actually getting the words to come out in the style you have chosen to use.

Now, this is obviously a very important matter, but it is more important at this stage not to let it prevent you from making a start. It is precisely the sort of consideration you should push to the back of your mind if it is weighing on you. Because writing is a task and a skill comparable to many others, the same conditions apply to it as to other jobs, most notably, for present purposes, that you can and will learn by actually doing the task. That is why it is often advisable to begin at any point in the text where you can write easily. Get started by any means possible and keep going, if necessary disregarding grammar, spelling, or anything else that inhibits you; the words, style, and sections will gradually begin to fall into place. Get started, and the voice—that is, the tone and attitude appropriate to your personality, the task, and the reader—of this particular piece of writing will probably begin to emerge. Get started, because if it doesn't come out right on the first attempt, there is still time to improve matters. Progress builds confidence, and confidence, as we know from many areas in life, is a catalyst that promotes the exercise of skill, while lack of confidence inhibits it. Don't think or hesitate for too long; make a start.

## Drafting

A draft is a fully written-out preliminary version of your piece of work, which serves as a basis for the final, finished version. A draft is something exciting because it represents a major step toward the completion of the task. It is also something reassuring because it is not the final version. It can be corrected. It can also be shown to other people and used to produce helpful feedback.

Only the most accomplished actors and directors manage to shoot a movie scene in a single take; only very accomplished and very lucky writers get it all right the first time. This is why most people find themselves advancing toward their goal by way of a number of drafts. The actual number of drafts depends on how long it takes you to satisfy your own requirements or those of the person who has commissioned you to write something. You should, in any event, allow time to make at least two drafts before you produce the final version.

This does not, however, mean that you have to write or type your whole piece out in full three times. Thankfully, drafting is no longer the laborious process that it was when everything was written out by hand, although the basic procedure is little changed. Before, longhand writers would write out their work; read through it again, crossing out whatever seemed unnecessary, incorrect, inappropriate, or poorly expressed and writing edits and additions between the lines and in the margins; and then write the whole thing out again as a clean copy. Many people still find it easier to revise on paper rather than on screen and therefore print out their work. If you prefer this method, be sure you leave fairly wide margins and double-space your text so that there is room for your corrections on the draft.

If you prefer to edit on screen, you can simulate the on-paper procedure fairly exactly by using the "Track Changes" tool in your word-processing program. It leaves everything you delete on the screen, but in a different color and with a line through it. It records all your additions in another color. Afterward, if you switch off the Track Changes tool, you will be left with a clean copy. Alternatively, you can make a copy of your first draft and in this new file make your corrections, additions, and deletions in it, then recopy the copy if you need to make further revisions. It is generally unwise to delete or make illegible earlier versions of your text until you are quite sure that the task is finished. More often than not, your second and third drafts will represent improvements on your first, but occasionally something that dissatisfied you at first proves, after all, to have merit. So, leave your options open. Allow yourself the ability to restore a piece of text.

It is up to you whether you compile a first draft of the whole work before you undertake any revision or whether you draft, revise, and redraft section by section. If the piece you are writing is fairly short, then it is definitely better to reach the end before you revise. Indeed, all other things being equal, it is probably better to begin with a complete first draft whatever the length of the piece. Part of the revision process is to compare the written-out version with your "mission statement" and your plan to make sure that you have achieved your original purpose and dealt with all your main points. This you can do properly only if you have a complete text to work with. Again, part of revision involves matching up the different sections to make sure that you do not repeat yourself and that you preserve a logical sequence and a consistent tone. Finally, it increases your confidence greatly to know that you have made it once through to the final page, and it motivates you to go back and finish off the job. Nevertheless, the alternative procedure can work equally well, and if you get stuck or run out of steam, working on an earlier section with a view to improving it can help to reengage you with the task and set you back on track.

The most important draft is the first. The most vital aspects of a first draft are that it should extend from start to finish and that it lacks nothing you intend to include. It will not be perfect, of course, but it will provide a firm basis on which you can build.

From the point of view of motivating yourself to begin, it may help to play down the first draft's importance. You may, for instance, be the sort of person who is not grammatical by nature or not a good speller and who feels that "If I even attempt to write 'correctly,' I will lose my concentration." You can tell yourself, quite truthfully, that "mistakes can always be corrected later," whether they are grammatical errors, stylistic infelicities, or less than perfect presentations of your ideas or arguments. A draft is only a draft, and the revised and corrected final version obviously outranks any draft.

On the other hand, especially if you are using modern word-processing technology, it is quite likely that the only time you write out your piece in full will be when you compose the first draft. The second and third drafts are likely to be revised versions of the first, rather than fresh versions completely rewritten from beginning to end. It will pay you, if you can, to provide a solid foundation.

As has been said several times before, different people have different work methods. Some people find it extremely difficult to leave anything in an unpolished state and become positively anxious at the thought that they may be leaving a litter of indifferently constructed sentences, poorly argued points, and textual inconsistencies behind them. They work at and rework the introduction until it says precisely what they want to say, and only then do they feel free to proceed. Other people get through the first draft in a blind rush. They are so frightened of losing their impetus, or their self-discipline, that they put anything down on paper anyhow. The only thing that matters is to reach the end. The first draft is simply raw material. The real work comes later.

The best policy for the majority of people probably lies somewhere between these two extremes. Proceed with deliberate speed. Continue to work steadily either from the beginning or from your best access point. It is important to keep up the momentum when drafting. If the piece is not too long, it may well benefit from being drafted in full during a single session. If that is not possible and you have to break up the drafting work, try not to succumb to the temptation to start revising. Simply read enough of the existing text to put yourself back in the picture and carry on. Write as well as you can, but do not worry too much about the finer points. Experiment, if you feel you need to, with different voices, but do not worry if an experiment does not work, so long as you have covered some of the necessary ground while you were experimenting. You must get to the end at all costs. If you start elsewhere than at the beginning, your draft is not complete until you have supplied the missing sections. You will probably find that as you go along you will fall into a writing style that you are comfortable with and that suits the occasion. You will probably also find that, even if you were not taking extreme care, you have produced a good deal of text that will stand up to scrutiny and that you can incorporate with minimal changes into your final version.

When you have finished the first draft, you should revise it (*see* chapter 3, page 72). You should also give serious thought to the issues that you may have had to put out of mind in order to get started. We shall now turn our attention to these details.

## YOUR AUTHORIAL VOICE

If you have ever listened to a classical singer talking about his or her career or a musical expert discussing this art form, you may have been struck by a tendency to refer to "the voice." Not my voice, your voice, his or her voice, but simply "the voice," as in "when Maria Callas made this recording, the voice was still in its prime." It is a strangely impersonal way of speaking. It makes it sound as if the vocal organ in question has a life of its own, independent of its possessor.

Whatever the precise reasons why musicians use that term, it is possible to see some sense in it. Even an ordinary person's singing voice may be somewhat different from his or her speaking voice, which we usually take to be his or her natural voice. There is nothing very surprising in that, for singing is a different activity from speaking. It requires you to pitch and project your voice deliberately, whereas speaking usually requires no conscious intervention, you simply open your mouth and speak as you were born to.

Just as everyone has a singing voice—good or bad, musical or unmusical—so everyone has a **writing voice.** And your writing voice relates to your natural speaking voice in much the same way as your singing voice does. It may not seem to you that you write differently from the way you talk. You have probably been told at some time or other that you should "write as you talk" and perhaps have followed that advice. Nevertheless, like it or not, there is probably a qualitative difference between the way you express yourself on paper and the way you express yourself by word of mouth.

To take an obvious example, unless you deliberately break them up, your words on paper will appear to come out in a continuous flow. There will be no little stops, hesitations, or coughs, no pauses while you search for the right word, no unintentional repetitions, no tailings off when you conclude a speech with a shrug of the shoulders or some other gesture. It may sound as if this refers only to the voice of the final version, from which all the little errors and infelicities have been removed, but this is not entirely the case. Just because writing, like singing, is less of a taken-for-granted activity than speaking and because it involves more deliberate effort, most people find that they are more "literate" when they use the written word. A sort of automatic politeness to paper kicks in when they are using a keyboard or pen.

Now, writing has certain obvious disadvantages compared with speaking that mainly have to do with the writer's comparative remoteness from the person whom he or she is addressing. The absence of the stops, hesitations, coughs, and gestures, referred to in the previous paragraph is, in fact, one of them. We are frequently told by psychologists and experts in human communications that a vast percentage of what we communicate is conveyed by other means than the words we utter, yet when we write, the words we put down are all we have. It is always possible to read between the lines, but that requires more subtlety perhaps than picking up the signals transmitted by someone's body language.

On the other hand, writing has one inestimable advantage that flows from the same source. Because we are not face to face with the addressee, we can perfect what we say before we commit to it. Through careful writing and thorough revision, we can ensure that what we say is only what we mean to say and conveys our message clearly. Furthermore, we can choose the voice we use.

It is perfectly possible to write as if you were someone completely different from the person you really are. Creative writers do it: They can tell their story from the point of view of any one of their characters, and to do this they temporarily adopt the personality of that character not only by expressing his or her attitudes but by using the sort of language and style that he or she might naturally be expected to use. Advertising copywriters do it: They usually strive to come across as the most energetic, empathetic, and enthusiastic characters on earth. Politicians do it—or their speechwriters do. You too can do it, if you are so minded. Sheltered behind the computer screen, you can put on any mask you choose.

This is not, however, intended as an argument in favor of insincerity, deception, or impressing other people by stealth. Most likely you will simply want to be yourself, but, as has been said, your writing voice is never quite the same as your natural voice, and you can and should exploit that little gap in at least two ways. You should deliberately adjust what you write to suit the person or people you are writing for, and you should select a tone that is appropriate to the circumstances.

## Adjusting to the Reader

A piece of writing is only ever as good as its ability to be understood by its readers. Sadly, this statement belongs not only in the category of obvious truths but also in that of frequently and unjustly neglected ones.

The terms of reference of this book prevent an extensive discussion of matters of writing style. For that you should consult its companion volume, *The Facts On File Guide to Style*. It can be said, however, that the first rule of style always was and still is "Be clear." There is an important corollary to that rule, however, that particularly concerns us here. Clarity lies ultimately in the eye of the reader, not in the eye of the writer.

It is not enough that a sentence or paragraph makes perfect sense to you; it must make sense to the reader, too, who will not be able to ask you to explain in more detail a sentence, idea, or section that remains unclear to him or her. Most readers are not blessed with infinite patience, either. They want your meaning to be immediately obvious. They may put up with a certain amount of obscurity in a poem or a piece of literary or philosophical prose; it is the price the ordinary mortal has to pay for a great mind's profundity. Readers also may be resigned to not fully understanding something written on a technical or academic subject that they know little about. But if they find that a piece of workaday prose requires the same degree of mental effort to understand it as they might normally expend on a crossword clue or a passage in a foreign language, they are apt to get exasperated—and with good reason.

It follows that if possible, you ought to identify your readers and gauge their likely level of understanding. If you are writing for publication, the publisher will certainly want to know what market you envisage for your work. If you offer a book on a scientific subject, say, the publisher would expect to present your material differently depending on whether your proposed work was targeted for professional scientists, high school students, children in elementary school, or the general public. It is obviously pointless trying to sell a book written for high-level experts to schoolchildren. It is equally pointless to try to persuade a local newspaper to print an article that really belongs in an academic journal.

The same, however, applies to work that is not written for publication. If you are writing about a business matter to a colleague in the same line of work, whom you can expect to be familiar with the intricacies of the trade, you should take a different approach to the task from the one you would take if you were writing on the same subject to an ordinary member of the public. Similarly, if you are writing to someone you have never met, your tone will differ from the tone you use with someone you know, let alone with an old friend.

There are occasions when you cannot specifically identify a reader, when you actually want what you write to be read by as many people as possible. The great American public, you hope, is out there eagerly awaiting the appearance of your work. It may be that the public has already shown its appreciation of your quirky and original style by buying your previous work in large quantities. If you are cold-calling the public, however, the obvious style to adopt is a plain, neutral style (*neutral,* as will be explained in a later subsection, does not necessarily mean your writing should be colorless or impersonal) that will be understandable by and acceptable to the majority of people. It is what we might call a "default" style of writing for use in most circumstances, and especially when the reader is anonymous.

It is impossible in a book of this size to exemplify all the different styles appropriate to the whole variety of readers, but for more information on the subject, see TONE (page 59). First, however, a little more needs to be said on the quality that should be a feature of all writing styles: clarity.

## Clarity

Writing clearly is not entirely easy, but neither is it particularly difficult. The requirements for clarity, essentially, are the following:

- What you write should be grammatically correct and conform to normal usage. Grammar is not an esoteric science. It is the foundation of our use of language—a common factor, as are the words that make up our vocabulary. Grammatical errors cause obscurity, not to mention the fact that they usually create an unfavorable impression of the writer. (For an in-depth discussion of grammar, see chapter 4.)
- The vocabulary and constructions you use should be as simple and straightforward as they can be without distorting your meaning. This does not mean that everything you write should be couched in words of only one or two syllables. It does mean, however, that when you have a choice between a simple word and a long and complicated word that mean the same thing, you should, as a rule, choose the simpler one. (See chapter 5 for a detailed look at vocabulary and usage.)
- You should always be aware that the reader's knowledge and vocabulary is not necessarily as extensive as your own. This does not mean that you should talk down to your reader. But it does mean that you should not assume the reader has done the same amount of preparation and research of the topic as you have. You should therefore be very careful about the use of specialized vocabulary.

As a result of its history and development, the English language is particularly rich in synonyms, different words that have essentially the same meaning. (It is perhaps no accident that the crossword puzzle was an English-language invention; the first newspaper crossword was published in a Sunday supplement to the *New York World* in 1913.) Although such words are usually almost interchangeable in meaning—*incarceration,* for example, means the same thing as *imprisonment,* just as *prestidigitation* equates to *conjuring, azure* to *sky blue, cogitate* to *think over,* and *festinately* to *in haste*—they are not the same in tone. The first words in each of the above pairs are more formal, literary, and even pretentious than their equivalents, and, more to the point, they are rarer in occurrence and less well known. While it would be wrong to deprive anyone of the pleasure of unearthing long-forgotten grandiose words, it would be equally wrong to suggest that a collector's interest in words has very much to do with the ordinary business of writing. Always choose the simpler word if it expresses your meaning just as well, and always choose the simpler construction, too. Try to avoid a pileup of phrases or clauses, as in:

> Previous to the last meeting of the committee, in view of the circumstances obtaining at that time, of which you were all informed beforehand by letter in accordance with standing orders and because I thought I owed you a personal explanation notwithstanding your general hostility toward me, which was a large factor in the circumstances referred to above, I tendered my resignation. . . .

This is a great deal of rambling language with a tiny bit of significant content included at the end. If you find yourself writing a sentence such as this one—it can happen to any of us in an unguarded moment—do not let it get away from you. Make sure you get to the point quickly, then unravel the rest of the information and present it in a simpler and clearer form. Often this will mean creating two or three sentences out of one:

> I tendered my resignation before the last committee meeting. I informed you all of my decision beforehand by personal letter, as I was bound to do by standing orders and common courtesy. Your general hostility toward me was, as you know, a major factor influencing my decision. . . .

(For a fuller discussion of these issues, see *The Facts On File Guide to Style.*)

Also avoid the use of specialized vocabulary, unless it is pertinent to your text. Slang falls in this category, because, by definition, slang is the language of an in-group. The in-group may be fairly large—all the people who came of age during a particular decade—or it may be comparatively small—all the people who work in the acting profession. Nevertheless, it remains an in-group, from which large sections of the population are excluded. This is what disqualifies slang—not its raciness or its tendency to date with great rapidity. There are obviously exceptions to this rule. You may be writing to or for other members of an in-group. You may feel the reader will get a special buzz from hearing the authentic voice of the young and cool or the hands-on professionals. You might want to individualize a fictional character by giving him or her an appropriate slang to speak. Nevertheless, for general, middle-of-the road intelligibility, avoid it. (*See also* SLANG, page 227.)

Colloquial language is a slightly different matter. By definition, most members of the population are likely to be familiar with it. The question of whether to use colloquialisms, however, relates mainly to the kind of tone you wish to adopt and is therefore dealt with in the following subsection on tone.

From the point of view of this discussion, what we ordinarily think of as technical and specialist vocabulary has a great deal in common with slang. It should be used with care because large sections of the population will be unfamiliar with it. It is very important, therefore, to know who your readers are likely to be if you have to write on a specialized subject. If you are a psychologist, paleontologist, or campanologist addressing your remarks to colleagues, then you are entitled to use freely the technical terminology of the science or art in question. If you are writing for the general public, however, you are not. It is a basic courtesy to the reader not to send him or her off to search in the dictionary when it can be avoided. If you are compelled to use a technical term, because no alternative word exists or because the technical term is effectively a piece of useful shorthand, then provide the reader with a brief explanation, which can be direct or indirect, the first time you use the word. For example,

> *A sphygmomanometer, the device doctors usually use to measure a patient's blood pressure, can often be adapted to serve this further purpose.*

or,

> *The line "And quench its speed in the slushy sand" is obviously intended to be onomatopoeic. Browning chooses his words to suggest the sound made by a small boat burying its prow in wet sand.*

The same rule applies if you need to use words from a foreign language. It is customary to put the foreign terms in italics. (*See also* FOREIGN WORDS AND PHRASES, page 193.)

> *Her attitude is perhaps best summed up by the French term* je-m'en-foutisme: *She couldn't care less about anything or anybody.*

Abbreviations and acronyms—with the possible exception of the very common ones that more or less everyone is certain to recognize (UN, UK, LA, NYC, NFL)—should also be explained on their first appearance:

> *Members of the ANA (the American Nurses Association) are holding their annual conference in Cleveland, Ohio, this year.*

(*See also* ABBREVIATIONS, page 202.)

Few writers actually set out to blind their readers with science; many, however, end up doing so because of a blind spot of their own. We are quick to recognize the difficulty of language from outside our own sphere of competence, but we expect everybody else to share our knowledge of our own specialties. It is a common experience in daily life to be baffled by an expert who rattles off an explanation of why the car's engine is not working, or why the computer has crashed, in terms that mean very little to us as lay people. There are obvious difficulties in writing about subjects in which we are not expert. There are also dangers, however, if we write for the general public as experts on our own subject, unless we pay very careful heed to the needs of our readership. This requires a leap of the imagination. We must attempt to put ourselves in our readers' shoes by imagining the sort of terms we would wish to be explained to us if the roles were reversed. Without treating members of the public as imbeciles or encumbering them with unnecessary explanations, we should not overtax their resources. It can be quite a difficult balancing act. This is where a candid friend, preferably one who does not share your specialties, can be an invaluable assistant. Ask him or her to read through your text for intelligibility. If your friend starts looking puzzled, take action.

## Tone

Tone in writing is similar to tone of voice. It expresses the attitude or emotion of the person writing. It is not difficult to express emotion in writing or to cause emotion in a reader. We can all think of pieces of writing that have seemed unbearably sad and made us want to weep or terribly funny and made us laugh out loud. On the other hand, it is not entirely easy. A simple sentence such as "Bring me my slippers, please" can be invested with various kinds of emotion in speech: It could be an imperious command or a gentle request. On paper it remains obstinately neutral unless it is accompanied by an explicit reference to the tone or context in which the words are used:

> *"Bring me my slippers, please," she said in an icy voice.*

It is, however, a fair assumption that most of what you write will be reasonably neutral in tone. You may, obviously, have occasion to write in an angry, complaining, enthusiastic, or affectionate tone in a letter or some other relatively short piece of writing—a review of a book or movie that you love or hate, for instance. But it would be difficult to sustain a strong emotional tone page after page after page—and it would probably be rather wearing for the reader.

A **neutral tone** is the broad middle ground in writing. It implies that the writer is using ordinary language, neither deliberately familiar nor deliberately highfalutin, without a strong emotional charge and without striving for special effect. It is the natural tone to adopt for conveying information, especially to nonspecialists, or for stating a case without pressuring the reader to accept your point of view. The word *neutral,* and the accompanying adjective *ordinary,* used above, however, may give the impression that such writing must be at best unexciting and at worst positively boring. That is a false impression and perhaps arises from a misconception of what writing is primarily about.

What is more important, the ideas and information that you have to communicate or the words you use to communicate them? In the vast majority of cases it will be the ideas and information. You do not want your words to call attention to themselves if in doing so, they distract the reader's attention from the message you are attempting to put across. Your words may cause distraction if they are ill-chosen, ungrammatical, or inadequate to the task, but they may do the same if they are self-consciously showy. If you had a rare and valuable object to display, would you put it in a transparent glass case or behind a stained glass window? Obviously, you would do the former. That, in the end, is the effect that neutrality in tone and language is intended to have. It is like a transparent envelope through which your ideas show clearly. To avoid boring your reader, ensure first that your material is interesting; stylistic considerations come second.

## Formality and Informality

The great advantage of the middle ground is that you can easily move out of it in any direction, toward greater formality or informality. A brief discussion of what is meant by these two terms in writing is in order here.

Formality implies a choice of more elevated vocabulary than usual and a stricter adherence to conventions, both grammatical and social. Informality implies the opposite: a more colloquial vocabulary, greater freedom with conventions, and, generally a greater closeness to the way most people use language in speech. These categories are not firmly fixed, and there is perhaps a tendency for the neutral tone to become more informal; nevertheless, they retain their usefulness.

As an example of the differences between the three, let us take a phrase from the previous paragraph:

> . . . *a greater closeness to the way most people use language in speech.*

If that may be taken as representing the neutral level, a more formal expression of the same idea might be the following:

> . . . *a closer approximation to the language of common speech.*

This more formal version uses fewer words and no verbs. It is neater and more trenchant in some respects, but it depends on the reader's understanding the word *approximation* in a sense other than the one in which it is most frequently used. Here it combines the sense of "closeness" and the sense of "approach" and does not mean a "rough equivalent." The reader must also understand that the word *common* is not intended to be in any way insulting. (Though "common speech" still seems to imply that the writer is commenting on things from a position of lofty authority.)

An informal version, on the other hand, might read

> . . . *getting closer to how people actually talk.*

This version dispenses with a noun and preposition combination ("closeness to"/"approximation to") in favor of the verb phrase "getting closer to," which for many people, especially traditionalists, would be considered informal simply because it contains the all-purpose word *get.* It also substitutes *talk* for the slightly more formal *speak.* In fact, it does what it says: It is probably closer to what most people would say.

Informal writing would allow the use of contracted verb forms, such as *can't, won't, would've,* and so on. These are probably the most obvious sign of an informal tone. In neutral and formal writing these forms should always be written out in full: *cannot, will not,* and *would have.* Informally, you might write "I can't help thinking . . ."; neutrally, this would become "I cannot help thinking . . ."; formally, it might evolve into "I cannot but think . . ."

The issue of strict grammatical correctness can occasionally cause problems with tone:

*Who stole the cookies from the cookie jar? Not I!*

"Not I" is, of course, grammatically correct, but very few people would ever say it, if they were asked such a question spontaneously in a real-life situation. If you are writing informally, there is no problem; you write "Not me!" which is what most people would say. If you are writing formally, there is no problem either; you write "Not I!" If you are trying to keep to the middle ground, this may make you stop and think. Do you write "Who did you talk to at the party?" or "To whom did you talk at the party?" Do you write "No matter who you ask, the answer is always the same" or "No matter whom you ask, the answer is always the same"? (For further discussion of *who* and *whom,* see chapter 4, pages 138, 154, and 159, and chapter 6, page 335.)

In both cases the second alternative is the grammatically correct one, and although you may sometimes feel you are being taken to a slighter higher level of formality than you are entirely comfortable with, you should obey the rules. Your writing voice, as was said earlier, is a different thing from your speaking voice, and it will be a somewhat more formal one. An exception may, however, be made for reported speech and dialogue, which should be placed within quotation marks. If you quote people talking, then let them talk as they talk.

When deciding whether to adopt a formal, informal, or neutral tone, it is again important to know your reader. The previous discussion of writer-reader relations focused mainly on intelligibility and involved an implicit assessment of the reader's intelligence level. In deciding whether to take an informal or formal tone, you have to assess the state of your personal relations with the reader and, more broadly, what degree of formality your reader is likely to feel most comfortable with, and to expect, in communications. Alternatively, there are conventions governing certain types of writing that will dictate the tone you choose. If, for example, you received a formal invitation of the type

*Mr. and Mrs. Alphonse T. Booker request the pleasure of the company of Mr. Noel Brooks and Ms. Lucia Hernandez at . . .*

you might, if you were best friends of Mr. and Mrs. Booker, write back, "Hi, thanks, great, we'll come." On the whole, however, you are more likely to respond in kind:

*Mr. Noel Brooks and Ms. Lucia Hernandez thank Mr. and Mrs. Alphonse T. Booker for their kind invitation to . . . and are delighted to accept.*

Similar conventions apply to certain kinds of essays, reports, and business correspondence.

By and large, however, communications are becoming more informal. If there are any conventions governing the exchange of e-mails—not to mention text messages—they all tend toward informality. We equate informality with friendliness, naturally enough, and want to put at ease the people we are corresponding with, so we usually write informally. We also, perhaps, want to show that we are ordinary, good-natured, unpretentious folks, and this too inclines us to informality. Finally, we are all pressed for time, and it is less troublesome to write something without particular regard for the finer points of grammar and language use.

Informality is fine in its proper place, which is, principally, in personal letters or other communications to friends or people we know quite well and in certain kinds of advertising copy and journalism. It can jar the reader, however, when it is used out of place. It is usually not appropriate to academic writing, letters to people we do not know well, and most writing that is directed at a large anonymous readership. For these situations, indeed, for most writing tasks, the neutral tone is preferable.

## Personal Pronouns for Authors

People sometimes feel anxious about how to refer to themselves when they are writing. They are not quite sure which is the proper personal pronoun to use to represent the authorial voice when expressing an opinion, for example, or referring the reader to a particular part of the text. There are three possible alternatives: to use *I,* to refer to yourself as *we,* or to avoid the use of a personal pronoun altogether as much as possible.

When a piece of work is written by a single author, there is no compelling reason not to use *I:* ". . . as I mentioned in the previous chapter"; "I should now like to broaden the discussion and consider two further points"; "In my opinion, neither of the two authors to whom I referred in the previous paragraph makes a convincing case for abolition." There is no convention that stipulates that a single author should refer to himself or herself as *we*. Individual authors sometimes use *we* as an act of self-effacement or to suggest that an impersonal authority is somehow responsible for the organization of the book and for its content, but this sounds rather old-fashioned nowadays. Too-frequent use of *I* should be avoided, as it should in a letter, where a succession of sentences all beginning "I did this . . ." and "I think that . . ." can give an impression of self-centeredness. This difficulty can usually be overcome by more imaginative sentence construction. A moderate use of *I* is entirely unobjectionable.

When a work has more than one author, the use of *we* is entirely appropriate. Some caution may be necessary to ensure that it is always obvious which *we* is being referred to. As it does in this book, *we* can be used to include the author(s), the reader(s), and possibly the rest of the human race. If *we* means the authors in most of the text, it is probably best to find some other way of being more inclusive.

If you dislike the use of any personal pronoun, then you can employ the passive voice and impersonal constructions to the same effect: "as mentioned in the previous paragraph . . ."; "as will be demonstrated in the next chapter . . ."; "at this point the discussion should be broadened to include two further points"; "It is fair to say that neither of the two authors referred to in the previous paragraph makes a convincing case for abolition." The only disadvantage of this method is that passive verbs can appear awkward and long winded: "It has several times been commented on in the course of this essay that there is a tendency to exaggerate on the part of this author. . . ." If you are using this convention, check carefully that your sentences are not straggling, and prune them if necessary: "This author's tendency to exaggerate has been commented on several times in the course of this essay. . . ." (For further discussion of the passive, see page 117.)

One final point should perhaps be made with respect to personal pronouns. The use of the pronoun *one* (discussed in chapter 4, under PRONOUNS, page 135) is generally relegated to more formal writing. It is not at all a good idea for an author to use it as a way of referring to himself or herself, because it sounds self-important: "One's space is limited, so one must forego the opportunity to comment further on this issue." It would be a pity, however, to lose the option of using this pronoun in its common generalizing sense of "people in general" or "anyone" or "I myself and other like-minded people," as in, "If one has nothing useful to say, then one had far better stay silent" or "But all one's efforts may be of no avail."

At least from the informal to neutral level, the use of *you* in this sense is now more usual and is generally acceptable. As with the use of *we*, however, care should be taken to make it clear to the reader that he or she is not being directly addressed. A sentence such as "If you have nothing useful to say, you had far better stay silent" sounds, without more context, as if it s being directed at someone in particular.

# COMPOSITION: PARAGRAPHS

Assuming that you have overcome any difficulties in getting started and you have decided what tone you should adopt toward your reader, you will now be in the process of putting together the body of your text, paragraph by paragraph.

A paragraph is the basic unit of any piece of writing. Its main function is to present information to the reader in a chunk of a manageable size. If you have read, or can imagine, a piece of writing that is not broken up into paragraphs, you will have some idea of the importance of manageability. (*See also* DIVISION INTO PARAGRAPHS, page 69.) Unbroken text is stressful to read. It is hard on the eye as well as on the mind. When novelists, as they occasionally do, produce a whole book that consists of unbroken text running perhaps for hundreds of pages, part of their purpose must be to stress the reader. Small pauses are as natural in writing as in speaking, and as necessary to the reader as to the listener.

Paragraphs are not arbitrary divisions of text. They are—or should be—consciously shaped units. The information that paragraphs present to the reader should be distinct. Paragraphs are not, of course, entirely self-contained because they form part of an ongoing argument, explanation, or discussion. Nevertheless, if you read a paragraph in isolation from the surrounding text, it ought to give the impression of being complete in itself.

The standard rule is one idea, one paragraph. A paragraph usually consists of a particular thought together with any explanatory or illustrative material connected with that thought. When you begin to deal with a new idea, you should begin a new paragraph:

> Charles Dickens was born in 1812 in Portsmouth, a naval base in the south of England. His father, John Dickens, worked as a clerk in the pay office of the Royal Navy. John Dickens had obtained his post through the influence of his father-in-law, who held a senior post in the pay office until he was revealed as an embezzler in 1810 and fled abroad to escape arrest.
>
> The family moved house frequently as a result of John Dickens's work. They spent some years in lodgings in London, before moving to Chatham, another naval base in Kent. There, Charles spent the happiest years of his childhood. . . .

The first paragraph deals mainly with Dickens's father and his connection with the Royal Navy. When the writer's attention turns to the places where Dickens spent his childhood, a new paragraph begins. Note, however, that the first sentence contains a reference to "John Dickens's work." This links the second paragraph back to the first and gives a sense of progression to the account. Where possible, it is a good idea to include "a hook" of this kind to establish a connection between one paragraph and the next.

It is also standard practice to begin a new paragraph when the point of view changes. On the whole, this happens more often in fiction than in nonfiction:

> Looking down from the 26th floor, Callaghan saw a man run out into the middle of the street, pull out a pistol, and point it at a car coming toward him from the direction of the lake. Callaghan tensed himself. The 26th floor was cut off from all outside sounds, but there was no sign of a shot. The car slid to a halt. A woman got out with her hands up. The man pushed her aside, got in, and drove off still waving the pistol out of the car window.
>
> Down in the street, Linda Jacowitz didn't know whether to curse or cry. . . .

The whole first paragraph describes what the character Callaghan perceives from the point of view of the 26th floor. When the action moves down to the street and the writer starts to describe Linda Jacowitz's reactions, a new paragraph is needed.

## The Topic Sentence

In many cases, the idea that the writer intends to deal with in the course of a paragraph will be expressed in one particular sentence. That sentence forms the nucleus of the paragraph and is often referred to as the topic sentence.

If you look back to the second paragraph of the previous subsection, you will see that the topic sentence is, in fact, the second sentence: "Its [the paragraph's] main function is to present information to the reader in a chunk of manageable size." It contains the basic idea that the paragraph is intended to convey. The first sentence serves as an introduction to it. The subsequent sentences discuss the concept of manageability and the disadvantages of presenting the reader with an unbroken run of text.

The topic sentence is the core of most paragraphs. For the writer, it is a guide to what belongs in a particular paragraph: Anything that falls within the paragraph should be related to the topic sentence. It has a similar function for the reader: It indicates to him or her what the paragraph is essentially about. Consequently, it is the sentence that it is most important to get right, that is, to make clear and, if possible, succinct.

A topic sentence ought, as a rule, to be fairly specific. If you choose to center your paragraph on a very general statement, you may saddle yourself with a task that you cannot accomplish within a paragraph of reasonable size. If, for example, your wrote as your topic sentence "Hamlet's encounter with his father ghost changes his whole worldview," you would be committing yourself to a discussion of virtually the entire play. This is an essay title rather than a topic sentence. If, instead, you wrote, "Hamlet's encounter brings about an immediate change in his behavior," then you would be limiting yourself to a discussion of the action following Hamlet's exchanges with the ghost in act I scene 5—a subject that can reasonably be dealt with in the space of a paragraph. Similarly, "Oil and gas supplies from the former Soviet Union are under threat" is less useful as a topic sentence than, for example, "Oil and gas supplies from southern areas of the former Soviet Union are particularly vulnerable to terrorist attack." By restricting the discussion to a particular geographical area and a specific kind of threat, the second example promises to handle a more manageable amount of information.

In order to help bind the paragraph together, it is sometimes useful to structure the topic sentence in such a way that it contains key words that recur within the remainder of the paragraph. Consider this example:

> Almost every American family possesses a useful and much neglected educational tool hidden away in drawer or cupboard and fished out maybe once or twice a year: a deck of cards. Card games aren't just fun; they're a great way of training children's memories, making them concentrate, and teaching them basic social skills. They also bring the whole family together for some quality time. Natural competitiveness quickly shows; it's that much more fun for the kids if they can beat Mommy or Daddy or Brother or Sister. But it won't be quality time if they can't get some fun out of just playing and maybe losing once in a while. Learning not to be a sore loser, that's a basic social skill; so is joining in wholeheartedly, and letting everyone have a turn. But they can't win if they don't concentrate. They have to watch those cards or they'll lose their chance. And if they can't remember what's on the table and what's still in the deck, they'll soon learn what it means to go bust!

This paragraph is written in an informal style, but the informality of its tone conceals a fairly formal structure. It has a topic sentence—the second sentence. It is couched in informal words, but it states the theme of the paragraph and contains key terms—*fun, memories, concentrate,* and *quality time*—most of which are woven back into the paragraph and directly hark back to the main theme. It is obviously possible to overdo this technique. Too much repetition, besides being a stylistic weakness, gives the impression of laboring a point. The reader usually requires only a gentle nudge to be kept on track, not a heavy hammering.

The position of the topic sentence within the paragraph is not fixed. Theoretically, it can come anywhere, but it seldom comes at or near the end, for the simple reason that you do not usually want to keep your reader hanging on for too long before giving him or her an explicit pointer to what the paragraph is about. It is often the first sentence, as in the paragraph above that begins "A topic sentence ought, as a rule, to be fairly specific." If your paragraph is, as it is often recommended that it should be, a miniaturized version of a longer structure, however, then it will often appear as the second or third sentence, depending on the length of the paragraph. (*See also* PARAGRAPH STRUCTURE below).

There is one further advantage of basing your paragraphs on topic sentences: These topic sentences ideally should originate from the preparatory work you have done before you start writing. Clear and careful notes worked into complete sentences can become the foundation stones of paragraphs when you write out the full version of your text. A fully worked-out plan could consist of a series of topic sentences corresponding to the paragraph arrangement of your text.

Nevertheless, not every paragraph has or needs a topic sentence. It is perfectly possible to produce a viable and well-written paragraph in which no single sentence is identifiable as the core and encapsulates the essential message. Such is the following example from Charles Dickens's 1854 novel *Hard Times:*

> In truth, Mrs. Gradgrind's stock of facts in general was woefully defective; but Mr. Gradgrind in raising her to her high matrimonial position had been influenced by two reasons. Firstly, she was most satisfactory as a question of figures; and, secondly, she had "no nonsense" about her. By nonsense he meant fancy; and truly it is probable that she was as free from any alloy of that nature as any human being not arrived at the perfection of an absolute idiot, ever was (Dickens 1984, 62).

This is a perfectly acceptable paragraph, but you could not really choose any one of its three sentences as having primacy over the other two. It comes from a novel, and there is no reason why a paragraph from a piece of creative writing should not have an identifiable core sentence. Not surprisingly, however, it is in writing that discusses a topic or works out an argument that the topic sentence most comes into its own.

## Paragraph Structure

Whether or not it contains a topic sentence, a paragraph should be a unit. It should hang together. Dickens's paragraph quoted above hangs together because it is all about the nature of Mrs. Gradgrind. And, though his intentions are satirical and the tone is comic, there is a definite logical progression. Mrs. Gradgrind is "woefully defective" in her stock of facts, and facts, as we have been told from the beginning of the book, are the be-all and end-all of Mr. Gradgrind's existence. Why then did he marry her? "Because she was satisfactory as a question of figures." Here Dickens is playing on the phrase *facts and figures*. She was unsatisfactory as to the former but satisfactory as to the latter, which is not to say that she was a mathematical genius, but that she came into the marriage with plenty of money. She also had "no nonsense" about her. This leads Dickens to specify what nonsense means to a man like Gradgrind, and thus he closes the paragraph. He truly closes it, too, for when you reach the end of that last sentence, you truly feel you have reached a pause. Everything has been said on this particular subject, and now it is time to speak of something else.

As briefly mentioned in the previous section, it is often recommended that a paragraph should mimic the arrangement of a larger piece of writing. It should have an opening, or introduction; a main body; and a conclusion, or close. This is good advice, though not always easily achievable within the space of a few sentences. A topic sentence, if you are using one, may form the introduction to the paragraph or be preceded by a separate introductory and usher in the main body. But it is usually not too difficult to construct the body of a paragraph. The ending may cause more difficulty, because it should "feel" like a close. The ending of a paragraph indicates a brief pause, because the writer is now about to treat a new topic. It is sometimes harder to introduce a silence than a point.

Let us briefly consider an example from a rather less exalted source than Charles Dickens. One of the paragraphs in the previous subsection concludes with the sentence "The reader usually requires only a gentle nudge to be kept on track, not a heavy hammering." The first draft of this sentence read slightly differently: "The reader usually requires a gentle nudge to be kept on track rather than a heavy hammering." During revision, it was felt that this sentence lacked "finality." If you were reading it aloud, it would be natural to keep your voice up at the end of it, because the way it is constructed requires a final stress on the word "hammering." The voice, however, usually falls before a pause. When the voice stays up, you expect the reader to go on and say something else—perhaps, in this instance, to illustrate or explain the difference between a "nudge" and a "hammering." That was not the intention in this paragraph. By sharpening the opposition from "a gentle nudge rather than a heavy hammering" to "only a gentle nudge, not a heavy hammering," the stress was moved away from the end of the sentence back onto the word *not*. This allows the voice to pronounce the last two words in a falling tone, and that, in turn, indicates a pause is coming and gives a better sense of finality. It may be added here as a general observation that reading your work aloud, or hearing it in your mind's ear as if it were being read aloud, is often a very good method of checking that it is indeed having the effect you intended.

## Paragraph Dimensions

There are no set rules for the size of paragraphs. A paragraph should be as long as the material it contains requires. A paragraph could consist of a single sentence, and as a sentence might only consist of a single word, the minimum size for a paragraph is one word. However, single-sentence, let alone single-word, paragraphs are comparatively rare and not necessarily preferred.

There is no upper limit on the size of paragraphs. In the hands of a skillful writer, a paragraph could be made to extend a whole page or more. The reasons given earlier for the existence of paragraphs, however, apply at all points. Text is easier to read and looks better on the page if it is broken up. If you embark on a paragraph that looks as if it is going to cover more than two-thirds of a page, it is usually wise to look for a way of dividing it into two or more smaller ones.

As a very rough guide, the average paragraph should contain not less than three sentences. This is the minimum usually needed for the introduction-body-conclusion pattern. Likewise, when you have written six or seven sentences, it is usually time to think of bringing the paragraph to a close. A lot depends, however, on the length of your sentences. Similarly, you should usually aim to fit three or four paragraphs onto a standard page. But there are a number of factors that can influence the size and number of your paragraphs.

First among these is the nature of your readership and of the piece you are writing. Certain types of writing, particularly tabloid journalism and writing for children, demand many short paragraphs, usually of only one or two sentences. The more sophisticated your readers, the longer you can make your paragraphs. You can safely assume that their attention span and their capacity to follow an argument will enable you to expand well beyond three sentences if you need to do so.

Second is the position of the paragraph within a section. It is usually recommended that the first and last paragraphs of a section be comparatively short. A couple of sentences should suffice to set the scene or get a discussion going, and also to bring the section to a close.

The third factor is the desirability of putting variety into your text. Wherever possible, you should vary the length of your paragraphs and also vary the lengths of the sentences within the paragraphs. A succession of uniform paragraphs spread uniformly across the page creates a regimented impression. For all its underlying planning and logic, a text should be something lively and not be entirely predictable. A varied arrangement of paragraphs indicates as much directly to the eye.

## Paragraphing and Dialogue

A particular paragraphing convention applies to the presentation of conversational exchanges. It is customary to start a new paragraph each time a person begins to speak and to include within the paragraph not only the attribution of the spoken words—that is, a phrase such as *he said, she answered,* or *they chorused*—but also any material that describes how the words were uttered or what the character was doing when he or she uttered them. The following example illustrates conventional treatment of written dialogue.

> "I don't think I can stand much more of this," said Henrietta. "If it gets any hotter I think I shall go insane! Why didn't you tell me it was going to be so—so *primitive!*"

> "Darling," replied Charles, in the soothing tone he reserved for such outbursts, "you did say you wanted to experience the real East."
>
> "I suppose you're telling me, it's all my fault." A large insect flew onto the veranda and began fluttering around her head. "Get away!" Henrietta shrieked, flapping at it wildly.
>
> Charles stood up and dispatched the intruder with a rolled-up copy of the *Straits Times*. This was not quite what he had imagined either, but he was certainly not in a mood to admit it.
>
> Peace returned briefly to the jungle clearing.
>
> "If you'd wanted the Singapore Hilton . . ." Charles began again.
>
> "I know what I said," she snapped. "You just didn't get what I meant!"
>
> Somewhere not too far away, an elephant trumpeted loudly.

Note that there is a new paragraph (of just one sentence) to describe the temporary silence in the setting. That sentence does not form part of Charles's reflections.

For further discussion of direct speech, see REPORTING SPEECH (page 167). For further discussion of the use of periods in direct speech, see PERIOD (page 354). For further discussion of the use of quotation marks and paragraphs, see QUOTATION MARKS (page 356).

## Division into Paragraphs

This discussion of paragraphs would not be complete without a brief demonstration of how a piece of undifferentiated text could be broken down. Imagine, if you like, that this writer, not wishing to be slowed while drafting, just presses ahead and produces the following:

> At the Mexico City Olympics in 1968, high-jumping set off in an entirely new direction that was to take it to unprecedented heights. Richard D. (Dick) Fosbury took gold for the United States that year with an entirely new jumping style of his own devising that came to be known as the Fosbury flop. Officials and spectators watched in amazement and dismay as Fosbury launched himself into the air, arched his back, went over the bar belly up, not belly down as in traditional jumping styles, and landed, apparently, on his head in the pit. They were amazed at his courage, at his success, and at the fact that he did not break his neck. They were dismayed by the thought of the spinal injuries and concussion that might result as, spurred on by Fosbury's success, young athletes tried to emulate his method. Since the early days when the high jump developed as a sport out of a desire by young men to show their daring and athleticism by leaping gates and hedges, it had been taken for granted that part of the skill lay in coming down safely on the other side. In most older belly-down styles like the straddle, the jumper's leading foot was the first part of the body that went over the bar and the first that came down on the other side to break the fall. Fosbury changed all that. His head went over the bar first and the rest of him followed, though he always insisted that it was his shoulders he landed on, not his head or neck. Despite Fosbury's Olympic success and the obvious

> effectiveness of the method, however, it took the best part of a decade before his flop became the predominant style among serious high jumpers. The replacement of the old-fashioned sand pit to land in by a very thick sponge mat made all the difference. Only the very brave are willing to risk their necks for glory.

This is a typical piece of first drafting that would benefit from several kinds of revision. But let us concentrate on breaking it down into paragraphs—or bringing out the paragraph breaks that are essentially already there. (You might like to try making it into paragraphs for yourself before reading the analysis below.)

The first two sentences constitute an introduction. At the end of the second sentence, the point of view changes. The writer introduces the "officials and spectators" and presents the event as seen through their eyes. A change of point of view necessitates a new paragraph. Two further sentences (both beginning with "they") continue the story from the same point of view. Next, the writer's attention seems to turn to the history of the sport, but the "topic element," as we might call it in this case, is mostly contained in the second part of that sentence: "it had been taken for granted [since the early days] that part of the skill lay in coming down safely on the other side." If we identify those words as containing the topic, then all of the next four sentences can be linked together as a unit. There might be an argument for separating out the two sentences that refer again to Fosbury, but against that it could be argued that Fosbury's method is being presented specifically in light of what had gone before. The last three sentences make quite an effective close, with again a possible option to let the very last sentence stand alone. The paragraphed version, awaiting further attention, would then look like this:

> At the Mexico City Olympics in 1968, high-jumping set off in an entirely new direction that was to take it to unprecedented heights. Richard D. (Dick) Fosbury took gold for the United States that year with an entirely new jumping style of his own devising that came to be known as the Fosbury flop.
>
> Officials and spectators watched in amazement and dismay as Fosbury launched himself into the air, arched his back, went over the bar belly up, not belly down as in traditional jumping styles, and landed, apparently, on his head in the pit. They were amazed at his courage, at his success, and at the fact that he did not break his neck. They were dismayed by the thought of the spinal injuries and concussion that might result as, spurred on by Fosbury's success, young athletes tried to emulate his method.
>
> Since the early days when the high jump developed as a sport out of a desire by young men to show their daring and athleticism by leaping gates and hedges, it had been taken for granted that part of the skill lay in coming down safely on the other side. In most older belly-down styles like the straddle, the jumper's leading foot was the first part of the body that went over the bar and the first that came down on the other side to break the fall. Fosbury changed all that. His head went over the

bar first and the rest of him followed, though he always insisted that it was his shoulders he landed on, not his head or neck.

Despite Fosbury's Olympic success and the obvious effectiveness of the method, however, it took the best part of a decade before his flop became the predominant style among serious high jumpers. The replacement of the old-fashioned sand pit to land in by a very thick sponge mat made all the difference.

Only the very brave are willing to risk their necks for glory.

## WRITING: AN OVERVIEW

- Get started. Especially if you have difficulties with the opening section, start at any point in your plan where you have plenty to say.
- Write your first draft in fairly long stretches; if possible, write out the whole piece. The most important thing about the first draft is that it should be complete. If necessary, ignore other factors until you have completed the first draft.
- Consider your readers and their expectations.
- Choose a tone that suits your readers and the type of piece you are writing. If in doubt, choose the neutral tone.
- Write paragraph by paragraph. Remember that the basic rule is one idea, one paragraph.
- Construct most of your paragraphs on the basis of a topic sentence.

When you have completed a draft, start revising it.

3

# Revising Your Document

For the purposes of this book, it is assumed that revision begins when you have completed the first draft and continues until you are completely satisfied with your text. Revision ends when you believe that your text is ready for submission to your intended reader.

This assumption is based on the recommendation, made earlier, that it is advisable to write out your text in full before you start a thorough and detailed attempt to improve it. If this goes against the grain for you—if you feel unhappy about moving too far ahead, leaving stretches of unimproved writing behind you—you can use the guidelines set out in this section to assist you with the revision that you do as you go along. Nevertheless, even if you feel, when you eventually reach the end, that what you have in front of you resembles an ordinary second draft more than an ordinary first draft, it is still important to conduct a thoroughgoing review of your whole piece along the lines recommended here.

It is perhaps useful at this point to remind ourselves what we are aiming to achieve. Your finished text should

- carry out the purpose that you set in your original mission statement;
- contain everything the reader needs in order to understand the information that you intend to share with him or her or the argument that you are putting forward;
- be clearly, logically, and consistently organized so as to convey the information or the argument effectively;
- be written in a tone and a manner that suits the type of work it is and the readership for which it is intended;
- hold the reader's interest not only through the material it offers but also by being written in a clear and lively style;
- be free of grammatical, spelling, and stylistic errors.

The purpose of revision is to ensure that the text does all this and that when it leaves your hands, it is as near perfect as you can make it.

## HOW TO REVISE

Revision requires critical thinking. The usefulness of critical thinking has already been referred to in this book in relation to evaluating the sources you use when assembling your material (*see* CRITICAL THINKING, page 17). But it is usually much easier to subject another person's work to dispassionate analysis than to cast a cold critical eye on your own.

The problem is that you know your own work too well. If it is a long piece that has required a good deal of research, you have quite likely lived with it for weeks if not months. You have struggled with it, slaved over it, put your all into it, and probably felt an enormous feeling of relief when you wrote or typed the final period. It may well seem to you to be full of good things. Even if you are aware that it is not entirely perfect, you may feel quite fond of it and proud of it. It is yours, after all. You may feel a natural reluctance to tamper with it. You may not even feel confident that if you attempt to change it, the results will be a genuine improvement.

All these are natural feelings that almost every writer experiences. You simply have to be stern with yourself. Revision is a vital part of the process. It is also another creative process. There need be nothing mechanical about it. You will almost certainly have second thoughts that are better thoughts. You will have new ideas—or find new and better ways of expressing your existing ideas—that will give the whole piece a lift. Steel yourself and sit down to go back to your work.

The first thing you need in order to be able to assess your work critically is to have some degree of distance from it. You need to come to it with fresh eyes. Ideally, when you come back to look at it again, you should regard it from the point of view of its intended reader or that of a disinterested outsider. It is quite difficult to do this by an effort of the imagination alone. By far the easiest way to achieve "distance" is to allow a period of time to pass between the completion of a draft and the beginning of revision. At least, leave the work overnight and come back to it fresh the next day. If possible, set it aside for a couple of days. Absence makes the head grow clearer. So, often, does a change of medium. This is why many writers prefer to edit on paper after they have written on screen. Printing out your work puts you in the position of a reader.

The other obvious way to achieve distance is to pass the work to somebody else and ask that person to comment on it. It is not usually advisable to do this, however, until you have made at least one effort to revise the piece yourself, especially if it is a piece of any length. If your first draft is fairly rough, it is unfair to show it to anyone while it is still unfinished in every sense except the minimal one—that you have made it once through to the end. If the person you show your work to is the sort who loves to take other people in hand and show them the "proper" way to do things, he or she may relish the task—but may end up taking over your authorial role, at least in part. On the other hand, any other person who is not so inclined may feel put upon when he or she realizes that there is still a very long way to go before the piece is finished and that you are expecting him or her to do the groundwork for you. These factors are in addition to the general problem that unless the person is used to being asked to pass an opinion on written work, he or she may find it hard to know exactly what to say to be helpful. Many a writer has had a piece of work handed back by a "candid friend" with a "that seems perfectly fine to me" and not known whether this means that the piece is good and readable, or the person thinks it is really dull and awful but does not want to say so, or he or she is really at a loss to make any constructive comments and merely wants to be vaguely encouraging. If you know someone who is willing to be candid and knows enough to be able to offer specific comments and advice, that person's help can be invaluable. You cannot, however, always rely on even the most willing and literate friend having the time to help you. In the last analysis, this is a job that you have to be able to do for yourself. If you can get help, that is a bonus.

It may also make things easier, especially if you have a fairly long draft to revise, to break the work of revision down into two separate phases. The first phase we might call **large-scale revision.** Here, you check the basic organization of the piece. You examine it for completeness and overall accuracy and ensure that the points follow one another in a logical sequence. You remove any material that seems to be superfluous, and you add anything that seems to be missing. The resultant reorganized text becomes your second draft. You then subject the second draft to the **small-scale revision.** In this second phase, you concentrate on matters of language and style. You check for grammatical accuracy, clarity of expression, and consistency in style. Again, you will add to and subtract from your text, but this time it is in order to improve the expression rather than the content.

It is quite likely that when you are essentially looking to make large-scale changes, you will spot some small-scale matters that need attention. If they can be easily dealt with—that is to say, you know immediately how to put them right—make the necessary changes. If they seem to be more complicated, mark them in some way and come back to deal with them when you are concentrating on the smaller-scale issues.

## REVISION CHECKLIST

This checklist is intended to cover everything that you need to consider when you are revising your text. It is couched in the form of questions that you should ask yourself and divided between the two phases of revision suggested previously.

### The First Phase

- Does the text fulfill the original purpose I had in mind when I began writing or the requirements of the writing task that I set?
- Does it cover all the relevant aspects of the subject?
- Does it contain any material that is irrelevant and ought to be removed?
- Are there any gaps in the material that need to be filled, or are there any sections where the material is thin or the argument seems weak and needs to be strengthened?
- Is all the material it contains accurate and accurately presented?
- Is the material presented in a clear and logical way? Will my readers receive the information I am presenting in the right order and will they be able to follow my arguments clearly?
- Is the language I am using suitable for my readers? Will they be able to understand it without too much effort?
- Am I using the right tone to address these readers?
- Have I used the same sort of language and the same tone consistently throughout the piece?

### The Second Phase

- Are my paragraphs well constructed?
- Are they linked so that argument flows easily from one paragraph to the next?
- Are my sentences well constructed? Are they clear and easy to read?
- Are there any excessively long sentences that would benefit from being broken down into shorter ones?
- Are there too many short sentences? Have I ensured that there is a reasonable variety in the length of my sentences?
- Is the language I have used clear and vigorous? Does it contain any clichés or inappropriate or mixed metaphors?
- Have I repeated any words or expressions too often?
- Are my grammar, punctuation, and spelling correct?
- Is my spelling consistent throughout the piece?
- Are all the headings and numbers styled consistently?
- Are there any peculiarities in my writing style that might put off the reader?

Let us now consider the two phases in more detail. It will be easier to do so, however, on the basis of an actual example.

## AN EXAMPLE OF REVISING A TEXT

Following is a short piece of writing as it might appear when the writer has completed the first draft. As usual, to be able to deal with the piece effectively we need to know the reason why it was written and the reader it was intended for. Let us suppose that a local dealership has decided to sponsor a competition for the best essay of not more than 600 words on the subject of "The Future of the Automobile." The first prize is $100 and publication in the local newspaper. The readers, therefore, are both the competition judges—say, the owner of the dealership, the editor of the newspaper, and a high school English teacher—and the rest of the townsfolk.

**The Future of the Automobile**

Is it possible to imagine a future in which the automobile plays no part? Yes, it is possible, but the prospect is a scary one. Imagine the highways of this country deserted. Imagine the streets of our great cities quiet. Imagine trade and industry at a standstill, for there are no vehicles left to take goods where they are meant to go. Imagine the sky and the ocean empty of powered vehicles, too, for whatever kills off the automobile is going to mean the kiss of death for the airplane, the ship, and the railroad too. A world at peace or a dead world? That is the question.

Our lives are shaped by our cars. The invention of the automobile at the end of the 19th century brought about a great leap forward in human freedom. A man who has his own transport is a free man. We are living in a go-where-you-like-any-time society. We like living in it and we are not going to give it up easily. And if the ordinary person could be persuaded or forced to part with his car, their are all the commercial interests—the companies who make vehicles, the companies who sell

> them, the companies who drill oil out of the ground, and the countries whose economies depend on oil—who are not going to lie down and watch themselves going bankrupt. Can you imagine them letting this happen? I can't.
>
> But the oil can't be drilled forever. It is a finite resource. We have gotten used to the prophets of doom not coming true. They said the oil would not last into the 21st century, but it has. However, one day it will run out.
>
> In the meantime, the pollution in our cities is getting worse, and the climate is changing. Emissions from internal-combustion engines have been identified as a major contributor to global warming. There would be some advantages from the disappearance of the automobile. Cleaner air, especially in the cities, and a more predictable climate.
>
> As I see it, human society is caught between a rock and a hard place. Our desire for freedom will prevent us from letting the automobile go, while our desire for survival will ultimately compel us to adapt to new global realities.
>
> What is the solution? Exercise is good for you, but I don't see any present or future politician being able to persuade the average American to give up his car in favor of walking or cycling. The answer must be to adapt the automobile to suit the realities. The first necessity is to discover a new fuel to drive the vehicles of the future.
>
> We know that automobile manufacturers are already experimenting with electric cars, but so far it has been difficult to store enough electricity inside to enable an electric-powered vehicle to go anything like as far as a gas-powered vehicle. For all we know they may have already discovered a new type of fuel source that does not have this disadvantage, but the rest of the world doesn't know about it yet.
>
> Peering into my crystal ball, I foresee that the automobiles of the future will run on hydrogen. Experiments to produce a hydrogen-powered car are already being made. There is an abundance of this gas on the earth—it is the most abundant element in the universe—and it can be burned without producing carbon dioxide—the gas that is most responsible for global warming.
>
> That is where the future of the automobile lies. It will be a smaller, cheaper machine for the benefit of the millions of people in the Third World who will one day want to enjoy the advantages that developed nations already enjoy. And it will run on hydrogen.

In its present form, the piece has 630 words, so it is over the limit and will need to be pruned. More important, in its present form it is unlikely to win any prizes. Let us see if by applying the questions in the checklist above, the writer can give this entry a better chance.

## The First Phase of Revision

The purpose of the first phase of revision is to deal with large-scale issues: Does the text fulfill the original purpose? No, it does not, in one obvious respect: It is too long. Does it fulfill the more general purpose of presenting an interesting account of the topic? Up to a point, perhaps. Does it cover all relevant aspects of the subject? The answer is again obviously no. There is a great deal more that could be said. But it is a very large topic, and the writer has rightly attempted to narrow it down. It is fairly obvious that he or she is not a technical or scientific expert who might have concentrated on seriously attempting to imagine the various ways in which automobile design and technology might evolve during the next 20 or 50 years. Instead, quite fairly, he or she has decided to concentrate on the basic idea that the future of the automobile will be determined by its indispensability to modern lifestyles on the one hand and its ecological impact on the other. If we ask whether all relevant aspects of the subject have been covered from this point of view in the space allowed, the answer is perhaps a cautious yes.

Moving on, is there any irrelevant material? Yes. On revising the text, the writer might, for example, question the relevance of pointing out that hydrogen is the most abundant element in the universe? Nobody is going to send spacecraft out to collect hydrogen to burn in vehicle engines on earth. Conscious that his or her scientific knowledge is slight, the writer has thrown in this tidbit to impress, yet a desire to impress is not a sufficient motive for including anything. This remark should be cut.

Are there gaps or thin sections? The writer might not feel very happy with the third paragraph. It seems "thin." Whether this is due to a lack of material or a fault in the writing is a moot point. The last sentence of that paragraph seems particularly weak. It tails off into nothing. The writer should mark that paragraph as requiring more attention.

Is the material accurate or accurately presented? There would seem to be some inaccuracies at least in the presentation. The first paragraph conjures up an empty sky and ocean and then goes on to mention the railroad, but railroad trains are not noted for their ability to fly or float. The writer might also, for instance, feel slightly uneasy about the second sentence of the second paragraph. Looked at more closely, it seems to suggest that widespread use of the automobile followed almost immediately on its invention, whereas it was only in the early decades of the 20th century and the introduction of mass-production techniques by Henry Ford that automobiles began to appear in large numbers. That sentence also needs adjusting.

Is the presentation clear and logical? There seems to be a lot of work still to be done in this respect. Two particularly glaring examples stand out: one at the beginning and one at the end.

The first paragraph ends with a question that is never answered: "A world at peace or a dead world?" To follow this up with "That is the question," when you have no intention of distinguishing between the two types of world and your discussion immediately moves on to another subject, makes matters worse. The writer should realize that the discussion has to be reorganized to make the question relevant, or that the question itself, dramatic-sounding as it is, has to be dropped. The second option would be the easier one.

The final paragraph introduces two new ideas: "the automobiles of the future will be smaller and cheaper" and "millions of people in the Third World" will want to own them. Where have these statements suddenly come from? The final paragraph should form a conclusion, and it is generally bad policy to introduce anything new when you are trying to draw the whole body of text together. If these ideas are to be retained, the writer should accommodate them elsewhere. The millions in the developing world might figure in the present second paragraph, which deals with the benefits of the automobile. The writer should perhaps try to include the idea of smaller and cheaper machines—smaller and cheaper by whose standards, incidentally?—in the paragraphs that envision new fuels.

The basic structure of the essay on a paragraph-by-paragraph basis is the following: a vision of the future without automobiles—lives are shaped by cars—oil is running out—pollution and climate change—human society between a rock and a hard place—adapt the automobile—new fuel sources/electricity—new fuel source/hydrogen—conclusion. This structure is essentially viable. It would probably benefit by being made more explicit. Rereading the text, the writer might spot that the "rock and a hard place" paragraph stands out from the others because it is the only one in which he or she comments directly on the situation. It might be recycled to provide a more explicit pointer to the direction the argument is going to take and/or to fill out the conclusion after the "new" material there is relocated.

The language used by the writer is unlikely to tax the reader's understanding. Its tone is rather uncertain, however, and is not consistently maintained. The piece begins on an almost rhetorical note with repeated injunctions to the reader to "imagine," and the first paragraph ends with the portentous "That is the question." By the end of the second paragraph, however, the tone has become much more informal: "Can you imagine them letting this happen? I can't." There are further instances of informality—"the oil can't be drilled forever," "Exercise is good for you, but I don't see . . ." and "Peering into my crystal ball . . ." (not so much informal, perhaps, as jokey)—interspersed with more neutral or formal elements. One sentence in the fourth paragraph does not sound like the rest of the piece at all: "Emissions from internal-combustion engines have been identified as a major contributor to global warming" gives the impression that it has been copied from a source and incorporated into the text without regard to whether it matches the style of the surrounding material. (Instructors, competition judges, and the like are usually quick to spot anything that stands out in this way.) It is to be hoped that the writer would recognize these inconsistencies and decide, given that this is a competition essay, that the best tactic is probably to reduce the informal element and bring everything closer to a neutral tone.

There is another aspect of the language in the first draft that the writer should attend to. At certain points, it is sexist or at the very least "noninclusive"; for example, "A man who has his own transport is a free man." A couple of sentences later, the writer seems to have second thoughts and refers to "an ordinary person." Nonsexist language should be used consistently throughout the piece.

## CUTTING AND PASTING

The first phase of revision may involve moving large sections of text into new positions. The easiest way to do this with a computer word-processing program is simply to select the portion of text you wish to relocate, use the Cut command in the Edit facility to remove it to the Clipboard, then, when you have moved the cursor to the position where you want the text to appear, use the Paste command in Edit to reintroduce it. If you have printed out your work to revise it, you can literally cut out sections with scissors and reposition them on a blank sheet of paper using paste or adhesive tape.

## The Second Stage of Revision

If the writer makes changes of the kind recommended in the previous subsection, the essay text may now look something like the following (new or repositioned material is shown in italics, and deletions from the first draft are shown in "strikethrough," having a line appear through text to indicate its omission):

**The Future of the Automobile**

Is it possible to imagine a future in which the automobile plays no part? ~~Yes, it is possible, but the prospect is a scary one.~~ Imagine the highways of this country deserted. Imagine the streets of our great cities quiet. Imagine trade and industry at a standstill, for there are no vehicles left to take goods where they are meant to go. Imagine the sky and the ocean empty of powered vehicles, too, for whatever kills off the automobile is going to mean the kiss of death for the airplane~~,~~ and the ship~~, and the railroad too. A world at peace or a dead world? That is the question.~~ *All this is possible. But the prospect is a frightening one.*

*As I see it, human society is caught between a rock and a hard place.* Our lives are shaped by ~~our cars~~ *the automobile.* ~~The invention of the automobile at the end of the 19th century~~ *When automobiles became widely available, they* brought about a great leap forward in human freedom. ~~A man who has his own transport is a free man.~~ People who have their own transport are free. We are living in a go-where-you-like-any-time society. We like living in it and we are not going to give it up easily. *Exercise is good for you, but I cannot see any present or future politician being able to persuade the average American to give up his car in favor of walking or cycling. And there are millions of people in the Third World who will one day want to enjoy the advantages that developed nations already enjoy.*

~~And~~ *Even* if the ordinary person could be persuaded or forced to part with his car, their are all the commercial interests—the companies who make vehicles, the companies who sell them, the companies who drill oil out of the ground, and the countries whose economies depend on oil—who are not going to lie down and watch themselves going bankrupt. Can you imagine them letting this happen? I ~~can't~~ cannot.

But *that is only part of the picture. Can we afford to be dependent on the automobile?* The oil ~~can't~~ *cannot* be drilled forever. ~~It is a finite resource.~~ We ~~have gotten~~ *are* used to the prophets of doom not coming true. They said the oil would not last into the 21st century, but it has. *But we cannot rely on their being wrong forever.* ~~However, o~~One day ~~it~~ *the oil* will run out. It is a finite resource.

In the meantime, the pollution in our cities is getting worse, and the climate is changing. ~~Emissions from i~~Internal-combustion engines ~~have been identified as a major contributor to~~ fuel global warming. There would be some advantages from the disappearance of the automobile.

Cleaner air, especially in the cities, and a more predictable climate.

~~As I see it, human society is caught between a rock and a hard place.~~ Our desire for freedom, *which* ~~will~~ prevents us from letting the automobile go, ~~while~~ *conflicts with* our desire for survival, *for which we need a livable planet*~~will ultimately compel us to adapt to new global realities.~~

What is the solution? ~~Exercise is good for you, but I don't see any present or future politician being able to persuade the average American to give up his car in favor of walking or cycling.~~ The answer must be to adapt the automobile to suit the realities. The first necessity is to discover a new fuel to drive the vehicles of the future.

We know that automobile manufacturers are already experimenting with electric cars, but so far it has been difficult to store enough electricity inside to enable an electric-powered vehicle to go anything like as far as a gas-powered vehicle. For all we know they may have already discovered a new type of fuel source that does not have this disadvantage, but the rest of the world ~~doesn't know about~~ *has no knowledge of* it yet.

~~Peering into my crystal ball,~~ I foresee that the automobiles of the future will run on hydrogen. Experiments to produce a hydrogen-powered car are already being made. There is an abundance of this gas on the earth, ~~—it is the most abundant element in the universe—~~ and it can be burned without producing carbon dioxide—the gas that is most responsible for global warming.

That is where the future of the automobile lies. It will *need to* be a smaller and more efficient~~, cheaper~~ machine *than the average American car of today, so as to reduce congestion, fuel consumption, and pollution in the ever-expanding cities of the world.* ~~for the benefit of the millions of people in the Third World who will one day want to enjoy the advantages that developed nations already enjoy.~~ And it will run on hydrogen.

The text is now ready for the second phase of revision, which involves subjecting a reorganized draft to more detailed stylistic examination. This particular second draft, incidentally, though better organized, is still some 30 words over length. This may in part be because the writer has still not entirely solved the problem of the conclusion and, having removed some material from it, has felt the need to add some more. It is not uncommon to find that revision proceeds at first on a basis of two steps forward and one step back. One reason for this is a natural reluctance to contemplate really radical change. To take two steps forward and not retreat at all, we need to be cruelly objective and not hesitate to reorganize and rewrite extensively if the piece fails any of the revision tests.

As far as length is concerned, however, the fact that a text is still slightly too long at this stage of revision need not be a serious problem. So, instead, let us imagine the writer applying the second-phase questions to the essay.

The paragraphing and paragraph-linking in the second draft are better than they were in the first. On the other hand, the writer might well think that the whole thing has not quite gelled yet. The repositioning of a sentence at the beginning of the second paragraph, for example, has made the structure slightly clearer, but that sentence is not a topic sentence for that paragraph. In fact, it is difficult to identify any sentence in the paragraph that constitutes a nucleus for the material it contains. "Our lives are shaped by the automobile" sounds as if it should perform this task, but the next part of the paragraph consists of short sentences that read more like separate thoughts placed next to one another, rather than thoughts connected to a central concept.

Part of the problem may lie in the type of sentences the writer uses. Applying the sentence questions dispassionately, the writer might well feel that the shorter sentences work best, but that there are possibly too many of them. The longer sentences do not suffer from being too complex; instead, they tend to straggle. For example, "Even if the ordinary person could be persuaded or forced to part with his car, their [there] are all the commercial interests—the companies who make vehicles, the companies who sell them, the companies who drill oil out of the ground, and the countries whose economies depend on oil—who are not going to lie down and watch themselves going bankrupt." This sentence would surely benefit from being tightened up. The parenthetical phrases between the dashes (the companies . . ., the companies . . .) are intended to emphasize the number and variety of the commercial interests that would be affected, but the same effect could be achieved more neatly: "Even if the ordinary person could be persuaded or forced to part with his [?] car, commercial organizations from vehicle manufacturers to oil companies and even nations would face being bankrupted. They would certainly not let this happen without a fight."

The language that the writer uses is simple and clear, and often vigorous. For example, the replacement sentence "Internal-combustion engines fuel global warming" has considerable punch through playing on the word *fuel*. However, the piece contains a number of clichés and inappropriate metaphors.

A cliché is a fixed phrase that has become overused. Clichés are usually neat, convenient, and superficially attractive phrases. The problem with them is that everyone finds them neat, convenient, and attractive, consequently they have been used over and over again. They are usually dead metaphors. When people use notorious clichés such as "go the extra mile," not only are they not, literally, going to walk five miles instead of four, but it never even enters their heads that what they are writing or saying has nothing to do with walking or distances. The metaphor is therefore dead. The phrase means no more than that they will make an extra effort.

The text under consideration contains several such phrases: "the kiss of death," for example, or "between a rock and a hard place" or "a great leap forward." It is very difficult not to use clichés. Even the most experienced writers may use them, if their attention lapses. Conscientious writers, however, ought to be ruthless about striking them from the text at the revision stage.

The writer of the example essay may have thought that "kiss of death" followed quite nicely the phrase "kills off the automobile," and that both brought a touch of racy vigor to the sentence. But if his or her conscience were really active, then "kill off" might, on second thought, seem a rather sloppy verb to use about the automobile, which is in no sense alive. It may seem a harsh judgment, but if "kiss of death" has to go, it is better that "kill off" goes too in order to make way for a new expression, perhaps something such as ". . . for whatever drives the automobile from the highway will inevitably and permanently ground the airplane and dock the ship." That formulation is more concrete and hardly less vigorous.

Are any words repeated too often? There are instances of repetition for effect ("Imagine . . . Imagine . . . Imagine . . ."), which is certainly allowable, and there is accidental repetition when the same word simply appears too many times within a short space, as *oil* perhaps does in the following passage: "The oil cannot be drilled forever. We are used to the prophets of doom not coming true. They said the oil would not last into the 21st century, but it has. But we cannot rely on their being wrong forever. One day the oil will run out."

Inexperienced writers sometimes think that the best way around this problem is to reach for the thesaurus, but if the writer substituted *petroleum* for *oil* in the third sentence and *gasoline* in the last, the passage would not be greatly improved. It would also be fairly obvious what he or she had done. If you find a word repeated, first try reconstructing the sentences in the passage and only then look for a synonym. And if you decide to use a synonym, make sure that it is a word of the same kind as the one it is intended to replace, not a much more formal or informal one that will upset the tone.

If the writer rewrote these sentences to eliminate one instance of the use of *oil,* he or she could take the opportunity to correct two other mistakes: *Oil* cannot be drilled; the *ground* or the *seabed* is drilled to extract oil. Likewise, only *prophecies* may not come true; *prophets,* on the other hand, can only be proved wrong (or right, as the case may be). An improved version might read: "We cannot go on drilling for oil forever. The prophets of doom have been wrong so far. They said the wells would run dry before the end of the 20th century. One day they will be proved right. Oil is a finite resource and will, in the end, run out."

There is a different kind of "repetition" a little further on in the passage that might possibly cause confusion. In the third paragraph from the end, the writer makes reference to a "gas-powered vehicle," meaning, presumably, a vehicle that runs on ordinary liquid fuel. *Gas* is so commonly used in this sense that we can easily forget that it is essentially an informal contraction of *gasoline.* But in the next paragraph the writer uses the word *gas* in its standard sense of, to quote *Merriam-Webster's Collegiate Dictionary,* 11th edition, "a fluid (as air) that . . . tends to expand indefinitely." Vehicles that run on liquefied petroleum gas already exist, and a vehicle that used hydrogen gas as its fuel could be correctly described as a "gas-powered vehicle." It makes sense, therefore, to change *gas-powered vehicle* in the third paragraph from the end to *gasoline-powered vehicle.*

The grammar and punctuation of the passage are fairly sound. Many misspellings, which are often really mistypings, such as *relaities* for *realities,* can be caught by a spell-checker. A spell-checker will not, however, alert you if you accidentally type *their* when you mean *there* (as this writer does), *fro* when you mean *for,* or *on* when you mean *one.* Always look out for the really common confusable terms, especially *its* and *it's* and *there, their,* and *they're.* It is a rather tedious procedure, but it may be worth conducting a computer search for each of these (using the Find command in the Edit facility) in order to make sure that you have not mistakenly used the one in place of the other. (Consistency in spelling is yet another matter, which is dealt with below. *See* CHECKING FOR CONSISTENCY, page 86.)

Are there peculiarities in the writing style? It requires a very special distancing effort to spot your own personal mannerisms, if you have any. Again, it is usually a question of tracking down repetition, but not single repeated words so much as repeated sentence elements or repeated formulations of a particular type. It may, for instance, strike the alert reader that this is the third sentence in a row that has been couched in an impersonal form beginning with the word *it*. The style chosen for this book has been kept deliberately impersonal (from the point of view of the authors), so there has been a great temptation to overuse this particular construction. But for the need to illustrate the point, the writers or editors would undoubtedly recast one or more of the sentences in this paragraph to ensure greater variety.

The writer of the example piece, on the other hand, seems to have a special fondness for a question-and-answer formula: "Is it possible to imagine . . .?" "Can you imagine them letting this happen? I cannot." "Can we afford to be dependent on the automobile?" There is nothing wrong with this way of initiating a discussion as such. It is only when a particular form of words recurs often enough to call attention to itself, and consequently perhaps distract the reader's attention from what is being communicated, that action needs to be taken.

Even when all the second-phase revision questions have been asked and answered, it is still worth carrying out two further procedures before proceeding to the third, and possibly final, draft. The first is to take a final look at any parts of the piece that have caused you particular difficulty at any stage. Often these will be—or will include—the introduction and the conclusion. The writer of the example essay has, as we have seen, had problems finding an adequate conclusion. The introduction, after a little revision, has seemed to be a sound, indeed quite a strong, passage of writing.

The second is to ask yourself as searchingly as you can whether, with all the changes you have made or are about to make, the piece now fulfills its original intention. This is perhaps a cue to check over what you regard as the strongest parts of the piece, those that caused you least trouble, your favorite sentences and paragraphs where you seemed to be able to hit the right note almost by instinct.

The great British lexicographer Dr. Samuel Johnson once recalled being given the following advice by a tutor at his university: "Read over your compositions, and where ever you meet with a passage that you think is particularly fine, strike it out." That instruction is unduly harsh. Nevertheless, it may serve as a timely reminder that it is possible to go wrong even when you think everything is going right, and that the piece as a whole is more important than any individual passage of apparently fine or successful writing.

Our essay writer, for example, might apply this final test to the generally strong introduction and realize that its very first sentence "Is it possible to imagine a future in which the automobile plays no part?" is very slightly skewed with respect to the title "The Future of the Automobile." The title obviously envisions that the essay will deal with the automobile as it will be in the future, not with the future and whether the automobile will play a part in it. In asking his or her reader to "imagine a future," the writer gets the emphasis slightly wrong. The sentence should be recast. If it read, for example, "Is it possible that the automobile has no future?" it would follow the lead of the title better and possibly give everything that follows a surer sense of direction.

## Approaching the Final Version

Here, then, is a third draft of the example essay, as it might look if all the corrections suggested above were incorporated and a general effort was made to tighten it up and cut it down to fit in the 600-word limit. (Corrections and additions to the second draft are given in italics, and deletions from the second draft are shown in strikethrough.)

**The Future of the Automobile**

Is it possible to imagine ~~a future in which~~ *that* the automobile ~~plays~~ *has* no ~~part~~ *future?* Imagine the highways of this country deserted. Imagine the streets of our great cities quiet. Imagine trade and industry at a standstill, for there are no vehicles left to take goods where they are meant to go. Imagine the sky and the ocean empty of powered vehicles, too, for whatever ~~kills off~~ *drives* the automobile *from the highway will inevitably and permanently ground* ~~is going to mean the kiss of death for~~ the airplane and *dock* the ship. ~~All this is possible. But the prospect is a frightening one.~~ *Can you imagine it? It is a possible and very frightening scenario.*

~~As I see it, human society is caught between a rock and a hard place.~~ *But most human beings are not yet ready to be frightened.* ~~Our lives are shaped by the automobile. When~~ The automobiles ~~became widely available, they brought about a great leap forward in~~ *increased* human freedom *in a way very few other inventions have.* ~~A man who has his own transport is a free man.~~ We ~~are~~ *like* living in a go-where-you-like-any-time society,~~. We like living in it~~ and we are not going to give it up easily. Exercise is good for you, but I cannot see any present or future politician being able to persuade the average American to give up his *or her* car in favor of walking or cycling. And there are millions of people in the *developing* ~~third~~ world who will one day want to enjoy the advantages that developed nations already enjoy.

Even if ~~the~~ ordinary ~~person~~ *people* could be persuaded or forced to part with ~~his~~ *their* cars, ~~their are all the commercial interests—the companies who make vehicles, the companies who sell them, the companies who drill oil out of the ground, and the countries whose economies depend on oil—who are not going to lie down and watch themselves going bankrupt. Can you imagine them letting this happen? I cannot.~~ *commercial organizations from vehicle manufacturers to oil companies and even nations would face being bankrupted. They would certainly not let this happen without a fight.*

But that is only part of the picture. Can we afford to *go on* being dependent on the automobile *and ignoring the frightening scenario?* ~~The oil cannot be drilled forever. We are used to the prophets of doom not coming true. They said the oil would not last into the 21st century, but it has. But we cannot rely on their being wrong forever. One day the oil will run out. It is a finite resource.~~ *We will not be able to drill for oil forever. The prophets of doom have been wrong so far. They said the wells would run dry before the end of the 20th century. One day, however, they will be proved right. Oil is a finite resource. It will in the end run out.*

In the meantime, the pollution in our cities is getting worse, and the climate is changing. Internal-combustion engines fuel global warming.

> There would be some advantages from the disappearance of the automobile. *We would have* ~~C~~cleaner air, especially in the cities, and a more predictable climate.
>
> Our desire for freedom, which prevents us from letting the automobile go, conflicts with our desire for survival, for which we need a livable planet.
>
> ~~What is the solution?~~ The ~~answer~~ *solution* must be to adapt the automobile to suit the new realities. The first necessity is to discover a new fuel to drive the vehicles of the future.
>
> We know that automobile manufacturers are already experimenting with electric cars, but so far it has been difficult to store enough electricity ~~inside~~ to enable an electric-powered vehicle to go ~~anything like~~ as far as a gaso*line*-powered vehicle. ~~For all we know they may have already discovered a new type of fuel source that does not have this disadvantage, but the rest of the world has no knowledge of it yet. I foresee that that the automobiles of the future will run on hydrogen.~~ *We have heard too of attempts* ~~Experiments~~ to produce a hydrogen-powered car ~~are already being made.~~ There is an abundance of this gas on the earth, and it can be burned without producing carbon dioxide—the gas that is most responsible for global warming. *If it is impossible to develop an electric vehicle that is capable of long journeys, perhaps hydrogen will do the job.*
>
> ~~That is where the future of the automobile lies. It will need to be a smaller and more efficient machine than the average American car of today so as to reduce congestion, fuel consumption, and pollution in the ever expanding cities of the world. And it will run on hydrogen.~~ *I do not personally believe that the frightening scenario will come true. Human beings have shown enormous ingenuity in the past in overcoming their problems, as they did when they invented the automobile to give the ordinary citizen the go-anywhere capability of the horse and the speed and strength of the railroad locomotive in a single machine. We need the automobile, and it does have a future. But in future it will have to go green.*

This represents a great improvement on the second and third versions. The writer remains within the word limit and has tightened up the piece considerably, notably by taking the idea of the "frightening" quality of the introductory scenario and, instead of dropping it after asking a useless question, using *frightening* as a keyword to link various parts of the argument together through to the radically altered conclusion.

It would tax the reader's patience to analyze this particular piece any further. You may well be able to spot places where the text could be further improved or have your own ideas on how to tackle the subject. The more important question, however, is, if this were your essay, would you be satisfied with it in its current state? Or, more broadly, at what point should you be satisfied with a piece of written work?

There is, unfortunately, no all-purpose answer to this question. You should continue to work on your text until you are reasonably satisfied that you can improve it no further and/or until the time you have available to work on it runs out. With luck, you will achieve satisfaction before your time expires. On the other hand, a piece of writing rarely reaches a state where it is absolutely perfect and cannot by any stretch of the imagination be improved. You need to strike a balance. The previous section has shown the kind of improvements that can be made by thorough revision. Revise until, in your judgment, the piece fulfills its purpose, is well organized, and reads easily and clearly, then let it go.

# CHECKING FOR CONSISTENCY

There are a series of small checks that are particularly important in extended pieces of work and that can be incorporated into the first and second stages of revision or into the proofreading stage or undertaken as a separate exercise. As they all have to do with consistency, it is convenient to deal with them together here.

Variety—in the construction of paragraphs and in the length of sentences, for instance—is an important element in writing, but there are certain particulars that you should try to keep the same throughout. The first of these is the level, or tone, of your writing. This point has been discussed more than once before, so it will suffice to remind you that you should generally avoid shifting—let alone suddenly lurching—from an informal to a formal mode, or vice versa: "With reference to your letter of October 24, it sucks!" or "I can't go bowling with you guys next Wednesday because I have a previous engagement."

Another issue is the spelling of particular words. It is not the case that every word has only one correct spelling (and any number of incorrect ones). For example, the word *livable* may also be spelled *liveable*. It is important, however, that you should choose one form, stick to it, and apply it to other similar words, such as *lovable* (not *loveable*) and *likable* (not *likeable*).

The same applies to the use of hyphens, punctuation with abbreviations, and capitalization. As noted at ABBREVIATIONS (page 202), the modern tendency is to omit periods, although they are sometimes used, and with certain abbreviations other punctuation marks are used. Any of the following four styles is possible (the first is probably the most standard), but a single style must be chosen and adhered to throughout a piece of writing.

> . . . animals, e.g., cats and dogs, are welcome . . .
> . . . animals, e.g. cats and dogs, are welcome . . .
> . . . animals e.g. cats and dogs are welcome . . .
> . . . animals eg cats and dogs are welcome . . .

(Similar styles with the use, or nonuse, of commas can be adopted with *i.e.* and *etc.*)

Certain words may be hyphenated, for example, *e-mail* or *email* and *good-bye* (or *good-by*) or *goodbye*. Certain words, especially proper names, must always have initial capital letters, but dictionaries label some words *"often cap,"* meaning that both forms are both acceptable (as in *webcam* and *Webcam*). You then have to choose which form you wish to use. The important point is that once you have decided which form you prefer, you should always use the word in that form wherever it occurs in

Finally, there may be two or more ways to refer to the same event or phenomenon—for instance, *World War II* or *the Second World War.* As before, choose whichever form you prefer and use it consistently for that and every related term (for example, *World War I* and *World War II,* or *the First World War* and *the Second World War*) on each appearance. (The Find facility in a word-processing program is often an invaluable help for searching out any oversights.)

## Consistency in Headings

In extended written texts, especially when you have written the material over a long period of time, it is important to check that headings are styled consistently. For example, in an essay on rites of passage, some headings might use a verb form—for example, "Marking the Initiation Ceremony"—while others might be styled with a noun—"Preparation for the Ceremony." These should be styled similarly throughout, for example, "Marking the Initiation Ceremony" and "Preparing for the Initiation Ceremony." Likewise, a separate check should be made that numbering (1., 1.1, etc.) or levels of hierarchy (*see* FORMAL PLANS, page 42) are consistent.

## Checking Text with Bullet Points

If you have included bullet points in your text, it is important to ensure that the opening (platform) text runs in grammatically with each individual bulleted line. Often the grammatical form of the words varies; for example,

Candidates should be

- Skilled to a high standard in a wide range of writing experience, including the production of fund-raising and educational materials
- Able to meet deadlines and organize workload, especially when priorities may conflict
- Able to work in a collaborative manner
- Have experience of staff supervision
- Be able to communicate the organization's aims clearly

This text should be revised to the following:

Candidates should be

- Skilled to a high standard in a wide range of writing experience, including the production of fund-raising and educational materials
- Able to meet deadlines and organize workload, especially when priorities may conflict
- Able to work in a collaborative manner
- Experienced in staff supervision
- Able to communicate the organization's aims clearly

As well as checking that the platform text runs in with each line grammatically and consistently, it is also important to check that the punctuation at the end of each bullet point is consistent. Contemporary trends are moving toward no punctuation at the end of each short bullet point, especially when these are shorter than a full sentence. The bulleted list may or may not have a concluding period at the end. When an individual bullet point consists of more than one sentence, however, normal punctuation rules should be adopted within the bullet point, such as a period at the end of the first sentence.

### Style Sheet

For extended pieces of writing, it can be very helpful to create a style sheet that lists the preferences used in the text, as in the following example.

, e.g.,
e-mail [hyphen]
good-bye [hyphen]
Internet [cap I]
lovable [*not* loveable]
Web site [cap W]

Numbers
Below 100, written out
50–5 [not 50–55]

## PROOFREADING

There are two points at which you may be required to proofread your text. If your work is not for publication, then when you have revised it until you are satisfied that you cannot improve it any further, you should print or type it out and read it carefully one last time. You are looking, essentially, for small matters that may have escaped your notice before: spelling mistakes that have not been caught by the spell-checker, errors in punctuation, or inconsistencies of the kind mentioned in the previous pages. By this time, you may well be so familiar with your text that it is very difficult to look at it with the close attention necessary to spot small mistakes. The best way to do this is to prevent yourself deliberately from getting into the flow. Read the text slowly sentence by sentence, with a brief pause at the end of the sentence. If you are still worried that your eyes are sliding over the text and may miss a mistake, try starting at the end and reading your sentences individually in reverse order.

If your work is being published, the publisher will usually send you a typeset copy (proofs or galleys). The proof copy shows you how your work will appear on the printed page. Your task is to go through it carefully and mark any corrections or alterations that you wish to make. You are looking for any errors that you may have overlooked before or that may have been introduced by the keyboarder or printer. Errors can creep in even if you have provided your work in electronic form (for example, an apostrophe or single quotation mark could come out straight ['] or curly [’] if text has been imported from different word-processing software.) You also have the opportunity to make any last-minute changes to the text, but these should be kept to a minimum as publishers may charge you for alterations made at proof stage that affect more than a specified percentage of the text. When making your corrections and edits, you will need to use special proofreading marks. Most publishers will provide you with a list of these marks and an explanation of how they are used. Proofreading symbols can also be found on the Web or in some style manuals and dictionaries.

# REFERENCES

## References to Books and Articles

If you are undertaking a piece of academic writing, you will need to provide references for any source that you quote or refer to. If you are not writing for academic purposes, you should still acknowledge in the text the sources of your material, but you can do this simply and generally, in the form such as "As R. T. Jones says in his book *George Eliot* . . ." or ". . . to quote Bea Smith's article in the *New York Times* . . ."

One simple and widely used system of reference is called the author-date system. As the name suggests, the system is based on the surname(s) of the author(s) and the work's date of publication. Under this system, when you refer to or quote from an author, you should include the surname and date in parentheses at some convenient point in the sentence, most often immediately following the quoted words or referenced thoughts, ideas, theses, and so on. You should also include a page number if you are making a direct quotation. Here are some examples: "Some authors insist the origins of the problem are genetic (Jones 1989; Smith 2003), others deny this (Henry 2004; Rasmussen 1996)" or "We may agree that 'Shakespeare got it wrong' (Bacon 1995, 37)." Note that, where more than one work or author is referred to, the reference data are separated by a semicolon, and the names are listed in alphabetical order or in chronological order according to date. The second reference in the first example sentence above could therefore be given as "(Rasmussen 1996; Henry 2004)." Either style is possible, but you should consistently follow one or the other.

The titles of books, whether referred to in the text or listed in a bibliography, should be in italics: *Martin Chuzzlewit* by Charles Dickens. The titles of articles in journals and newspapers should be shown in quotation marks; the names of the publications in which the articles appear should be shown in italics: "The Queen and the Workers" by A. Beille in *Beekeeper's Quarterly.*

At the end of your piece you will need to provide a list of all the works that you have referred to in the text and that you have used in your research; they should be listed alphabetically by surname(s) of the author(s). This reference list may be called a Bibliography, References, or Works Cited. It is advisable, as was recommended earlier, to make a note of the details that you will need for your references while you are doing your research.

When you list a book, you need to provide its title, the name(s) of the author(s), the publisher's name, and the place and date of publication. You list these details in the following order: author's surname, author's given name(s) or initials, title, place of publication, publisher's name, date of publication. Below is an example.

Biene, D. *The Making of Honey.* Cambridge, Mass.: Hive Press, 1996.

An alternative style lists the date of publication before the title:

Biene, D. 1996. *The Making of Honey.* Cambridge, Mass.: Hive Press.

When you list a journal article, you follow roughly the same procedure, but you must give the volume and issue numbers of the journal, as well as the page number. (These will usually be shown on the front cover and the title page).

Beille, A. "The Queen and the Workers." *Beekeeper's Quarterly* 72, no. 4 (2001): 22–23.

or

Beille, A. 2001. The Queen and the Workers. *Beekeeper's Quarterly* 72, 4: 22–23.

Note that there are no quotation marks around the title when it appears in the second type of reference list.

If the work you refer to happens to be part of a volume to which several authors have contributed, show it as follows:

Smoker, A. "Drones." In *Bees for Beginners.* Edited by James B. Combe. New York: Cider Press, 1999.

or

Smoker, A. 1999. Drones. In *Bees for Beginners,* edited by James B. Combe. New York: Cider Press.

If the work has more than one author, show the first author's surname followed by his or her given name or initials. The following author's or authors' names should appear in the normal order of given names, then surname.

Combe, James B., D. Biene, and Julia Van Bij. *The Uses of Beeswax.* Los Angeles: Politz and Drung, 1987.

or

Combe, James B., D. Biene, and Julia Van Bij. 1987. *The Uses of Beeswax.* Los Angeles: Politz and Drung.

If a person is the editor of a book rather than its author, the abbreviation *ed.* should come immediately after the name. If more than one work by the same author(s) is cited then a long (3-em) dash may be used to avoid repeating the name, also for works where that author's name is first in a list of coauthors.

Your reference list should cite the authors' names in alphabetical order. Multiple works by the same author can be listed in order of their date of publication or in alphabetical order by title of publication. All works produced by an author as an individual are listed before any works where his or her name is followed by the names of coauthors. Oftentimes all original works by an author are listed before any that he or she may have edited or translated, followed by any that were prepared with coauthors. Following are two examples of a bibliographical list:

Beille, A. "The Queen and the Workers." *Beekeeper's Quarterly* 72, no. 4 (2001): 22–23.
Biene, D. *The Making of Honey.* Cambridge, Mass.: Hive Press, 1996.
Combe, James B. *Telling the Bees.* New York: Cider Press, 2002.

———, ed. *Bees for Beginners.* New York: Cider Press, 1999.
Combe, James B., D. Biene, and Julia Van Bij. *The Uses of Beeswax.* Los Angeles: Politz and Drung, 1987.
Smoker, A. "Drones." In *Bees for Beginners.* Edited by James B. Combe. New York: Cider Press, 1999.
Van Bij, Julia, and A. Smoker. "The Nutritional Value of Royal Jelly." *Apiarist Magazine* 1, no. 2 (1993): 5–7.
Beille, A. 2001. The Queen and the Workers. Beekeeper's Quarterly 72, 4: 22–23.
Biene, D. 1996. *The Making of Honey.* Cambridge, Mass.: Hive Press.
Combe, James B., ed. 1999. *Bees for Beginners.* New York: Cider Press.
———. 2002. *Telling the Bees.* New York: Cider Press.
———, D. Biene, and Julia Van Bij. 1987. *The Uses of Beeswax.* Los Angeles: Politz and Drung.
Smoker, A. 1999. Drones. In *Bees for Beginners,* edited by James B. Combe. New York: Cider Press.
Van Bij, Julia, and A. Smoker. 1993. The Nutritional Value of Royal Jelly. *Apiarist Magazine* 1, 2: 5–7.

Referencing is a large subject. Your publisher or your instructor or school may have a special way of presenting references, which you obviously should follow. Either of the above styles should serve most purposes when no other instructions are given. For a more detailed account of the subject, including more obscure and special cases, consult *The Chicago Manual of Style* (Chicago: University of Chicago Press).

## References to Internet Sources

Each Internet source quoted or referenced to in your text should also be included in your bibliography. Citations should include the complete name of the author, the title of the work (article or paper or Web page), the name of the online source (publication, news service, organization, Web site, etc.), the URL of the Web document, and the date the document was posted or last updated or the date you downloaded it. If the source is an e-zine or is transcribed from a serial publication, such as a newspaper or magazine, use the date it was posted. If the document is a company, organization, or personal Web page that is continually revised and updated, indicate when it was last updated. If such information is unavailable, record the date on which you downloaded the page. Following are some examples:

Dereksen, Wilfried. "Elections in Venezuela." Electoral Web Sites. Available online. URL: http://www.agora.stm.it/elections/election/venezuel.htm. Updated on April 13, 1998.
Fulford, Pam. "8 Million People Can't Be Wrong." Beauty Net: The Virtual Salon for Beauty, Wellness and Style. Available online. URL: http://www.beautynet.com/ViewStories.html?Id=581&category=Skin%Zocare. Downloaded on December 29, 2004.
Glaister, Dan. "Landmark Hollywood Hotel to Become a School." *The Guardian.* Guardian Unlimited. Available online URL: http//www.guardian.co.uk/usa/story/0,12271,1305566,00.html. Posted on September 16, 2004.

Make a careful note of the punctuation. Italics are unnecessary for Web site names unless the Web document appears in an online publication such as the *New York Times* or *Science News*.

## REVISION: AN OVERVIEW

- If possible, allow a period of time to pass between finishing a draft and beginning its revision.
- Divide the work of revision into two phases.
- In the first phase correct and improve on the large scale. Consider whether you have fulfilled your purpose, covered all your material, presented the content accurately, organized the content well, and maintained an appropriate tone consistently.
- In the second phase correct and improve on a smaller scale. Consider paragraph and sentence construction, the quality of your language, clichés and repetitions, and grammatical correctness.
- Proofread your work and make final consistency checks.
- Make a reference list, if required.
- Submit your work to the reader.

# WRITING FUNDAMENTALS

# INTRODUCTION

Part I of this book has guided you through the process of preparing to write and then actually writing and revising a text. You have been shown how to build a structure, but no attention has yet been given to the nuts and bolts that hold this structure together. These nuts and bolts—the principles and conventions that underpin all communication in the English language—are the subject of Part II. They include the rules of grammar as they have developed over the centuries; the actual words we use; and the special symbols universally adopted in English as a way of punctuating written texts.

Many people feel an instinctive anxiety whenever the word *grammar* is mentioned, and very few would claim to have a perfect understanding of grammatical rules. Grammar is also not taught as formally in schools as it once was. Yet all native speakers and writers of English have been absorbing the conventions of English grammar since earliest childhood through what they hear and what they read. In reality, we all know more about English grammar than we think we do.

Grammar, put simply, controls the ways in which words and phrases interact. If there were no agreed rules of grammar, it would be as correct to say *her see I* as to say *I see her,* and nobody could be sure who had actually seen whom. Without grammar, individual words and phrases would have no universally understandable relationship with one another, and communication would be reduced to the simplest level. It is only because words are divided into categories such as verbs and nouns and because nouns, verbs, adjectives, adverbs, and so on can be grouped together in an orderly way to form clauses and sentences that sophisticated communication is possible.

This does not mean, unfortunately, that every rule of English grammar is absolutely clear and entirely beyond question. Although many rules can be treated as more or less permanent, the English language is constantly changing. New words and new ways of using words are being introduced all the time, while old words are acquiring new meanings. Sometimes, the only option is to describe the various possible ways in which something may be written and to leave the rest to the reader's personal preference. But this is as it should be, for any language serves its users, not the other way around.

Besides the chapter on grammar, Part II of this book includes chapters on the actual words we use. It deals in particular with such issues as spelling, slang, words that are easily confused with one another, and how to avoid the use of terms that may be considered insensitive or politically incorrect. It also explores how new words are formed (for instance, through the addition of prefixes and suffixes or through borrowings from other languages) in order to help demystify terminology that may otherwise appear unfamiliar or difficult. A better understanding of the origins of words and of the rules to which they conform brings greater confidence in using them and should lead to an improvement and enlargement of the reader's and writer's personal vocabulary.

Another chapter is dedicated to punctuation. Words may be the big animals in the language environment, but those little insects, the punctuation marks, play just as vital a role. It is as important to know how to use periods, commas, and quotation marks correctly, as it is to know how to use a verb or a noun. This chapter covers not only the rules for correct punctuation but also the pitfalls that too often await the unwary.

Part II concludes with a chapter on reference resources—other places writers may turn to in the quest to improve their use of language, together with tips on how to use them—and finally a glossary of grammatical terms. So, to return to the original metaphor, here are the nuts and bolts. See how they all fit together, then go and build with greater confidence.

# 4

# Grammar

## INTRODUCTION

The rules of grammar provide the framework that shows how the words of a language are put together and used. They create relationships between different words, dictating their order and the way they behave in different contexts, and so change what would otherwise be an indecipherable jumble into a meaningful sentence.

Every language has its own grammar. The grammar of the English language has many things in common with other modern languages, such as French and German, but it also has many quirks of its own with which all writers need to be at least partially familiar. Grammar is widely taught in schools, but most English speakers unconsciously learn the key features at a young age through the example of others. Learning is a continuing process. Like vocabulary, grammar continues to evolve, and what was anathema to one generation may become perfectly acceptable to the next. This process of change can often be controversial, however, and what is judged "poor English" is often faulted on grammatical grounds.

English grammar is commonly thought of in traditional terms, deriving many of its golden rules from classical Latin, but in reality it may be seen to respond (albeit slowly) to the language as written and spoken every day. Modern English grammar increasingly allows greater leeway for informal usages and for the varied influence of regional variations, fashionable trends, and modern jargon. There is no one single formal authority presiding over the rules of English grammar. It is instead built on established practice, as reinforced by education and popular prejudice.

The standard of grammar expected in one context may not be the same as that expected in another. The grammar of informal spoken English, for instance, is much less rigorous than that of formal written English. This goes beyond the obvious fact that the visual cues and intonations of spoken English are necessarily replaced in writing by punctuation and tone. The same level of grammatical strictness is not automatically expected in written communications between friends, for example, as it is in official reports, technical documents, or formal job applications. Allowances also have to be made for regional characteristics and dialects in different parts of the English-speaking world. Nonetheless, many basic rules of English grammar are upheld throughout the English-speaking world. Some aspects are universally considered plain right or wrong.

As well as providing the writer with the actual rules, grammar also gives us the linguistic terms that we can use to distinguish and discuss the many and varied aspects of the written word. Grammar has several specialized branches. These include the study of words (morphology); the study of how words change in different tenses, cases, and persons (inflection); the study of how new words are formed (derivation); the study of the structure of phrases, clauses, and sentences (syntax); the study of meaning (semantics); the study of language in actual use (pragmatics); the study of speech sounds (phonetics); and the study of punctuation. These and many other specialized grammatical terms are listed and explained at the end of this book.

# NOUNS

A noun is a word that variously denotes a thing, person, place, quality, state, action, or concept (for example, *man, house, idea, piece, speed, color*). It serves as the subject of a verb and can be singular or plural. Plural forms are usually distinguished by the addition of a final *s* (*beds, lions, trees*), although other plural forms are commonly encountered (*life/lives, marsh/marshes, mouse/mice, phenomenon/phenomena, woman/women*). Nouns can be replaced by pronouns, such as *it* or *they* (*see* PRONOUNS, page 135).

## Types of Nouns

There are several different types of nouns. Once the characteristics of the different types of noun are learned, it is relatively easy to distinguish between them. Details of the different types are given below. (*See also* NOUN PHRASE, page 148.)

### PROPER NOUNS

Proper nouns (also called **proper names**) refer to specific people, places, and things and begin with a capital letter. They include personal names (*Henry, Simone*); place-names (*America, Himalayas, Oslo, Pacific, Sahara, White House*); formal titles (*Sergeant, Reverend*); titles of literary, artistic, or other works (*the Bible,* Great Expectations, *Bill of Rights*); forms of address (*Dr., Mrs.*); languages (*English, Mandarin*); organizations and institutions (*New York Times, Red Cross, Roman Catholic Church*); events and festivals (*Superbowl, Easter*); and months and days of the week (*January, Monday*). In contrast to common nouns (see below), proper nouns are rarely encountered as plurals, although there are occasions in which they may be employed in such a fashion (*Thanksgivings of the past, a gift for both Alices*). They are not usually introduced by an indefinite article such as *a* or *the,* although there are exceptions:

> ***That** car is a Ford.*
> *This was not the Paris of her dreams.*

Some proper nouns, such as place-names, may be considered concrete nouns, while others, such as days of the week, are considered abstract nouns (see next page).

## COMMON NOUNS

Common nouns include all nouns that are not otherwise classified as proper nouns (for example, *ambition, duck, lasso, pencil, weakness*). They do not usually begin with a capital letter and are usually preceded by an indefinite article such as *a* or *the*. Note that some common nouns (such as *state* in *an affair of state*) may also be categorized as proper names, depending upon the context (as in *State Department*).

## COUNTABLE NOUNS

Countable nouns are nouns that can be counted and thus have a plural form (*fox/foxes, ocean/oceans, wasp/wasps*). Countable nouns are always prefaced in the singular (and often in the plural) by indefinite articles such as *a* or *the* or by such possessives as *my* or *our* (*a hole, the restaurant, my brother, our holiday*), except where they operate like uncountable nouns in such phrases as *at school* (see below).

## UNCOUNTABLE NOUNS

Uncountable nouns are nouns that represent something that cannot be counted (*dampness, frustration, steam, wastage, water*). They are thus not generally referred to in the plural. Most abstract nouns may be categorized as uncountable. They are not normally prefaced by an indefinite article such as *a* or *the*, but occasionally take one, as shown below with *mess* and *understanding:*

*A mess of pottage.*
*A basic understanding of Greek.*

Note that some nouns can qualify as both countable and uncountable nouns according to the way in which they are employed (*a glowing light/in failing light, a third time/time past, a low-fat food, buy some food*). Other nouns that are uncountable by themselves may become countable when made part of a countable noun phrase (*a moment of inspiration, a pair of scissors, a piece of news*).

## CONCRETE NOUNS

Concrete nouns are nouns that refer to things that have some kind of actual physical existence (*air, building, rock, string*). Note, however, that concrete nouns may also operate as abstract nouns in some circumstances (see below). Depending on the context, concrete nouns may be variously categorized as countable (*birds, flowers, walls*) or uncountable (*lace, rainfall, saliva*).

## ABSTRACT NOUNS

Abstract nouns are nouns that refer to ideas, emotions, or other concepts that do not have an actual physical existence (*despair, intention, strength, wish*). Note that some abstract nouns may also qualify as concrete nouns, depending on the way in which they are employed (*the root of a plant/the root of the problem, speak in a whisper/a whisper of doubt*). Some abstract nouns are countable (*dreams, fears, triumphs*), while others are uncountable (*charity, ignorance, paleness*).

Abstract nouns are often created through the addition of a formulaic ending to an existing noun, adjective, or verb. Examples of endings used to create abstract nouns from existing nouns include *-cy* (*accuracy, tenancy*), *-dom* (*kingdom, martyrdom*), *-hood* (*boyhood, sisterhood*), *-icide* (*infanticide*), *-ism* (*magnetism, marxism*), and *-ship* (*gamesmanship, generalship*). Examples of endings used to create abstract nouns from existing adjectives include *-ism* (*feminism, naturalism*), *-ity* (*fragility, minority*), *-ness* (*coolness, weariness*), and *-th* (*depth, hundredth*). Examples of endings used to create abstract nouns from existing verbs include *-age* (*breakage, linkage*), *-al* (*perusal, rehearsal*), *-ance* (*annoyance, performance*), *-ation* (*confirmation, imagination*), *-ence* (*emergence, reference*), *-ery* (*mockery, trickery*), *-ing* (*drowning, talking*), *-ion* (*action, regulation*), *-ment* (*government, statement*), and *-ure* (*closure, seizure*).

## COLLECTIVE NOUNS

A collective noun denotes a particular group of people, animals, or things. Confusion sometimes arises over the question of whether collective nouns when used in the singular should take a singular or plural verb. In cases where the collective noun in question is understood to refer to a class of things of a certain kind, rather than to a grouping of one particular thing, the general rule is that the noun always takes a singular verb, as follows:

*The furniture has been put into storage.*

Where a collective noun refers to people in general, or to a broad grouping of people, it is generally treated as plural and takes a plural verb:

*The people deserve an answer.*

In many other cases, however, it is not always clear which should be used, and it is often up to the writer to decide which choice to make, since either form is acceptable:

*The committee is undecided.*
*The committee are undecided.*

The use of a singular verb underlines the unity of a group as a single entity, while the choice of a plural verb emphasizes its composition of many individuals. Whichever choice is made, it is important that it is reflected in associated words or phrases in the same sentence, as in the following:

*The committee is undecided, but it meets again in the morning.*
*The committee are undecided, but they meet again in the morning.*

Consistency is essential in these cases, and it is incorrect to treat a collective noun as plural and yet attach a singular possessive pronoun, or vice versa (*the committee has decided the proposal does not meet with their approval; the committee have decided the proposal does not meet with its approval*). Similarly, where a collective noun is in the singular, its singular state should be reflected in any attached adjectives, even though the accompanying verb may be plural:

*This troupe are all professional dancers.*

Where the collective noun is made plural, any attached adjectives become plural in the usual way:

*These herds will all move south in the winter.*

Note that some collective nouns are uncountable and cannot be rendered in plural form, as is the case with the names of commercial organizations and other institutions (as in *the FBI*).

Many groups have their own specific collective nouns, sometimes unique to themselves, and mistakes made in identifying these occur frequently. Some collective nouns are more widely known than others, and in the less common cases it may be considered pedantic to use the more strictly correct form (for instance, *clamor* or *yoke*) rather than a more general term (such as *flock* or *herd*).

The following list includes some of the more familiar collective nouns, as well as some of the less widely known.

| Individuals | Collective Noun(s) | Individuals | Collective Noun(s) |
|---|---|---|---|
| actors | cast/company/troupe | cranes | herd/sedge/siege |
| airplanes | flight/squadron | crocodiles | bask |
| angels | host | crows | murder |
| antelopes | herd | cubs | litter |
| arrows | sheaf | dancers | troupe |
| asses | pace | deer | herd |
| badgers | cete | dogs | pack |
| bears | sloth | dolphins | school |
| beavers | colony | ducks | paddling/team |
| bees | swarm | eagles | convocation |
| bells | peal | eggs | clutch |
| birds | flock/flight | elephants | parade |
| bishops | bench | elks | gang |
| boars | singular | experts | panel |
| bowls | set | ferrets | business |
| bread | batch | finches | charm |
| buffaloes | herd | fishes | shoal |
| camels | caravan | flies | swarm |
| cards | deck/pack | flowers | bouquet/bunch/posy |
| cars | fleet | foxes | skulk |
| cattle | drove/herd | frogs | army |
| chickens | brood | geese | gaggle/skein |
| choughs | chattering | goats | tribe |
| coots | covert | golf clubs | set |
| cormorants | flight | grapes | bunch/cluster |

*(continues)*

*(continued)*

| Individuals | Collective Noun(s) | Individuals | Collective Noun(s) |
|---|---|---|---|
| grasshoppers | cloud | porpoises | school |
| guillemots | bazaar | pups | litter |
| gulls | colony | quails | bevy |
| hares | husk | rabbits | bury/nest |
| hawks | cast | rags | bundle |
| hens | brood | rats | colony |
| herons | siege | ravens | unkindness |
| herrings | glean/shoal | rhinoceroses | crash |
| horses | string | rooks | building/clamor |
| hounds | pack | runners | field |
| insects | swarm | sailors | crew |
| kangaroos | troop | sails | suit |
| kittens | kindle | seals | herd/pod |
| laborers | gang | sheep | flock |
| larks | exaltation | ships | fleet/flotilla/squadron |
| leopards | leap | soldiers | army |
| lions | pride | sparrows | host |
| locusts | plague | squirrels | dray |
| magistrates | bench | starlings | murmuration |
| magpies | tittering | stars | cluster/constellation |
| minstrels | troupe | steps | flight |
| monkeys | troop | swallows | flight |
| musicians | band/orchestra | swifts | flock |
| nightingales | watch | thrushes | mutation |
| onions | rope | tigers | ambush |
| otters | family | toads | knot |
| owls | parliament | trees | clump |
| oxen | drove/herd/team/yoke | turkeys | rafter |
| parrots | pandemonium | turtles | turn |
| partridges | covey | whales | gam/pod/school |
| peacocks | muster | wolves | pack/rout |
| pearls | rope/string | woodcocks | fall |
| penguins | rookery | woodpeckers | descent |
| pheasants | nye | worshippers | congregation |
| pigs | litter | zebras | zeal |
| plovers | congregation | | |

## Plurals of Nouns

The plurals of nouns can take a number of different forms, of which three are classed **regular** endings. Most nouns are made plural through the simple addition of an *-s* at the end (*dogs, keys, radios, wheels*). Nouns that end with the letters *-ch, -s, -sh, -x,* and *-z* generally take the ending *-es* (*batches, crosses, fishes, boxes, quizzes*). Nouns that end in a consonant and *-y* have the plural ending *-ies* (*armies, babies, cities, ladies, stories, territories*). This last rule does not always apply, however, in the case of proper nouns, which sometimes take the regular *-s* ending (*the O'Reillys*). (*See also* comments in the section on SPELLING, page 180.)

These so-called regular endings are not the only form of plural nouns. There are a number of **irregular** plurals that can cause confusion because they do not follow set rules.

Some nouns ending with *-f* or *-fe,* for instance, take the plural ending *-s* (*beliefs, griefs, gulfs, roofs*), while others take the ending *-ves* (*calves, halves, selves, thieves, wolves*). There is no set rule here, and the only way to master the difference is to become familiar with each individual case. Note that in certain instances either ending, *-fs* or *-ves,* is acceptable, although one form may be preferred or more common (*dwarfs/dwarves, hooves/hoofs, scarves/scarfs*). Whichever choice is made, it is important to be consistent and at all costs to avoid using both forms in the same piece of writing.

In general, the spelling of singular nouns that end in *-is* is altered to *-es* in the plural (*axis/axes, crisis/crises*). But note that some follow the regular ending rule of *-es* (*iris/irises, trellis/trellises*).

Many nouns ending with *-o* take an *-s* ending (*ghettos, pianos, solos, videos*). Others, however, take an *es* ending (*echoes, tomatoes, volcanoes*). There is no rule governing such words, although words ending with *-o* that are abbreviated versions of longer words always take an *-s* ending (*photos, rhinos*). Once again, there are a number of nouns that can be made plural through the addition of either *-s* or *-es,* and neither version is more correct than the other, although one is invariably preferred in the dictionary (*cargoes/cargos, zeros/zeroes*).

Nouns that end with *-on* sometimes assume an *-s* ending in the plural (*cartons, coupons*), But others take an *-a* ending (*criterion/criteria*), while still others may take either ending (*automaton/automatons* or *automata*).

Nouns that end in *-um* sometimes take the plural ending *-a* (*bacterium/bacteria, stratum/strata*). Others, however, take the regular ending *-s* (*conundrum/conundrums*). As before, there is a further group that may take either ending (*aquariums/aquaria, referendums/referenda*).

Nouns that end in *-us* usually take the ending *-i* in the plural (*nucleus/nuclei, stimulus/stimuli*), although others take *-ses* (*bonus/bonuses, genius/geniuses*). Some words, however, are equally correct with either ending (*radiuses/radii, syllabuses/syllabi*).

Some nouns, notably animal names, are identical in both their singular and plural forms. Examples of such nouns (sometimes called **zero plurals**) include *aircraft, crossroads, deer, fish* (though *fishes* is also found), *series,* and *sheep.* This class of nouns also includes some nationalities (*Chinese, Sudanese*).

Other irregular plural forms defy categorization. Thus, the plural of *mouse* is *mice* (although the plural of *house* is *houses,* not *hice*). Other examples include *child/children, foot/feet, goose/geese, man/men,* and *woman/women.*

The list on the following page details some of the more common irregular plural forms.

| Singular Noun Ending | Irregular Plural Noun Ending |
|---|---|
| -an | -en |
| -f | -fs/-ves |
| -fe | -ves |
| -is | -es/-ises |
| -ld | -ren |
| -o | -s/-es |
| -on | -s/-a |
| -oose | -eese |
| -oot | -eet |
| -ouse | -s/-ice |

Nouns borrowed from foreign languages pose a particular problem, since their plural forms may sometimes be created by adding an *-s* according to English-language rules or other times by following the convention of the original language. Sometimes both alternatives are considered acceptable, as is the case with words from French ending in *-eau* (*chateaus/chateaux, gateaus/gateaux, tableaus/tableaux*). Words taken from Latin and Greek sometimes retain the plural as it appeared in the original language (*fungus/fungi, larva/larvae, phenomenon/phenomena*), but on other occasions simply acquire an *-s* in the plural form (*era/eras, quota/quotas*). Again, there are circumstances when there is more than one choice of permissible ending (*formulas/formulae, octopuses/octopi*).

Words ending in *-ex* or *-ix* tend to adopt the plural ending *-es* (*complex/complexes, prefix/prefixes*). Some, however, can also take the irregular plural ending *-ices* (*appendix/appendices, index/indices*).

As a general rule, when there is a choice between a regular plural ending (such as *-s*) and an irregular one (such as *-ices*), the approach adopted by many users is to employ the regular ending in everyday use and to reserve the irregular ending for more formal or technical contexts. This principle should be treated with caution, however, since the different plurals may in some circumstances convey different meanings: *media,* for instance, refers to means of communication and does not mean the same as *mediums,* which refers (among other things) to people who claim to act as conduits of communication with the afterworld. Guidance as to the best choice to be made in specific circumstances is given in most good dictionaries.

Nouns that have distinct singular and plural forms are known as **variable nouns.** Nouns that are found only in either their singular or plural form, but not in both, are formally called **invariable nouns** (*cardboard, cattle, jolliness, people, series*). Particular notice should be taken of a small class of invariable nouns that end in *-s* (and thus might be assumed to be plural) but are in fact singular and should thus take singular verbs (*checkers, mathematics, news*):

*Checkers is a great game.*
*The news has just come through.*

It should also be noted, though, that some apparently plural nouns ending with *-s* may refer to a single item (*goggles, scissors, trousers*), even though they take a plural verb:

*My goggles are all steamed up.*
*Those are my trousers.*

Words that end in *-ics* may be the cause of confusion since they act as singular nouns in some circumstances but as plurals in others:

*Politics is not an exact science.*
*The chairman's politics are not up for discussion.*

It should be remembered, however, that on occasion plural words ending in *-ics* may still have the singular form *-ic* (*tactic/tactics*).

Another problematic area that can lead to errors concerns the plurals of compound nouns (nouns that comprise more than one word; see below) and the difficulty of knowing which word should take a plural ending. When the compound noun consists of a noun and an adjective, the noun should be made plural (*courts martial, poets laureate*), though in everyday use it is common for the plural ending to be tacked onto the second word. When a compound noun consists of two nouns, usually the second noun should be made plural (*town clerks*), although exceptions exist (*sergeants major*). Where a compound noun comprises a noun together with a prepositional phrase or adverb, the plural ending is attached to the noun (*fathers-in-law, fly-by-nights, lookers-on*). In those cases where a compound noun does not actually contain any nouns, then the plural ending is added at the end (*go-betweens*).

## Gender of Nouns

In many languages it is important to know whether a noun is masculine or feminine because all nouns have a gender, which influences the form of associated pronouns and other parts of speech. In English, however, the gender of nouns is far less important, and most nouns are considered gender neutral.

The issue of gender is, however, sometimes relevant, particularly as it is expressed in pronouns (*he, she, his, hers,* etc.) linked to the noun in question. (Pronouns are discussed in depth later in this chapter, page 135.) Most nouns (for example, *brick, bicycle, pen, shirt,* etc.) can be categorized as **inanimate nouns** that do not have a gender and are thus rendered as *it* or *its* when reduced to pronouns. Others, however, are classed as **animate nouns** and are clearly specifically masculine or feminine by their very nature (*man, woman, brother, sister*), an identity that is reflected in their pronoun forms:

*Your mother said she would take us home.*
*The tall man wants his hat back.*

Some nouns may be either masculine or feminine, depending on the context:

*That cat is never slow to defend his territory from other males.*
*Our cat never leaves her kittens.*

Most nouns that have a masculine or feminine identity relate to people (**personal nouns**) or to male and female animals (**nonpersonal nouns**) Nonetheless, *it* is still normally used in circumstances where the gender is either unknown or not germane to the context:

*The baby has dropped its rattle.*
*Give the dog its ball.*

Note, however, that in recent years the identification of gender in nouns has become a slightly contentious issue, with determined attempts being made in some quarters to resist the usual convention of assuming nouns to be masculine where both sexes are actually being referred to:

*This building is a testament to man and his imagination.*
*The good athlete takes his training seriously.*

One alternative is to opt for *his* or *her* in such circumstances (*a pupil and his or her parents*), although some people find this usage awkward. An alternative is to use a plural (*pupils and their parents*).

A small number of apparently genderless nouns referring to inanimate objects are traditionally treated as having a specific gender, usually feminine. These include various means of transport, machinery, and countries:

*The new boat made her maiden voyage last week.*
*The law applies throughout Britain and her dominions.*

In recent years this custom is also being set aside for more gender-neutral forms. (*The new boat made its maiden voyage last week. The law applies throughout Britain and its dominions.*)

Many nouns have different masculine and feminine forms (*brother/sister, cock/hen, king/queen, man/woman*), which are widely understood. The most common of these include feminine nouns created by adding the ending *-ess* to an existing masculine noun (*author/authoress, lion/lioness, manager/manageress, murderer/murderess*). Care should be taken in using many of these, however, since they may be considered patronizing or sexist, particularly as relating to jobs and official positions. It may be safer to opt either for an alternative that is understood to include both sexes (*author, manager*) or for a more neutral term that does not have any gender overtones at all (*police officer, salesperson*). (*See also* SENSITIVE TERMS, page 219.)

The issue of linguistic sensitivity does not extend to the many alternative names for males and females of other species besides the human race. The following list details some of the more commonly encountered of these.

| Species | Male | Female |
|---|---|---|
| antelope | buck | doe |
| bear | boar | sow |
| bird | cock | hen |
| bobcat | tom | lioness |
| cat | tom | queen |
| cattle | bull | cow |
| chicken | cock | hen |
| cougar | tom | lioness |
| deer | stag | doe |
| dog | dog | bitch |

| Species | Male | Female |
|---|---|---|
| duck | drake | duck |
| eagle | eagle | eagle |
| elephant | bull | cow |
| fish | cock | hen |
| fox | dog | vixen |
| goat | billy-goat | nanny-goat |
| goose | gander | goose |
| hare | buck | doe |
| horse | stallion | mare |
| lion | lion | lioness |
| ox | bullock | cow |
| pheasant | cock | hen |
| pig | boar | sow |
| rabbit | buck | doe |
| rhinoceros | bull | cow |
| seal | bull | cow |
| sheep | ram | ewe |
| swan | cob | pen |
| tiger | tiger | tigress |
| whale | bull | cow |
| wolf | dog | bitch |

## Possessive Nouns

Possessive nouns are nouns that are altered to show that they have some right of possession or ownership over whatever follows. In English the possessive (or **genitive**) case is usually indicated by the addition of *'s* to the noun in question (*a day's work, Bob's house, the giraffe's neck, the deceased's wishes*). The noun itself remains otherwise unchanged. The same rule applies to singular nouns that end with an *s* (*a manageress's income, the walrus's nose*), as it also does to singular proper nouns of one syllable (*James's bag, Wes's car*). Note, however, that in the case of proper nouns of more than one syllable it is considered acceptable to add either *'s* or *'* (single apostrophe without the *s*) (*Charles's room* or *Charles' room*). The convention for plural nouns that end in an *s* is to add an apostrophe only (*the actors' union, the voters' choice*). Plural nouns that end in a letter other than *s* take *'s* as elsewhere (*the brethren's prayers, the men's pay, on the mafia's orders*).

As regards inanimate objects, the usual method of indicating possession is through the insertion of *of* (*the bottom of the heap, the last of his friends*). This alternate method may also sometimes be applied to people and animals (*the fate of the president, the wings of a dove*). In certain cases—so-called **double genitives, double possessives,** or **post-genitives**—both *of* and the possessive ending *'s* or *'* (apostrophe) may be used together (*some relations of Helen's*).

In the case of noun phrases, the correct procedure is to attach the *'s* or *'* ending to the last word of the phrase (*the court of appeal's decision, the queen of England's family*).

It should be noted that the presence of a genitive ending does not necessarily indicate possession. Note the absence of a possessive relationship in various familiar figurative phrases, expressions of time, and where the possessive construction is interpreted as meaning "by" rather than "of" (*a stone's throw, in two days' time, the government's retraction of aid*).

## Compound Nouns

Nouns are sometimes employed adjectivally (as **modifiers**) in combination with other nouns to form single terms called compound nouns (*road rage, coffee mug, people carrier, carport, drugstore, house paint*). Note that in some cases it is usual to join the two words with a hyphen, whereas elsewhere the words may be combined as one or else kept separate. When an open compound noun is used adjectivally, it is usual for a hyphen to be inserted (*people-carrier manufacturer*).

There are various ways in which compound nouns may be formed. Some result from the combination of two nouns (*beach patrol, soundwave, theater-goer*). Others are formed from the combination of a noun and an adjective (*lieutenant general, mother superior*) or an adjective and a noun (*darkroom, sweetheart*); of a noun and an adverb (*looker-on, passer-by*); of a verb and an adverb (*breakup, go-between*); of a noun, a preposition or conjunction, and another noun (*rum and coke, sister-in-law*); of an adverb or preposition and a noun (*downtown, underworld*); of a single letter and noun (*B movie, T-shirt*); or some other combination (*has-been, wannabe*).

When making compound nouns plural, it is generally correct to make the noun part of the compound plural (*demigods, hangers-on*). When the compound noun consists of two nouns, the second noun takes the plural ending (*beekeepers, house owners*). In the case of compound nouns comprising a noun with a preposition and another noun, it is the first noun that takes the plural ending (*brothers-in-law, men-about-town*) whereas compound nouns created through the combination of a noun with a conjunction and another noun have the plural ending on the second noun (*two whisky and sodas*). When the compound noun contains no nouns at all, the plural ending is attached to the final part (*also-rans, spin-offs*). Note that in a few cases there is more than one acceptable form (*courts-martials/court-martials*).

## Nouns as Verbs

Nouns are occasionally reinvented as verbs, although caution should be exercised against employing them in this manner too often, particularly in formal contexts, as the practice is disliked by many people. The practice has nonetheless gathered pace in recent years, with such (*new usages*) as the following:

*The president hopes to progress the project rapidly over the next 10 years.*
*The property will be gifted to the university.*
*The organ was helicoptered to the hospital.*

Such reinventions are frequently criticized when first encountered, but many have slowly won acceptance as verbs in their own right. Examples of so-called **deverbal nouns** that overcame initial opposition to win general acceptance include *chair, head, host,* and ***question.***

# ADJECTIVES

Adjectives are words that give descriptive information about a noun (*blue, black, fast, slow, round, square, large, small,* etc.). They are usually placed close to the noun to which they refer.

## Types of Adjectives

Adjectives can be subdivided into groups according to their position in relation to the noun and according to whether they can be used to make comparisons. Note that some adjectives can be used in one or more positions.

### ATTRIBUTIVE ADJECTIVES

Adjectives that are placed before a noun are termed attributive adjectives (*a* ***new*** *car,* ***black*** *clouds,* ***great*** *ambitions, a* ***quiet*** *moment*). A number of adjectives can be used only before nouns and not elsewhere in a sentence (*the* ***principal*** *component,* ***utter*** *confusion, a* ***former*** *partner*).

### PREDICATIVE ADJECTIVES

Adjectives that follow a verb are called predicative adjectives (*the ball is* ***blue****; time is* ***short***). Note that some adjectives may only be used as predicatives:

*The monster is* ***alive.***
*The child is* ***asleep.***

Most of these solely predicative adjectives begin with *a-* (*adrift, afraid, alive, alone, awake,* etc.).

### POSTPOSITIVE ADJECTIVES

Adjectives that follow a noun or pronoun are called postpositive adjectives (*the president* ***elect****, times* ***past****, nothing* ***serious***). These may take the form of a verb with an *-ed* ending (*something* ***borrowed****, those* ***concerned***). Note that some adjectives may be used only as postpositives and cannot be placed elsewhere in a sentence (*food* ***aplenty****, time* ***immemorial***).

### GRADABLE/UNGRADABLE ADJECTIVES

Adjectives can be categorized as either gradable or ungradable. Gradable adjectives are capable of varying in amount or quality, whereas ungradable adjectives are not. Gradable adjectives can be qualified by such modifiers as *completely, fairly, quite, too, totally,* and *very* (*completely empty, fairly warm, quite expensive, too high, totally disorganized, very stupid*). Ungradable adjectives (*impossible, real, unique,* etc.) cannot normally be qualified by such modifiers.

### COMPARATIVE AND SUPERLATIVE

Many adjectives may be rendered in comparative and superlative forms that allow two or more nouns to be compared. The superlative form denotes the relationship between three or more nouns:

*This is the fastest of the three locomotives.*
*That is the best track on the CD.*

The comparative form refers to the relationship between two nouns:

*This beer is stronger than that one.*
*That is the better of the two paintings.*

In their simplest form comparative and superlative forms are created through the addition of the suffix *-er* (the comparative form) or *-est* (the superlative form) to the stem word:

*This is the larger of the two houses.*
*That is the broadest part of the structure.*

When creating comparative or superlative, if the adjective ends in a single vowel followed by a single consonant, the consonant is doubled:

*Give her the bigger coat.*
*Fold the pastry where the dough is thinnest.*

When the adjective ends in a consonant and *-y,* the final letter becomes an *-i* before the addition of the suffix:

*She was the prettiest girl in her year.*
*That certainly looks like the easier option.*

Note that in a small number of cases it may be acceptable to leave the final *-y* unchanged (as in *drier* or *dryer*). In the case of adjectives that end in a consonant and *-e* the final *e* is not doubled (*closer, palest*).

Alternatively, an adjective may be preceded by *more* (the comparative form) or *most* (the superlative form) rather than having a suffix added.

*He is the more talented of the two brothers.*
*The emperor controls the most powerful army in the field.*

The general rule is that the suffixes *-er* and *-est* are always employed in the case of one-syllable words and of two-syllable words ending in *-y* (*dirty, filthy*), *-le* (*feeble, subtle*), *-ow* (*hollow, shallow*), and *-er* (*clever*), whereas the words *more* or *most* (or *less* and *least*) are applied to other two-syllable words and to words of three or more syllables (*more horrific, most beautiful, less harrowing, least attractive*). Some adjectives are correct in either form (*heavier/more heavy, flakiest/most flaky*). In the case of compound adjectives (see below), similarly, either method may be used (*more strong willed, stronger-willed*). There are various circumstances in which these rules do not apply, however, as is the case sometimes when two adjectives (even monosyllabic ones) are compared with each other (*less arrogant than cheeky*) or when the accuracy of an adjective is being questioned (*no more wise than I am*).

Note that there is also a small number of irregularly formed comparatives and superlatives, such as *good/better/best* and *bad/worse/worst.*

Particular care should be taken not to confuse comparatives and superlatives or to use them in the wrong context. Comparatives should be confined to comparisons between two persons or things, while superlatives should be used when referring to more than two things:

*He is one of the most talented artists on the scene.*
*He is the more talented of the two artists.*
*This is the less desirable of the two possible outcomes.*

In addition, there is a third category of adjective used to make comparisons of persons or things judged to be on a similar level with each other. These usually employ the formula *as [adjective] as:*

*This tree is as old as that one.*
*His explanation is as good as yours.*

Comparatives and superlatives are frequently employed in advertising slogans in order to proclaim the advantages of a particular product or service (*a better solution, a fuller flavor, the simplest way*). (For further information on spelling the comparative and superlative forms, see page 180.)

### ABSOLUTE ADJECTIVES

Many adjectives, such as *complete, empty,* or *total,* have no comparative or superlative senses and are generally incapable of being modified by such words as *slightly, very,* or *quite.* Note, however, that some absolute adjectives are capable of being modified by the addition of *almost, nearly,* or *virtually:*

*The venture was an almost total loss.*
*The tiger is a nearly extinct species in this part of the world.*
*This was a virtually unparalleled achievement.*

In the remainder of cases modifiers are only rarely applied to absolute adjectives, usually either for effect or to emphasize an even closer approach to perfection than that already attained:

*His hopes are very much alive.*
*A fuller account of the battle will never be written.*

## Use of Adjectives

Care should be taken not to use adjectives too frequently, as they tend to slow down a reader and may bury the essential facts of a sentence in too much detail. They should also be avoided where they are tautological and add nothing to the meaning of a sentence. Some adjectives are more precise in meaning than others: The adjective *nice* should be treated with particular caution because it tends to be greatly overused (***nice** food, a **nice** house, a **nice** person*), despite the fact that it conveys relatively little in terms of hard information. It is usually possible to find an alternative for such adjectives with a little effort (***tasty** food, an **attractive** house, a **pleasant** person*).

It is generally good policy to avoid using several adjectives together, except where they are used to convey precise factual information (*a tall, blonde-haired, blue-eyed woman*). They should also be used with restraint in formal or factual writing, since many adjectives tend to have emotional or judgmental overtones.

Adjectives are sometimes employed as nouns (*the* ***homeless****, the* ***Japanese****, the* ***rich***). The technical term for such adjectives (which are usually used in the plural form) is **nominal adjectives.** Exceptions in which nominal adjectives appear in the singular include various words ending in *-ed* (*one's* ***beloved****, the* ***accused***) and certain abstract terms (*attempt the* ***impossible***). Nouns, in return, are sometimes employed as attributive adjectives, in which role they are known as **adjectival nouns** (*a* ***plastic*** *fork, a* ***steel*** *helmet, a* ***wood*** *panel*).

Some adjectives may also be employed as adverbs (*wipe* ***clean****, laugh* ***loud***), while similarly some adverbs function as adjectives (*a* ***slow*** *process, a* ***late*** *arrival*). It is not always easy to distinguish whether a word is an adjective or an adverb: The most practical test is to check whether the verb *be* in the sentence can be replaced with another verb, such as *seem* or *appear.* If it can, then the word in question is an adjective (*he is annoyed, they are rich*). If it cannot, then the word in question is an adverb (*he is absent, they are inside*).

Many verbs can also be adapted for use as adjectives. These are commonly characterized by *-ed* or *-ing* endings and are technically known as **participial adjectives** (*the* ***elected*** *representative,* ***interesting*** *discoveries*). They may also include irregular *-en* endings (*a* ***broken*** *engagement, a* ***fallen*** *tree*). Note that participial adjectives may also be encountered in comparative and superlative forms (*a more promising plan, his most battered hat*). They can be used in both attributive and predicative contexts:

*It was a most entertaining show.*
*The show was most entertaining.*

Some participial adjectives may take the prefix *un-* in order to form new words (*unbroken, unsold, untied*).

Adjectives are not always embedded in sentences and may sometimes be employed on their own as one-word exclamations, usually followed by an exclamation mark (*Great! Sensational! Wonderful!*). They may also be encountered in verbless clauses in which the verb is implied but not actually written:

*Reply today, if [that is] possible.*
*Ignore this section, where [it is] inapplicable.*

## Order of Adjectives

When two or more adjectives are strung together before a noun, the order in which they are placed is subject to various conventions. The usual practice is to place more general adjectives referring to size, shape, age, and so on (*close, large, thick, old,* etc.) before adjectives derived from verbs (*deadly, flattened, interesting, worrying,* etc.). The latter in turn come before adjectives denoting color (*dark, green, yellow,* etc.), adjectives referring to nationality or region (*northern, South American,* etc.), and nouns used as adjectives or adjectives derived from nouns (*steel, woolen*, etc.).

> *He served them a delicious yellow Thai curry in his comfortable, brightly-lit uptown steel-and-chrome apartment.*

Note, however, that these rules are not set in stone, and that the order may be altered for poetic effect or where a particular adjective is more closely linked to the noun, among other reasons.

Conventions vary concerning the punctuation of strings of adjectives. The usual rule is to place commas between two or more adjectives where they all refer directly to the same noun (in other words, *and* could be inserted between them without disrupting the meaning): *a soft, sweet voice; deep, dangerous waters*. Commas are not employed, however, where one or more of the adjectives form a compound with the noun (in other words, *and* could not be inserted without disrupting the sense): *an imposing country house, an epic adventure film*. (*See also* COMMA, page 342.)

Adjectives are sometimes connected through such linking words as *and, but, if,* and *or*. Such connections can link both predicative and attributive adjectives:

> *The atmosphere was lively but friendly.*
> *She seemed anxious and afraid.*
> *He moved into an apartment of convenient, if modest, character.*
> *They are looking for pots of white or cream paint.*

Certain adjectives are so commonly linked that they are almost automatically associated with one another, even to the point of being considered clichés, and thus should be used sparingly, if at all, in formal contexts (*bright and early, nice and hot, right and proper*).

For discussion on the hyphenation of adjectives, as in *a red-wine bottle* and *a red wine bottle*, see HYPHEN (page 350).

## Compound Adjectives

Caution should be exercised in the use of compound adjectives, which consist of two or more words (*dark-haired, first-class, heat-resistant, mud-covered, off-white, wine-colored*). Compound adjectives are often useful as a means of providing more exact information about something and in most cases are unlikely to meet with disapproval, but some examples are prone to overuse and many of the more recently coined versions are considered jargonistic or slangy. Such inventions as *user-friendly* (and its many subsequent variants, from *eco-friendly* to *family-friendly*) and euphemistic constructions such as *financially challenged* or *stylistically challenged* (spin-offs of *physically challenged*) have acquired the status of clichés and should be used sparingly, if at all, in formal writing.

Note that some compound adjectives are conventionally written with a hyphen (*English-speaking, house-owning, well-known*), while others are usually written as one or two separated words (*carsick, coal black, sky blue*). For more information on hyphenation, see HYPHEN (page 350).

# DETERMINERS

Determiners include a wide range of words that fulfill a crucial role in the formation of sentences. As well as the definite and indefinite articles, such as *a* and *the,* they include numerals and various other words that serve to specify particular objects or persons or indicate their number (*all, each, few, much, that,* for example). They function in a similar fashion to adjectives and are always positioned before the noun to which they refer. Note, however, that they may also be used as pronouns, and many determiners (such as *all* and *some*) are applicable in both roles.

In some cases it is perfectly possible for a noun to be preceded by more than one determiner at a time (*all or some of the team, each and every time*) or by a determiner and one or more adjectives (*a few short moments, each individually handcrafted item, that very heavy load*).

There are some restrictions concerning the type of nouns to which determiners may be applied. Certain determiners (*a, an, each, either, neither,* and *one*) may be applied only to singular countable nouns:

*Each book must be returned by the due date.*
*This is an example of creative thinking.*

Other determiners (*both, few, many, several, these,* etc.) may be used only with plural countable nouns:

*Both men know that their reputations are under threat.*
*Several of these flowers are hybrids.*

While *one* may refer only to a single countable noun, numerals above one may be applied only to plural countable nouns (*two persons, ninety-nine times out of a hundred*).

Such determiners as *least, less, little,* and *much* are applicable only to uncountable nouns (*least disturbance, less chance, little hope, much trouble*).

## Definite and Indefinite Articles

The most commonly encountered determiners are the so-called definite and indefinite articles, respectively, *the* and *a*. *The* refers to something already referred to or otherwise certainly identified, often because it is the only object under consideration (*the paper in front of you, the first contestant, the last chance*), whereas *a* is less specific and could refer to any one thing (*a pointed look, a good meal*). In some circumstances, *a* may be interpreted as meaning *one* (*place a coin on the table*), or, alternatively, as *per* (*twenty miles a day*). Note that *a* is used only before singular nouns (*a building*), though *the* can be applied to both singular and plural nouns (*the cat, the raindrops*).

Convention dictates that *a* becomes *an* when preceding a noun beginning with a vowel (*an apple, an envelope*). The same rule applies to abbreviations that are pronounced as though they begin with a vowel, even though they actually begin with a consonant (*send an SOS*). Conversely, words that begin with a vowel that sounds like a consonant are preceded with *a* (*a unicorn*). Words that begin with the letter *h* can cause particular confusion in this context, since both *a* and *an* are sometimes considered acceptable depending on variations in pronunciation such as aspiration of the *h* (*a hotel/an hotel, an herb/a herb*).

Articles are not usually necessary before proper nouns, and in some circumstances it is also possible to omit the article before other nouns. Articles may be omitted before both countable nouns (*stay for tea, go by foot, lie in bed*) and uncountable nouns (*love hurts, pressed for time*) and also before plural nouns (*responsible adults, paid employees*).

# VERBS

Verbs can be defined as words of doing or being and typically constitute the grammatical center of a sentence. These words of action constitute a large and important class of words whose forms vary according to tense or mood.

Verbs usually follow the subject of a sentence, although there may be one or more intervening words:

*I love that hat.*
*That man is a stranger.*
*You very nearly got yourself killed.*

There are situations, however, in which a verb may precede the subject:

*Floating on the water was a single petal.*
*Waiting on the mat was a letter.*

## Types of Verbs

Verbs can be subdivided into two broad groups of **regular** and **irregular verbs.** Regular verbs, which account for the majority, follow a standard pattern in their various tenses, whereas irregular verbs follow nonstandard patterns, which are much less predictable. (See pages 118–122 for lists of regular and irregular verbs.)

All grammatically correct sentences must contain a phrase with a **finite verb,** meaning the verb has both a subject and a specific tense, number, and person, as appropriate (*he* ***stands*** *alone; the ball* ***dipped;*** *they* ***are*** *all tired*). Verbs that are not finite cannot by themselves constitute a complete sentence and do not change to reflect singular and plural or tense (***going*** *to bed,* ***walking*** *by the river*). The nonfinite forms of a verb include the infinitive, the present participle, and the past participle. (*See* INFINITIVES, page 123, and PARTICIPLES, page 124.)

Verbs can also be subdivided into **transitive** and **intransitive** categories. Transitive verbs must have a direct object (*find peace, love skiing, see something*) unless they are being used in the passive tense (*admired by some*) (see below about passive verbs). Intransitive verbs do not have to have a direct object (*time will tell; the temperature is dropping*). They include numerous verbs of movement (*the moon is rising; the tide is coming in*). Some verbs are always transitive or intransitive, but many may be employed either as transitive or as intransitive in different contexts (*he turned the car around; the car turned around*). The same verb can have a different meaning depending on whether it is being used transitively or intransitively (*they staggered the new arrivals to avoid congestion; he staggered down the road*).

In the case of **reflexive verbs,** the subject and object are the same (*she helped herself; the baby amuses itself with a rattle*). Note that some verbs (*perjure oneself; pride oneself*) are always reflexive, whereas others are more versatile (*admire oneself/admire someone else; prepare oneself/prepare a meal*).

**Auxiliary verbs** represent another class of verbs that are used in combination with other verbs to vary their meaning or tense. They are usually placed in front of the main verb and include *be, can, do, have, may, must, shall,* and *will,* among other verbs (*they are lost; she did not approve; he had gone*). Most auxiliary verbs can be used only in combination with other verbs (so-called **modal verbs**):

> *It **might** rain later.*
> *I **may** go with you.*
> *He **shall** call tomorrow.*

The verbs *be, have,* and *do* (sometimes called **primary verbs**), however, can also be used independently:

> *My dog **is** a prizewinner.*
> *They **have** several victories to their credit.*
> *In the event, he **did** nothing.*

The auxiliary verbs *can* and *could* are used to express ability (*we can run fast; she could tell he was lying*), while *must* and *should* are used to express obligation (*you must come early; he should do what he's told*). *Would* is used to express wishes (*we would like to come; would you hold this hammer for me*), and *may* and *might* are used to express possibility (*that may be possible; it might not be too late*). With the exceptions of *be* and *have,* all auxiliary verbs are followed by the infinitive form (without *to*) of the main verb (*we can hear, you must go, they might disagree*). The verb *be* is widely used to create the passive form of many verbs (*she was defeated; they were arrested*).

The auxiliary verb *do* is often employed for emphatic effect:

> *We do know how to have a good time, don't we?*
> *They did promise to pay us back.*

It is also frequently employed in the construction of questions:

> *Do you know the man who lives next door?*
> *Did you go abroad this year?*

Another class of words that closely resembles auxiliary verbs concerns such verbs and verb phrases as *be able to, dare, going to, had better, need to, **ought to, used to,*** and *would rather.* Like auxiliary verbs, these also come before the main verb, which is rendered in the infinitive (without *to*):

*She was **able to** be of assistance.*
*They are **going to** pay for the trip.*
*She **had better** go before he gets back.*
*The system **needs to** be cleaned up.*
*His mother **used to** work for the government.*

Not all verbs that appear before the main verb are necessarily categorized as auxiliary verbs. Some may be more accurately categorized as **catenative verbs** (*appear, begin, come, expect, get, happen, help, manage, seem, want*):

*This **appears** to be the right door.*
*Things **began** to look better.*
*She **happens** to be his sister.*

Like auxiliary verbs, catenative verbs are used in front of a main verb in its infinitive form (including *to*). Note that catenative verbs are sometimes used in combination with one another:

*She **managed to seem** to be surprised.*
*As time passes we **begin to get** to know each other better.*

Verbs that serve to link a subject to a word or phrase describing it are termed **linking** or **copular verbs:**

*The garden **is** lovely at this time of year.*
*The sky **became** cloudy.*

Some words belong to a class of verbs that have their origins in nouns. In recent years the practice of adapting nouns for use as verbs has gathered pace, but it should be treated with caution, as many people dislike verbs created in this manner (***trash** one's opponents*). Some verbs created by this process never win wide acceptance, while others are absorbed into the language over the course of years and become part of the standard vocabulary. (*See also* NOUNS, page 98.)

Verbs in which the action of the verb is performed by the subject are termed **active verbs** (*the baby **cried**, the couples **danced***). Verbs in which the subject is affected by the action of the verb are termed **passive verbs** (*the door **was broken** by the force; the protesters **were handcuffed** by the police*). The following examples demonstrate how the subject of an active verb becomes the object of a passive verb (usually preceded by the word *by*):

*The fox caught the bird. [active]*
*The bird was caught by the fox. [passive]*

Passive construction is generally formed by the auxiliary verb *be* followed by the past participle of the verb concerned:

*The table was repaired by an expert.*
*The road has been reopened.*

Note that only transitive verbs can be used in the passive tense, because intransitive verbs lack a subject. Note also that it is not possible to render reflexive verbs in the passive mood. Conversely, some passive verbs cannot be made active (*we are supposed to agree*).

Passive verbs have many uses, but care should be taken not to fall into the habit of using them in place of more vigorous active verbs. Overuse of passive verbs can make a passage seem contrived and ponderous to read. In many cases it is possible and preferable to replace a passive verb with a simpler active equivalent. (*See also* PHRASAL VERBS, page 131.)

## Principal Parts

The principal parts of a verb are those forms of a verb upon which the various inflected versions are based. They include the infinitive, the present participle, the past tense, and the past participle. Regular verbs follow a standard pattern, with an *-ing* ending being added to the infinitive to form the present participle and an *-ed* ending being added to form both the past tense and the past participle. Irregular verbs, however, vary considerably, particularly in the form taken for the past participle. Examples of the principal parts of some frequently used verbs follow.

### REGULAR VERBS

| Infinitive | Present Participle | Past Tense | Past Participle |
|---|---|---|---|
| aim | aiming | aimed | aimed |
| arrive | arriving | arrived | arrived |
| assume | assuming | assumed | assumed |
| climb | climbing | climbed | climbed |
| describe | describing | described | described |
| destroy | destroying | destroyed | destroyed |
| fail | failing | failed | failed |
| hate | hating | hated | hated |
| love | loving | loved | loved |
| mutter | muttering | muttered | muttered |
| open | opening | opened | opened |
| peel | peeling | peeled | peeled |
| play | playing | played | played |
| please | pleasing | pleased | pleased |
| pretend | pretending | pretended | pretended |
| remember | remembering | remembered | remembered |
| start | starting | started | started |
| succeed | succeeding | succeeded | succeeded |
| turn | turning | turned | turned |
| visit | visiting | visited | visited |
| walk | walking | walked | walked |
| work | working | worked | worked |

## IRREGULAR VERBS

| Infinitive | Present Participle | Past Tense | Past Participle |
|---|---|---|---|
| abide | abiding | abode/abided | abode/abided |
| arise | arising | arose | arisen |
| awake | awaking | awoke/awaked | awoken/awaked |
| be | being | was/were | been |
| bear | bearing | bore | borne/born (*See* WORDS OFTEN CONFUSED) |
| beat | beating | beat | beaten/beat |
| become | becoming | became | become |
| begin | beginning | began | begun |
| bend | bending | bent | bent |
| bet | betting | bet/betted | bet/betted |
| bid | bidding | bade/bid | bidden/bid |
| bind | binding | bound | bound |
| bite | biting | bit | bitten/bit |
| bleed | bleeding | bled | bled |
| bless | blessing | blessed/blest | blessed/blest |
| blow | blowing | blew | blown |
| break | breaking | broke | broken |
| breed | breeding | bred | bred |
| bring | bringing | brought | brought |
| broadcast | broadcasting | broadcast/broadcasted | broadcast/broadcasted |
| build | building | built | built |
| burn | burning | burned/burnt | burned/burnt |
| burst | bursting | burst/bursted | burst/bursted |
| buy | buying | bought | bought |
| catch | catching | caught | caught |
| choose | choosing | chose | chosen |
| cling | clinging | clung | clung |
| come | coming | came | come |
| cost | costing | cost | cost |
| creep | creeping | crept | crept |
| cut | cutting | cut | cut |
| deal | dealing | dealt | dealt |
| dig | digging | dug | dug |
| dive | diving | dived/dove | dived/dove |
| do | doing | did | done |
| draw | drawing | drew | drawn |
| dream | dreaming | dreamed/dreamt | dreamed/dreamt |
| drink | drinking | drank | drunk/drank |
| drive | driving | drove | driven |
| dwell | dwelling | dwelled/dwelt | dwelled/dwelt |
| eat | eating | ate | eaten |
| fall | falling | fell | fallen |
| feed | feeding | fed | fed |

*(continues)*

*(continued)*

| Infinitive | Present Participle | Past Tense | Past Participle |
|---|---|---|---|
| feel | feeling | felt | felt |
| fight | fighting | fought | fought |
| find | finding | found | found |
| flee | fleeing | fled | fled |
| fling | flinging | flung | flung |
| fly | flying | flew | flown |
| forbear | forbearing | forbore | forborne |
| forbid | forbidding | forbade/forbad | forbidden |
| forecast | forecasting | forecast/forecasted | forecast/forecasted |
| forget | forgetting | forgot | forgotten/forgot |
| forgive | forgiving | forgave | forgiven |
| forsake | forsaking | forsook | forsaken |
| freeze | freezing | froze | frozen |
| get | getting | got | got/gotten |
| give | giving | gave | given |
| go | going | went | gone |
| grind | grinding | ground | ground |
| grow | growing | grew | grown |
| hang | hanging | hung/hanged (*See* WORDS OFTEN CONFUSED) | hung/hanged (*See* WORDS OFTEN CONFUSED) |
| have | having | had | had |
| hear | hearing | heard | heard |
| heave | heaving | heaved/hove | heaved/hove |
| hew | hewing | hewed | hewed/hewn |
| hide | hiding | hid | hidden/hid |
| hit | hitting | hit | hit |
| hold | holding | held | held |
| hurt | hurting | hurt | hurt |
| keep | keeping | kept | kept |
| kneel | kneeling | knelt/kneeled | knelt/kneeled |
| know | knowing | knew | known |
| lay | laying | laid | laid |
| lead | leading | led | led |
| leap | leaping | leaped/leapt | leaped/leapt |
| learn | learning | learned/learnt | learned/learnt |
| leave | leaving | left | left |
| lend | lending | lent | lent |
| let | letting | let | let |
| lie | lying | lay | lain |
| light | lighting | lit/lighted | lit/lighted |
| lose | losing | lost | lost |
| make | making | made | made |
| mean | meaning | meant | meant |
| meet | meeting | met | met |
| mislay | mislaying | mislaid | mislaid |
| mislead | misleading | misled | misled |

| Infinitive | Present Participle | Past Tense | Past Participle |
|---|---|---|---|
| mistake | mistaking | mistook | mistaken |
| mow | mowing | mowed | mowed/mown |
| overtake | overtaking | overtook | overtaken |
| pay | paying | paid | paid |
| plead | pleading | pleaded/pled | pleaded/pled |
| prove | proving | proved | proved/proven |
| put | putting | put | put |
| quit | quitting | quit/quitted | quit/quitted |
| read | reading | read | read |
| ride | riding | rode | ridden |
| ring | ringing | rang | rung |
| rise | rising | rose | risen |
| run | running | ran | run |
| saw | sawing | sawed | sawed/sawn |
| say | saying | said | said |
| see | seeing | saw | seen |
| seek | seeking | sought | sought |
| sell | selling | sold | sold |
| send | sending | sent | sent |
| set | setting | set | set |
| sew | sewing | sewed | sewn/sewed |
| shake | shaking | shook | shaken |
| shed | shedding | shed | shed |
| shine | shining | shone/shined | shone/shined |
| shoot | shooting | shot | shot |
| show | showing | showed | shown/showed |
| shrink | shrinking | shrank/shrunk | shrunk/shrunken (*See* WORDS OFTEN CONFUSED) |
| shut | shutting | shut | shut |
| sing | singing | sang/sung | sung |
| sink | sinking | sank/sunk | sunk |
| sit | sitting | sat | sat |
| slay | slaying | slew | slain |
| sleep | sleeping | slept | slept |
| slide | sliding | slid | slid |
| slit | slitting | slit | slit |
| smell | smelling | smelled/smelt | smelled/smelt |
| sneak | sneaking | sneaked/snuck | sneaked/snuck |
| sow | sowing | sowed | sown/sowed |
| speak | speaking | spoke | spoken |
| speed | speeding | sped/speeded (*See* WORDS OFTEN CONFUSED) | sped/speeded (*See* WORDS OFTEN CONFUSED) |
| spend | spending | spent | spent |
| spill | spilling | spilled/spilt | spilled/spilt |
| spin | spinning | spun | spun |
| spit | spitting | spit/spat | spit/spat |

*(continues)*

*(continued)*

| Infinitive | Present Participle | Past Tense | Past Participle |
|---|---|---|---|
| split | splitting | split | split |
| spoil | spoiling | spoiled/spoilt | spoiled/spoilt |
| spread | spreading | spread | spread |
| spring | springing | sprang/sprung | sprung |
| stand | standing | stood | stood |
| steal | stealing | stole | stolen |
| stick | sticking | stuck | stuck |
| sting | stinging | stung | stung |
| stink | stinking | stank/stunk (*See* WORDS OFTEN CONFUSED) | stunk (*See* WORDS OFTEN CONFUSED)) |
| stride | striding | strode | stridden |
| strike | striking | struck | struck/stricken |
| string | stringing | strung | strung |
| strive | striving | strove/strived | striven/strived |
| swear | swearing | swore | sworn |
| sweep | sweeping | swept | swept |
| swell | swelling | swelled | swelled/swollen |
| swim | swimming | swam | swum |
| swing | swinging | swung | swung |
| take | taking | took | taken |
| teach | teaching | taught | taught |
| tear | tearing | tore | torn |
| tell | telling | told | told |
| think | thinking | thought | thought |
| thrive | thriving | thrived/throve | thrived/thriven |
| throw | throwing | threw | thrown |
| thrust | thrusting | thrust | thrust |
| tread | treading | trod/treaded | trodden/trod |
| unbend | unbending | unbent | unbent |
| undergo | undergoing | underwent | undergone |
| understand | understanding | understood | understood |
| undertake | undertaking | undertook | undertaken |
| undo | undoing | undid | undone |
| upset | upsetting | upset | upset |
| wake | waking | woke/waked | woken/waked |
| wear | wearing | wore | worn |
| weave | weaving | wove/weaved | woven/weaved |
| weep | weeping | wept | wept |
| win | winning | won | won |
| wind | winding | wound | wound |
| withdraw | withdrawing | withdrew | withdrawn |
| withhold | withholding | withheld | withheld |
| wring | wringing | wrung | wrung |
| write | writing | wrote | written |

## Infinitives

The infinitive is the basic form of a verb, unaffected by tense, number, or person. It is usually preceded by *to*. Without the *to*, the infinitive also supplies the imperative form of a verb and all the forms of the present tense except the third person singular.

The infinitive is frequently used (without *to*) after various auxiliary verbs (*you must try, they may return*). It is also used (with *to*) after adjectives (*hard to understand, quick to agree*) and nouns (*a chance to excel, the time to move*) and, sometimes, in combination with other verbs (*try to behave, play to win*).

The infinitive may be used in the sense of *in order to:*

*To fly you don't need to grow wings.*

It may also be employed as a verbal noun as an alternative to a verb's *-ing* form (formally called the **gerund**):

*She started to run.*
*To smile in the face of adversity is a sign of great mental strength.*

Note, however, that infinitives are not always interchangeable with gerunds: *She wanted to go,* for instance, could not be rendered in the form *she wanted going.* Similarly, *he regretted calling* cannot be rendered *he regretted to call.* It should be noted that even when the two are interchangeable, the switch may result in a change in meaning: *They stopped to eat* does not mean the same as *they stopped eating.*

## Split Infinitives

It is traditionally considered incorrect for an adverb to be placed between the *to* and the infinitive form of a verb (*to **boldly** go, to **gently** rock*). This most problematic of all grammatical rules has its origins ultimately in Latin grammar, although acute sensitivity over the issue is a relatively recent phenomenon.

In many other modern languages, such as French, the infinitive is usually expressed as a single word and thus can never be interrupted by other words. In English, where the infinitive consists of two words, any associated adverb should either precede the *to* or follow the verb (***boldly** to go, to rock **gently***). In practice, however, this rule is often ignored. The majority of speakers are probably unaware of the convention and may break infinitives with more than one adverb or even whole phrases: *We want to **definitely and without reservation** know what is intended.* Those who are aware of the rule may take serious exception to such slips, and the split infinitive remains a bone of contention between those who consider it a bastion against sloppy usage and those who believe it to be nothing more than a manifestation of linguistic pretentiousness. Criticism of the split infinitive is a frequent subject of discussion in the media. For many people it marks the front line in the struggle between good and bad style, particularly when written.

Some careful speakers and writers avoid splitting infinitives at all costs, even when the alternatives are less than ideal (***never** to let her go/to **never** let *her go*). Very occasionally, however, it may be employed deliberately to useful, ironical effect: *Everybody has to* ***sometimes*** *break the rules*. A compromise position agreed between many contemporary speakers and writers is to accept the splitting of infinitives where the only alternatives available are even more unwieldy and undesirable. In colloquial or poetic contexts, a split infinitive may often sound more natural than the more correct alternative: *We hope to* ***really*** *let go on this holiday.*

Particular care should be exercised when moving adverbs in relation to split infinitives because doing so can affect the meaning and may lead to ambiguity. Thus, *they decided to* ***cautiously advance*** may be rendered as *they decided to advance* ***cautiously*** or as *they decided* ***cautiously*** *to advance,* each of which has a different meaning.

## Participles

All verbs have present participle and past participle forms. **Present participles** are formed through the addition of an *-ing* ending to the infinitive stem (*being, trying, walking*). Note that when an infinitive has an *-e* ending, the final *e* is usually dropped before the *-ing* is added (*coming, solving*). Other exceptions include a number of verbs ending with *-ie* in the infinitive, which replace it with a *y* in the present participle (*dying, tying*), verbs that end in *-c,* which acquire a *k* (*panicking, frolicking*), and verbs that end in *-d, -m, -n, -r, -t,* etc., in which the final letter is doubled (*plodding, swimming, running, purring, patting*).

Present participles are used in various clauses and to express the continuous forms of verbs (*going solo, riding bareback*). They can also assume the role of nouns known as **gerunds** (*don't criticize my dancing; swimming is fun*) and adjectives (*choking gas, a stunning revelation, soaking clothes*).

Problems can arise when using a present participle with a pronoun. Many people are uncertain as to which type of pronoun to employ before the participle concerned. The rule is that if the participle has its own subject (meaning that the participle is actually a gerund, acting more like a noun than a verb), then the possessive pronoun is correct.

*How about my bringing something to eat?*

If the participle is acting more like a verb than a noun, then the possessive form should not be used:

*Do you mind me singing?*

**Past participles** are variously formed through the addition of an *-ed* ending to the infinitive stem (*ended, loaded, started*) or, in the case of irregular verbs, through the affixing of one of a variety of other established endings (*brought, chosen, gotten, sawn, shone, taken, taught*). Note that some irregular verbs have identical present tense and past participle forms (*cut, hit, let, split*). In other instances the past participle differs from the past tense (*did/done, flew/flown, went/gone*), or there are two alternatives for both the past tense and the past participle (*burned/burnt, dreamed/dreamt, leaped/leapt, showed/shown, spilled/spilt, spoiled/spoilt*). In U.S. English the *-ed* form is more commonly used than elsewhere in the English-speaking world.

Participles can be used in a number of different ways. As well as forming the perfect tenses and passive forms of verbs, they are commonly encountered serving as adjectives (*a falling star, a broken chair, a startled look*). They can also be employed as a means of introducing a sentence:

*Tied to the post, a large fierce dog snarled at all passersby.*
*Being unavoidably detained, he knew he would be late for the meeting.*

Caution should be exercised in the use of introductory participles because they can easily become unintentionally attached to the wrong noun in the sentence that follows:

*Determined to win, the contest was far from over.*
*Being ravenously hungry, the meal was a great relief.*

In some circumstances an introductory participle may be unrelated, or at least uncertainly connected, to any subject in the ensuing sentence, in which case it is termed a **dangling participle** (otherwise called an **unattached participle** or **unrelated participle**):

*Lost in thought, the twilight soon became night.*
*Listening to the song, her mood improved.*

Careful writers avoid creating dangling participles by placing them next to the noun to which they refer and thus making the link between the participle and the subject unambiguous. Participles that are uncertainly linked to the subject that follows still have their uses, however. They are particularly useful as prepositions or conjunctions, regardless of their relationship with the subjects that follow:

*Talking of politics, did you see the news tonight?*
*Bearing in mind the weather, they were lucky to get back home so soon.*
*Having said that, things may change.*

## Agreement

Verbs must agree with the subject in terms of number and person. Regular verbs in present tense follow a standard pattern in their expression of the various different persons, with the third person singular being distinguished by the addition of *-s* or *-es:*

| Person | Present-Tense Regular Verb |
|---|---|
| I (first person singular) | call/kiss/run/see/talk |
| you (second person singular) | call/kiss/run/see/talk |
| he/she/it (third person singular) | calls/kisses/runs/sees/talks |
| we (first person plural) | call/kiss/run/see/talk |
| you (second person plural) | call/kiss/run/see/talk |
| they (third person plural) | call/kiss/run/see/talk |

Verbs that end with *-y* lose the final *y* in the third person singular and are replaced by an *i* and *-es* (*flies, spies, tries*). Verbs that end with *-o* usually add an *-es* ending (*does, goes*).

Irregular verbs in the present tense may change more dramatically from one person to another, particularly in the case of the third person singular:

| Person | Present-Tense Irregular Verb |
|---|---|
| I (first person singular) | am |
| you (second person singular) | are |
| he/she/it (third person singular) | is |
| we (first person plural) | are |
| you (second person plural) | are |
| they (third person plural) | are |
| | |
| I (first person singular) | have |
| you (second person singular) | have |
| he/she/it (third person singular) | has |
| we (first person plural) | have |
| you (second person plural) | have |
| they (third person plural) | have |

In sentences where the subject consists of more than one noun, confusion can sometimes arise over the identification of the noun with which the verb should agree. Such confusion is particularly troublesome when one competing noun is singular and another plural:

> ***Some*** *of the team, including the captain,* ***have*** *expressed support for the decision.*
> ***One*** *of the teams* ***is*** *to be disqualified.*

Linking the verb to the correct subject is particularly complicated when the phrase *either . . . or* is used. The general rule here is that if both subjects are singular, then the verb is singular, too:

> *Either the driver or his wife knows the answer.*

If one of the subjects is plural, however, then the verb agrees with the subject that immediately precedes it:

> *Either the president or his advisers are responsible for this change.*

The same rule applies to the person of the verb:

> *Either you or I am going next.*
> *Either you or your parents are going next.*

## Tenses

In order to express distinctions in time, verbs possess present, future, and past tenses. The present and past tenses are frequently expressed through changes in the form of the main verb, but other tenses tend to rely on the use of auxiliary verbs.

## PRESENT TENSES

The present tense is used to describe either events that are currently taking place or states or conditions that exist in a context in which time is irrelevant. It is generally formed by taking the infinitive verb stem and making minor changes specifically to the ending of the third person singular to designate their person (*I believe, he pretends, she speaks, it cools*). The major exception to this rule is the verb *to be* (*I am, you are, he/she/it is, we are, they are*).

The present tense can also be used to refer to events in the future:

*We invade next week.*
*They arrive tomorrow.*

It can, in certain circumstances such as newspaper headlines, also be used to refer to past events:

*Veteran actor dies in Hollywood.*
*Masked men rob bank.*

In many contexts the verb is required to describe an action that is continuing to take place (*crying, falling, wanting*). In order to express this sense of a **continuous present** (as a tense, also called the **present progressive**), the verb *to be* is added and conjugated, while the main verb becomes a participle with the *-ing* ending (*see* PARTICIPLES, page 124, for further explanation):

*I am writing to you from a hilltop.*
*They are hoping for an improvement soon.*
*The pupils are working hard this term.*

## PAST TENSES

The past tense in its various forms refers to events that have already taken place. In its simplest form it is expressed through the addition of an *-ed* ending to the verb stem (*banned, rolled, summoned*)

*He interrupted me before I could finish.*
*The response surprised them.*

Note, though, the exceptional case of the verb *to be,* which varies in the past tense according to the persons involved (*I was, you were, he/she/it was, we were, they were*).

When referring to events in the relatively recent past, the usual course is to employ the **present perfect** by adding the auxiliary verb *have* to the past participle (*-ed* ending) of the verb concerned (*see* PARTICIPLES, page 124, for further explanation):

*We have traveled through dangerous territory.*

Another option is to employ the basic past tense in such contexts:

*They already left.*
*We just arrived.*

The perfect tense is often used instead of the simple past tense in questions:

*Have you packed yet?*

It may also be preferred to the simple past tense in order to emphasize that an action has been completed:

*Yes, I have tidied my room.*

Finally, when the intention is to describe a past action that is still taking place in the present, the usual solution is to employ the present perfect tense:

*She has decided she has no option but to resign.*
*They have lived here all their lives.*

The formula when expressing the **continuous past** (or **past progressive**), used to describe something that was still taking place at the time in question, is to apply the verb *to be* and add the verb ending *-ing* (present participle):

*As we were passing the building, there was an explosion.*
*He was thinking of applying for the post.*

Sometimes it is necessary to refer to something that happened before the past time being described, in which case the usual solution is to employ the **past perfect** (or **pluperfect**) **tense.** The past perfect is formed by combining the past tense of *have* and the past participle:

*They had seen the film before, so they already knew the ending.*
*When he had completed his rounds, he settled down at his monitor.*

## FUTURE TENSES

The future tense in its various forms refers to events that have yet to take place. It is usually formed through the addition of the auxiliary verbs *will* or *shall* to the infinitive of the verb concerned:

*It will be an interesting contest.*
*We shall arrive at the coast in an hour.*

Both *will* and *shall* are commonly reduced to *'ll* (I'll, we'll). In many circumstances both *shall* and *will* can be used to express determination or insistence:

*You will behave when we get there.*
*We shall have our revenge.*

Note, however, that the present tense can also be used to express events in the future:

*She is to resign next week.*
*It remains to be seen.*
*He is to be promoted shortly.*
*The tree is about to fall.*
*The news may be bad.*

## SEQUENCE OF TENSES

When there are multiple conjugated verbs in a sentence certain set rules come into play to ensure that their tenses harmonize—a system known as the **sequence of tenses.** The clause containing the most important verb is identified as the main clause (***we heard** that they had gone*), while the clause or clauses containing lesser verbs are identified as subordinate clauses (*we heard **that they had gone***).

The tense of the subordinate clause is often the same as the tense of the main clause:

*I think it is time to stop.*
*He says he is fine.*
*She thought he was being rude.*

This is not always the case, however, since the two clauses may refer to two different times:

*I wish that I had met her earlier.*
*We think that was a bad idea.*

If the main clause is in the future tense, then the subordinate clause is most likely to be in the present tense:

*They will want to eat as soon as they arrive.*
*I will contact you once the train pulls into the station.*

If the main clause is in the past tense, and the subordinate clause refers to some permanent state of affairs, then the subordinate clause is most likely to be in the present tense:

*He realized that some things are too important to leave to chance.*

If the main clause is in the past tense, and the subordinate clause refers to the future, then the subordinate clause is most likely to be in the past tense:

*We knew they would survive.*

(*See also* REPORTING SPEECH, page 167.)

## Moods of Verbs

Verbs can be rendered in three basic "moods": the indicative, the imperative, and the subjunctive. The **indicative** mood of a verb is the basic and most frequently encountered form, used in simple statements of fact and in questions (*the sky is blue; have you no shame?*).

The **imperative** mood of a verb is used for giving orders and is identical to the infinitive in form. When written down, the imperative is often emphasized with the addition of an exclamation point at the end of the word or the sentence in which it appears:

*Be quiet!*
*Come here!*
*Stop talking and pay attention!*

The same convention applies to the negative form of the imperative, which is usually introduced by the verb *do:*

*Don't do that!*
*Do not block this driveway!*

Note, though, that the imperative may also be used in less emphatic contexts, often in relation to instructions:

*Connect the printer to the computer.*
*Come to our party.*
*Please close the gate.*

The **subjunctive** mood of a verb relates to the expression of possibilities or wishes. In most verbs it is based on the third person singular of the present tense, with any final *-s* being removed (*be that as it **may**; lest she **disagree***). Note, however, that in the case of the verb *be,* the subjunctive form in past tense is *were,* not *was* (*if I were to come; as it were*)—hence the technical term ***were*-subjunctive.**

Clauses containing subjunctives are commonly introduced by *that:*

*We insist that he come at once.*
*It is important that she sign the agreement today.*

These clauses, which typically feature such verbs as *ask, demand,* and *suggest,* are formally known as **mandative subjunctives.**

Other clauses containing subjunctives are introduced by *if, as if, as though,* or *supposing:*

*If the situation were to change, there might be an opening.*
*She acted as though she were a young girl.*
*I am prepared to go, supposing I were chosen.*

Other subjunctive clauses include a number of commonly encountered standard phrases, such as *if need be* and *suffice it to say.* These are formally termed **formulaic,** or **optative, subjunctives.**

A particular source of confusion concerns the use of the verb *be* as a subjunctive, especially in the past tense, in the context of phrases beginning with *if*. Where something hypothetical is being proposed *were* is the correct form to use because the mood is subjunctive:

*If that were to happen, I would be worried.*

If, however, a statement of fact or probability is being proposed, then *was* is the correct form, representing the indicative mood:

*If he was ill, he seems to have recovered now.*

Overuse of the subjunctive mood should be avoided, because it can sound more formal than simpler alternatives. One way to avoid overuse of subjunctives is to insert the word *should (lest she should disagree).*

## Phrasal Verbs

Phrasal verbs are constructed through the combination of an existing verb with an adverb or preposition, or both (*carry on, come across, do up, leave out, look after, look forward to, run over, try out*). The object of the verb usually follows the adverb or preposition (*do up the parcel; look after the child*).

Caution should be exercised in relation to phrasal verbs, since they often have secondary, often figurative, meanings that are not obvious from their superficial appearance. Some uses of phrasal verbs are literal in their meaning (*go out after dinner; tie up the dog*), while others acquire extended meanings (*go out with a girl; tie down with work; tie up all day; visit with one's parents*). Note that there is some risk involved in extending ordinary verbs in such a way where they are not already well established, because such coinages may be considered nonstandard slang.

## Negation

In order to turn a statement into the negative the usual method is to insert the word *not* after the main verb or the first auxiliary verb:

*We are not millionaires.*
*He was not wearing a suit.*
*They were not being fair.*

In cases where the main verb or the auxiliary verb is not *be*, the correct procedure is to insert the auxiliary verb *do* before the word *not*:

*I do not have the documents you are talking about.*
*We did not go shopping today.*

Note, however, that for poetic effect *not* occasionally follows the main verb:

*Where she lives now I know not.*

In common use *not* is habitually shortened to *n't* (*can't, hadn't, mustn't, weren't*) to reflect everyday pronunciation, but care should be taken not to use these reduced forms in formal contexts.

Difficulty can arise when clauses containing the phrase *used to* are put into the negative. One option is to treat *used to* as a main verb and employ *didn't* as its auxiliary verb:

*We didn't used to come here.*

Some people, it should be noted, will reduce *used* to *use* in such circumstances:

*He didn't use to be so unfriendly.*

A better option is to treat *used to* as an auxiliary verb and add *not* or *n't* to make it negative:

*She used not to mind such interference.*

*Not* may also be used in combination with such words as *any* or *either* to make a sentence negative:

*She did not say anything to the police officer.*
*They may not want either of these dresses.*

In other circumstances it is possible to make a statement negative through the use of various words that in themselves express a negative quality. These include such pronouns as *nobody* and *nothing,* such adverbs as *never* and *nowhere,* and the determiner *no:*

***Nobody** saw them enter.*
*There is **nothing** in the cupboard.*
*They will **never** succeed.*
*There is **nowhere** to go around here.*
*There are **no** easy solutions.*

Particular caution should be exercised in avoiding **double negatives,** sentences in which two negatives are employed. The result is that the two negatives cancel each other out, and the intended meaning is reversed. The phrase *I was not in no holdup,* an apparent denial of being present when a crime was committed, actually means *I was in a holdup,* as the negatives have canceled each other out. Note, however, that very occasionally a double negative is not necessarily incorrect:

*He didn't say he wouldn't come.*
*We couldn't not let her in.*

# ADVERBS

Adverbs are words that provide further information about how, when, and where something takes place. They may consist of a single word (formally termed a **simple adverb**), two words joined together (called a **compound adverb**), or an **adverbial phrase** (*see* ADVERBIAL PHRASE, page 151).

Adverbs may be formally subdivided into adverbs of manner, adverbs of degree, adverbs of time, and adverbs of place. **Adverbs of manner** refer to the manner in which something is done or takes place. Examples include *angrily, carefully, eagerly, easily, energetically, happily, loudly, movingly, quickly, quietly, sadly, slowly, smoothly, tightly,* and *wistfully:*

*She dropped lightly to the floor.*
*The train moved jerkily forward.*
*They tackled the task enthusiastically.*

**Adverbs of degree** describe the degree to which something is done. Examples include *barely, completely, considerably, deeply, greatly, hardly, highly, immensely, partly, rather, strongly,* and *utterly.*

*They were greatly interested.*
*The result was immensely impressive.*
*She was rather drunk by the end of the evening.*

Among the adverbs of degree are the so-called **intensifiers**, which can be used to intensify adjectives or other adverbs. Examples include *absolutely, altogether, barely, completely, desperately, enough, extremely, fairly, hardly, quite, rather, remarkably, scarcely, slightly, somewhat, terribly, thoroughly, too,* and *very:*

*The wind was blowing very strongly.*
*His wife is fairly good-looking.*
*It is a terribly disappointing result.*

**Adverbs of time** describe the time when something is done or takes place. Examples include *always, currently, daily, frequently, immediately, later, now, often, recently, soon, then, today, tomorrow,* and *yesterday:*

*He turned up late.*
*They left the city yesterday.*
*I will be there soon.*

**Adverbs of place** refer to the location where something is done or takes place. Examples include *above, anywhere, away, below, down, forward, here, in, nearby, nowhere, out, somewhere, there,* and *up:*

*Get here as soon as you can.*
*It is snowing outside.*
*There is a hotel nearby.*

Other categories of adverbs include those that express the probability of something (*certainly, possibly, probably*), those that restrict or specify (*exactly, only, particularly*), and those that make clear what is being discussed (*about, on, over*). It is also possible to create a further class comprising the word *how* and certain adverbs that begin with *wh-* (*when, where, why*), which are used to introduce relative clauses, ask questions, and link clauses:

*Where is she going?*
*It was turning into a day when nothing was going right.*
*We know where the key is.*
*There is a reason why the clock has stopped.*

The *wh-* adverbs are often strengthened through the application of the adverb *ever,* especially in informal contexts:

*How ever did you get here so quickly?*
*What ever were you thinking?*
*Where ever are your clothes?*

Caution should be taken, however, not to confuse these adverbs used for emphasis with the more straightforward adverbs *however, whatever, wherever,* etc., which are always written as one word:

*However difficult the task, it is worth persevering.*
*Whatever happens, I will be here.*
*Wherever she goes, trouble follows.*

Adverbs can be attached to several other classes of word. They can modify verbs (*dance gracefully, die slowly*), adjectives (*slightly damp, very cold*), or other adverbs (*reasonably quickly, quite well*). On occasion an adverb may modify a whole clause or sentence:

*Critically the play was well received.*
*Sadly, the campaign achieved nothing.*

Alternatively it may modify a noun phrase (*quite a blow, the layer below*) or a preposition (*just above, not since then*).

Care should be taken with such **sentence adverbs** when the adverb concerned relates more closely to the speaker than to the content of the ensuing sentence, since such imprecision may incur disapproval:

*Personally I wouldn't dream of spending so much.*

Another way of categorizing adverbs is to separate them according to their role within a sentence. The majority of adverbs may be classed as **adjuncts,** adverbs that relate to the verb or to the whole sentence (*wave **wildly**, leave **yesterday***). Others may be grouped under the title **subjuncts,** which relates to adverbs that play a subordinate role in a sentence (*pass the bottle, **please***). A third group are called **disjuncts,** adverbs that refer to the style or content of a sentence (*generally, perhaps, undoubtedly*). A final group of so-called **conjuncts** includes adverbs that link clauses, sentences, or paragraphs (*alternatively, besides, finally, firstly, however, instead, likewise, meanwhile, nevertheless, overall, secondly, similarly, so, therefore*).

Adverbs are commonly formed by adding an *-ly* or *-ally* ending to an adjective (*coyly, softly, tactically, basically*). Note that in a few cases the spelling of the adjectival stem may alter with the addition of the adverbial ending (*easily, truly*). (See also page 181.) Some adverbs, however, retain their adjectival form and do not require an *-ly* ending (*arrive late, sink low*). Other adverbial endings include *-ward*, or *-wards* (*downward, upward*), *-ways* (*sideways*), and *-wise* (*clockwise*).

Note that many adverbs can be used in comparative and superlative contexts (*more completely, less quietly, most richly decorated*) and may have specific comparative and superlative forms as in the case of *fast* and *hard* (*fast/faster/fastest, hard/harder/hardest*). Some may have irregular comparative and superlative forms (*well/better/best, badly/worse/worst*).

## Position of Adverbs

Adverbs are usually placed next to the simple verb between the parts of a verb (*they have never met; she is rarely defeated*), although they can be placed virtually anywhere within a sentence:

*She walked slowly through the garden.*
*Slowly she walked through the garden.*
*She walked through the garden slowly.*

Adverbs should not be placed between a verb and its direct object, however. The length of the object clause determines whether an adverb should be placed before or after the verb:

*She tidied the room quickly.*
*She quickly tidied the room that she had slept in.*

Note that the positioning of an adverb can alter the meaning of the sentence:

*Only the president can order a sale.*
*The president can only order a sale.*
*The president can order a sale only.*

Careless positioning of an adverb can sometimes lead to ambiguity:

*He whispered faintly romantic words.*

In this example the adverb *faintly* may be confusingly interpreted as applying either to the verb *whispered* or to the adjective *romantic*.

The safest option is usually to position the adverb next to the word to which it relates. If it modifies another adverb or an adjective, it should be placed immediately before that adverb or adjective (*quite good progress, very gently*). (*See also* SPLIT INFINITIVES, page 123.)

# PRONOUNS

A pronoun is a word that can be used in place of a noun, noun phrase, or (occasionally) a whole clause, to refer to someone or something. Pronouns are invaluable as a means of avoiding lengthy repetition of words already mentioned. As replacements for nouns, they behave exactly as nouns do, acting as subject, object, and complement to the verb as required.

## Types of Pronouns

Pronouns can be subdivided into various categories. **Personal pronouns** are the largest and most important category of pronouns. They are used to refer to a specific person or thing and include such words as *I, you, he, she, it, we,* and *they.*

The correct choice of pronoun in a given context depends firstly upon whether it is the subject or object of the sentence. If it is in the **subject case,** the correct choice depends next upon which **person** it represents.

Personal pronouns can be subdivided into three persons. The first person is the speaker (singular or plural), who is represented by *I* or *we.* The second person is the person the speaker is directly addressing, represented by *you* (the same for both singular and plural). The third person is a person or object as discussed by the first and second persons and represented by *he, she, it* if singular, according to gender, and by *they* if plural:

*I spoke.*
*We agreed.*
*You failed.*
*It started.*
*They sat down.*

Note that the personal pronoun *one,* which is sometimes used in formal contexts where an impersonal tone is appropriate, behaves in much the same way as *he, she,* and *it,* taking a third person verb ending:

*One needs to be cautious when discussing such contentious issues.*

If a pronoun is serving as the object of a sentence, or if it follows a preposition, then it goes into the **object case.** The first person thus becomes *me* or, in the plural, *us,* while the second person remains *you,* and the third person becomes *him* or *her,* or, in the plural, *them* (*it* and *you* remain the same):

*Help me.*
*Don't tell us.*
*She hit you.*
*Look at them.*

Confusion often arises regarding personal pronouns when the writer is unclear about the rules surrounding the subject and object forms, specifically when a pronoun follows a preposition. The rule is that prepositions should always be followed by the object form of a personal pronoun, so *with my husband and me, between you and me,* and *good-bye from Jim and me* are correct (but *with my husband and I, between you and I,* and *goodbye from Jim and I* are not). Note that the rule stands regardless of the number of pronouns following the preposition.

**Reflexive pronouns** are a smaller group of pronouns that refer to the subject of the clause or sentence within which it is placed, and indicating that the subject and object of the verb are one and the same. Reflexive pronouns are formed by adding *-self* (singular) or *-selves* (plural) to the objective or possessive form of the personal pronoun (*myself, yourself, himself, herself, itself, oneself, ourselves, yourselves, themselves*):

*She prided herself on her sense of direction.*
*The cooker will turn itself off after three hours.*

Note that reflexive pronouns do not necessarily come immediately after the verb, but may follow a preposition:

*He was annoyed with himself for his cowardice.*
*You should be ashamed of yourself.*

Reflexive nouns feature in a number of widely familiar stock phrases:

*They were beside themselves with fear.*
*She isn't herself today.*
*He lives all by himself.*
*It's good to have the place all to ourselves.*

Mistakes commonly occur when a writer is tempted to replace a personal pronoun with a reflexive pronoun. Note that it is incorrect to replace a phrase such as *Bob and I have to go* with *Bob and myself have to go*. Note also that it would be incorrect to replace a sentence such as *Father needed provisions, so I got some things for us and him* with *Father needed provisions, so I got some things for us and himself* because *Father* is not the subject of the verb *got*.

**Possessive pronouns** are personal pronouns that indicate possession (*mine, his, hers, its, ours, theirs, yours*). They can serve as either the subject or the complement of the verb, as required, and do not vary in form wherever they are placed:

*That seat is yours.*
*Mine is that house over there.*
*It ruined our holiday.*

*Whose* is the possessive form of *who* or *whom:*

*Whose are those shoes?*

Note that it is incorrect to render any version of the possessive pronoun with an *'s* ending; *yours* and *theirs* are the correct forms.

**Demonstrative pronouns** such as *this* and *that* (singular) and *these* or *those* (plural) are used to distinguish between things being referred to:

*This is my hat; that is yours.*

The term *demonstrative* indicates the role of such pronouns in demonstrating which of several things are being referred to. Note that *this* and *these* usually refer to things close at hand, while *that* and *those* refer to things farther away:

*Come and look at this.*
*Let's go and have a look at those.*

**Interrogative pronouns** are used to introduce questions. Five in number, they all begin with *wh-* (*what, which, who, whom, whose*):

*What would you like to drink?*
*Which door leads outside?*

Interrogative pronouns do not change in form, whether singular or plural. They are closely related to such interrogative adverbs as *how, when, where,* and *why.*

The one aspect of interrogative pronouns that sometimes causes problems is that relating to the use of *who* or *whom. Who* is the subject pronoun and is thus the correct form to use in such questions as *who sings better?* and *who wrote that letter to him? Whom* is the object pronoun and is thus correct in such phrases as *whom should we tell? to whom should this message go?* and *whom are you waiting for?* Note, however, that in everyday usage these distinctions are often ignored and *who* is frequently used in the place of *whom* without provoking much comment.

**Relative pronouns** such as *that, which, who, whom,* or *whose* are used to introduce relative clauses (clauses that provide further information about the noun they follow). They vary slightly in use. *Which* and *that* are used with reference to things, although on occasion *that* may also be applied to people. *Who* and *whom* are reserved for people. *Whose* is applied to people or things:

*He hired the last horse that remained in the stable.*
*He is the one who denounced us.*
*She returned to me the old book, which is now in tatters from her man handling it.*
*He is the architect whose works you have been admiring.*

*That* and *which* should not be considered to be interchangeable. *That* is employed restrictively to focus the attention on a particular category or thing (*the coat that you were buying; the course that she was taking*), whereas *which* is used nonrestrictively to tack on additional information about something already mentioned (*the house, which stood on the corner; she objected, which came as a surprise to no one*). Note that *that* is not preceded by a comma, whereas *which* is preceded by a comma, parenthesis, or dash. (See also the section on relative clauses, page 154.)

Commonly the relative pronoun may appear with a preposition inserted immediately in front of it:

*This is the bag in which the box was found.*
*She is the woman with whom he made his escape.*

Note that *when* and *where,* which are more correctly **relative adverbs,** can also be used in a similar way at the beginning of a relative clause.

**Emphatic pronouns** are reflexive pronouns used in order to add emphasis within a sentence:

*I* ***myself*** *have seen the ghost on a number of occasions.*
*This is not a criticism of the government* ***itself,*** *but of the policy it is enforcing.*

Emphatic pronouns are identical in form to reflexive pronouns (*myself, himself,* etc.). They are usually placed immediately after the noun or pronoun they refer to, although there are occasions when they may be placed farther away:

*She did not do the last of the jobs* ***herself,*** *but trusted her assistant to do it for her.*

**Indefinite pronouns** are pronouns that refer to a group of people or objects in general terms, without specifying more precisely who or what is meant (*all; anybody; anyone; anything; both; each; either; everybody; everyone; everything; nobody; no one; none; nothing; one; some; somebody, something*). Some indefinite pronouns (*anybody, anyone, everybody, nobody, one, somebody,* etc.) are reserved for references to people, while others (*anything, everything, nothing, something,* etc.) are only used of things. A third group of indefinite pronouns (*all, none, some,* etc.) may be freely applied to both people and inanimate objects.

It is possible to subdivide indefinite pronouns into two groups, compound pronouns (*anybody, everything,* etc.) and pronouns that are followed by *of* (*all, some,* etc.). Compound pronouns can serve as the subject or object of a verb or may be placed after a preposition (*everybody agreed; listen to something*). Note that compound pronouns are always treated as singular, even though they may represent a number of people or things (*everyone is coming*). Pronouns that may be followed by *of* may generally be defined as expressions of quantity (*all, most,* etc.) and may be treated as singular when used with or in the place of a singular or uncountable noun, or as plural when used with or instead of a plural noun:

*All of the town is included/All is included.*
*All of the geese are dead/All are dead.*

The pronouns *another, each, either,* and *neither* are always treated as singular as they all refer to only one person or thing:

*Another has gone this morning.*
*Each has its advantages.*
*Neither is ideal.*

Conversely, the pronouns *both, few,* and *many* are always treated as plural as they necessarily refer to more than one person or thing:

*Both have gone missing.*
*Few are left now.*
*Many have died since then.*

Note that the pronouns *less, least, little,* and *much* are always singular, since they usually refer to uncountable nouns:

*Little is better than none at all.*
*Much remains to be discovered.*

The pronoun *one* operates both in the singular (*one is mine, one is yours*) and in the plural, in the form *ones* (*which ones are mine?*).

**Reciprocal pronouns** are pronouns employed when there is some kind of mutual relationship between the persons or things being referred to. They take the form *each other* or *one another* and are always used with a plural subject:

*Her parents detest each other.*
*If we help one another we will soon get the job done.*

In choosing between *each other* and *one another* the convention is to use *each other* when referring to two people or things (*the twins love each other*) and *one another* when there are more parties involved (*we must all look after one another*). This rule is not set in concrete, however, and is often disregarded.

Note that a reciprocal pronoun may serve as the object of a verb or may follow a preposition (*salute one another, look at each other*). In most circumstances, reciprocal pronouns refer to people or animals, but they can also be applied to inanimate things:

*The carriages bumped into each other.*
*The raindrops raced one another cross the windshield.*

## Gender of Pronouns

The same conventions that govern the attribution of gender to nouns also hold true for pronouns. The pronouns themselves only reflect gender, however, in their third person singular forms (*he, she, it, himself, herself, itself*). Masculine pronouns *he* and *him* are used in the place of masculine nouns, while feminine pronouns *she* and *her* are used as replacements for feminine nouns. Where the noun has no particular gender, *it* and *its* is usually employed as a replacement. *It* is also the usual choice of pronoun when the gender is unknown:

*The baby shook its rattle.*

Problems can arise when a pronoun is understood to refer to people of either sex in relation to a word such as *anyone or someone,* because there is no singular pronoun that is accepted as including both genders. This question is less of an issue in the plural, since *they* and *themselves* have no particular gender, but in the singular it is not always appropriate to opt for *it* as an impersonal alternative. One cannot say, for example, *anyone is entitled to its opinion.* Historically, the usual solution has been to treat such words as masculine and opt for *he* or *his* (*anyone is entitled to his opinion*), but in relatively recent times the chauvinism of such an assumption of masculinity has made such a solution contentious. Even in the example given above, *the baby shook its rattle,* a writer risks causing offense. Many writers on childcare now adopt the approach of assuming all babies to be female (*the baby shook her rattle*) when spoken of in general terms. Others switch between gender from one paragraph to the next.

One alternative in non-gender-specific circumstances is to use *he or she* or *his or her* (*anyone is entitled to his or her opinion*), but this option can create clumsy constructions that do not bear regular repetition. This alternative is particularly awkward in terms of the reflexive pronoun (*the mystery guest will reveal himself or herself to the audience at the end of the show*). In practice, the more common solution in recent years has been to avoid the use of a singular noun in the first place and so keep everything in the plural:

*Citizens in a free state are all entitled to their opinion.*
*Her parents have indicated their opposition to the decision.*
*Members of the audience are on their feet.*

Some even have taken to treating general pronouns such as *anyone* or *someone* as plural in form to maintain gender neutrality (*anyone is entitled to their opinion*), although this is unacceptable to many.

## PREPOSITIONS

A preposition is a word that shows the relation of a noun, phrase, or clause to the rest of the sentence. Prepositions are typically small in size (*above, after, at, before, below, down, during, for, in, into, off, on, out, over, under, up, with, without*), but they are among the most useful words in the language, linking together the various elements of a sentence. A preposition and the element it links with are formally referred to as a **prepositional phrase.**

Prepositions can be used to link many different kinds of sentence elements, the words following a preposition being formally termed the **prepositional complement.** The prepositional complement may be a noun phrase, a pronoun, an adverb, or another prepositional phrase, as illustrated, respectively, in the following examples:

*The man ran out of* ***the house.***
*These chocolates are for* ***you.***
*Is there any light in* ***here?***
*The aircraft emerged from* ***behind a cloud.***

When a preposition refers to two complements in the same sentence, it does not necessarily have to be repeated:

*She went shopping with her mother and father.*
*They know lots about music and painting.*

The preposition should be repeated, however, if there is any risk that by not doing so the meaning of the sentence may be misconstrued. *His mother was thinking about going abroad and about writing a book,* for example, may not mean the same thing as *his mother was thinking about going abroad and writing a book.* (In the first example the implication is that the activities of *going abroad* and *writing a book* are not necessarily linked, while in the second example they are more likely to be.)

All the prepositions so far described have consisted of just one word (so-called **simple prepositions**), but there are other prepositions that consist of two or more words (called **complex prepositions**). These behave in exactly the same way as simple prepositions. They include such constructions as *according to, ahead of, apart from, as far as, as for, as to, as well as, away from, because of, but for, by means of, close to, due to, except for, further to, in accordance with, in addition to, in case of, in face of, in spite of, instead of, in terms of, in view of, near to, next to, on account of, on behalf of, on top of, out of, owing to, regardless of, up to, with reference to,* and *with regard to.*

It is sometimes easy to become confused between prepositions and adverbs or conjunctions, particularly because a number of words may operate as either without any change in appearance. The preposition *onto* (*get onto the table*), for instance, may also be encountered in the form of the adverb *on* together with the preposition *to* (*go on to the end*). The preposition *until* (*they slept until sunrise*), meanwhile, may also be found functioning as a conjunction (*they slept until the sun rose*). The best way to determine whether a word is operating as a preposition or an adverb is to try placing the word in a different part of the sentence and seeing if it is still grammatically acceptable. If it is, then the word in question is probably operating as an adverb. In the case of conjunctions, the rule is that if the clause that follows the word in question can stand independently as a sentence, then the word under examination is a conjunction, not a preposition.

## Position of Prepositions

Prepositions are often placed before the noun or pronoun to which they refer:

*The dog hid under the table.*
*She walked into town.*

This is not always the case, however, and prepositions may be positioned elsewhere, including at the end of a sentence. Conventional wisdom (which has its roots in the rules of Latin grammar) insists that prepositions should never be placed at the end of a sentence, but rigid observance of this rule and attempts to find an alternative can lead to the construction of much more clumsy sentences. A sensible compromise is to relax the rule where placing a preposition at the end of a sentence is the most natural solution, as in the following examples:

*There is nothing to worry about.*
*Go and see what the children are up to.*
*She is a difficult person to live with.*

*She gave the child a book to look at.*
*This was something we had all hoped for.*

In practice, most people find nothing objectionable about a sentence that ends with a preposition in spoken English but will generally seek out an alternative sentence structure that allows a preposition to precede its complement when writing formally. It should be noted that it is not incorrect to end a sentence with *in, off, on,* etc., when these words are operating as adverbs.

## Meanings of Prepositions

Preposition may also be categorized according to their meaning. **Prepositions of space** include many of the most frequently encountered prepositions. They may be subdivided into prepositions that refer to a position (*across, at, in, on,* etc.), prepositions that describe a position relative to another (*above, among, away from, behind, below, between, in front of, next to, off, opposite, out of, under,* etc.), prepositions of movement (*across, along, down, over, past, through, under, up,* etc.), prepositions of movement toward somewhere (*in, into, on, onto, to,* etc.), or prepositions of movement away from somewhere (*away from, from, off, out of,* etc.).

**Prepositions of time** are another significant group. They variously refer to periods of time (*during, for, since, throughout, until,* etc.), to particular points in time (*at, by, in, on,* etc.), or to points in time relative to other points in time (*after, before,* etc.).

Other groups of prepositions include **prepositions of cause** (*at, because of, on account of, out of,* etc.), **prepositions of manner or means** (*as, by, like, with, without,* etc.), **prepositions of accompaniment** (*with, without,* etc.), **prepositions of support** or **of opposition** (*against, for, with,* etc.), **prepositions of possession** (*of, with, without,* etc.), **prepositions of concession** (*despite, in spite of, notwithstanding,* etc.), and **prepositions of addition** or **of exception** (*apart from, as well as, besides, but, except,* etc.).

Some prepositions belong to more than one category and mean different things according to the context. The preposition *at,* for instance, may be used as a preposition of space (*arrive at the venue*), as a preposition of time (*leave at dusk*), as a preposition of cause (*offended at her remarks*), as well as in other guises.

In some cases several different prepositions can be equally legitimately attached to the same word and still mean the same thing. A particularly contentious example of this phenomenon is *different,* which can be variously combined with the prepositions *from, to,* and *than.* Many people insist that *different from* is the only correct form, though in reality there is no real case against the use of any of the alternatives.

*The international situation is different from what it was in the postwar years.*
*The international situation is different than it was in the postwar years.*

Many prepositions have become fixed as part of established phrases and idioms, which have widely familiar figurative meanings. These include such phrases as *at arm's length, from bad to worse, start from scratch, through and through,* and *with open arms,* among many more.

# CONJUNCTIONS

Conjunctions are words or phrases that serve to link words, clauses, or sentences. Including such ubiquitous words as *although, and, because, but, if, or, so, unless, when,* and *while,* they represent one of the most frequently used classes of words in the English language. Conjunctions can be subdivided into coordinating conjunctions, subordinating conjunctions, and correlative conjunctions.

**Coordinating conjunctions** (or **coordinators**) are conjunctions that are used to connect words and clauses of the same grammatical type. They include *and, but, or, then,* and *yet:*

*You and I.*
*It looks good but tastes horrible.*
*Would you like tea or coffee?*
*An afternoon of rain, then sun.*
*Gone yet not forgotten.*

Coordinating conjunctions can be used to link adjectives (*wet* ***and*** *warm, black* ***or*** *white decisions*), adverbials (*out of time* ***and*** *out of luck, slowly* ***but*** *surely*), noun phrases (*a box of crayons* ***and*** *a pad of paper, a slice of cake* ***or*** *a couple of biscuits*), and even main sentence clauses:

*You must go to school,* ***and*** *I must get off to work.*
*She has not yet received the document,* ***but*** *I know what the report will say.*

The conjunctions *but* and *yet* can be used only to connect two sentence elements, whereas *and* and *or* can connect two or more:

*We're lost* ***and*** *scared* ***and*** *want to go home.*
*You can advance* ***or*** *retreat* ***or*** *surrender.*

In such lists the usual convention is to replace all but the last conjunction with a comma (*red, white, and blue*), but on occasion the additional conjunctions are left in place, generally for reasons of emphasis.

Where a coordinating conjunction connects two clauses that share a common verb there is no need to repeat the verb:

*He is old yet still charming.*
*They were tired but willing.*

In circumstances where the conjunction connects two or more subjects, note that a plural verb is usually required, unless the subjects effectively represent a single entity or concept:

*Mars and Jupiter have both been extensively surveyed.*
*Peanut butter and jelly is a surprisingly tasty combination.*

Care should be taken to choose the appropriate conjunction according to the nature of the relationship between the subjects under discussion. There are important differences in meaning between the various conjunctions, and in most circumstances they are not interchangeable.

The conjunction *and* is used where two or more persons or objects are added to each other or otherwise combined (*inside and outside, cold and lonely*). Note that the order of the parts linked by *and* can usually be reversed, although the order of some phrases is established by convention and is rarely altered (*food and drink, good and bad*). An exception to this rule is where *and* is used to place events in the order in which they happened:

*She opened the tin and emptied it out.*
*They unlocked the door and went in.*

*But* differs from *and* in that it is used to link two opposing concepts or express a contrast:

*She likes men with moustaches but hates beards.*
*He wants bread but not butter.*
*The weather in the morning was cold but bright.*

When *but* is used in the sense of *except*, it is not always clear whether it is being employed as a conjunction or as a preposition and whether it should be followed by an object or subject pronoun (*all but she/all but her*). The usual solution here is to opt for a subject pronoun if it comes in the middle of the sentence (*all but he had an alibi*) but to employ an object pronoun if it comes at the end of the sentence (*commendations went to all but him*).

Care should be taken not to use *but* to link harmonious concepts or to use *but* in the same sentence as *however*, because essentially they mean the same thing. Note that it is also incorrect to insert a comma after *but*.

*Or* is used to express a choice or alternative:

*Would you like to carry this bag or that one?*
*It is either a crow or a raven.*

When *or* connects two singular subjects, it is correct to use a singular verb. When it links plural subjects a plural verb should be employed:

*Tom or Sue knows the way.*
*Blues or pinks are this year's colors.*

If *or* connects singular and plural subjects, the verb should agree with the subject that is nearest to it:

*One large spoonful or two small ones are enough.*
*Two small spoonfuls or one large one is enough.*

**Subordinating conjunctions** (or **subordinators**) are conjunctions that are used to connect a subordinate clause (usually an adverbial) to a main clause.

They include *after, although, because, before, except, for, if, in case, in order that, since, though, unless, until, when, where, whereas,* and *while:*

> *They will lose the election,* ***because*** *they have no popular support.*
> *This won't happen* ***unless*** *we get permission from the state authorities.*
> *I will help out,* ***when*** *we run short of staff.*

The correct choice of subordinating conjunction depends on the intended meaning. Some conjunctions (*after, as, before, till, until, when, while,* etc.) express time:

> *The game was effectively lost* ***after*** *the team's star athlete was injured.*
> *They talked it over* ***while*** *waiting for the train.*

Others (*where, wherever,* etc.) express place:

> *The land* ***where*** *dragons live is far away.*
> *He is recognized* ***wherever*** *he goes.*

Other subordinating conjunctions (*because, for, since,* etc.) express a reason:

> *She left* ***because*** *she had an appointment elsewhere.*
> *They said little,* ***since*** *there was nothing left to be done.*

Yet another group of subordinating conjunctions (*in order that, in order to, so that,* etc.) express a purpose:

> *The flight was postponed* ***in order that*** *the delayed passengers could get there.*
> *Take the pan from the heat* ***so that*** *the mixture cools.*

The subordinating conjunction *so* expresses a result:

> *He did not reply,* ***so*** *she left the room.*

A further group of subordinating conjunctions (*as long as, if, in case, providing, unless,* etc.) express a condition:

> *We will get home tonight,* ***providing*** *there are no problems on the road.*
> *He will receive the money next week,* ***unless*** *there is a delay.*

The subordinating conjunctions *although, even if, if, though,* etc., express concession:

> *They did not deserve to win,* ***although*** *they played well enough.*
> *I will get there,* ***even if*** *I have to walk all the way.*

Such subordinating conjunctions as *whereas,* and *while,* express contrast:

*This house has no garage, **whereas** the other has parking for three cars.*
*Her mother is a vegetarian, **while** her father loves meat of all kinds.*

The subordinating conjunction *except* (*that*) expresses exception:

*He'd like to help out, except (that) he's away that weekend.*

A last group (*as, as if, as though, like,* etc.) express comparison or similarity:

*He set to work at once, **as though** he had been doing the job for years.*
*They behaved **like** there was no tomorrow.*

Some subordinating conjunctions have more than one meaning:

*The flame flickered **as** [at the same time as] the wind began to rise.*
*You must go, **as** [because] you do not have permission to be here.*

Note that a subordinating conjunction is normally placed at the start of the subordinate clause it serves to link, often at the beginning of the whole sentence when the subordinate clause comes before the main clause:

***As** you arrived last, you must go to the end of the line.*
***After** they had finished their meal, the family went outside.*
***Before** it started raining, we were playing outside.*

**Correlative conjunctions** are conjunctions that include such pairs as *either . . . or* and *neither . . . nor* and are always used together:

*You must either agree to our conditions or tear up the contract.*
*They have neither wealth nor property.*

These two examples of correlatives can be further categorized as coordinating correlatives, along with *both . . . and* and *not only . . . but also:*

***Both** the army **and** the navy must be prepared to accept cuts in funding.*
*Such an action is **not only** foolish **but also** shortsighted.*

Another category includes the subordinating correlatives *hardly . . . when, if . . . then, less . . . than, more . . . than, scarcely . . . when,* so . . . *that,* and *such . . . that:*

***Hardly** had the door closed **when** the ceiling fell in.*
***If** the money is not forthcoming **then** the deal is off.*
***Such** was his horror at the crime **that** he immediately handed himself over to the police.*

### Use of Conjunctions

Many people consider it incorrect to begin a sentence with a conjunction such as *and* or *but*. Although conjunctions are often used in this manner in spoken English, it is best to avoid their use in formal written contexts. There are some circumstances, however, when writers will choose to break this convention in order to draw attention to a tacked-on phrase or sentence:

*Such behavior is antisocial. And illegal.*
*She loves to dance. And how!*

Note that the use of *or* at the beginning is less contentious and more frequently encountered:

*It may rain later. Or it may not.*

## PHRASES, CLAUSES, AND SENTENCES

### Phrases

A phrase is a group of words that function together in their respective roles as noun, verb, adjective, adverb, preposition, etc. (*a white rabbit, blue as the sky, go away, deeply moved, at the top of the stairs, in connection with*). A phrase does not by itself usually constitute a complete sentence and is not synonymous with a **clause,** which always contains a finite verb and may comprise one or more phrases belonging to different categories. In the clause *the sun had set in the west,* for instance, *the sun* is a noun phrase, while *had set* is a verb phrase and *in the west* is a prepositional phrase. The different categories of phrases are described below.

#### NOUN PHRASE

A noun phrase is composed of a noun or pronoun and any accompanying modifiers and determiners (*an old gray cat, a cat with a grey coat, a cat that has a grey coat*). It can variously play the role of subject, object, or complement within a clause or sentence:

***That song** is great. [subject]*
*We love **that song**. [object]*
*That is **a great song**. [complement]*

Noun phrases can also include single nouns or pronouns or a single noun preceded by *a* or *the* (*a man, the woman*). Examples of cases where a noun phrase may consist of only a single word include sentences where the second word in a noun phrase has been omitted, because it is unnecessary in order to make the meaning clear:

*We must get the **doctor's** [clinic/office/house/etc.].*
*They were staying at **Bill's** [house/apartment/etc.].*

When two noun phrases immediately follow one another and refer to the same person or thing, they are said to be in **apposition:**

*Alison, my sister, arrives tomorrow.*
*This model, the latest in this line, is very popular.*

Note that noun phrases that are in apposition are often capable of being transposed without changing the meaning and are set apart by commas. Further, either phrase can be left out without destroying the sentence. This rule does not always apply, however, as when the two phrases are separated by words such as *namely* or *for example:*

*This was written by the greatest Elizabethan playwright, namely Shakespeare.*
*He likes the work of modern artists, for example Picasso.*

There are also occasions when noun phrases in apposition depend on each other to make the meaning clear and should not be separated by commas. If either was removed the reader may not understand what is being referred to:

*The plant* ***myosotis*** *grows as a weed in many gardens.*

Here, without the phrase *the plant,* it might not be clear what *myosotis* is; without the word *myosotis,* it might be unclear what plant is being referred to.

## ADJECTIVE PHRASE

An adjective phrase consists of an adjective together with various modifiers offering further information (*fairly clever, very hot, deep enough, happy to come*). Modifiers that are placed before the so-called **head adjective** are formally termed **premodifiers** (***quite*** *cold,* ***too*** *bright*), while modifiers that appear after the head adjective are called **postmodifiers** (*quiet* ***enough***, *better* ***than ever***).

Premodifiers are often adverbs (*fairly, quite, too,* etc.). In some cases it is possible for more than one adverb to be used in this way:

*The ride was* ***nearly too*** *exciting.*
*The shower was* ***very quickly*** *over.*

Premodifiers in adjective phrases can also be adjectives themselves:

*He sat in an* ***old*** *red armchair.*
*The sea was* ***deep*** *blue.*

Sometimes they may be no more than a repetition of the adjective they describe:

*It was a* ***sad,*** *sad day for all concerned.*
*They waited for a* ***long,*** *long time, but it never happened again.*
*The storm became* ***wilder*** *and wilder.*

Note that adjective phrases may be used in different parts of a sentence, being placed either before the noun (*a deeply shocking event, a surprisingly good outcome*) or after the verb (*we were very pleased; the water is too shallow*).

Postmodifiers take several different forms. They may be adverbs (*loud* ***enough***), phrases beginning with a preposition (*fond* ***of cheese,*** *irritated* ***by the noise***), or clauses variously beginning with *than, that,* an infinitive, a word ending with *-ing,* or a word beginning with *wh-*:

*It was raining harder* ***than ever.***
*He was sorry* ***that he would not be there.***
*The knot was difficult* ***to undo.***
*They were busy* ***unloading the cargo.***
*She was uncertain* ***which way to go.***

Alternatively, an adjective phrase may be followed by a combination of the above forms, such as an adverb and an infinitive (*cold* ***enough to snow***) or a clause beginning with *than* and a prepositional phrase (*fonder* ***than ever of music***). Whatever their form, postmodifiers are usually placed in a predicative position after the verb:

*The rope was not* ***long enough.***
*The children were* ***eager to start.***
*She was* ***sure that she could get there in time.***

Note that in some circumstances an adjective phrase may have both premodifiers and postmodifiers:

*She was* ***very glad of their help.***
*They were* ***more lucky than most.***

## VERB PHRASE

A verb phrase includes the verb element in a clause or sentence and may consist of a single word or more than one word:

*They* ***lived*** *in a small house on the edge of town.*
*The dog* ***was running*** *in a circle after its tail.*
*She* ***would have said*** *something if present.*

As these examples indicate, a verb phrase contains a main verb, which conveys the central meaning of the phrase (*he* ***walked*** *into the house*), and often one or more auxiliary verbs, such as *is, can, had, might,* and *should,* that have a subsidiary role:

*Her mother* ***is sleeping*** *upstairs.*
*You* ***can see*** *for miles from here.*
*They* ***should prepare*** *for trouble.*

Auxiliary verbs are an essential part of verb phrases when used in questions:

*Did you hear the explosion?*
*Can you reach that box?*

They are also necessary when using verb phrases in negative sentences with *not* (or *n't*):

*He **did** not drop the ball.*
*They **could** not get home in time.*

In questions the auxiliary verb is placed before the subject:

***Have** you seen the news?*
*What **was** she thinking?*

Where a question contains a verb phrase that has more than one auxiliary verb, the rule is to put just the first auxiliary verb in front of the subject:

***Have** you been registered?*
***Could** he have been mistaken?*

The same approach applies to negative sentences with *not* (or *n't*), the *not* (or *n't*) being placed after the first auxiliary verb:

*I **am** not wearing a seatbelt.*
***Shouldn't** he have taken that road?*

(*See also* PHRASAL VERBS, page 131.)

### ADVERBIAL PHRASE

An adverbial phrase is made up of a group of words based on an adverb or preposition. This group of words plays the role of an adverb within a clause or sentence. A phrase built on an adverb may include additional words placed both in front of and after the adverb (*as soon as possible; oddly enough; very slowly*). Phrases beginning with prepositions are very common and consist of the preposition and the prepositional complement functioning adverbially as a unit (*in town, with luck*). (*See also* adverbial clause explained immediately below.)

## Clauses

A clause is a meaningful group of words that includes a subject and a predicate and typically forms part of a complete longer sentence. There are two main types of clause.

A **main clause** (or **independent clause**) is complete in itself and so is capable of existing independently as a sentence:

***He ordered the fish,** because that was the only choice left.*
*As there was nothing left to do, **she decided to go home.***

A sentence must include at least one main clause. Often a complete sentence is no more than a single independent clause:

*I stayed at home.*
*She worked all night.*
*He knows the truth.*

Some sentences (sometimes called **multiple sentences**) consist of two or more main clauses, any of which could be taken out of context and used as a complete sentence in its own right:

*They won the race, but they did not break the record.*
*She turned down the offer, and today she is one of the richest women in America.*

A **subordinate clause** (or **dependent clause**) is not complete in itself and so is incapable of standing alone as an independent sentence. Subordinate clauses typically begin with such words as *although, because, if,* or *when,* all of which imply that there is more to be said:

***Although the time had come,*** *nothing was ready.*
*He ordered the fish,* ***because that was the only choice left.***
***When the others arrive*** *I will light up the barbecue.*

It is also possible to subdivide clauses according to the type of verb phrase they contain. A clause that contains a finite verb phrase is called a **finite clause,** while one containing a nonfinite verb phrase is termed a **nonfinite clause.** (*See* TYPES OF VERBS, page 115.)

An **adverbial clause** is a clause that provides information about the verb, such as when, where, how, and why something is performed. It may or may not contain a verb itself. Adverbial clauses are typically introduced by such words as *because, if, when, where,* or *while:*

*I need the money* ***because we need a new car.***
*There will be a riot* ***if nothing is done.***
*She nodded her head approvingly* ***when she heard what had happened.***
*That is the shed* ***where the boat is kept.***
*Tell the crew to eat* ***while they are working.***

An **appositive clause** is a clause that adds further detail about a preceding abstract noun (for example, *idea, belief, decision*):

*There was no option but to continue, despite the fact* ***that there was little hope of success.***
*The notion* ***that they could do the job themselves*** *had not occurred to them.*

Note that appositive clauses always begin with *that.* Some appositive clauses are restrictive, meaning that they cannot be removed without essential information being lost:

*He refuted the claim* ***that the accusation had no grounds.***

Others are nonrestrictive, or capable of being removed without the essential meaning of the sentence being lost:

> *The government's argument (**that such a change would be too expensive**) has been dismissed by critics.*

See below for more on restrictive and nonrestrictive clauses.

A **comment clause** is a short clause that is added to a sentence in order to express a view about what is being conveyed. Comment clauses can be inserted at virtually any point in a sentence and are enclosed by commas:

> *The whole class, **he was sorry to say,** had failed to meet expectations.*
> ***What's more,** another delivery is not expected until next week.*

Note that comment clauses are nonrestrictive in nature and can be removed without altering the sense of the surrounding sentence.

Comment clauses vary in composition. Some comprise a subject and verb (*you know; I guess; it seems*) or a subject, verb, and complement (*I'm sorry to say; as it happens*). Others comprise a subject and verb introduced by the word *as* (*as I said; as you know*) or consist of a clause variously introduced by *what* (*what's more; what is strange*).

Comment clauses can be used for various different effects. Such phrases as *I know* and *I'm sure* convey certainty:

> *Such a move, I know, will anger our opponents.*
> *That is against the rules, I'm sure.*

*I suppose* and *I think* are among the comment clauses commonly used to convey speculation or uncertainty:

> *That is the way home, I think.*
> *The family have moved north, I believe.*

Hope, regret, and other emotions can be conveyed through the use of such comment clauses as *I hope, I'm afraid,* or *we fear:*

> *This is the start of a bright new chapter, we hope.*
> *There is nothing left to eat, I'm afraid.*

Other comment clauses, such as *you see,* are used in relation to explanatory material or where something is being made clearer:

> *This, you see, is how the system works.*

A final category of comment clauses is used to address the reader directly:

> *This is the corridor to the kitchens, as you know.*
> *The dress created quite an impression, don't you think?*

Caution should be used in relation to such comment clauses as *you know* and *I mean,* which are commonly employed to fill gaps in spoken English, often purely to buy the speaker time to think, but are considered too casual in most formal written contexts.

A **comparative clause** is a form of clause used when comparing persons or things. Comparative clauses may be subdivided into two categories, the first relating to comparisons between equivalent persons or things and the second to persons or things that are not equivalent to each other.

Comparative clauses relating to persons or things that are equivalent to each other employ the construction *as . . . as:*

*He is as reckless as his father is cautious.*
*This apple is as sweet as that one.*

Many familiar idiomatic phrases take the form of comparative clauses linking equivalents of various kinds: *as clear as day, as good as gold, as light as a feather.*

Where a comparison is being made between persons or things that are not equivalent a so-called **comparative element** is employed. Comparative elements may comprise either an adjective ending in *-er* (*longer, older*) or a phrase with the word *more* or *less* combined with a subordinate clause beginning with *than.* When someone or something is being compared with a higher or greater equivalent, the word ending *-er* or *more* is used:

*He is younger than his sister.*
*She has more money than the queen has.*
*Children today are more environmentally aware than previous generations were.*

When the comparison is with a lesser equivalent the word *less* (or *fewer* if in relation to plurals) is used:

*They are less eager to go now than they were last night.*
*There are fewer options now than there were 24 hours ago.*

In addition to adjectives, comparative elements can include noun phrases (*more weapons, a warmer temperature*), adverbs or adverb phrases (*more steadily, less fully*), or pronouns (*fewer, more*).

Note that when parts of the subordinate clause in comparative clauses are parallel in construction to the main clause, they are commonly omitted because they merely repeat what has already been stated:

*He is as frightened as you [are].*
*We are selling more units now than [we were] last month.*

A **relative clause** provides further information about the subject or object of a sentence that it follows, acting in much the same way as an adjective phrase. Some relative clauses begin with the words *that, which, who, whom,* or *whose* (called **relative pronouns**), while others begin with the words *when* or *where* (called **relative adverbs**):

*Mrs. Brainerd, whom I greatly respect, is a popular teacher among the students.*
*The man* ***who broke the bank at Monte Carlo*** *moved on to Las Vegas.*
*This is the snake* ***that escaped last week.***
*That was her favorite food* ***when she was young.***
*This is the house* ***where we shall live when we retire.***
*The book, which was first published in 1970, has brought in steady royalties.*

Note that the relative pronouns *which* and *whom* are sometimes preceded by a preposition:

*This is the room* ***in which the murder happened.***
*She was the author* ***by whom the book was written.***

In such cases it is incorrect to replace *which* with *that* or *whom* with *who.*

The relative adverbs *when* and *where* may on occasion be replaced by such phrases as *at which, in which, on which,* etc.:

*That was the day on which the war ended.*
*This was the place at which the peace was signed.*

Relative clauses can be subdivided into two categories. A **restrictive clause** (or **defining clause**) conveys essential information without which the rest of the sentence would be unclear. It is usually introduced by *that,* or *who:*

*My brother* ***who works in finance*** *may be able to advise us.*

The clause here is restrictive, because without it, the reader would be unsure which of several possible brothers is the one being referred to. The following examples are also restrictive:

*The car* ***that he bought*** *was nearly 10 years old.*
*The path* ***that she followed*** *led through a dark wood.*

When *that* refers to the object of a restrictive clause, it may be omitted altogether:

*The car [that] he bought was nearly ten years old.*
*The path [that] she followed led through a dark wood.*

The same applies to *whom:*

*She was the woman [whom] he had seen earlier in the evening.*

In all other cases, however, the relative pronoun should never be omitted.

A **nonrestrictive clause** (or **nondefining clause**) provides additional or explanatory information that is not essential to the sentence and could be omitted without the reader becoming confused about who or what is being referred to:

*My brother, **who works in finance,** may be able to advise us.*

Here the clause is nonrestrictive because there is only one possible brother being referred to and therefore no doubt about the person specified. Note the addition of commas here, which help distinguish a nonrestrictive clause from a restrictive clause. By extension, it is incorrect to place commas or dashes around a restrictive clause. For further discussion on the use of commas in relative clauses, see COMMA (page 342).

If a nonrestrictive clause refers to a thing, it should begin with the relative pronoun *which:*

*This ring, which belonged to my grandmother, has now been passed to my daughter.*
*Madrid, which is the capital of Spain, recently suffered a terrorist attack.*

Confusion often arises over the use of *who* and *whom* in relative clauses. Both are used only in relation to people. *Who* is used where the noun is the subject of the verb, while *whom* is correct when it is the object:

*No one has come forward to defend the people who committed this act.*
*He is the politician whom the voters trust most.*

Some writers replace *who* or *whom* with *that* in restrictive clauses. Others consider this incorrect:

*Let me introduce you to the people that made all this possible.*

A third type of relative clause is the **sentential relative clause,** in which the clause refers not to a particular word but to an entire clause or to the remainder of the sentence:

*The captain said the ship was sinking—which caused panic among the passengers.*

Sentential relative clauses are typically introduced by the pronoun *which:*

*She paused before replying, which gave him time to collect his thoughts.*
*They failed the test, which came as no surprise to their teacher.*

They may also, however, begin with *by which, for which, in which,* etc.:

*The president applauded the initiative, by which he meant the people behind it.*
*The lieutenant abandoned his post, for which he was later reduced to the ranks.*

Care should be taken not to interpret sentential relative clauses incorrectly, because there is sometimes room for more than one possible reading:

*The chairman came into the house, which was remarkable.*

Here, for instance, it is equally possible that the adjective *remarkable* refers to the action of the chairman coming into the house as that it refers to the house itself. Only the context in such cases can make the correct interpretation clear. The best alternative in such cases is to rewrite the sentence so that no such confusion arises.

## Sentences

A sentence comprises a meaningful and grammatically complete unit consisting of one or more words. To be grammatically correct a sentence must start with a capital letter, include a verb, and end with a period, exclamation point, or question mark. In practice, however many sentences lack verbs. Verbless sentences are often used for effect, sometimes to emphasize the previous sentence:

*Nothing had changed. Nothing at all.*
*Things will work out. With luck.*

### PARTS OF A SENTENCE

Sentences are composed of a number of different parts, which are governed by various conventions and rules, although personal or house style is also a significant factor to bear in mind while writing. The five basic parts of a sentence are the subject, the verb, the object, associated complements, and associated adverbials.

#### *Subject*

The subject of a sentence is the person or thing that the sentence is about and is usually the person or thing that carries out the action of the verb:

***The principal** made a speech to the whole school.*
***That dog** will bark if a stranger approaches the house.*
***She** left work early that afternoon.*
***Life** is full of surprises.*

The subject usually appears toward the beginning of a sentence and precedes the verb, but sometimes it appears elsewhere. In questions, for instance, the subject is generally placed after the verb or the first auxiliary verb:

*Where is **my bag**?*
*Did **you** eat yet?*
*When will **the train** arrive?*

The subject often appears after the verb for reasons of emphasis:

*Down went **his opponent**.*
*Gone were all **her dreams**.*

The subject also often appears after the verb in the reporting clause that follows direct speech (*see* REPORTING SPEECH, page 167):

> *"Come in," said* ***the doctor.***
> *"Tell me everything," whispered* ***Helen.***

A subject may be made up of a single noun or pronoun or a longer phrase:

> ***They*** *liked each other.*
> ***Climbing mountains with friends*** *is his favorite pastime.*
> ***Why he died*** *has yet to be explained.*

It may also consist of two or more nouns or pronouns:

> ***Cats and dogs*** *are popular pets.*
> ***You and I*** *can share the cost.*

It is also possible for the subject to consist of the *-ing* form of a verb (a gerund):

> ***Collecting stamps*** *is his favorite pastime.*
> ***Walking*** *is good for the health.*

Note that sometimes the subject may be a subordinate clause:

> ***What we ask*** *is to be left in peace.*

The form of the subject decides the form of the verb, regardless of which comes first. If the subject is singular, the verb must also be in the singular; if the subject is plural, the verb must also be plural. This is known as **concord,** or **agreement.**

> ***He likes*** to go *fishing.*
> ***They know*** *what will happen if they misbehave.*

Sometimes it is not always immediately clear whether the verb should be singular or plural. Note, for instance, the form of the verb in the following examples:

> *A collection of objects was brought out for inspection.*
> *The aims of the policy are threefold.*

In the first example a singular noun (*collection*) is linked to a plural noun (*objects*) by *of.* In the second example a plural noun is similarly linked to a singular noun. In both cases the verb follows the form of the first noun, which is the subject of the sentence (followed by a prepositional phrase). At times, there is scope for some flexibility in such cases, depending on whether the writer wishes to emphasize the unity of the group of objects or persons or to highlight them as individuals:

*A number of items have been retrieved from the well.*
*A group of teenagers were waiting outside.*
*The squad of new recruits was drawn up in two ranks.*
*A row of trees was destroyed in the blast.*

### *Verb*

Verbs, which are discussed in detail elsewhere in this chapter (page 115), often play the central role in a sentence and convey the most essential information:

*She* ***broke*** *the window.*
*They* ***stopped*** *at the light.*

On other occasions, though, the verb may be no more than a connecting word linking the subject with other parts of a sentence. Typical of such **linking verbs** are the verbs *be, seem,* and *feel:*

*The aim of this change in direction is to improve profit margins.*
*The storm seems to have blown over.*
*Something felt funny about the whole business.*

### *Object*

The object of a sentence usually follows the subject and the verb and denotes the person or thing that is affected by the verb. There are two types of object.

A **direct object** is a person or thing directly affected by the verb:

*The boy caught* ***the ball.***
*The bird ate* ***the seed.***
*Discussing politics bores* ***her.***

Where it is not immediately obvious what the object of the sentence is, one solution is to ask a question about the sentence beginning with *what* or *who/whom* (*what did the boy catch? what did the bird eat? whom does discussing politics bore?*).

An **indirect object** is an additional object that sometimes appears with certain verbs, notably verbs relating to the act of giving. It designates the person or thing to which or for which the action occurs.

*He sold his car to* ***her.***
*She bought a new leash for* ***the dog.***
*The noise gave* ***the horse*** *a fright.*
*They gave* ***their parents*** *a surprise party.*

If it is not obvious whether an object is indirect, the easiest way to identify it is by asking yourself a question about the sentence beginning with *to whom, to what, for whom,* or *for what* (*to whom did he sell his car? for what did she buy a new leash? to what did the noise give a fright? for whom did they give a surprise party?*).

Indirect objects are usually employed alongside direct objects, but sometimes the meaning of the direct object is absorbed by the indirect object and the direct object is omitted altogether. In the following examples the indirect objects have effectively made the direct objects (in brackets) redundant:

*She served* ***the customers*** *[a drink].*
*I told* ***them*** *[something].*

Where a sentence contains both a direct and an indirect object, the indirect object appears first, unless preceded by a preposition, such as *for* or *to:*

*He wrote* ***the man*** *[indirect object]* ***a dedication*** *[direct object] in his new book.*
*Tell* ***me*** *[indirect object]* ***the truth*** *[direct object].*

Both direct and indirect objects may consist of more than one noun or pronoun:

*Give* ***the child at the door*** *some money.*
*Pass me* ***the book with the yellow cover.***

They may also consist of a subordinate clause:

*She'll sell the car to* ***whoever offers the most money.***
*We'll take* ***what she gave us*** *into the house.*
*They know* ***why the team keeps losing.***

Both types of object may also consist of the *-ing* form of a verb (acting as a gerund):

*The pupils all enjoy* ***singing.***
*The priest refused to give* ***dancing in the streets*** *his approval.*

### *Complement*

In some sentences what follows the verb is termed a complement instead of an object because it simply adds more information about the subject or object of the verb. Complements commonly appear with a certain class of verbs (**linking verbs** or **copular verbs**) that serve primarily to link parts of the sentence (*appear, be, become, feel, grow, seem,* etc.):

*In her youth she was* ***a champion rider.***
*That seems* ***a foregone conclusion.***
*The night grew* ***dark.***

A complement that relates to the subject (termed a **subject complement**) is usually placed after the verb:

*Her clothes were totally* ***unsuitable.***
*He is* ***a much-admired writer and thinker.***

A complement that relates to the object of the verb (a so-called **object complement**) consists of the direct object and all associated, descriptive words, usually placed after the object:

*She painted* ***the town red.***
*They crowned* ***her queen.***
*This will make* ***the journey shorter.***

A complement may consist of a single word or a longer phrase. Most complements take the form of an adjective or a noun phrase:

*The boat is* ***a catamaran.***
*The woman became* ***angry.***
*The box was* ***empty.***

Others, however, may be a pronoun or a longer clause:

*This is* ***it.***
*That is* ***something to be discussed.***

### *Adverbial*

The **adverbial** refers to the part of the sentence that includes additional information about the verb. It many cases it comprises a single-word adverb:

*Look* ***closely*** *at the detail.*
*She wept* ***bitterly.***

On other occasions it may consist of an adverbial phrase:

*The deal collapsed* ***relatively soon afterward.***
*Let's get together again* ***really soon.***

In some cases the adverbial is made up of a phrase starting with a preposition:

*He slept* ***in a chair.***
*The fox wriggled* ***under the wire.***

It is also possible for a noun phrase to serve as an adverbial:

*We return* ***next week.***
*He retired* ***last year.***

Sometimes the adverbial consists of a subordinate clause:

*The audience applauded* ***after watching his performance.***
*They acted* ***because they feared an outbreak of violence.***

Note that it is possible to encounter more than one adverbial in a single sentence:

> *The package will be delivered* **by hand,** *we are promised,* **later the same day.**

The adverbial is normally placed after the verb, usually at the end of the clause or sentence. On occasion, however, it may also appear at the start of the sentence or after the subject and before the verb:

> ***Because of failing light*** *the game finished early.*
> *The general* ***slowly*** *raised his hand.*

It should be noted that some verbs are not grammatically complete without the addition of an appropriate adverbial:

> *Several bodies lay* ***on the ground.***
> *He put the gun* ***back in its holster.***

## STRUCTURE OF SENTENCES

The usual order of the grammatical elements within a clause or sentence is subject, verb, object/complement/adverbial:

> *The man [subject] closed [verb] the window [object].*
> *The old lady [subject] became [verb] tearful [complement].*
> *The detective [subject] watched [verb] from the shadows [adverbial].*

Many sentences may include more than one object or a combination of object and adverbial or object and complement:

> *The boy [subject] told [verb] his sister [object] a lie [object].*
> *The teacher [subject] wrote [verb] a report [object] very soon afterward [adverbial].*
> *This machine [subject] makes [verb] complex tasks [object] simple [complement].*

In all such cases everything that follows the subject is called the **predicate.**

There are a number of other possible structures, for instance, object, verb, subject, or object, subject, verb:

> *"Stop!" [object] ordered [verb] the police officer [subject].*
> *"Hold this," [object] he [subject] commanded [verb].*

In questions the order is often verb, subject, complement/adverbial:

> *Are [verb] you [subject] comfortable? [complement]*
> *Is [verb] her mother [subject] inside? [adverbial]*

Sometimes the adverbial appears first:

*Away went the train.*

The form of certain parts of the sentence may influence the form of other parts of the sentence. The conventions relating to **concord**, or **agreement**, affect verbs and associated subjects and possessive pronouns, and in certain circumstances they also apply to subjects and subject complements and to objects and object complements. Hence, if the subject of a verb is in the singular, then so must be the verb: *The girl is over there.* If the subject of a verb is in the plural, then so must be the verb: *The girls are over there.* Note, however, that there is never a requirement for an object and a verb to agree:

*The aircraft has four engines.*
*The hotel has few facilities.*

Other examples of instances where concord is of importance include the subjects and objects of reflexive verbs, which should always harmonize:

***He** blamed **himself** for the accident.*
***She** worked **herself** into an early grave.*

Subjects and possessives that precede related nouns have to be in agreement, too:

***They** lost **their** stake money.*
***We** love **our** new house.*

Subjects and subject complements should also be in concord where the complement consists of a noun or pronoun:

***He** is **a fool.***
***Those** are **less valuable items.***

The same is also true of objects and object complements where the complement consists of a noun or pronoun:

*She considered **him a good friend***
*He thought **them genuine antiques.***

The above rules hold true in most cases, but there are exceptions. In particular, confusion can sometimes arise where verbs apparently break the rules and appear in concord with the meaning of a subject (in terms of singular or plural) instead of following it grammatically (a phenomenon known as **notional concord**):

*Twenty dollars is too much to pay.*

Conversely, sometimes it may also be considered correct for the verb to agree with the part of the subject closest to it (**proximity concord**):

*A selection of products have been reduced in price.*

## TYPES OF SENTENCES

Sentences can range from verbless **minor sentences** of a single word (*When? Really? No!*) or a brief phrase (*No way! For sale. What now? No, of course not!*) to **major sentences** containing a verb and, in their fuller form, one or more clauses, including a subject, a verb, an object, and various modifiers. Major sentences, which can include statements, questions, instructions, exclamations, interjections, and vocatives, are not necessarily long and may be no more than a word or two. The most important requirement is that they are complete:

*See?*
*I know.*
*Help me!*
*You're kidding.*

Minor sentences do not contain a verb, but must make sense and be presented in sentence form. They can include exclamations, interjections, greetings, instructions, sayings, and shortened questions:

*What a shame!*
*Good evening.*
*For rent.*
*No swimming.*
*Cigarette?*

Sentences that contain more than one clause are sometimes termed **multiple sentences,** while those that comprise a single clause are called **simple sentences.** Multiple sentences can be further divided into **compound sentences** and **complex sentences.** Compound sentences contain two main clauses linked by a connecting word such as *and, but,* or *or:*

*She turned off the power, and the house went dark.*
*He called for help, but there was no one in the vicinity.*

Complex sentences contain a main clause and a subordinate clause and begin with *after, because, before, if, when, while,* etc.:

*I will call the office after I have finished here.*
*The team has taken shelter in the dugout while the storm continues.*

### *Statement*

A statement is a sentence that conveys information of some kind. It usually contains a subject, which precedes the verb, and ends with a period:

*The war has ended.*
*If nothing else happens, the case will be closed.*

Note that in some circumstances the subject may follow the verb:

*In went the crowd.*

### Question

A question is a sentence in which the writer or speaker requests a response. Questions usually contain a subject, which follows the verb (or part of it), and typically end with a question mark:

*Will you try again?*
*Is it snowing?*
*Are you better?*

Some questions can be answered with a simple affirmative or negative, while others (such as questions beginning with *how, what, when, where, who,* or *why*) require more extensive replies:

*What are you doing tonight?*
*Who are you going to meet?*
*Why did you do that?*

In the case of so-called **rhetorical questions,** it is often clear that the writer does not actually expect a reply and is merely using a question form to make a point or express frustration or some other emotion:

*Why do I have to do everything myself?*
*Why do things like this always happen to me?*

Another form of question is the **tag question,** in which a simple statement of fact is turned into a question by the addition of a tag such as *isn't it?* or *don't you?*:

*It's a great car, isn't it?*
*You like this color, don't you?*

Tag questions often invite a particular response to the question, but there are cases where no reply is actually invited at all, and the question is really operating as a statement:

*This is a real mess, isn't it?*
*They're not coming back, are they?*

Sometimes their purpose is to make a suggestion (*you don't have any ideas, do you?*), to make a request (*you couldn't lend me a hand, could you?*), or to convey anger or another strong emotion (*they didn't bother to tell me, did they?*).

### Directive

Directives include commands, instructions, requests, and warnings. **Commands** usually incorporate an imperative verb but do not necessarily have a subject. They often conclude with an exclamation mark, which conveys greater force:

*Pay attention!*
*Come here!*
*Don't do that!*

**Instructions** also contain an imperative verb and usually lack a subject. In contrast to commands, they do not usually end with an exclamation mark:

*Do not touch.*
*Press here.*
*Watch your head.*
*Bring to a boil.*

Some directives are less insistent than others. Some, indeed, are little more than polite requests or invitations to do something:

*Come in.*
*Have a seat.*
*Come to a party.*
*Join us over here.*
*Have a good time.*

Such entreaties are sometimes prefaced by the verb *do*, which serves to make an instruction sound more polite or adds emphasis to it:

*Do have a biscuit.*
*Do tell me all about it.*

### *Exclamation*

Exclamations are a type of sentence conveying surprise, anger, or other strong emotions. They may comprise major or minor sentences, varying in length from a single word to relatively lengthy clauses, and usually end with an exclamation point:

*Unbelievable!*
*Oh, no!*
*Don't do that!*

Some of the most commonly encountered exclamations begin with *how* or *what*:

*How lovely it is here!*
*What a fantastic performance!*

Exclamations differ in structure from statements and questions in that the object or complement often precedes the subject:

*How sad it was!*
*What a night that was!*

Sometimes, however, they may resemble negative questions in form, distinguished only by the exclamation point at the end:

*Isn't it awful!*
*Aren't they adorable!*

### *Interjection*

An interjection is a category of exclamation incorporating words used to express anger, surprise, pain, etc. Most interjections consist of a single word followed by an exclamation point (*ah! ha! mmm! oh! ouch! ugh! yes!*). Some are ordinary vocabulary words (*cool! great! thanks!*), while others have no other use (*hey! phew! ssh!*).

In most cases the use of interjections should be confined to spoken English, because they are widely considered too casual for most formal written contexts. They appear most often in direct reported speech (see the following main section).

> *"Hey! Quit spying on me!"*
> *"Mmm! This tastes great!"*

Particular care should be taken with regard to obscene or blasphemous expletives, which are very likely to cause offense, particularly when used in the wrong context.

Some interjections are inserted in the middle of sentences, typically to express hesitation, and therefore need no exclamation point:

> *We are—er—reluctant to commit further resources.*
> *Your services will—ah—no longer be needed.*

Elsewhere they can express delight, approval, gratitude, disappointment, disbelief, and other emotions.

### *Vocative*

A vocative is a word or phrase that specifies the person being addressed. It can take the form of a name (*Ted, Mr. Jones, Trigger*), a family title (*Father, Mom, Junior*), a term of endearment (*darling, sweetheart*), a job title (*nurse, governor*), a title of respect (*sir, your majesty*), an insult (*fool, numskull*), or a generic term for a particular group (*children, men*).

Vocatives may be variously used to draw the attention of a particular person, to distinguish an individual from a group, or to express attachment (or other feeling) toward a particular person. It is generally the case that vocatives are followed by a comma or period:

> *Come inside, sir, and we'll see what we can do.*
> *John, telephone the school.*
> *Good morning, Mr. Smith.*

## REPORTING SPEECH

Special rules apply to the reporting of speech in written form. In **direct speech** the words that a person has said are repeated exactly, usually enclosed by quotation marks:

> *"Would you like a coffee?" she inquired politely.*
> *"Tell me," he said at last, "everything you know about the organization."*
> *He whispered, "There's someone in the room."*

In **indirect speech** (otherwise called **reported speech**) the gist of what has been said is communicated without the actual words being repeated and without the insertion of quotation marks:

*He said he was less worried about his daughter now than he had been.*
*She asked where her husband was.*

In either form, sentences containing speech comprise two clauses: the reporting clause and the reported clause.

A **reporting clause** introduces or sets the tone for the reported clause. The reporting clause consists of a subject and a verb of speaking or writing, as well as any other related information (*Roger said; answered Tom; they shouted angrily*). In indirect speech the reporting clause always precedes the reported clause, but in direct speech it may be placed before, after, or in the middle of the reported clause. When it is inserted after or in the middle of the reported clause, it is set off by commas, and the verb is often placed before the subject (*said his mother; replied Bill*). When the reporting clause is placed at the beginning of the sentence, it is usual to follow it with a comma or colon, which appears before the opening quotation marks. It is also the convention to insert any closing punctuation related exclusively to the direct speech before the closing quotation marks (*see* QUOTATION MARKS, page 356). Note how the punctuation differs between reported clauses made up of one sentence and others made up of more than one sentence, particularly how a capital letter is used to reopen the quotation when it comprises multiple sentences:

*"Hold on a moment," she said, "while I think about that."*
*"Hold on a moment," she said. "We need to think about that."*

Where a text has two or more people involved in a conversation, it is common for the reporting clause to be omitted once it has been established whose turn it is to speak.

*"What do you mean by that?" demanded Higgins.*
*"What do you think I mean?" responded Davies.*
*"I'm not sure."*
*"Let me know when you are."*

Note also that the convention of beginning a new paragraph with each new speaker aids in distinguishing the individuals in a conversation (*see* PARAGRAPHING AND DIALOGUE, page 68).

The reporting clause may be omitted in so-called **free indirect speech:**

*She could not believe what he was telling her—how he had lost all their money, and how he could not remember the name of the man who had cheated him.*

It may also be left out in the case of so-called **free direct speech** (typically where the writer is expressing his or her own thoughts):

*I bought the house in the end, even though it's a ruin. Why do I love it so much?*

If the previous example were rendered in direct speech, the last two sentences would be separated by *I thought, I told myself,* or a similar construction.

A **reported clause** includes what was said or written, with or without quotation marks, as appropriate. In indirect speech what has been said or written is usually introduced by *that* or a word beginning with *wh-*:

*She said* ***that she would never go back there again.***
*The teacher told us* ***where they should look for the child.***
*He asked* ***which suitcase was ours.***

Note that in practice the word *that* may actually be omitted, but any *wh-* word must remain in place:

*He promised us [that] he would win.*
*She said [that] she would phone.*
*He asked what they were planning to do.*

Certain changes are made when direct speech is converted to reported speech. As well as the reporting clause being (usually) moved to the start of the sentence, personal pronouns are usually changed, (from *I* to *he* or *she*, from *we* to *they*, and from *you* to *I* or *we*, etc.), and changes to references to time and location may also need to be made:

*"There is no need to go until tomorrow," he said. [direct speech]*
*He said there was no need to go until the following day. [reported speech]*
*"Nothing will be decided until you get back from vacation," they told her. [direct speech]*
*They told her that nothing would be decided until she got back from vacation. [reported speech]*

Sometimes when converting, the words *if* or *whether* need to be inserted:

*"Is there any money left in the budget?" he asked. [direct speech]*
*He asked if there was any money left in the budget. [reported speech]*
*"Has the news been released yet?" they asked. [direct speech]*
*They asked whether the news had been released yet. [reported speech]*

Note that the tense of the verb in the reported clause changes from the present tense to the past tense:

*"I have no interest in the matter," she said. [direct speech]*
*She said she had no interest in the matter. [reported speech]*
*"I'm thinking about it," he assured us. [direct speech]*
*He assured us he was thinking about it. [reported speech]*

Similarly the future tense *will* changes to *would:*

> *"I will write something for the occasion," a local composer suggested. [direct speech]*
> *A local composer suggested he would write something for the occasion. [reported speech]*
> *"Time will tell," she commented. [direct speech]*
> *She commented that time would tell. [reported speech]*

The simple past tense in turn is transformed into the past perfect (pluperfect) tense:

> *"We hoped to get in free," they admitted. [direct speech]*
> *They admitted they had hoped to get in free. [reported speech]*
> *"We were trying to prevent an outbreak of violence," the police said. [direct speech]*
> *The police said they had been trying to prevent an outbreak of violence. [reported speech]*

(*See also* SEQUENCE OF TENSES, page 129.)

# 5

# Words in Use

## INTRODUCTION

As well as acquiring a good working knowledge of grammar, it is useful to be aware of how words are formed and how they are used in practice. Many pitfalls exist in language usage, and it is essential to know how to avoid making common mistakes.

Few people would claim perfect confidence in terms of usage, but the issues that often cause perplexity can usually be settled with little difficulty when the various relevant rules are understood and applied. Lack of familiarity with these rules lies at the root of much of this uncertainty. This chapter therefore surveys the vocabulary of English, including sections on word formation, words and phrases borrowed from other languages, and abbreviations. The chapter also discusses rules of spelling and how to refer to numbers, times, and dates in written texts. Finally, the chapter gives guidance on sensitive terms in such areas as gender, race, and physical and mental capability and discussion of the usage of slang.

## VOCABULARY

### Introduction

The term *vocabulary* may be defined as all the words that make up a language. Words are the basic units of speech and writing, and a wide vocabulary is generally respected as a sign of learning and intelligence. The choice of the right word can be of crucial importance in a person's daily dealings, whether it be in winning an argument, impressing a potential employer, pleasing or flattering another person, or conveying respect or seriousness of purpose.

It is estimated that there are some 1 billion speakers of English around the world (including those who speak English as a second language). The number of words a person may include in his or her personal vocabulary depends on a variety of factors, not least his or her age and education. Estimates of the size of the average English speaker's vocabulary range from 10,000 to 12,000 words for a 16-year-old to anything between 20,000 and 60,000 for a college graduate. It has been calculated that William Shakespeare drew on a vocabulary of between 18,000 and 25,000 words in his various writings.

Inevitably, every speaker or reader of English encounters hitherto unfamiliar words on a regular basis. Most people add new words to their vocabulary more or less unconsciously in the course of their everyday experience through imitation of what they hear others say, either face to face or via broadcast media, or from what they read in books, newspapers, and other written documents. It is, however, possible to widen your vocabulary in a more deliberate manner through the use of dictionaries, thesauruses, and other word books. Some people doggedly read a page or two of a dictionary every day in order to increase their vocabulary. Many more find that when they look up a word in a dictionary they are easily beguiled into reading neighboring entries that were formerly unfamiliar to them, or they find themselves browsing at random.

It may be useful to note that there is a difference between a person's **passive vocabulary** (the words he or she understands) and a person's **active vocabulary** (the words he or she actually uses). Every speaker or writer of English exercises personal discretion in deciding which words are suitable for use in formal contexts and which are acceptable only in informal surroundings. Making mistakes in this regard risks social embarrassment or, in the case of applying for a job or attracting a sponsor for instance, material disadvantage. However wide a person's active and passive vocabularies may be, there are always a number of words about which the person concerned is uncertain, whether it be with regard to their meaning, spelling, or usage. Removing this uncertainty by checking a word in a dictionary or other source enables a person to use that word with more confidence and in the right context (though, in view of the size of the English vocabulary, its place in an individual's lexicon of unfamiliar words is very likely to be quickly taken by another new word).

Each individual's personal vocabulary develops as he or she goes through life according to the influences of fashion, slang, the jargon of new technologies, and regional usages, to name but a few factors. Understanding new words is often important. Leaving aside the option of consulting a dictionary or other written authority, sometimes their meaning can be guessed at by their context or through knowledge of similar related words. Some appreciation of how words are formed can also help in unraveling meaning, and several aspects of word formation, spelling, and usage are discussed in the following pages.

## Understanding English Vocabulary

It is a common complaint among people learning to write and speak English that many words apparently fail to follow the same set of rules. Thousands of commonly used words behave in an irregular manner, taking unexpected and seeming unpredictable forms in the plural or in the past tense, for example. Words that sound the same may be spelled differently and be totally unconnected in meaning. Others may look completely different but actually mean exactly the same thing. The more one examines the vocabulary of English, the more it seems to disobey the rules.

In order to unravel these complexities, it is very helpful to have a broad understanding of how the language has acquired its volatile modern vocabulary, which is both its greatest glory and its deepest mystery. A brief overview of the historical development of the English vocabulary may help in appreciating and understanding the sometimes illogical ways in which different words behave, apparently in response to contradictory sets of rules.

Much of the answer lies in the fact that the vocabulary has been drawn not from one but from many different sources. Roughly half of the existing vocabulary of English was derived originally from Anglo-Saxon (Germanic) sources spoken in Britain from the fifth century A.D. to the Norman Conquest (1066), while the other half has been absorbed from French and other Romance languages or from other, more exotic borrowings from more far-flung parts of the world.

During the Old English period (c. 450–c. 1100) there were four main dialects of English: Northumbrian, Mercian, Kentish, and West Saxon. West Saxon gradually emerged as the dominant form, especially as regards writing, and many important Latin texts were translated into English using this particular form. From these Anglo-Saxon dialects came many ordinary vocabulary words in everyday use today, typically characterized by brevity, directness, and simplicity (*and, dead, house, is, sun*), and reflecting the influence of the island's Norse-speaking invaders in the fifth century (*dirt, squeak*). Many of these words were derived ultimately from a Proto-Indo-European language spoken in western Asia around 5000 B.C. This language was the origin of numerous other languages spoken in Europe and Asia, hence the obvious similarities between words across many languages spoken around the world.

The Middle English period (c. 1100–c. 1500) saw English divided into five main dialects, namely Northern (developing from Northumbrian), West Midlands and East Midlands (developing from Mercian), South Western (developing from West Saxon), and South Eastern (developing from Kentish). The vocabulary was further broadened through the introduction of French as the language of England's Norman invaders. As the language of the ruling class in England, French was considered more refined and sophisticated than the native English tongue and together with Latin became the formal and more complex language of high society and academia until English became the standard written form in the 15th century. Many of the multisyllabic words in common use today are of French, Latin, or Greek origin, although this fact does not necessarily mean that their simpler English equivalent was abandoned (hence the great richness of the modern English vocabulary, which frequently offers a number of choices for the same word). Sometimes the directness and clarity of an Anglo-Saxon version of a word is considered preferable to its more abstract French- or Latin-derived form (for example, *kill* instead of *eliminate* or *eradicate*); sometimes the latter may be preferred exactly because it is less direct or provocative or because it sounds more impressive.

Modern English describes the form of the language as used since around the year 1500. This period has witnessed the borrowing of many more words from other parts of the world as English-speaking peoples have come into contact with other cultures through exploration, colonization, and commerce. Source languages have ranged from Albanian and Afrikaans to Scandinavian and Welsh (*see* FOREIGN WORDS AND PHRASES, page 193). The vocabulary of modern English has been further extended through the adoption of thousands more Greek and Latin words, especially in the fields of science and academic study.

The process of change in the vocabulary is unceasing. The coining of new terms and the emergence of new meanings or usage are constant. Recent influences upon the vocabulary's development have included an explosion in technical terminology and jargon since the middle of the 20th century, necessitated by the commercialization of technology and the advent of the computer age.

## Word Formation

A greater understanding of how words operate can be gleaned through knowledge of the various processes by which they are formed and of the various classes into which they can be categorized beyond their basic grammatical identity as nouns, verbs, adjectives, and so on.

The study of the origin and development of words is called **etymology.** The best source of information about the etymology of a particular word is a good dictionary, although it is also possible to consult books dedicated to the study of word origins. The larger dictionaries often provide additional etymological information about individual words, suggesting which language a word might have come from as well as, perhaps, its original form and an indication of when it first appeared in the English language. Thus, to take one example, consulting a good dictionary about a word such as *soldier* will reveal the etymological information that it entered the English language in the 13th century, being derived from the Old French *soude* (meaning "army pay"), which itself came from the Late Latin *solidus* (meaning "gold coin" and originally "firm").

Because the English language as we know it is the product of a thousand years or more of continual (and continuing) development, many words have changed their spelling or meaning one or more times over the centuries. This factor may be of some significance if a reader is reading (or writing) a book or document of a historical character, whether it be a play by William Shakespeare or a legal paper dating back 100 years. Words that have famously, and sometimes unpredictably, changed their meaning include *nice* (formerly meaning *dainty* or *delicate* but now more generally indicating anything satisfactory in nature) and *gay* (formerly meaning *jolly* or *bright* but now relating almost exclusively to homosexuality).

Relatively few words in English are the product of pure invention, and most have evolved from or are related to other words. A large proportion of words in English are **blends** resulting from the combination of two or more existing words (*see* PORTMANTEAU WORDS on the next page). Another substantial class of words owes its existence to the addition (*see* PREFIXES AND SUFFIXES, page 185) or removal (*see* BACK FORMATION on the following page) of various affixes to existing words, which again may provide a clue as to meaning (thus *aqua-* signifies something to do with water, while *psycho-* indicates a connection with psychology). A relatively small number of words called **eponyms** began life as surnames, in which case the life of the person concerned may give an idea of the field to which a particular term is relevant: for instance, *newton* (after British physicist Isaac Newton) and *sousaphone* (after U.S. composer John Philip Sousa).

Of those words that have sprung up apparently independently of other existing words, there is usually no alternative but to have their meaning explained directly, either by another person or through consulting a dictionary or other written source. Many such words begin as taboo slang usages or obscure technical jargon before winning general acceptance into mainstream vocabulary. A great many more initially unfathomable words comprise borrowings from other languages, among them Latin, Greek, Arabic, Persian, French, and German, as well as more exotic sources such as Chinese, Hindi, and Kiswahili (*see* FOREIGN WORDS AND PHRASES, page 193).

## PORTMANTEAU WORDS

Some words are formed through the combination of two or more smaller words, resulting in a so-called portmanteau word (or **blend**) that incorporates the meanings of the original two words. Typically the new word is formed by taking the first part of one word and attaching it to the last part of another word. Widely familiar examples include *brunch* (from *breakfast* and *lunch*), *motel* (from *motor* and *hotel*), *docudrama* (from *documentary* and *drama*), and *smog* (from *smoke* and *fog*). By this process whole groups of words may be built through combining a particular stem (for example, *info*) with a host of other words (*infotainment, infomercial, infopreneurial*).

Note that portmanteau words are not always the product of two whole words but may be arrived at through the combination of one whole word with part of another word (thus, *foodie, dopey,* etc.). Most portmanteau words are coined as convenient responses to changing linguistic demands but, however useful, typically meet, on first introduction, with some resistance from those who consider them clumsy and artificial. Nonetheless, countless portmanteau words have entered the language and appear as a matter of course in respected dictionaries.

Because of doubts about the authenticity of many portmanteau words, especially when they are newly coined, they are sometimes written with a hyphen between the two parts of the word (as in *no-brainer* or *de-skilled*). These hyphens tend to be omitted as the word wins general acceptance.

## BACK FORMATION

Back formation describes a method of forming new words through the reduction of longer words by the removal of an assumed affix (which does not usually in reality exist). The majority of words formed in this manner are verbs derived from nouns or adjectives, although there are also examples of adjectives, adverbs, and nouns created in this way. Another group of words created through back formation consists of singular nouns derived from plural nouns. Most new words formed by back formation attract disapproving attention when first introduced and are likely to be considered grammatically incorrect. They are often dismissed as jargon or slang and widely disliked, but this negativity has not prevented hundreds of examples from being absorbed into mainstream usage, often within very few years. Some caution should be exercised, therefore, in using relatively recently coined back formations, especially in formal contexts.

The following table lists some accepted source words and the new words created from them through the process of back formation:

| Source Word | Back Formation |
|---|---|
| automation | automate |
| babysitting | babysit |
| burglar | burgle |
| curiosity | curio |
| diagnosis | diagnose |
| disgruntled | gruntled |
| donation | donate |
| dry cleaning | dry-clean |
| editor | edit |
| enthusiasm | enthuse |
| emotion | emote |
| extradition | extradite |
| groveling | grovel |
| house hunting | house-hunt |
| lazy | laze |
| liaison | liaise |
| oration | orate |
| pease | pea |
| peddler | peddle |
| reminiscence | reminisce |
| sculptor | sculpt |
| self-destruction | self-destruct |
| sightseeing | sightsee |
| statistics | statistic |
| taxicab | taxi |
| television | televise |
| typewriter | typewrite |

# SPELLING

For many people the correct spelling of words in the English language poses a considerable challenge, and few would claim perfect understanding of the various rules involved and the seemingly countless exceptions to them. Some justify inaccurate spelling by pointing out that the general meaning is usually still communicated, but this assumption is risky because even minor errors in some circumstances can lead to significant changes in meaning. In some cases, furthermore, misspellings may be interpreted as a reflection of a writer's carelessness or even ignorance and work against success in, for instance, job applications.

The problem stems chiefly from the historical fact that English spelling developed on the basis of etymologies (that is, the origins of words) as much as it did upon the phonetic qualities of words (that is, how they actually sound to the ear). In this, English differs from many other major languages, in which spellings are often largely phonetic. As a result of this process the way a word in English looks does not necessarily echo the way it sounds, just as the way it sounds is not necessarily obvious from the way it is spelled.

A single letter of the alphabet in English may represent more than one sound, or even no sound at all (as, for instance, is the case with the *b* in *subtle* or the *p* in *psychic*). Conversely, a single sound may be represented by not just one but by several different letters or by particular combinations of letters (as, for instance, is the case with the sound *oo*, which may be written as *oo, ou, ue,* or *ew,* among other ways). One tip here, though not an infallible one by any means, is that if a vowel sound is short, it is more likely to be represented by a single letter (*step, tap, whip*) than by multiple letters. Note, however, the role of the diphthong (that is, the addition of an upward gliding *y* sound to the sound of a vowel) in transforming what may look like a short sound into a longer one (as in *make, fight, lout, boat, boy*). The situation has been further complicated over the centuries through the absorption of numerous foreign words, whose different cultural origins are reflected in their spelling, and through long-term shifts in pronunciation.

In reality, however, the rules governing spelling in the English language are not quite so wayward and illogical as they may first appear, and there are general conventions that can provide guidance. Most people are taught to read as children either by sounding letters or by looking for recognizable visual patterns within unfamiliar words, methods that rely upon the fundamental truth that similar-looking arrangements of letters within different words are likely to sound the same and perhaps even be linked in meaning. Thinking of longer words in terms of their subsidiary parts (prefix, root, and suffix) may be helpful.

One way to learn how to spell a word is to "look, cover, write, check" (that is, look at the word, cover it up, write it down from memory, and then check to see if this new word matches the covered one). Another safeguard when uncertain how a word should be spelled is to write down the possible alternatives: In most cases the correct version will reveal itself simply by "feeling right." When these methods fail, the simplest solution is to look up the word in a dictionary.

## Spelling Rules

### -ABLE/-IBLE

The rule governing words ending with the suffixes *-able* and *-ible* dictates that words that have been borrowed from Latin generally take the suffix *-ible,* whereas *-able* is applied to all other words (and is much the most frequently encountered). This rule is of limited value, though, since it depends on a knowledge of the etymology of a given word. The best alternative way to choose a suffix is to see whether removal of the suffix would leave a complete word: If that is the case, then the correct suffix to use is probably *-able.* Note, however, that there are a number of words that do not obey this rule (for instance, *formidable, probable, accessible*). The final letters of a word before the suffix may provide another clue: If the word ends with a soft *c* or soft *g* or with the letters *ns, ss, ct, pt,* or *st,* then it is likely that *-ible* will be the correct form (*invincible, illegible, responsible, impossible, indestructible, susceptible, combustible*), although, again, there are exceptions (*intractable, unacceptable*).

If the above tests fail, the only solution is to familiarize yourself with the most common examples of both forms. Note that new coinages of this kind always take the suffix *-able;* no new words ending in *-ible* are being created.

The following lists include examples of commonly encountered words ending in *-able* or *-ible*. (*See also* WORDS ENDING IN -E, page 182.)

### -able

acceptable
adaptable
admirable
affable
affordable
agreeable
amenable
amiable
bearable
breakable
capable
comfortable
comparable
contactable
dependable
despicable
detestable
disagreeable
durable
employable
enjoyable
estimable
expandable
expendable
fashionable
flammable
formidable
hospitable
implacable
inevitable
intolerable
invariable
invulnerable
irritable
laughable
likable (or likeable)
lockable
malleable
marriageable
memorable
obtainable
palpable
peaceable
perishable
pitiable
probable
readable
reasonable
respectable
separable
tolerable
unacceptable
unflappable
unbearable
unbreakable
uncomfortable
unfashionable
unforgivable
unmissable
unobtainable
unreasonable
unrespectable
unshockable
unsinkable
untouchable
untraceable
unworkable
variable
viable
vulnerable
washable
watchable
workable

### -ible

accessible
admissible
audible
collapsible
collectible
combustible
compatible
comprehensible
contemptible
credible
deducible
defensible
destructible
digestible
divisible
edible
eligible
expressible
fallible
feasible
flexible
forcible
gullible
horrible
illegible
implausible
impossible
inaccessible
inaudible
incomprehensible
incontrovertible
incorrigible
incredible
indefensible
indelible
indestructible
indivisible
inedible
inexhaustible
infallible
inflexible
insensible
intangible
intelligible
invincible
invisible
illegible
indestructible
irascible
irresistible
irresponsible
irreversible
legible
negligible
ostensible
perceptible
permissible
plausible
possible
reducible
reprehensible
responsible
reversible
sensible
susceptible
suggestible
tangible
terrible
unintelligible
unsusceptible
visible

## -AR/-ER/-OR

It is easy to confuse these word endings, particularly since speakers often pronounce them in an identical fashion. The general rule is that the suffix *-er* (or simply *-r*) is the most likely ending used in the sense of "person who does this," but there are a limited number of exceptions where -*or* is the correct form and an even smaller number where -*ar* is appropriate. The following lists include examples of commonly encountered words ending in -*ar*, -*er*, or -*or*.

***-ar***

| | | |
|---|---|---|
| beggar | friar | scholar |
| burglar | liar | |

***-er***

| | | | |
|---|---|---|---|
| builder | farmer | leader | producer |
| dancer | fighter | lover | rider |
| designer | gunner | maker | ruler |
| driver | hunter | manufacturer | teacher |
| employer | keeper | miner | thinker |
| explorer | laborer | painter | worker |

***-or***

| | | | |
|---|---|---|---|
| actor | director | janitor | supervisor |
| author | distributor | persecutor | surveyor |
| aviator | governor | prosecutor | survivor |
| conductor | inheritor | prospector | tailor |
| contractor | inspector | reflector | visitor |
| contributor | inventor | resistor | |
| defector | investor | sailor | |

## -ED/-ING

Confusion can sometimes arise over the addition of the verb endings -*ed* and -*ing*, which can have varying effects upon the verb stem. In most cases the addition of such suffixes requires no change to the stem itself (*blinked, blinking; talked, talking*). There are exceptions, however, in which the stem may be altered. In the case of words that end in a consonant plus -*y*, the -*y* is dropped and the suffix -*ed* becomes -*ied*, while in certain words that end with a vowel plus -*y*, the usual rule of adding -*ed* is similarly dropped in favor of -*id*. The following list gives examples of such exceptions:

| | | |
|---|---|---|
| cry | crying | cried |
| fry | frying | fried |
| lay | laying | laid |
| pay | paying | paid |
| say | saying | said |
| spy | spying | spied |
| try | trying | tried |

(*See also* PARTICIPLES, page 124.)

## -EI-/-IE-

The letter combinations of -*ei*- and -*ie*- often express the same *ee* sound and are easily confused. In order to tell them apart most people rely on the time-honored rule "i before e except after c," and this advice is generally effective. Note, however, that a more complete rule is "i before e except after c, when the sound is long ee."

For examples of words that obey this well-known rule and of some of the few exceptions to it see below. Note particularly that the rule does not apply in words where *-ei-* represents the sound *ay.*

### *Examples*

| | | | |
|---|---|---|---|
| achieve | deceit | piece | sieve |
| belief | deceive | receipt | thief |
| brief | diesel | receive | wield |
| ceiling | field | relieve | yield |
| chief | grief | shield | |
| conceit | niece | shriek | |
| conceive | perceive | siege | |

### *Exceptions*

| | | | |
|---|---|---|---|
| ageism | Fahrenheit | neither | sovereign |
| beige | fancies | policies | species |
| caffeine | feign | protein | veil |
| codeine | foreign | reign | vein |
| counterfeit | freight | rein | weigh |
| deign | inveigle | seize | weight |
| eight | neigh | skein | weir |
| either | neighbor | sleigh | weird |

## -ER/-EST

The addition of *-er* and *-est* suffixes to adjectives to create comparative and superlative forms does not usually necessitate any change in the stem word (*large, larger, largest; small, smaller, smallest*), but there are occasions when a change is required.

In the case of words that end in a silent *-e*, this last letter is dropped when a suffix beginning with a vowel is added (*pale, paler, palest*). When a word ends with a consonant followed by *-y*, the final *-y* is replaced by *-i* before the suffix (*cheery, cheerier, cheeriest*). One-syllable words with a short vowel sound and ending in a single consonant have the final consonant doubled before the suffix (*glad, gladder, gladdest*). (*See also* COMPARATIVE AND SUPERLATIVE, page 109.)

## -ES/-S

The suffix *-s* is usually added in order to make a noun plural or to alter the present tense of verbs in the third person singular (*he, she,* or *it*). In cases where words end in *-ch, -s, -sh, -x,* or *-z,* however, *-es* is the appropriate form. See the lists below for examples.

### *-es*

| | | | |
|---|---|---|---|
| boxes | catches | lashes | pitches |
| blushes | chintzes | masses | sexes |
| bushes | foxes | matches | taxes |

***-s***

aims
caps
dogs
fires
hills
horses
joints
lawns
pillars
ropes
snakes

## -FS/-VES

Most nouns are made plural by the simple addition of an *-s* ending, but there are exceptions. The general rule is that plurals of nouns that end in a single letter *f* take the form *-ves,* although again there are exceptions to this.

***-fs***

beliefs
briefs
chiefs
dwarfs
griefs
gulfs
proofs
roofs

***-ves***

calves
halves
leaves
loaves
ourselves
scarves
sheaves
shelves
themselves
thieves
wives
wolves

## -IES/-YS

Nouns that end with *-y* are sometimes made plural by the simple addition of an *-s,* while others take the ending *-ies*. The rule is that the *-ys* ending applies where the word ends with a vowel plus *-y,* while the *-ies* ending is applied where the word ends with a consonant before the final *-y.*

***-ies***

armies
babies
charities
families
fancies
flies
homilies
huskies
lilies
pennies
skies
spies
sundries

***-ys***

bays
boys
days
holidays
journeys
pathways
rays
toys
trays
ways

## -ILY/-LY

Most words of one syllable that end in *-y* simply have *-ly* added in their adverbial form (*coy, coyly*), but there are a few exceptions to this rule in which the stem word is transformed (*day, daily; dry, drily*). In the case of words with more than one syllable that end in *-y,* the correct procedure is to replace the *-y* with *-ily* (*happy, happily; merry, merrily; unsteady, unsteadily*).

## -LLY/-LY

The general rule is that if an adjective ends in *-l,* then its adverbial form will take an *-lly* ending (*occasional, occasionally; playful, playfully*). Note, however, that if an adjective ends in *-ll*, the adverbial form is also spelled *-lly*, not with a triple *l* (*dull, dully*).

## -NES/-NNES

The creation of new nouns by the addition of the suffix *-nes* to an existing word can sometimes lead to confusion about the correct spelling. The rule is that if the existing word already ends with *-n*, the new word ending should be spelled *-nnes* (*meanness, thinness*).

## -OES/-OS

Most nouns ending in *-o* take an *-s* in the plural. There are, however, a number of exceptions to this rule that take the ending *-es*. Note that in a number of cases both ending are considered correct (for instance, *cargoes* and *cargos* or *volcanoes* and *volcanos*). Words ending in *o* that are shortened versions of longer words always take an *-s* ending (*photos*). The third person singular of the present tense of most verbs ending in a consonant and *-o* is formed by adding *-es* (*goes, vetoes*).

***-oes***

| | | | |
|---|---|---|---|
| buffaloes | grottoes | mangoes | tomatoes |
| dominoes | haloes | mottoes | tornadoes |
| echoes | heroes | potatoes | torpedoes |

***-os***

| | | | |
|---|---|---|---|
| cameos | folios | radios | silos |
| chinos | pianos | rhinos | studios |

## WORDS ENDING IN -E

The general rule is that when a suffix beginning with a vowel is added to a word that ends in *-e*, this final letter is dropped (*debate, debatable; monotone, monotonous; stare, staring, stared*). There are a few exceptions to the basic rule where dropping the *-e* might lead to confusion with other superficially similar but otherwise unrelated words (as in *singe, singeing*, as distinct from *sing, singing*). The final *-e* is also retained in the case of words ending with a soft *c* or *g* sound where the suffix begins with *a* or *o* (*changeable, peaceable, unmanageable*). Note that in a number of cases alternative spellings of the same word with and without the final *-e* before the suffix are considered acceptable (*likable, likeable; unsalable, unsaleable*).

Where an adjective ends with a consonant followed by *-le*, the adverbial form is created by replacing the final *-e* with *-y* (*horrible, horribly; subtle, subtly*). The final *-e* is usually retained in the case of suffixes beginning with a consonant, although there are rare exceptions to this rule (*truly; wholly*). (*See also* -ER/-EST, page 180.)

## WORDS ENDING IN -Y

Most words that end with a consonant plus *-y* have the *y* replaced by *i* when a suffix is tacked on (*beauty, beautiful; happy, happiness; marry, marriage*). There are a small number of exceptions to this rule, however, in which the

-*y* is either retained or replaced by *e* (*shyly, slyly, beauteous, piteous*). Words that end with a vowel plus -*y* usually retain the -*y* when combined with a suffix beginning with a vowel (*annoyance, joyous*).

## DOUBLING OF CONSONANTS

The doubling of consonants within words is the root cause of many spelling problems. There is no single rule that governs such doubling, but there are underlying guiding principles. Words that end with a single consonant have that consonant doubled when adding a suffix beginning with a vowel (*thin, thinner, thinnest; whip, whipping, whipped*). Another guideline is that the final consonant of a word is doubled when the addition of a suffix turns it into a word of a different class (*dig, digger; stop, stoppable*). Note also that the final consonant is often doubled with the addition of the suffix -*y* (*grit, gritty; sun, sunny*).

In the case of words with more than one syllable, the rule is that the final consonant doubles when the stress falls on the last syllable (*forget, forgetting; commit, committed; repel, repellent*) but not when the stress falls elsewhere (*bias, biased; carpet, carpeted; envelop, enveloped; unparalleled*).

The number of words with doubled consonants is far too large to make learning each one individually a realistic prospect. Perhaps the best approach is to think of such words as belonging to one of three categories of words, namely those with no double consonants, those with one pair of double consonants, and those with two (or more) pairs of double consonants. The following lists include examples of words with one pair and with two or more pairs of double consonants. (*See also* COMMONLY MISSPELLED WORDS, page 184.)

### *Words with One Pair of Double Consonants*

abbreviation
aberration
abyss
accede
accelerate
accident
accomplish
account
accurate
addendum
addition
affect
allergy
ammonia
aggrieved
appropriate
approval
approximate
arrest
assist
baffle
barrel
barricade
beginning
biennial
blubber
brilliant
cattle
cherry
collapse
collect
college
commemorate
commit
consummation
corridor
current
desiccated
disappear
disappoint
dissatisfied
dissemble
discuss
exaggerate
exceed
excellent
excess
garrulous
gorilla
happening
harass
illustrate
immediate
immigrate
imminent
immobile
immoral
kennel
kittenish
lasso
lattice
lullaby
massacre
medallion
millionaire
mutter
necessary
occasional
occult
occur
paraffin
parallel
passion
predecessor
proceed
procession
professional
proffer
purring
quarrel

*(continues)*

*(continued)*

questionnaire
resurrect
rosette
satellite
scissors
sheriff
slippery
sufficient
summer
syllable
terrible
terror
tomorrow
trigger
tyranny
vaccinate
vacillate

### *Words with Two or More Pairs of Double Consonants*

abbess
access
accessory
accommodation
accidentally
address
addressee
assassin
assessment
cassette
commission
committed
crossbreed
embarrass
guerrilla
happiness
mattress
millennium
oppress
possession
succeed
unnecessary

## Commonly Misspelled Words

The following list includes some of the more commonly misspelled words. (*See also* WORDS OFTEN CONFUSED, page 229.)

aberration
abbreviation
abysmal
accelerate
accessory
accommodate
accommodation
achieve
achievement
acoustics
acquaint
acquiesce
acrylic
address
adjourn
admissible
adolescent
advantageous
aggravate
ancillary
annihilate
anoint
anonymous
Antarctic
appalling
Arctic
asphalt
asphyxiate
assassinate
assessment
assimilate
authoritative
autumn
bankruptcy
beautiful
beginner
beginning
besiege
billionaire
bourgeois
buoyant
bureaucracy
caffeine
calendar
Caribbean
ceiling
census
chief
colossal
colleague
commemorate
commiserate
commissionaire
commitment
committee
concede
conceit
conceive
conscience
conscientious
conscious
consensus
corollary
corroborate
credibility
curriculum
deceive
definitely
desiccated
desperate
detach
dialogue
diarrhea
diphtheria
diphthong
disappear
disappoint
discipline
ecstasy
eighth
embarrass
embarrassed
embarrassment
exaggerate
exceed
excite
exhilarate
exorbitant
extrovert
exuberant
fascinate
fatigue
February
fluorescent
foreign
foreigner
forfeit
forty
four
fourth
friend
gauge
grammar
granddaughter
guarantee
guard
guerrilla
harass
harassed
harassment
height
heinous
hemorrhage
heterogeneous
honorary

hygiene
hypocrisy
idiosyncrasy
illegible
impeccable
inconceivable
indefinitely
independent
indispensable
innocuous
inoculation
inseparable
intercede
itinerary
jeopardize
legacy
liaise
liaison
lieutenant
liquefy
loose
lose
maintenance
maneuver
martyr
Massachusetts
medicine
Mediterranean
millennium
millionaire
miniature
minuscule
miscellaneous
mischievous
Mississippi
misspell
mnemonic
mortgage
necessarily
necessary
niece
noticeable
occasionally
occurrence
omission
omit
omitted
oscillate
parallel
paralleled
parliament
peccadillo
perceive
perennial
perseverance
personnel
playwright
pneumatic
Portuguese
possess
practitioner
precede
preceding
preparation
privilege
proceed
pronunciation
psychiatry
pursue
questionnaire
queue
receipt
receive
recommend
reconnaissance
relevant
relieve
remembrance
reminiscent
rendezvous
repertoire
resistant
responsible
restaurant
resuscitate
rhyme
rhythm
Romania
sacrilege
sacrilegious
schizophrenia
secretary
seize
separate
sergeant
sheriff
siege
skillful
subterranean
success
successful
suddenness
supersede
tariff
temporarily
temporary
threshold
traveler
truly
unnecessary
unwieldy
vaccination
vacuum
variegated
veterinary
Wednesday
weight
weird
whether
wholly
withhold

# PREFIXES AND SUFFIXES

Many longer single words can be broken down into constituent elements, namely a stem word providing the base of the longer word and any segments (**affixes**) added onto it. Affixes can be subdivided into **prefixes** (added to the beginning of the stem word) and **suffixes** (added to the end of the stem word).

A basic knowledge of the way in which prefixes and suffixes operate can be very useful when trying to work out the meaning of an otherwise unfamiliar word. By linking an unfamiliar coinage with a more familiar word sharing the same prefix or suffix, you can often make an educated guess about the new word's meaning. By the same token, it is worth spending time becoming conversant with the meaning of common prefixes and suffixes if only to avoid confusing them and thus being misled as to a word's actual meaning.

## Prefixes

A prefix may be added to the beginning of an existing word to form an entirely new coinage, usually an elaboration of the original word. Sometimes, for instance, the prefix serves to provide a new verbal form of an accepted noun (such as *befriend* from *friend*) or converts a noun into an adjective (as with *antiterrorist* or *prohunting*). Sometimes it may be used to create a new word signifying the opposite of the original (usually the case with such prefixes as *de-*, *dis-*, *in-*, *non-*, and *un-*). Often, by a process known as **assimilation,** a prefix indicating the opposite of something is adjusted in form to match the existing word, as for instance in the case of *in-*, which transforms as a prefix to produce such words as *irregular* (from *regular*), *illegible* (from *legible*), or *immortal* (from *mortal*).

Many prefixes are married to the original without any kind of break, but some are tacked onto the original word with a hyphen, especially where the new word is felt to be a slightly cumbersome or relatively unfamiliar development of the original or where it is agreed the prefix needs to be kept distinct to promote clarity of meaning (as in *self-harm* or *pro-Chinese*). Often the hyphen may be dropped subsequently as the application of the prefix becomes more widely accepted. For discussion on the use of hyphens with prefixes, see HYPHEN (page 350).

Restraint should be exercised in the creation of new coinages through the addition of prefixes, since some readers may find such compounds as *macroscopic* or *megabucks* jargonistic or slangy. Some compounds, however, produced by the addition of a prefix have continued in use long after the original word has disappeared from the common vocabulary. Examples of this phenomenon include such words as *uncouth* and *unkempt*. In some cases, the prefix has become so well known it has assumed the status of a word in its own right (as in *anti, extra,* and *ultra*).

The application of prefixes and suffixes accounts for a substantial proportion of new additions to the English language (particularly true in relation to technological jargon). Knowing what a prefix means can assist greatly in the deciphering of a new word upon first encounter. The majority of prefixes come ultimately from Greek and Latin, and knowledge of these languages can provide a clue to their meaning.

The following table lists some of the more common prefixes, together with their meanings and examples of words created through their use:

| Prefix | Meaning(s) | Example(s) |
|---|---|---|
| a- | not | asymmetry |
| ab- | away from | abduct |
| ad- | toward | advance |
| aero- | air | aerodynamic |
| ambi- | both | ambidextrous |
| ante- (*See* WORDS OFTEN CONFUSED) | before | antecedent |
| anthrop(o)- | human | anthropology |
| anti- (*See* WORDS OFTEN CONFUSED) | against | antiwar |
| aqua- | water | aquarium |
| arch- | chief | archenemy |
| astro- | stars | astronaut |
| audio- | sound | auditorium |
| auto- | self | autobiographical |
| be- | surround | besiege |
| | cause to be | befriend |

| Prefix | Meaning(s) | Example(s) |
|---|---|---|
| bi- | two | bipolar |
| biblio- | book | bibliography |
| bio- | biological | biodiversity |
| by- | near | bystander |
| | secondary | by-product |
| centi- | hundred | centimeter |
| chron(o)- | time | chronology |
| circum- | around | circumnavigate |
| co-/col-/com-/con-/cor- | together | combination |
| | | correlate |
| contra- | opposite | contradict |
| counter- | against | counterpart |
| crypt(o)- | hidden | cryptography |
| cyber- | computer | cyberspace |
| de- | remove | deduct |
| | do the reverse | decelerate |
| deca- | ten | decahedron |
| deci- | one-tenth | decimal |
| demi- | half | demigod |
| di- | two | dialogue |
| dia- | through | diameter |
| dis- | not | dissimilar |
| | opposite | disconnect |
| duo- | two | duologue |
| dys- | abnormal | dysfunctional |
| e- | electronic | e-mail |
| eco- | ecological | ecotourism |
| electr(o)- | electricity | electromagnetic |
| em-/en- | put in or on | enthrone |
| | surround | enmesh |
| | | embrace |
| | cause to be | enthrone |
| end(o)- | inside | endoscope |
| epi- | above | epidermis |
| | after | epilogue |
| equi- | equal | equitable |
| Eur(o)- | European | Eurocentric |
| ex- | former | ex-boxer |
| | out of | exclude |
| extra- | outside | extracurricular |
| for- | reject | forgo |
| | prohibit | forbid |
| fore- | in front of | forehead |
| geo- | earth | geology |
| giga- | billion | gigawatt |
| hect(o)- | hundred | hectare |
| hemi- | half | hemisphere |
| hemo- | blood | hemorrhage |

*(continues)*

*(continued)*

| Prefix | Meaning(s) | Example(s) |
|---|---|---|
| hepta- | seven | heptathlon |
| hetero- | other | heterosexual |
| hexa- | six | hexagonal |
| homo- | same | homosexual |
| hydro- | water | hydroelectric |
| hyper- (*See* WORDS OFTEN CONFUSED) | huge | hypermarket |
| | excessive | hyperactive |
| hypo- (*See* WORDS OFTEN CONFUSED) | under | hypothermia |
| ig-/il-/im-/in-/ir- | not | ignominious |
| | | improbable |
| | | insoluble |
| il-/im-/in-/ir- | into | infiltrate |
| infra- | below | infrared |
| inter- (*See* WORDS OFTEN CONFUSED) | between | intermediary |
| intra- (*See* WORDS OFTEN CONFUSED) | within | intravenous |
| intro- (*See* WORDS OFTEN CONFUSED) | inward | introvert |
| iso- | equal | isobar |
| kilo- | thousand | kilometer |
| macro- | large | macrocosm |
| mal- | bad | malfunction |
| mega- | huge | megabucks |
| meta- | change | metamorphosis |
| | concerned with | metamathematics |
| | behind or after | metaphase |
| micro- | very small | microbe |
| mid- | middle | midterm |
| milli- | one thousandth | millimeter |
| mini- | small | minimal |
| mis- | incorrect | misfire |
| mon(o)- | one | monorail |
| multi- | many | multiple |
| neo- | new | neologism |
| neuro- | nerves | neurotic |
| non- | not | nonverbal |
| ob- | against | obstacle |
| oct(a/o)- | eight | octagon |
| omni- | all | omnivorous |
| ortho- | correct | orthodox |
| out- | beyond | outreach |
| | outside | outhouse |
| over- | above | overcoat |
| | too much | overheat |
| pan- | universal | pantheon |
| para- | beside | paramilitary |
| | beyond | paranormal |
| pent(a)- | five | Pentagon |
| peri- | around | perimeter |

| Prefix | Meaning(s) | Example(s) |
|---|---|---|
| phil- | loving | philanthropist |
| photo- | light | photograph |
| physio- | natural | physiology |
| | physical | physiotherapy |
| poly- | many | polygamy |
| post- | after | postgraduate |
| pre- | before | prenuptial |
| pro- | for | pro-Chinese |
| | substitute for | pronoun |
| proto- | first | prototype |
| pseudo- | false | pseudonym |
| psycho- | mind | psychologist |
| pyro- | fire | pyromaniac |
| quad- | four | quadruple |
| re- | again | restart |
| | back | return |
| retro- | backward | retroactive |
| self- | self | self-abuse |
| semi- | half | semiretired |
| socio- | society | sociologist |
| sub- | below | subterranean |
| super- | more than | supercriminal |
| supra- | above | supranational |
| sur- | over | surcharge |
| | beyond | surpass |
| sym-/syn- | together with | sympathetic |
| | | synchronous |
| techno- | technology | technophobia |
| tele- | at a distance | television |
| the(o)- | God | theology |
| thermo- | heat | thermodynamic |
| trans- | across | transcontinental |
| tri- | three | triumvirate |
| turbo- | turbine-driven | turbo-charged |
| ultra- | beyond | ultraviolet |
| | extremely | ultrasensitive |
| un- | not | uncontested |
| | opposite | unleashed |
| under- | below | underpass |
| | less than | underestimate |
| uni- | one | unicycle |
| vice- | deputy | vice-chancellor |
| video- | visual | videotape |

## Suffixes

Suffixes are sometimes appended to stem words to form new words, which can include nouns, verbs, adjectives, and adverbs. The addition of such suffixes as *-s* or *-ed* creates the inflected forms of verbs (as in *walks, walked, walking*) or indicates the plural of nouns (as in *cars, tables, wasps*).

The following table lists some of the more common suffixes, together with their meanings and examples of words created through their use:

| Suffix | Meaning(s) | Example(s) |
|---|---|---|
| -able (*See* SPELLING RULES, page 177) | capable of | readable |
| | causing | comfortable |
| -age | of a group | baggage |
| | action | passage |
| | state | bondage |
| | fee | postage |
| -aholic/-oholic | addicted to | alcoholic |
| -al | action | rebuttal |
| | relating to | practical |
| -an | belonging to, coming from | European |
| | typical of | Elizabethan |
| -ance/-ancy | indicating a state or condition | resemblance |
| -ant | causing or performing | pleasant |
| -ar (*See* SPELLING RULES, page 178) | of, belonging to, or like | linear |
| -ary | of or related to | cautionary |
| | connected with | missionary |
| -ate | possessing | fortunate |
| | having a certain function | electorate |
| -atic | of the nature of | problematic |
| -ation | action, state, or condition | discoloration |
| -cide | killing | suicide |
| -cy | state or quality | lunacy |
| -dom | state or condition | freedom |
| | domain | earldom |
| | group of persons | officialdom |
| -ed | in the past | happened |
| | possessing | quickwitted |
| -ee | recipient | addressee |
| | of a specified group | devotee |
| -eer | concerned with | engineer |
| -en | become | whiten |
| | made of | earthen |
| -ence/-ency | state, condition, or quality | benevolence |
| -ent | causing or performing | astringent |
| -er (*See* SPELLING RULES pages 178, 180) | more | slower |
| | doing or involved in | worker |
| | living in | New Yorker |
| | characterized by | teenager |
| -ery/-ry | place of activity | brewery |
| | group of things | crockery |
| | condition | slavery |
| | the practice of | wizardry |

| Suffix | Meaning(s) | Example(s) |
|---|---|---|
| -es | plural | bushes |
| -ese | place of origin or language | Japanese |
| -esque | of a specified character | statuesque |
| -ess | feminine | waitress |
| -est | most | longest |
| -ette | small | kitchenette |
| | feminine | majorette |
| -fold | multiplied by | threefold |
| -ful | characterized by | soulful |
| | able to or helpful | useful |
| | amount specified | mouthful |
| -fy/-ify | make or become | petrify |
| -gon | angle | polygon |
| -hood | state, condition | childhood |
| | body of persons | priesthood |
| -i | of a region or people | Pakistani |
| -ian | belonging to, coming from | Egyptian |
| | expert in | technician |
| -ible (*See* SPELLING RULES, page 177) | capable of | collectible |
| | causing | contemptible |
| -ic/-ical | relating to | comical |
| -ice | practice of | service |
| -ics | a science or art | optics |
| | a specified activity | acrobatics |
| -ide | a chemical compound | bromide |
| -ie | informal name for | nightie |
| | affectionate diminutive | lassie |
| -ine | of or relating to | divine |
| -ing | past participle | walking |
| | action or result | wedding |
| | material | sheeting |
| -ion | action, process, or result | celebration |
| -ious | by or full of | ambitious |
| -ish | of or relating to | foolish |
| | somewhat | yellowish |
| | of a country or language | English |
| | approximately | tennish |
| -ism | doctrine, theory, or system | socialism |
| | action, process, or result | exorcism |
| | condition or quality | modernism |
| | prejudice or discrimination | ageism |
| -ist | adherent or follower | communist |
| | involved in a particular field | botanist |
| | user of | motorist |
| | characterized by | pessimist |
| -ite | follower of | Jacobite |
| | fossil or mineral | dolomite |
| | native or inhabitant of | Israelite |

*(continues)*

*(continued)*

| Suffix | Meaning(s) | Example(s) |
|---|---|---|
| -itis | disease or condition | peritonitis |
| -ity | state or condition | fragility |
| -ive | having the quality of | massive |
| | causing | digestive |
| -ize/-ise | make or become | sterilize |
| -less | free from | fearless |
| -let | diminutive form of | booklet |
| -like | resembling | lifelike |
| -ling | diminutive form of | duckling |
| -logy | science or subject | astrology |
| -ly | having the quality of | manly |
| | happening regularly | weekly |
| -man | person fulfilling a role | salesman |
| -ment | action, result, or state | agreement |
| -most | the furthest | innermost |
| -ness | condition, state, or quality | eagerness |
| -nik | practitioner or supporter of | refusenik |
| -oid | resembling | anthropoid |
| -or (*See* SPELLING RULES, page 178) | person or thing doing something | actor |
| | activity, condition, or state | horror |
| -orya | place where | dormitory |
| | having a quality | illusory |
| -ous | full of | glorious |
| -phile | lover of or loving | Anglophile |
| -phobia | fear of | agoraphobia |
| -s | plural | bees |
| -'s | of or belonging to | person's |
| -ship | condition, quality, or state | comradeship |
| | skill | workmanship |
| | group of | fellowship |
| -some | causing | tiresome |
| -ster | belonging to | gangster |
| -th | adjectival number | fourth |
| | process or state | growth |
| -ty | state or condition | frailty |
| -ward/-wards | expressing direction | backward |
| -ways | expressing direction or manner | lengthways |
| -wise | in such a manner | likewise |
| | with regard to | moneywise |
| -woman | woman fulfilling a role | Scotswoman |
| -y | characterized by | lucky |
| | affectionate diminutive | sonny |
| | act of doing something | inquiry |
| | condition, quality, or state | jealousy |

# FOREIGN WORDS AND PHRASES

Many words and phrases in the English language have been absorbed from other cultures through the centuries. Their meaning in the source language has in most cases been preserved, although the pronunciation may have changed, sometimes quite radically. Some foreign words or phrases (such as *pajamas* or *tempo*) have become so familiar to English speakers they are treated no different from any others, but many more (such as *de rigueur* or *persona non grata*) are still treated as essentially foreign words and may be picked out in italics within a written text (*see* ITALICS, page 352). Take note, however, that foreign proper nouns or names of foreign institutions (for example, München, Folketing, Universidad de las Américas) are not italicized. On plurals of foreign words and phrases, see page 104.

Because their linguistic roots are different, it is not always easy to discern the meaning of such words and phrases, unless the reader has some prior knowledge of the language in question. It is not, however, necessary to be well read in the source language to use a word or phrase that has been absorbed into modern English. By spending a little time familiarizing yourself with the meaning of some of the more useful examples (many of which are commonly encountered in everyday speech and writing), it is easily possible to add them to one's own passive, or even active, vocabulary. It soon becomes apparent that many seemingly alien words and phrases extracted from foreign languages have relatively simple meanings, and writers should not be afraid of considering their use where the context seems appropriate. Overuse of such words and phrases in the wrong context should, however, be avoided, because their inclusion can make a piece of writing seem mannered and pretentious.

The following table lists some of the more commonly used foreign words and phrases adopted by English speakers and writers, together with their source language and meaning:

| Word or Phrase | Source | Meaning |
|---|---|---|
| ab initio | Latin | from the beginning |
| ab origine | Latin | from the beginning of the world |
| abseil | German | to lower oneself by rope |
| a cappella | Italian | unaccompanied |
| accelerando | Italian | getting faster |
| actualité | French | truth |
| actus Dei | Latin | act of God |
| ad absurdum | Latin | to the point of absurdity |
| adagio | Italian | at a relaxed pace |
| addendum | Latin | addition or appendix |
| à deux | French | for two people |
| ad finem | Latin | to the end |
| ad hoc | Latin | for this special purpose |
| adieu | French | farewell |
| ad infinitum | Latin | to infinity |

(continues)

*(continued)*

| Word or Phrase | Source | Meaning |
|---|---|---|
| adios | Spanish | farewell |
| ad lib | Latin | spontaneous, extemporized |
| ad nauseam | Latin | interminably |
| Adonis | Greek | handsome young man |
| ad rem | Latin | to the purpose |
| aegis | Greek | auspices |
| affidavit | Latin | written statement |
| aficionado | Spanish | enthusiast |
| agent provocateur | French | spy, secret agent |
| agitprop | Russian | propaganda |
| agoraphobia | Greek | fear of open spaces |
| aide-de-camp | French | military aide |
| aide-mémoire | French | reminder |
| à la | French | in the manner of |
| à la carte | French | from a separately priced menu |
| à la mode | French | fashionable |
| al dente | Italian | lightly cooked |
| al fine | Italian | to the end |
| alfresco | Italian | in the open air |
| algebra | Arabic | arithmetic using letters |
| alias | Latin | an assumed name |
| alibi | Latin | defensive plea |
| allegro | Italian | brisk |
| alma mater | Latin | a person's place of education |
| al segno | Italian | repeat from the point indicated |
| alter ego | Latin | a person's other self |
| alumnus | Latin | former student |
| amanuensis | Latin | assistant |
| amigo | Spanish | friend |
| amok | Malay | wild, uncontrollably |
| amour propre | French | self-esteem |
| ancien régime | French | the old order |
| andante | Italian | moderately slowly |
| angst | German | anxiety |
| anno Domini | Latin | year of the Lord |
| annus mirabilis | Latin | year of wonders |
| anorak | Danish | weathproof jacket |
| ante meridiem (A.M.) | Latin | before noon, morning |
| apartheid | Afrikaans | racial segregation |
| aperitif | French | alcoholic appetizer |
| a posteriori | Latin | empirically |
| apparatchik | Russian | underling |
| a priori | Latin | deductive |
| apropos | French | opportunely, relevant |
| archipelago | Italian | chain of islands |
| argot | French | dialect, idiom |
| armada | Spanish | fleet, large group |

| Word or Phrase | Source | Meaning |
|---|---|---|
| Armageddon | Greek | final battle |
| arpeggio | Italian | notes of a chord |
| assassin | Arabic | murderer |
| à trois | French | for three people |
| attaché | French | diplomatic officer |
| au contraire | French | on the contrary |
| au courant | French | up-to-date |
| au fait | French | well-informed |
| auf Wiedersehen | German | farewell |
| au gratin | French | with cheese |
| au naturel | French | naked |
| au pair | French | foreign family help |
| au revoir | French | farewell |
| avant-garde | French | in the forefront |
| badinage | French | banter |
| baguette | French | small loaf of white bread |
| baksheesh | Persian | bribe or gratuity |
| balaclava | Russian | knitted headwear |
| bandanna | Hindi | cloth worn on the head or around the neck |
| barbecue | Spanish | open-air grill |
| basque | French | tight-fitting bodice |
| bazaar | Persian | market or store |
| beau geste | French | noble gesture |
| beau monde | French | high society |
| belle | French | beautiful girl |
| berserk | Old Norse | frenzied |
| bête noire | French | detested person or thing |
| bijou | French | small but elegant |
| billet-doux | French | love letter |
| bistro | French | café or wine bar |
| bivouac | French | rudimentary encampment |
| blasé | French | indifferent |
| blitz | German | intensive assault |
| bona fide | Latin | in good faith |
| bonanza | Spanish | lucky success |
| bon appétit | French | enjoy your meal |
| bonhomie | French | geniality |
| bonjour | French | good morning |
| bon mot | French | quip, witticism |
| bon viveur | French | lover of the good life |
| bon voyage | French | farewell |
| boudoir | French | lady's bedroom |
| bouquet garni | French | mixed herbs |
| bourgeois | French | middle-class |
| boutique | French | shop |
| brasserie | French | small restaurant |
| bric-a-brac | French | odds and ends |

*(continues)*

*(continued)*

| Word or Phrase | Source | Meaning |
|---|---|---|
| brio | Italian | vivacity |
| buenas noches | Spanish | good night |
| cabaret | French | nightclub entertainment |
| cadenza | Italian | closing passage |
| cadre | French | select group of persons |
| canapé | French | appetizer |
| canoe | Spanish | small lightweight boat |
| canyon | Spanish | deep valley |
| capo | Italian | chief |
| carpe diem | Latin | seize the moment |
| carte blanche | French | free license |
| casus belli | Latin | cause of hostilities |
| cause célèbre | French | notorious scandal or person |
| caveat | Latin | warning |
| caveat emptor | Latin | let the buyer beware |
| c'est la guerre | French | expression of resignation |
| c'est la vie | French | that's life |
| chargé d'affaires | French | diplomatic officer |
| chef d'oeuvre | French | masterpiece |
| che sarà sarà | Italian | what will happen, will happen |
| chez | French | at the house of |
| chiaroscuro | Italian | light and shade |
| chic | French | fashionable |
| chutzpah | Yiddish | self-confidence, audacity |
| ciao | Italian | farewell |
| cliché | French | overused expression or theme |
| coiffure | French | hairstyle |
| comme ci comme ça | French | so-so |
| compos mentis | Latin | sane |
| concierge | French | doorkeeper, porter |
| contretemps | French | argument, something unfortunate |
| cordon sanitaire | French | protective barrier |
| cortège | French | retinue |
| coup de grâce | French | fatal blow |
| coup d'état | French | revolution |
| crèche | French | day nursery |
| crème de la crème | French | the very best |
| crescendo | Italian | increasing in volume or force |
| cri de coeur | French | heartfelt appeal |
| cum laude | Latin | with honors |
| curriculum vitae | Latin | career record |
| debacle | French | disaster |
| debut | French | first appearance |
| de facto | Latin | actually |
| déjà vu | French | already seen or experienced |
| de jure | Latin | by right |
| démodé | French | outmoded |

| Word or Phrase | Source | Meaning |
|---|---|---|
| denouement | French | final outcome |
| de rigueur | French | required |
| deus ex machina | Latin | contrived solution |
| diktat | German | official command |
| diminuendo | Italian | decreasing in volume |
| distingué | French | distinguished |
| distrait | French | distracted |
| ditto | Italian | as before |
| dolce vita | Italian | the soft life |
| doppelgänger | German | double |
| double entendre | French | double meaning |
| dramatis personae | Latin | cast of a performance |
| du jour | French | of the day |
| eau de toilette | French | scented perfume |
| ecce homo | Latin | behold the man |
| éclat | French | acclaim, ostentation |
| élan | French | enthusiasm, zest |
| émigré | French | emigrant |
| éminence grise | French | power behind the scenes |
| en bloc | French | collectively |
| enchanté | French | charmed |
| encore | French | again |
| en croûte | French | in pastry |
| en famille | French | at home |
| enfant terrible | French | unruly rebel |
| en masse | French | in a body |
| ennui | French | boredom |
| en passant | French | incidentally, by the way |
| en route | French | on the way |
| ensemble | French | group |
| en suite | French | in a series, connected |
| entente | French | agreement between nations |
| entente cordiale | French | cordial agreement |
| entre nous | French | between ourselves |
| entrez | French | enter or introduction |
| ergo | Latin | therefore |
| erratum | Latin | error |
| esprit de corps | French | team spirit |
| et alia (et al.) | Latin | and others |
| et cetera (etc.) | Latin | and so on |
| eureka | Greek | I have found it |
| ex cathedra | Latin | with official authority |
| exempli gratia (e.g.) | Latin | for example |
| ex gratia | Latin | voluntary |
| exit | Latin | goes out |
| ex libris | Latin | from the library of |
| ex officio | Latin | by virtue of a person's office |

*(continues)*

*(continued)*

| Word or Phrase | Source | Meaning |
|---|---|---|
| exposé | French | revelation, exposure |
| ex post facto | Latin | after the fact, retrospective |
| extempore | Latin | unprepared |
| factotum | Latin | general assistant |
| fait accompli | French | irreversible deed |
| farrago | Latin | jumble |
| faux | French | artificial |
| faux pas | French | social blunder |
| femme fatale | French | dangerously seductive woman |
| fête | French | festival, fair, party |
| fiancé | French | man engaged to be married |
| fiancée | French | woman engaged to be married |
| fiasco | Italian | chaos, disaster |
| fiesta | Spanish | festival |
| fin de siècle | French | end of the century |
| finesse | French | refinement, adroitness |
| flambé | French | in flaming liquor |
| forte | Italian | loud |
| fracas | French | clamor, uproar |
| garni | French | served with a garnish |
| gateau | French | cake |
| gauche | French | awkward |
| genre | French | category, style |
| ghetto | Italian | minority quarter of a city |
| gigolo | Italian | paid male escort |
| goujon | French | strip of chicken or fish |
| goulash | Hungarian | meat stew |
| gourmet | French | lover of fine food |
| graffiti | Italian | words written in a public place |
| gratis | Latin | free |
| gravitas | Latin | solemnity |
| guerrilla | Spanish | irregular soldier |
| habeas corpus | Latin | court writ |
| habitué | French | regular frequenter |
| hasta la vista | Spanish | farewell |
| haute couture | French | high fashion |
| haute cuisine | French | elaborate cuisine |
| hoi polloi | Greek | common herd |
| hors de combat | French | out of action |
| hors d'oeuvre | French | appetizer |
| hubris | Greek | pride, self-confidence |
| ibidem (ibid.) | Latin | in the same place |
| idem (id.) | Latin | already mentioned |
| id est (i.e.) | Latin | that is |
| imbroglio | Italian | confusion |
| impasse | French | deadlock |
| impresario | Italian | promoter, sponsor |

| Word or Phrase | Source | Meaning |
|---|---|---|
| in absentia | Latin | in the absence of |
| in camera | Latin | privately |
| incognito | Latin | under a concealed identity |
| incommunicado | Spanish | not in communication |
| in extremis | Latin | at the point of death |
| in flagrante delicto | Latin | caught redhanded |
| ingénue | French | naive young woman |
| in loco | Latin | instead of |
| in memoriam | Latin | in memory of |
| in situ | Latin | in its natural position |
| in toto | Latin | completely |
| in transit | Latin | on the way |
| in utero | Latin | in the womb |
| in vino veritas | Latin | in wine there is truth |
| in vitro | Latin | in a test tube |
| ipso facto | Latin | by the very fact |
| je ne sais quoi | French | indefinable quality |
| jihad | Arabic | holy war |
| joie de vivre | French | enjoyment of life |
| juggernaut | Hindi | unstoppable force or object |
| junta | Spanish | ruling political faction |
| kamikaze | Japanese | suicidal |
| kaput | German | dead, out of action |
| kitsch | German | cheap, lacking in taste |
| kudos | Greek | prestige |
| laissez-faire | French | free choice |
| largesse | French | generosity |
| leitmotif | German | recurring theme |
| lèse-majesté | French | disrespect |
| libretto | Italian | text of a musical show |
| lingua franca | Italian | common language |
| locum tenens | Latin | temporary substitute |
| macho | Spanish | aggressively male |
| maelstrom | Dutch | whirlpool, turbulence |
| maestro | Italian | composer, conductor, master |
| mafia | Italian | criminal organization |
| magnum opus | Latin | masterpiece |
| maître d'hôtel | French | headwaiter |
| malaise | French | unease |
| mañana | Spanish | tomorrow, the indefinite future |
| manifesto | Italian | declaration of policy |
| mano a mano | Spanish | direct confrontation |
| manqué | French | would-be |
| matériel | French | equipment, ammunition |
| mea culpa | Latin | I am to blame |
| mélange | French | medley |
| melee | French | confused struggle |

*(continues)*

*(continued)*

| Word or Phrase | Source | Meaning |
|---|---|---|
| memento mori | Latin | a reminder that you must die |
| ménage | French | household |
| ménage à trois | French | relationship of three people |
| merci | French | thank you |
| moccasin | Algonquian | soft shoe |
| modus operandi | Latin | method, procedure |
| modus vivendi | Latin | practical compromise |
| mogul | Persian | magnate |
| mot juste | French | appropriate word |
| mutatis mutandis | Latin | with the necessary changes made |
| nada | Spanish | nothing |
| née | French | born |
| nil desperandum | Latin | never despair |
| nirvana | Sanskrit | spiritual enlightenment |
| noblesse oblige | French | the obligations of nobility |
| noli me tangere | Latin | do not touch me |
| nom de guerre | French | pseudonym |
| nom de plume | French | pen name |
| nonpareil | French | person or thing without equal |
| non sequitur | Latin | illogical conclusion |
| nota bene (NB) | Latin | note well |
| nouveau riche | French | newly rich |
| obiter dictum | Latin | incidental remark |
| objet d'art | French | work of art |
| oeuvre | French | artistic or literary work |
| opere citato (op cit) | Latin | in the work cited |
| opus | Latin | work |
| outré | French | eccentric |
| padre | Italian/Spanish/ Portuguese | priest |
| pampas | Spanish | grassy plain |
| panache | French | style, flamboyance |
| paparazzi | Itaiian | press photographers |
| par excellence | French | beyond compare |
| parvenu | French | newly rich, upstart |
| pas de deux | French | duet for two dancers |
| passé | French | outdated |
| passim | Latin | mentioned here and there |
| pastiche | French | imitation |
| patio | Spanish | terrace |
| patois | French | local dialect |
| peccadillo | Spanish | minor vice |
| penchant | French | inclination, liking |
| per annum | Latin | each year |
| per capita | Latin | for each person |
| per procurationem (p.p.) | Latin | on behalf of |
| per se | Latin | in itself |
| persona non grata | Latin | inadmissible person |

| Word or Phrase | Source | Meaning |
|---|---|---|
| petit bourgeoisie | French | lower middle class |
| piano | Italian | softly |
| piazza | Italian | open square |
| pièce de résistance | French | chief attraction |
| pied-à-terre | French | temporary residence |
| placebo | Latin | something that soothes or placates |
| plaza | Spanish | square |
| plus ça change | French | the more things change, the more they are the same |
| por favor | Spanish | please |
| post hoc | Latin | after this |
| post meridiem (P.M.) | Latin | afternoon, evening |
| postmortem | Latin | autopsy |
| postscriptum (P.S.) | Latin | written afterward |
| précis | French | summary |
| premiere | French | first performance |
| prima facie | Latin | on the face of it |
| pro bono publico | Latin | for the good of society |
| pro forma | Latin | as a matter of form |
| pronto | Spanish | promptly |
| pro rata | Latin | in proportion |
| protégé | French | pupil |
| quid pro quo | Latin | something for something |
| quod erat demonstrandum | Latin | what had to be demonstrated |
| quorum | Latin | group of people |
| raison d'être | French | motivation |
| rappel | French | to descend by rope |
| rapport | French | harmonious agreement |
| re | Latin | regarding |
| recherché | French | choice, rare |
| rendezvous | French | prearranged meeting |
| repertoire | French | rehearsed performances, skills, etc. |
| répondez s'il vous plaît (RSVP) | French | please reply |
| résumé | French | summary |
| risqué | French | improper, indelicate |
| roué | French | rake, profligate |
| safari | Kiswahili | hunting trip |
| sangfroid | French | self-possession |
| sans souci | French | carefree |
| savoir faire | French | assured confidence |
| sic | Latin | thus |
| sic passim | Latin | so throughout |
| sierra | Spanish | mountain range |
| siesta | Spanish | nap |
| sine qua non | Latin | something essential |
| sobriquet | French | epithet, nickname |
| soirée | French | social gathering in the evening |
| sotto voce | Italian | in an undertone |

(continues)

*(continued)*

| Word or Phrase | Source | Meaning |
|---|---|---|
| spiel | German | chatter, talk |
| status quo | Latin | existing state of affairs |
| sub judice | Latin | under consideration by the court |
| subpoena | Latin | legal summons |
| sub rosa | Latin | confidential |
| sui generis | Latin | unique |
| table d'hôte | French | fixed price menu |
| tacit | Latin | implied, understood |
| tempus fugit | Latin | time flies |
| terra firma | Latin | dry land |
| tête-à-tête | French | private conversation |
| thug | Hindi | gangster, ruffian |
| timbre | French | tone |
| tour de force | French | remarkable feat or display |
| tout le monde | French | everybody |
| trompe l'oeil | French | optical illusion |
| trousseau | French | bridal possessions |
| tsunami | Japanese | tidal wave |
| ultra vires | Latin | beyond the power of |
| vendetta | Italian | feud |
| verbatim | Latin | word for word |
| verboten | German | forbidden |
| via | Latin | by way of |
| vis-à-vis | French | regarding |
| viva voce | Latin | by word of mouth |
| voilà | French | there |
| volte-face | French | about-face |
| vox populi | Latin | the voice of the people |
| wunderbar | German | wonderful |
| wunderkind | German | child prodigy |
| zeitgeist | German | spirit of the time |

# ABBREVIATIONS AND SYMBOLS

## Abbreviations

The reduction of words, phrases, and titles to simple abbreviations allows a convenient means of expressing longer terms in shortened form. This device saves time and also helps the writer (or speaker) to keep sentences clear and concise.

Abbreviations are accepted in a wide range of contexts, from technical documents to spoken speech, and can be employed in virtually any field of endeavor, from science and technology to politics and business. As a general rule, however, they should be used sparingly or not at all in more formal documents.

An abbreviation can belong to one of several categories according to the manner in which it has been created. Sometimes the abbreviation consists of just the first letter or letters of the word or words (thus, *f* for *forte, abr.* for *abridged,* and *CBS* for *Columbia Broadcasting System*). Sometimes it is formed from a contraction of the original word by removing all the letters between the first and last (for example, *Dr.* for *Doctor*). Others are arrived at through the extraction of certain key letters from within a word (as in *Mgr.* for *Monsignor* and *Cdr.* for *Commander*).

Many abbreviations are familiar to all readers, but others may need some explanation. The usual convention is to give the full word or title followed by the abbreviation in parentheses on first use and thenceforth to give the abbreviated form alone. Care should be taken when an abbreviation has more than one meaning and the context does not make it clear which meaning is intended: *n/a,* for instance, could be intended as *not available* but interpreted by another as *not applicable.* If there is any doubt that an abbreviation might not be understood, it is always best to use the full form.

Perhaps the most confusing aspect of the use of abbreviations concerns the inclusion or omission of periods, which is to a large extent a matter of personal taste. In times gone by it was expected that a period would be placed after each letter to indicate that it was a shortened form of a word, but in recent times periods have been omitted with increasing frequency, chiefly in the interests of presenting a cleaner, neater, more modern-looking script. A period is usually added when the abbreviation is a contraction that includes the first and last letters of a word (as in *Mr., Lt.*) and is generally omitted where a letter is not an abbreviation for a whole word (as in *TV*). Opinion is divided when the abbreviation comprises the first part of a word. Some people insist that such abbreviated words as *abbrev.* (for *abbreviated*) or *rev.* (for *revised*) should always be followed by a period and further that this rule should also apply to single letters representing a person's first name. Others, however, commonly leave periods out in such cases. When an abbreviation with periods ends a sentence, it is not correct to add a second period. (*See also* PERIOD, page 354.)

Whatever decision a writer takes over the inclusion of periods in abbreviations, the golden rule is to remain consistent throughout a document and never to use periods in some abbreviations and leave them out in other similar abbreviations.

Some abbreviations are always rendered in capital letters (as in *U.S.* or *YMCA*), while others are usually written in lower-case letters or may be written either way. Occasionally the convention changes as the abbreviation becomes more familiar. The possibility of confusion between abbreviations customarily written in lower-case letters and ordinary vocabulary words means that such abbreviations are more often written with periods between the letters to distinguish them. In some cases, notably when the abbreviation is of Latin words, it is customary to put the abbreviation in italics (as *v.* or *vs.* for *versus*). Certain abbreviations are commonly written in SMALL CAPITALS, for example, A.D. (or C.E.), B.C. (or B.C.E.), A.M., and P.M.

Abbreviations are usually made plural through the addition of *-s* or *-es* in much the same way as in the case of a complete word or words (thus, *IDs* for *identities* and *DOSes* for *disk operating systems*). If the abbreviation ends with a period it is usual to add the *-s* or *-es* after the final period (thus, *a meeting of D.A.s*). Note, however, that the reverse applies if the abbreviation is a shortened word that ends in a single period (thus, *capts.*). Another exception concerning plurals relates to the abbreviations for weights and measures, which remain in the singular even when actually plural (thus, *45 in.* or *90 cm*). In some rare cases the plural is indicated by doubling the final letter (as in *pp.* for *pages*).

In spoken and written sentences abbreviations take *an* if they begin with a vowel sound (as in *an amp* or *an LCD*). Regarding pronunciation of abbreviations, there is no easy way to tell whether an abbreviation should be pronounced as a word in itself or spelled out. The simplest solution is either to imitate what other people do with the word or to consult a dictionary. In most instances they are pronounced by spelling out each letter in turn, unless they happen to be acronyms (see below).

## ACRONYMS

Acronyms are abbreviations that constitute pronounceable names or words. Many organizations deliberately choose names that will spell out a pronounceable word when reduced to an abbreviation, believing that people remember such acronyms much more easily than other abbreviations. Well-known examples include *ALGOL* and *UNESCO*.

When written down, acronyms are usually rendered in capital letters and never have periods between each letter. Some acronyms are so familiar that they have come to be treated as words in their own right, are indistinguishable from other words, and are written in lower-case letters. Examples of this phenomenon including *radar* (which originally stood for *radio detecting and ranging*) and *laser* (*light amplification by stimulated emission of radiation*).

The following table offers a selection of the more commonly encountered abbreviations and acronyms, together with the words they represent:

| Abbreviation | Meaning |
|---|---|
| A | associate of |
| AA | Alcoholics Anonymous |
| AA(A) | anti-aircraft (artillery) |
| AB | able-bodied seaman |
| abbr(ev). | abbreviation |
| ABM | antiballistic missile |
| abr. | abridged |
| ABS | antilock braking system |
| AC | air-conditioning; aircraftman; *ante Christum* (before Christ) |
| ac | alternating current |
| a/c | account |
| ACAD | auto computer-aided design |
| ACTH | adrenocorticotrophic hormone |
| ad. lib. | *ad libitum* (at pleasure) |
| A.D. | *anno Domini* (in the year of our Lord) |
| A-D | analog-to-digital |
| ADC | aide-de-camp |
| ADH | antidiuretic hormone |
| Adj. | adjutant |
| adj. | adjective |
| Adm. | admiral; admission |

| Abbreviation | Meaning |
|---|---|
| ADP | adenosine diphosphate |
| adv. | adverb |
| AFV | armored fighting vehicle |
| AGM | air-to-ground missile; annual general meeting |
| AGR | advanced gas-cooled reactor |
| AH | *anno Hegirae* (in the year of the Hegira) |
| AI | artificial intelligence |
| AID | artificial insemination by donor |
| AIDS | acquired immuno deficiency syndrome |
| AIH | artificial insemination by husband |
| AK | Alaska |
| aka | also known as |
| AL | Alabama |
| ALCM | air-launched cruise missile |
| ALGOL | algorithmic language |
| alt. | altitude |
| AM | amplitude modulation; *anno mundi* (in the year of the world) |
| A.M. | *ante meridiem* (before noon) |
| amp | ampere; amplifier |
| AMU | atomic mass unit |
| anon. | anonymous |
| AOB | any other business |
| approx. | approximately |
| APR | annual percentage rate |
| Apr. | April |
| AR | Arkansas; autonomous republic |
| ASA | American Standards Association |
| asap | as soon as possible |
| ASEAN | Association of South East Asian Nations |
| ASM | air-to-surface missile |
| AST | Atlantic Standard Time |
| AU | astronomical unit |
| AUC | *ab urbe condita* (in the year from the foundation of Rome); *anno urbis conditae* (in the year of the founding of the city) |
| Aug. | August |
| AV | audiovisual; Authorized Version (Bible) |
| Ave. | avenue |
| AWACS | Airborne Warning and Control System |
| AWOL | absent without leave |
| AZ | Arizona |
| b. | born |
| BBC | British Broadcasting Corporation |
| B.C. | before Christ |
| B.C. | British Columbia |
| B.C.E. | before common era |
| BCG | bacille (bacillus) Calmette Guérin |
| Blvd. | boulevard |
| BP | blood pressure |

*(continues)*

*(continued)*

| Abbreviation | Meaning |
|---|---|
| Bp | bishop |
| bps | bits per second |
| BSE | bovine spongiform encephalopathy |
| BVM | Blessed Virgin Mary (Beata Virgo Maria) |
| C | Celsius; centigrade; century |
| c. | *circa* (about) |
| CA | California |
| ca. | *circa* (about) |
| CAD | computer-aided design |
| cap. | capital |
| Capt. | captain |
| CAT | computerized axial tomography |
| CB | citizens' band |
| CBS | Columbia Broadcasting System |
| CCTV | closed-circuit television |
| CD | compact disc; corps diplomatique |
| Cdr. | commander |
| Cdre. | commodore |
| CD-ROM | compact disc read-only memory |
| C.E. | common era; Christian era |
| cert. | certified |
| CET | Central European Time |
| cf. | *confer* (compare) |
| CFC | chlorofluorocarbon |
| CFS | chronic fatigue syndrome |
| CGS | centimeter-gram-second |
| CIA | Central Intelligence Agency |
| cif | cost, insurance, and freight |
| C-in-C | commander-in-chief |
| cm | centimeter |
| CNN | Cable News Network |
| CO | Colorado; commanding officer |
| c/o | care of |
| COBOL | Common Business Oriented Language |
| COD | cash on delivery |
| COED | computer-operated electronic display |
| Col. | colonel |
| Comdr. | Commander |
| COMECON | Council for Mutual Economic Assistance |
| conj. | conjunction |
| cons. | consecrated |
| Corp. | corporation |
| Cpl. | corporal |
| CPR | cardiopulmonary resuscitation |
| CPS | characters per second |
| CPU | central processing unit |
| CST | Central Standard Time |

| Abbreviation | Meaning |
|---|---|
| CT | Connecticut |
| CV | curriculum vitae |
| CVS | chorionic villus sampling |
| d. | died |
| D.A. | District Attorney |
| D&C | dilation and curettage |
| DBS | direct broadcasting from satellite |
| D.C. | District of Columbia |
| dc | direct current |
| DDT | dichloro-diphenyl-trichloroethane |
| DE | Delaware |
| Dec. | December |
| del. | *delineavit* (he/she drew it) |
| Dem. | Democrat |
| dept. | department |
| DG | *Dei gratia* (by the grace of God) |
| DIA | Defense Intelligence Agency |
| DIY | do-it-yourself |
| DJ | disc jockey |
| DNA | deoxyribonucleic acid |
| do. | *ditto* (the same) |
| DOA | dead on arrival |
| DOC | Department of Commerce |
| DOD | Department of Defense |
| DOE | Department of Energy |
| DOL | Department of Labor |
| DOS | disk operating system |
| DOT | Department of Transportation |
| DP | data processing |
| Dr. | doctor |
| DST | daylight saving time |
| DTP | desktop publishing |
| DV | *Deo volente* (God willing) |
| DVD | digital video disc |
| E | east |
| ea. | each |
| EARM | electrically alterable read-only memory |
| EC | European Community |
| ECG | electrocardiogram |
| ECOSOC | Economic and Social Council (of the United Nations) |
| ECT | electroconvulsive therapy |
| EEG | electroencephalogram |
| e.g. | *exempli gratia* (for example) (*See* WORDS OFTEN CONFUSED) |
| e-mail | electronic mail |
| EMF | electromotive force |
| EMU | electromagnetic unit |
| ENIAC | electronic numeral indicator and calculator |
| EPA | Environmental Protection Agency |

*(continues)*

*(continued)*

| Abbreviation | Meaning |
|---|---|
| EPOS | electronic point of sale |
| ER | Elizabetha Regina (Queen Elizabeth); emergency room |
| ESA | European Space Agency |
| ESP | extra-sensory perception |
| esp. | especially |
| EST | Eastern Standard Time |
| est. | estimate |
| ETA | estimated time of arrival |
| et al. | *et alia* (and others) |
| etc. | *et cetera* (and so on) |
| et seq. | *et sequentia* (and the following) |
| EU | European Union |
| excl. | excludes |
| ext. | exterior/extended; extension |
| F | Fahrenheit |
| *f* | *forte* (loud) |
| FAA | Federal Aviation Administration |
| FAO | Food and Agriculture Organization (United Nations) |
| FBI | Federal Bureau of Investigation |
| FDA | Food and Drug Administration |
| Feb. | February |
| fec. | *fecit* (made this) |
| fem. | feminine |
| *ff* | *fortissimo* (very loud) |
| FHA | Federal Housing Administration |
| FHWA | Federal Highway Administration |
| FILO | first in, last out |
| FL | Florida |
| fl. | *floruit* (flourished) |
| FM | frequency modulation |
| foll. | followed |
| FORTRAN | formula translation |
| FPS | foot-pound-second |
| Fri. | Friday |
| ft. | foot, feet |
| FTAA | Free Trade Area of the Americas |
| FWA | Federal Works Agency |
| GA | Georgia |
| GATT | General Agreement on Tariffs and Trade |
| GB | Great Britain |
| GBH | grievous bodily harm |
| GDP | gross domestic product |
| Gen. | general |
| GHQ | general headquarters |
| GI | government issue |
| GIGO | garbage in, garbage out |
| GMT | Greenwich Mean Time |

| Abbreviation | Meaning |
|---|---|
| GNP | gross national product |
| GOC | general officer commanding |
| GSA | General Services Administration |
| GU | Guam |
| GUT | grand unified theory |
| GW | gigawatt |
| HE | His/Her Excellency |
| HF | high frequency |
| HH | His/Her Highness; His/Her Honour; His Holiness |
| HI | Hawaii |
| HIH | His/Her Imperial Highness |
| HIM | His/Her Imperial Majesty |
| HIV | human immunodeficiency virus |
| HJS | *hic jacet sepultus* (here lies buried) |
| HM | His/Her Majesty |
| HMO | health maintenance organization |
| HMS | His/Her Majesty's Ship/Service |
| Hon. | Honorary; Honorable |
| hp | horsepower |
| HQ | headquarters |
| HR | House of Representatives |
| HRH | His/Her Royal Highness |
| HRT | hormone replacement therapy |
| HTML | hypertext markup language |
| I. | island |
| IA | Iowa |
| IAEA | International Atomic Energy Agency |
| IATA | International Air Transport Association |
| ibid. | *ibidem* (in the same place) |
| IBM | International Business Machines |
| ICAO | International Civil Aviation Organization |
| ICBM | intercontinental ballistic missile |
| ID | Idaho; identification |
| id. | *idem* (already mentioned) |
| i.e. | *id est* (that is) (*See* WORDS OFTEN CONFUSED) |
| IHS | Iesus Hominum Salvator (Jesus the Savior of Mankind) |
| IL | Illinois |
| ILO | International Labor Organization |
| IMF | International Monetary Fund |
| IN | Indiana |
| in. | inch, inches |
| Inc. | incorporated |
| incl. | includes |
| INRI | Iesus Nazarenus Rex Iudeorum (Jesus of Nazareth, King of the Jews) |
| inst. | *instant* (current month) |
| INTELSAT | International Telecommunications Satellite Organization |
| interj. | interjection |
| Interpol | International Criminal Police Commission |

*(continues)*

*(continued)*

| Abbreviation | Meaning |
|---|---|
| intr. | intransitive |
| IOC | International Olympic Committee |
| IOU | I owe you |
| IPA | International Phonetic Alphabet |
| IQ | intelligence quotient |
| IRBM | intermediate-range ballistic missile |
| IRC | International Red Cross |
| IRS | Internal Revenue Service |
| Is. | islands |
| ISBN | International Standard Book Number |
| ISDN | integrated services digital network |
| ISP | Internet service provider |
| ISSN | International Standard Serial Number |
| IT | information technology |
| IUD | intrauterine device |
| IVF | in vitro fertilization |
| Jan. | January |
| Jul. | July |
| Jun. | June |
| KGB | Komitet Gosudarstvennoye Bezhopaznosti (Committee of State Security) |
| kHz | kiloHertz |
| KJV | King James Version (Bible) |
| KKK | Ku Klux Klan |
| km | kilometer |
| KO | knockout |
| kPC | kiloparsec |
| KS | Kansas |
| kW | kilowatt |
| kWh | kilowatt hour |
| KY | Kentucky |
| LA | Los Angeles; Louisiana |
| LAPD | Los Angeles Police Department |
| lat. | latitude |
| lb. | pound |
| lc | lower case (printing) |
| LCD | liquid-crystal display |
| LED | light-emitting diode |
| loc. cit. | *loco citato* (in the place cited) |
| long. | longitude |
| LPG | liquefied petroleum gas |
| LSD | lysergic acid diethylamide |
| Lt. | lieutenant |
| Ltd. | limited (liability) |
| LV | luncheon voucher |
| LW | long wave |
| m | meter; mile |
| M. | Monsieur |

| Abbreviation | Meaning |
|---|---|
| MA | Massachusetts |
| Maj. | major |
| Mar. | March |
| masc. | masculine |
| MASH | Mobile Army Surgical Hospital |
| max. | maximum |
| MC | master of ceremonies |
| MD | managing director; Maryland |
| MDMA | methylenedioxymethamphetamine |
| ME | Maine; myalgic encephalomyelitis |
| mg | milligram |
| Mgr. | Monsignor |
| MH | Medal of Honor |
| MI | Michigan; Military Intelligence |
| MIA | missing in action |
| min. | minimum; minute |
| MIRV | multiple independently targeted reentry vehicle |
| ml | milliliter |
| Mlle. | Mademoiselle |
| MLR | minimum lending rate |
| mm | millimeter |
| Mme. | Madame |
| MMF | magnetomotive force |
| MN | Minnesota |
| MO | medical officer; Missouri |
| MODEM | modulator/demodulator |
| MOH | Medal of Honor |
| Mon. | Monday |
| MP | Military Police |
| MPC | megaparsec |
| mph | miles per hour |
| Mr. | Mister |
| MRA | Moral Rearmament |
| Mrs. | Mistress (married woman) |
| MS | manuscript; Mississippi; multiple sclerosis |
| MSG | monosodium glutamate |
| MST | Mountain Standard Time |
| MT | Montana |
| Mt. | Mount; million tonnes |
| MV | merchant vessel; motor vessel |
| MW | medium wave |
| N | north |
| n. | noun |
| n/a | not applicable; not available |
| NAACP | National Association for the Advancement of Colored People |
| NAFTA | North American Free Trade Agreement |
| NASA | National Aeronautics and Space Administration |
| NASDA | National Space Development Agency |

*(continues)*

*(continued)*

| Abbreviation | Meaning |
|---|---|
| NATO | North Atlantic Treaty Organization |
| NB | *nota bene* (note well) |
| NBA | National Basketball Association |
| NBC | National Broadcasting Corporation |
| NC | North Carolina |
| NCO | noncommissioned officer |
| ND | North Dakota |
| NE | Nebraska; northeast |
| NFC | National Football Conference |
| NFL | National Football League |
| NH | New Hampshire |
| NHL | National Hockey League |
| NICAM | near instantaneously companded audio multiplex |
| NIMBY | not in my back yard |
| NIV | New International Version (Bible) |
| NJ | New Jersey |
| NM | New Mexico |
| NMR | nuclear magnetic resonance |
| no. | number |
| Nov. | November |
| NPS | National Park Service |
| NRA | National Recovery Administration; National Rifle Association |
| NSA | National Security Agency |
| NSC | National Security Council |
| NT | New Testament |
| NV | Nevada |
| NW | northwest |
| NY | New York |
| NYC | New York City |
| NYPD | New York Police Department |
| NZ | New Zealand |
| OAPEC | Organization of Arab Petroleum Exporting Countries |
| OAS | Organization of American States |
| OAU | Organization of African Unity |
| OB | outside broadcast |
| ob. | *obiit* (died) |
| OCR | optical character recognition/reader |
| Oct. | October |
| OED | *Oxford English Dictionary* |
| OH | Ohio |
| OHP | overhead projector |
| OK | Oklahoma |
| ONO | or near offer |
| op. | *opus* (work) |
| op. cit. | *opere citato* (in the work cited) |
| OPEC | Organization of Petroleum Exporting Countries |
| OR | Oregon |

| Abbreviation | Meaning |
|---|---|
| OS | Old Style (calendar) |
| OT | Old Testament |
| oz. | ounce |
| *p* | *piano* (softly) |
| p. | page |
| PA | Pennsylvania; personal assistant |
| PC | personal computer; politically correct |
| PCP | phenylcyclohexylpiperidine |
| PDR | precision depth recorder |
| PE | physical education |
| PGA | Professional Golfers' Association |
| PH | Purple Heart |
| PHS | Public Health Service |
| PIN | personal identification number |
| Pl. | Place |
| pl. | plural |
| P.M. | *post meridiem* (after noon) |
| PMS | premenstrual syndrome |
| pop. | population |
| POW | prisoner of war |
| pp. | pages |
| p.p. | *per procurationem* (on behalf of) |
| PR | proportional representation; public relations; Puerto Rico |
| prep. | preposition |
| PRO | public relations officer |
| Prof. | professor |
| PROM | programmable read-only memory |
| pron. | pronoun |
| P.S. | postscript |
| PST | Pacific Standard Time |
| pt. | point |
| PTFE | polytetrafluoroethylene |
| PTO | please turn over |
| PVA | polyvinyl acetate |
| PVC | polyvinyl chloride |
| Pvt. | private |
| PWA | Public Works Administration |
| PWR | pressurized-water reactor |
| QCD | quantum chromodynamics |
| QED | quantum electrodynamics; *quod erat demonstrandum* (which was to be proved) |
| q.v. | *quod vide* (which see) |
| RAF | Royal Air Force |
| RAM | random access memory |
| RC | Red Cross; Roman Catholic |
| Rd. | road |
| RDA | recommended daily allowance |
| REM | rapid eye movement |

*(continues)*

*(continued)*

| Abbreviation | Meaning |
|---|---|
| Rep. | representative; Republican |
| Rev. | reverend |
| RI | Rhode Island |
| RIP | *requiescat in pace* (rest in peace) |
| RMS | root mean square |
| RN | Royal Navy |
| RNA | ribonucleic acid |
| ROM | read-only memory |
| RPG | rocket propelled grenade |
| RPM | resale price maintenance; revolutions per minute |
| RRP | recommended retail price |
| RSI | repetitive strain injury |
| RSVP | *répondez s'il vous plaît* (please reply) |
| RTA | road traffic accident |
| S | south |
| s. | second |
| SAE | stamped addressed envelope |
| SALT | Strategic Arms Limitation Talks |
| SAM | surface-to-air missile |
| SASE | Self-addressed stamped envelope |
| Sat. | Saturday |
| SC | South Carolina |
| SD | South Dakota |
| SDI | strategic defense initiative |
| SE | southeast |
| SEATO | South-East Asia Treaty Organization |
| Sen. | senator |
| Sept. | September |
| SHF | super-high frequency |
| SI | Système International (International System) |
| SIDS | Sudden Infant Death Syndrome |
| sing. | singular |
| SLR | single-lens reflex |
| SOR | sale or return |
| SOS | save our souls |
| sq. | square |
| SS | Schutzstaffel (Protective Squad) |
| SSA | Social Security Administration |
| SSN | Social Security Number |
| SSR | Soviet Socialist Republic |
| St | saint; street |
| START | Strategic Arms Reduction Talks |
| STD | sexually transmitted disease |
| Sub. Lt. | sublieutenant |
| Sun. | Sunday |
| SW | short wave; southwest |
| SWF | single white female |

| Abbreviation | Meaning |
|---|---|
| TASS | Telegrafnoe Agentsvo Sovetskovo Soyuza (Telegraph Agency of the Soviet Union) |
| TB | tuberculosis |
| TBA | to be announced |
| TCP | trichlorophenylmethyliodialicyl |
| Thurs. | Thursday |
| TN | Tennessee |
| TNT | trinitrotoluene |
| tr. | transitive |
| Tues. | Tuesday |
| TV | television |
| TVA | Tennessee Valley Authority |
| TVP | textured vegetable protein |
| TX | Texas |
| TXT | text file |
| uc | upper case (printing) |
| UFO | unidentified flying object |
| UHF | ultra-high frequency |
| UHT | ultra-high temperature |
| UK | United Kingdom |
| UN | United Nations |
| UNCTAD | United Nations Conference on Trade and Development |
| UNESCO | United Nations Economic, Scientific and Cultural Organization |
| UNHCR | United Nations High Commission for Refugees |
| UNICEF | United Nations Children's Fund |
| UNO | United Nations Organization |
| UNRWA | United Nations Relief and Works Agency for Palestine Refugees in the Near East |
| UNSC | United Nations Security Council |
| URL | uniform-universal resource locator |
| U.S. | United States |
| USA | United States Army; United States of America |
| USAF | United States Air Force |
| USAID | United States Agency for International Development |
| USCG | United States Coast Guard |
| USDA | United States Department of Agriculture |
| USES | United States Employment Service |
| USIA | United States Information Agency |
| USMC | United States Marine Corps |
| USN | United States Navy |
| USS | United States Ship |
| USSR | Union of Soviet Socialist Republics |
| UT | Utah |
| UV | ultraviolet |
| v. | versus |
| VA | Virginia |
| vb. | verb |
| VCR | videocassette recorder |

*(continues)*

*(continued)*

| Abbreviation | Meaning |
|---|---|
| VD | venereal disease |
| VDU | visual display unit |
| VHF | very high frequency |
| VHS | video home system |
| VI | Virgin Islands |
| VIP | very important person |
| VLF | very low frequency |
| VOA | Voice of America |
| vol. | volume |
| vs. | versus |
| VT | Vermont |
| VTR | videotape recorder |
| W | west |
| WA | Washington |
| WASP | white Anglo-Saxon Protestant |
| WBA | World Boxing Association |
| WBC | World Boxing Council |
| Wed. | Wednesday |
| WHO | World Health Organization |
| WI | Wisconsin |
| WMO | World Meteorological Organization |
| wt. | weight |
| WTO | World Trade Organization |
| WV | West Virginia |
| WWF | World Wildlife Fund |
| www | World Wide Web |
| WY | Wyoming |
| WYSIWYG | what you see is what you get |
| yd. | yard |
| YMCA | Young Men's Christian Association |
| yr. | year |
| Yrs | yours |
| YUPPIE | young upwardly mobile professional |
| YWCA | Young Women's Christian Association |

## Symbols

The use of symbols in the place of words is an accepted practice that works as long as all parties are familiar with their meaning. Mathematical and scientific symbols are essential to the understanding of formulae and calculations, but other symbols (such as & and #) are best reserved for note taking and other informal contexts.

| Symbol | Meaning | Symbol | Meaning |
|---|---|---|---|
| & | and (ampersand) | # | number |
| * | *see* note (asterisk) | + | plus |

| Symbol | Meaning | Symbol | Meaning |
|---|---|---|---|
| - | minus | % | percent |
| × | multiplied by | @ | at |
| + | divided by | $ | dollar(s) |
| = | equals | ¢ | cents(s) |
| ≠ | does not equal | £ | pound(s) sterling |
| < | less than | € | euro(s) |
| > | greater than | © | copyright |
| ≤ | less than or equal to | ® | registered |
| ≥ | greater than or equal to | ™ | trademark |

# NUMBERS

In some contexts it is appropriate to render numbers as figures, while in others it is better to write out numbers in full. One widely held convention recommends writing numerals out in full from zero to nine (or ten) and thereafter rendering them as figures. Variants of this rule advise writing out all numbers below 20 or alternatively 100 in full.

In mathematical, technical, or statistical documents, it is probably best to render all numbers as figures, but in more imaginative writing such as a story or poem it is probably best to write all numbers out in full. Where you choose to combine smaller numbers written out in full and larger numbers written as numerals it may be best to avoid having both forms in the same sentence and, if they are close to each other, rendering both numbers in the same form (*earn between two and twenty dollars a day; a margin of error ranging from 5 to 55 percent*). Note that the same choice between numerals and letters exists in relation to the expression of fractions, which may be variously rendered according to the context in which they appear (*one-quarter; three-quarters; ⅞*).

## Cardinal and Ordinal Numbers

Numerals can be divided into cardinal numbers (*one, two, three, four, five,* etc.) and ordinal numbers (*first, second, third, fourth, fifth,* etc.). Most ordinal numbers are formed by adding the suffix *-th* to the cardinal number concerned (*sixth; sixty-seventh; two hundredth*). The exceptions are *first, second,* and *third.* Note that in certain cases the final *-e* of the cardinal number is dropped and the last letter may change to form the equivalent ordinal number (*fifth; eighth; ninth; twelfth; twentieth*).

## Large Numbers

Large numbers are often rendered as numerals with commas dividing them into groups of three digits. These delineate thousands, millions, or other large amounts (*1,000, 10,000, 100,000, 1,000,000*). The use of commas in numbers of four figures or more is preferable, although many choose to do without them. Note that commas are never used in relation to yearly dates (*in the year 1459*), unless the year referred to has more than four digits (*50,000* B.C.).

In the case of unfeasibly large numbers or numbers with many zeros, the convention in mathematical and technical contexts is to express the magnitude of a number in the form of a superscript numeral ($10^9$ = billion, $10^{12}$ = trillion, etc.) after the first figure, or in less technical documents to make use of such vocabulary words as *million, billion,* and *trillion.* Note, however, that there is scope for confusion in what these words represent in terms of figures, as they are sometimes defined differently in France, the United States, Germany, and the United Kingdom.

| Term in United States | Numeral |
|---|---|
| million | 1,000,000 |
| billion | 1,000,000,000 |
| trillion | 1,000,000,000,000 |

When discussing such large figures, it is conventional to omit the final *-s* in the plural form (*two million, six billion, three trillion*).

For further discussion of the use of commas with numbers, see COMMA (page 342), and the use of hyphens with numbers, see HYPHEN (page 350).

## Dates

Dates can be rendered in various different ways, some written out more fully than others. The most succinct way to render a date of the year is to reduce it to purely numerical form in the order: month of the year, day of the month, and year (as in *1/31/05* or *1.31.05*). A less concise form, possibly less abrupt in character and thus more suitable for informal use, is to combine words and figures in the style of *January 31, 2005.* In imaginative writing it is usual to write out dates in full (*the twenty-second of August*).

Years are usually rendered as figures and are rarely written out in full. In informal circumstances they may, however, be abbreviated to just two numbers in the belief that it is unnecessary to be more specific (*back in '98; the '39–'45 war*). Decades and centuries are commonly rendered in abbreviated form using a combination of words and figures. Examples of alternative styles for decades include *the 1800s* and *the 1970s,* as well as the fully written version (*the seventeen-forties; the nineties*). Note that there is no need to place an apostrophe before the *s.* Examples of the style for centuries, apart from the fully written style (*the twenty-first century*) include *21st century* or *21 c.*

Years (and centuries) prior to the birth of Christ are labeled *before Christ,* abbreviated to B.C. Years after the birth of Christ are labeled *anno domini* (meaning "year of our Lord"), abbreviated to A.D. Note that B.C. and A.D. are often rendered in SMALL CAPITALS in printed texts. By convention B.C. comes after the date, while A.D. goes before the date (*320 B.C.; A.D. 781*). This last rule does not apply, however, in all circumstances, as for instance in *built in the ninth century A.D.* Note that there is an alternative dating system for years that avoids reference to the life of Christ, in which the initials *B.C.E.* (*before common era*) and *C.E.* (*common era*) follow the year. *B.C.E.* corresponds to *B.C.,* while *C.E.* is the equivalent of *A.D.*

In expressing a range of dates, as for instance in a person's birth and death dates, the usual convention is to render them separated by a dash (*1604–76*). Note that in such cases there is no need to preface the figures with any introductory words such as *from, to,* or *between.* The same rule applies to figures in other kinds of number ranges (*repeat 20–30 times, pages 73–78,*

*300–400 years ago*). Where a range links numbers that begin with the same first digit, you can sometimes omit the first digit (or preceding digits) in the case of the second number (*50–5; 160–2*), but this depends largely on your personal preference or the demands of a particular house style. On occasion, this style can cause confusion. For further discussion of the use of the dash in dates, see DASH (page 347).

### Time

It is possible to express the time in either words or figures, the choice depending largely on the context (*1:30; half-past one*). It is the convention to indicate times between midnight and noon by adding A.M., the abbreviated form of *ante meridiem,* and the times between noon and midnight by adding P.M., the abbreviated form of *post meridiem.* Note that A.M. and P.M. are often rendered lower case (*a.m., p.m.*) and sometimes without periods (*am, pm*). Care should be taken to avoid such phrases as *shortly after 11:30* P.M. *at night,* which are tautological.

## SENSITIVE TERMS

Some words are overtly controversial and should be used with care since the use of the wrong word in some contexts can cause serious offense. Typically, such words refer to such politically sensitive topics as gender, race, and physical and mental capability. The correct choice of term in such circumstances is heavily influenced by prevailing public opinion, and a word that may be approved of one year may easily fall from favor the next. It is clearly sensible to be aware of current feeling about such sensitive terms, but you should also take care not to fall into the trap of using ultra-correct words that could cause you to be accused of being unduly pedantic or jargonistic. Often the appropriate choice may be influenced by the audience at which your writing or speech is directed (words that may be considered acceptable in private conversation will not necessarily meet with approval in a newspaper article, for instance).

A selection of the more commonly encountered words that fall within this category is discussed in the following list:

**Aboriginal** The word *Aboriginal* refers to the indigenous people of Australia and has now largely replaced *Aborigine* as the preferred modern term.

**Aborigine** *See* ABORIGINAL.

**accessible** The adjective *accessible* is often used with reference to access for people with impaired mobility, specifically for people in wheelchairs. It is free of any derogatory overtones and is consequently widely used, often in hyphenated form (*a wheelchair-accessible building*).

**actor** The term *actor* is now understood to refer to performers of both sexes. *Actor* and *actress* are still in common use, however, and are unlikely to cause offense in most circumstances.

**actress** *See* ACTOR.

**African American** This term, applied to an American of African descent, is often used as an alternative to BLACK and has now largely replaced the earlier usage *Afro-American.* This latter term should be avoided since it has acquired derogatory overtones.

**Afro-American** *See* AFRICAN AMERICAN.

**American Indian** *See* NATIVE AMERICAN.

**Asian** *Asian* is now the preferred term for a person originating from East Asia, replacing the former term *Oriental.*

**author** The term *author* is now commonly employed in reference to writers of either sex. The term *authoress* may be considered condescending by some people and is best avoided.

**authoress** *See* AUTHOR.

**bartender** The word *bartender* has now replaced to some extent the former terms *barman* and *barmaid. Barman* is still fairly commonly used in relation to male bartenders, but *barmaid* is more contentious and is best avoided.

**black** The term *black* (usually spelled without an initial capital letter) is now used in preference to most other alternatives to describe a dark-skinned person of African origin. The former terms *Negro, Negress,* and *colored* (a word that was inclusive of all nonwhites) are now considered offensive, the latter partly through its association with the apartheid policies of South Africa. Note, however, that the negative associations of the ordinary vocabulary word *black* with evil and misfortune (*a black day, a black outlook*) mean that *black* remains a sensitive term, the use of which may make some people feel uncomfortable. Note particularly that the slang word *nigger,* from *Negro,* has long since been considered offensive, except when in jocular use between black people themselves. *See also* AFRICAN AMERICAN; PERSON OF COLOR; WHITE.

**blind** *See* VISUALLY IMPAIRED.

**businessman/businesswoman** *See* EXECUTIVE.

**cameraman/camerawoman** *See* CAMERA OPERATOR.

**camera operator** This term has now largely replaced the former job descriptions *cameraman* and *camerawoman* on the grounds that there is no justification for making a distinction based on gender when both people perform the same job. Note that the same gender-neutralizing formula may be applied to numerous other jobs (for example, *winch operator*).

**Caucasian** *See* WHITE.

**chair/chairperson** The terms *chairman* and *chairwoman* were among the most prominent casualties when the language began to be purged of such gender-specific words from the 1960s onward. Many people, however, dislike the rather clumsy alternative *chairperson* and even more disapprove of *chair,* which is considered jargonistic and ugly. The term *chairman* is still heard, but *chairwoman* is more contentious and is best avoided.

**chairman/chairwoman** *See* CHAIR/CHAIRPERSON.

**challenged** The term *challenged* is sometimes used in relation to people who are subject to a mental or physical disability of some kind (*physically challenged*). In formal contexts, at least, it has to some extent replaced such previous usages as *DISABLED* (although this word is still heard) and *blind* (now *visually challenged*). Care should be taken not to use the term to excess, however, since such vogue terms as *vertically challenged* (for *short in height*) or *follicularly challenged* (for *bald*) are disliked by many people and are generally confined to humorous or facetious contexts.

**cleft lip** This phrase is now the preferred term to describe a congenital split in the upper lip. It replaces the former usage *harelip,* which is now likely to cause offense.

**clergyman/clergywoman** *See* MEMBER OF THE CLERGY.

**colored** *See* BLACK.

**congressman/congresswoman** *See* MEMBER OF CONGRESS.

**conjoined** The term *conjoined* is now the preferred adjective to describe people who are born physically joined to each other. It replaces the former term *Siamese twins.*

**craftsman/craftswoman** *See* CRAFTWORKER.

**craftworker** This term is in widespread use as a replacement for the gender-specific *craftsman* and *craftswoman.* A less commonly adopted alternative is *craftsperson.*

**deaf** *See* HEARING IMPAIRED.

**deaf-mute** *See* PROFOUNDLY DEAF.

**deprived** *See* DISADVANTAGED.

**disabled** The adjective and noun *disabled* has emerged as perhaps the safest choice of word when referring to people who have a physical or mental impairment of some kind. It replaces such former terms as *crippled, defective,* and *handicapped,* all of which should be avoided since they have derogatory or negative overtones. Note, however, that caution should be exercised even in the use of *disabled,* since it, too, may be considered to have negative connotations. It is sometimes preferable to opt for such alternatives as *physically challenged* or the admittedly less elegant *differently abled* or *person with disabilities* (although some people will object to such coinages on the grounds that they are unduly jargonistic). *See also* CHALLENGED.

**disadvantaged** This term is sometimes employed as a more acceptable alternative to *poor,* which has strong negative connotations. Other alternatives include *deprived* and UNDERPRIVILEGED.

**dumb** Care should be taken in the use of *dumb* in its sense of "mute" or "unable to speak," since the word has come to be dominated by its other, informal sense of "stupid." In order to avoid any implication that the inability to speak arises from innate stupidity, it is best to use an alternative term, such as *mute* (though this word too can cause offense) or *speech impaired. See also* PROFOUNDLY DEAF.

**dwarf** *See* PERSON OF RESTRICTED GROWTH.

**Eskimo** *See* INUIT.

**-ess** The suffix *-ess* is sometimes added to nouns to create a specifically feminine variant (*manageress, murderess*), but such usages may be considered patronizing or sexist. Increasingly the original masculine noun form is applied to both sexes (*author, host*). Note, however, that in a few cases the *-ess* ending is never dropped, typically when denoting aristocratic rank (*duchess, princess*). Note also that caution should be exercised in the use of other related suffixes, such as *-ne* and *-ette* (*comedienne; usherette*).

**-ette** *See* -ESS.

**European** *See* WHITE.

**executive** Those directly involved in business are particularly sensitive to gender issues and the need to demonstrate an impartial approach to the sexes in order to avoid accusations of bias on gender grounds. In response to this, the gender-neutral term *executive* (or *business executive*) is now widely preferred to *businessman* or *businesswoman,* although these more traditional terms are by no means redundant.

**firefighter** The term *fireman* has been largely replaced by the gender-neutral *firefighter* since women have come to assume a significant role in the fire service. Although *fireman* has not entirely disappeared, its counterpart *firewoman* has never won wide acceptance.

**fireman/firewoman** *See* FIREFIGHTER.

**gay** The adjective *gay* originally meant "cheerful" or "lighthearted" but should be used with care in this sense, as the term is now more usually interpreted as meaning "homosexual" (*gay marriage, gay rights*). The term *gay* has been wholly accepted by the homosexual community and is unlikely to cause offense, although many people regret the effective loss of the word in its original sense. Note, however, that the term is sometimes assumed to refer specifically to homosexual men and is less commonly used of homosexual women, who are more likely to be described as being *lesbian.*

**geriatric** The use of the word *geriatric* as a descriptive term for an "elderly person" is avoided by some people since it is widely interpreted as having derogatory overtones, with an emphasis on incompetence resulting from advanced age. Similar care should be taken, however, over such alternatives as *old person, person of advanced years,* and *senior citizen.*

**handicapped** *See* CHALLENGED; DISABLED.

**harelip** *See* CLEFT LIP.

**hearing impaired** The term *hearing impaired* is often employed, particularly in formal contexts, as a more neutral alternative to *deaf,* which is felt by many people to have negative connotations. *Hearing impaired* is generally preferred to another contemporary alternative, *aurally inconvenienced.* By extension, people with perfect hearing may be termed *hearing people. See also* PROFOUNDLY DEAF.

**Indian** *See* NATIVE AMERICAN.

**Inuit** The term *Inuit* is the preferred term for an indigenous inhabitant of the northernmost United States, Canada, and Greenland, formerly called an *Eskimo.* The modern prejudice against *Eskimo* lies in its literal meaning of "eater of raw flesh" (while *Inuit* has the more innocuous meaning of "people"). Note, however, that *Inuit* does not usually extend to inhabitants of the Aleutian Islands and Siberia, who are also traditionally known as *Eskimos.*

**learning difficulties** This phrase is one of several terms now commonly used in reference to people who find the mastering of simple skills a challenge (*to be diagnosed with learning difficulties*). Such people may also be described as *learning disabled,* although this term and other similar usages may be considered jargonistic outside formal contexts.

**lesbian** *See* GAY.

**man/woman** *See* PERSON.

**mankind/womankind** The term *mankind* is sometimes used to refer to the whole of humanity, regardless of gender (whereas *womankind* refers specifically to females). The term should be used with caution, however, since it is likely to be considered offensive, particularly where gender issues are being discussed. It may be safer to use such neutral alternatives as *the human race, human beings,* or even *humankind.*

**member of congress** This term is often used as a gender-neutral alternative to *congressman* and *congresswoman,* although the latter terms are still in fairly frequent use.

**member of the clergy** This term is increasingly being used as a replacement for the gender-specific *clergyman* and *clergywoman. Clergywoman* in particular has never been popular, although the more politically neutral *member of the clergy* is occasionally itself considered clumsy. The more concise *cleric* is an acceptable alternative.

**Miss/Mrs./Ms.** It is important to know the difference between these three alternative titles for women, all of them abbreviated forms of *Mistress. Miss* is traditionally the correct form to choose for a girl or young unmarried woman, while *Mrs.* is appropriate for a woman who is or has been married. The more recent coinage *Ms.* is used when the marital status of a woman is unknown. Note that both *Mrs.* and *Ms.* are conventionally written with a period after them. In modern usage many women dislike being addressed as *Miss* or *Mrs.* because of the automatic assumption being made about their marital status. They are more likely to prefer the neutral *Ms.* Note, however, that *Ms.* is disliked by some (mainly older) people because of its feminist associations.

**Mrs.** *See* MISS/MRS./MS.

**Ms.** *See* MISS/MRS./MS.

**native** As a noun meaning "indigenous inhabitant," *native* should be used with care since it may easily cause offense, having acquired various derogatory connotations over the years. The term is unlikely to meet with opposition when used in its widest sense but may well be a cause of resentment when understood to imply "uncivilized barbarian" or "nonwhite" (*murdered by natives; violence between natives and colonizers*).

**Native American** This description is now considered the preferred term when referring to the indigenous inhabitants of North America and their modern descendants. It replaces such former terms as *Red Indian* and *Indian,* which are now considered unacceptable. *Red Indian* is particularly likely to cause offense with its reference to skin color. Both *Red Indian* and *Indian* are, in any case, derived from a factually incorrect historical assumption (based on the mistaken conclusion of early American explorers that they had arrived in the East Indies). Note also that the term *American Indian* has in recent times won increasing acceptance as an alternative to the over-repetition of *Native American* in a given text.

**-ne** *See* -ESS.

**Negress/Negro** *See* BLACK.

**nonwhite** *See* WHITE.

**Oriental** *See* ASIAN.

**partially sighted** *See* VISUALLY IMPAIRED.

**person** The word *person* can refer to either a male or a female, and it is occasionally chosen in preference to the gender-specific *man* or *woman*. In the same way, *-person* is often used as a suffix in replacement of *-man* or *-woman* to form such neutral terms as *sportsperson, salesperson, spokesperson,* etc. Another alternative applicable to people of either sex is *individual*.

**person of color** This phrase is sometimes employed as a less provocative alternative to such terms as *colored* or *nonwhite*. It does not meet with universal approval, however, being a somewhat labored coinage in the opinion of many people. *See also* BLACK.

**person of restricted growth** This phrase is sometimes advanced as a politically acceptable term for a person of unusually short stature. Though clumsy and jargonistic, it is widely considered preferable to *dwarf*. *Midget* is entirely unacceptable, now regarded as offensive because of its derogatory overtones. In the United States the term *little person* is gaining currency.

**person with disabilities** *See* DISABLED.

**poet** The term *poet* is now widely understood to refer to poetry writers of either sex. The feminine equivalent *poetess* is considered condescending and old fashioned and is very rarely encountered.

**poetess** *See* POET.

**policeman/policewoman** *See* POLICE OFFICER.

**police officer** The term *police officer* is now generally preferred to the gender-specific *policeman* or *policewoman,* although these are still in use.

**profoundly deaf** The term *profoundly deaf* has now largely replaced the terms *deaf-mute* and *deaf-and-dumb* to describe a person who is both unable to hear and unable to speak because of the negative connotations of the latter terms. *Deaf-and-dumb* is considered particularly offensive since it may suggest that the person concerned is incapable of communication of any kind.

**Red Indian** *See* NATIVE AMERICAN.

**salesgirl/salesman/saleswoman** *See* SALESPERSON.

**salesperson** The term *salesperson* has now largely replaced such former gender-specific terms as *salesgirl, salesman,* and *saleswoman.* The term *salesgirl* is doubly contentious, referring both to the person's gender and age.

**sculptor** The term *sculptor* was formerly used only for males but is now applied equally to females. The former term *sculptress* has now been largely replaced.

**sculptress** *See* SCULPTOR.

**Siamese twins** *See* CONJOINED.

**spokesman/spokeswoman** *See* SPOKESPERSON.

**spokesperson** The term *spokesperson* is now often preferred to the gender-specific *spokesman* or *spokeswoman,* although these are by no means out of use.

**sportsman/sportswoman** *See* SPORTSPERSON.

**sportsperson** The terms *sportsman* and *sportswoman* are commonly used, but there are circumstances where the gender-neutral *sportsperson* is preferable (*an opportunity for sportspersons everywhere*). Care should be taken over the use of this term and similar coinages, however, since they tend to operate less effectively when applied to one gender or the other rather than to both.

**squaw** This term originally denoted a woman of Native American origin, but since the word has been used more widely as a derogatory term for any woman, regardless of ethnic origin, its use has become controversial and should be avoided in all contexts. The implication is that the woman in question is subservient to her husband or occupied solely with her domestic role.

**underprivileged** The term *underprivileged* has emerged as a preferred alternative to *poor,* denoting people who lack opportunities to improve their comparatively low standard of living. *See also* DISADVANTAGED.

**visually impaired** The term *visually impaired* is now widely preferred to *blind* when referring to people with impaired eyesight. *Blind* is now avoided because of its negative associations and also because it does not reflect the many different degrees of visual impairment. It is considered particularly insensitive to use the impersonal plural form *the blind.* Other acceptable modern alternatives to *blind* include *visually challenged, unsighted,* and *partially sighted* (this last term being reserved for people with at least some vision).

**waiter** The term *waiter* was formerly reserved for males only, with *waitress* being used for females. Increasingly, however, *waiter* has come to be applied to both sexes, although *waitress* is by no means obsolete.

**waitress** *See* WAITER.

**weather forecaster** The term *weather forecaster* is often preferred to the gender-specific *weathergirl* or *weatherman.* The term *weathergirl* in particular may be considered condescending.

**weathergirl/weatherman** *See* WEATHER FORECASTER.

**white** The noun *white* is considered generally acceptable in descriptions of a person's skin color, but note that the term *nonwhite* is more controversial and should be avoided on the grounds of its negative connotations. An alternative is to refer instead to a person's geographical origins by using the terms *Caucasian* or *European.*

**worker** The term *worker* is usefully gender-neutral and is widely preferred to *workman* or *workwoman. Workwoman* itself has never enjoyed wide acceptance.

**workman/workwoman** *See* WORKER.

# SLANG

Great care should be taken regarding the use of slang outside the context of ordinary everyday speech. Slang may be defined as including any examples of vocabulary or idioms that do not belong within the standard forms of a language and are likely to be considered unacceptable in formal contexts. Many people use slang words as a mainstay of daily conversation, peppering their discourse with them in order to convey what they have to say with more immediacy or color. Slang is often described as the language of the common people and can be vibrant, vigorous, and original. It can also identify membership of a particular social class, trade, age group, or geographical region.

Slang is constantly changing. Slang words tend to be metaphorical in nature and in most cases are relatively short-lived, in many cases coming into and going out of fashion within a few years. The incautious use of outdated or unfamiliar slang can make the user look anachronistic and behind the times. One phenomenon that can cause confusion concerns the reworking of existing words by giving them new meanings, as was the case with *gay* (originally meaning "cheerful" or "brightly colored," later adopted as an offensive slang term for "homosexual," then adopted by homosexuals themselves and in due course entering the language as a generally accepted term and not a slang usage). Other examples include the adjectives *bad, cool,* and *wicked,* all of which have enjoyed new slang incarnations as superlatives in recent years.

Other slang terms are arrived at through the contraction or abbreviation of longer words, often to a single syllable (thus, *biz* for *business* or *vibes* for *vibrations*). Such coinages represent the least offensive end of the slang spectrum, but they should still be employed with care, since they may be considered too casual for formal contexts.

In the wrong context, slang words can alienate or seriously offend a reader. A person who employs slang words inappropriately risks being accused of using "bad language" (though some might argue whether any such thing exists). Even more contentious is the use of the coarser vulgarisms sometimes categorized as **taboo slang.** As a general rule it is best to avoid any word belonging to this category in written contexts and to exercise care in their use even in daily speech, particularly bearing in mind the expectations and sensitivities of a specific reader or audience. Overuse also tends to blunt their impact, both in spoken and in written contexts. Taboo slang typically includes references to religious, sexual, defecatory, or drugs imagery. An alternative course is to use a milder euphemism or the technical name for something (although such words may sound stilted in spoken communication among friends or peers).

A last category of slang words concerns the use of expletives, which can vary considerably in strength and character. As expressions of raw passion, many people would consider expletives of one kind or another indispensable in daily conversation, while still being aware that their use in written language is more contentious. As with all other slang, it is best to avoid the insertion of expletives in all but the most informal of written contexts, such as personal letters or passages of reported speech.

The following list includes a few examples of informal and slang equivalents of formal words:

| Formal | Informal/Colloquial | Slang |
|---|---|---|
| angry | mad | pissed |
| attractive | sexy | hot |
| automobile | car | wheels |
| deranged | crazy; mad | loony |
| excellent | fine | cool |
| friend | buddy; pal | main man |
| impressive | great | mega |
| lunatic | madman | headcase |
| pleasing | nice | sweet |
| satisfactory | all right | OK; okay |
| unintelligent | stupid | dumb |

# 6

# Words Often Confused

Certain words are easily confused because they look or sound similar—although they may have quite distinct meanings—or because their meanings are closely linked. The choice between different words meaning the same thing may depend on the grammatical context. The simplest solution in these cases is to find another word altogether, but taking a little time to become familiar with such confusable words and their differences allows writers to employ them with confidence and expand the number of words in their vocabulary. The following includes some of the more commonly confused words.

**a/an** The rule regarding these indefinite articles is that *a* is always used before words or abbreviations beginning with a consonant sound (*a dog, a hospital, a sound*), while *an* is used before words or abbreviations beginning with a vowel sound or with a letter that sounds like a vowel (*an inch, an FBI operative, an S bend*). Note, however, that *an* is used before many words beginning with a silent *h* (*an hour, an heiress, an honest opinion*). One exception to the general rule concerns words beginning with a *yoo* sound, usually represented by *u* or *eu:* In these cases the correct indefinite article is *a* (*a united front, a Eurasian species*). In a small number of cases (mostly words beginning with the letter *h*) *a* or *an* are both considered acceptable (*a historic moment, an historic occasion; a heroic figure, an heroic episode*), the choice depending largely on regional pronunciation.

**abrogate/arrogate** These similar-sounding verbs have distinct meanings. *Abrogate* means "abolish" or "annul" (typically, a treaty or other arrangement), while *arrogate* means "seize or appropriate for oneself without justification."

**abuse/misuse** *Abuse* and *misuse* are close in meaning, but there is a distinction between them. *Abuse* implies deliberately wrong or improper treatment of someone or something (*substance abuse, child abuse*), while *misuse* merely describes incorrect or unorthodox use, either intentional or unintentional (*misuse of the equipment, misuse of their opportunities*). Note also that as a verb *misuse* rarely applies to treatment of people, whereas *abuse* may:

*His parents abused him as a child.*

**accede/exceed** These two verbs have different meanings. *Accede* means "agree" (*accede to their demands*), while *exceed* means "be superior to" or "go beyond" (*exceed all expectations*). Note that unlike *exceed*, *accede* is always followed by *to*.

**accept/except** The verbs *accept* and *except* should not be confused since they have contrasting meanings, despite the similarity in their sound. *Accept* means "receive" or "agree to"; *except* means "leave out," "omit," or "exclude":

*He accepted the gift.*
*She accepted their argument.*
*Everyone must pay the entrance charge, children excepted.*

Note that while *except* exists as a preposition, meaning "excluding," and conjunction, meaning "otherwise than," as well as a verb, *accept* exists only as a verb.

**access/excess** The nouns *access* and *excess* vary in both meaning and pronunciation. *Access* means "entry" or "means or right of approach" (*access to the courtyard, Internet access, access to the collection*), while *excess* means "surplus" or "overindulgence" (*an excess of good things, a life of excess*). As regards pronunciation, the stress always falls on the first syllable in *access* but on the first or second syllable in *excess*.

**activate/actuate** These two verbs are similar in meaning, both signifying "make active" or "put into operation." *Activate* is the more commonly used word (*activate the boiler*), *actuate* being reserved chiefly for technical or formal contexts:

*The computer is actuated by a series of impulses.*

*Actuate* is also used where an element of personal motivation is implied:

*The decision was actuated by fear.*

**actuate/activate** *See* ACTIVATE/ACTUATE.

**adapt/adopt** These two verbs are similar in appearance but are unrelated in meaning. *Adapt* means "adjust" or "modify" (*adapt to changed circumstances; adapt an engine to run on diesel fuel*), whereas *adopt* means "accept" (*adopt the policy as your own*) and also has the specific meaning "take as your child" (*adopt a baby*).

**adherence/adhesion** The nouns *adherence* and *adhesion* both come from the verb *adhere*, meaning "to stick," but differ slightly in meaning. *Adherence* means "loyalty" or "obedience" (*adherence to official policy, adherence to the party*), while *adhesion* more literally refers to "attachment" or "sticking together" (*adhesion of the stamp to the letter*).

**adhesion/adherence** *See* ADHERENCE/ADHESION.

**administer/administrate** These two verbs both mean "manage," "supervise," or "direct":

*The state is administered from the capital.*
*It is possible to administrate your affairs from abroad.*

*Administer,* however, has additional meanings that *administrate* lacks. In certain contexts *administer* can signify "give" or "apply":

*The nurses administered first aid.*
*The punishment was administered personally by the principal.*

**administrate/administer** *See* ADMINISTER/ADMINISTRATE.

**admission/admittance** These two nouns have the same meaning of "permission" or "right to enter," but there are subtle differences in their usage. *Admission* is the standard form (*admission to the auditorium, admission charge*), while *admittance* tends to be reserved for more formal contexts:

*He was granted admittance to the royal court.*
*She was refused admittance to the library.*

*Admission* can also mean "confession" or "acknowledgment":

*The policeman recorded his admission of guilt.*
*We await an official admission of the true state of affairs.*

**admittance/admission** *See* ADMISSION/ADMITTANCE.

**adopt/adapt** *See* ADAPT/ADOPT.

**adverse/averse** These two adjectives are easily confused because their meanings overlap. *Adverse* means "antagonistic," "hostile," "unfavorable," or "contrary" (*an adverse reaction, an adverse result*), while *averse* means "opposed" or "disinclined":

*She was not averse to the suggestion.*
*He was averse to change.*

Note that in *adverse* the stress usually falls on the first syllable, but in *averse* it always falls on the second syllable.

**advice/advise** The words *advice* and *advise* are related in meaning but should not be confused. *Advice* is a noun meaning "counsel" or "formal notification" (*she offered him some good advice; receive advice of the government's decision*), whereas *advise* is the related verb meaning "to offer advice" or "notify" (*he was advised to be wary; they were advised of the decision*).

**advise/advice** *See* ADVICE/ADVISE.

**affect/effect** The verbs *affect* and *effect* are usually pronounced the same and are thus frequently confused. *Affect* means "influence" or "change":

*This development may affect the outcome.*
*The match was affected by the weather.*

*Effect* is used in formal contexts and means "bring about" or "carry out":

*He effected a comprehensive victory over his enemies.*
*The desired changes were effected immediately.*

Note that *effect* is generally more commonly used as a noun (meaning "result").

**allowed/aloud** These two words are completely separate in meaning but are sometimes confused because they share the same pronunciation. *Allowed* is the past participle of the verb *allow:*

*These changes will not be allowed.*

*Aloud* means "audible":

*He did not voice his opinion aloud.*

**all ready/already** There are differences in meaning between *all ready* and *already* and care should be taken not to confuse them. The phrase *all ready* means "in a state of readiness":

*The captain reported that the men were all ready to disembark.*

*Already* is an adverb meaning "at or by a particular time":

*The deed was already done.*

Note that *already* is the correct form when employed as an intensifier in informal speech:

*Enough already!*

**all right/alright** Confusion often arises over the correct spelling of *all right* and *alright*. Although both forms are encountered, *all right* is considered the only strictly correct version, and *alright* is best avoided.

**all together/altogether** The words *all together* and *altogether* have different meanings but are sometimes confused. The phrase *all together* means "at the same time or place" (*arrive all together*), whereas *altogether* means "entirely" or "all told":

*It does not mean that we have given up altogether.*
*That brings the total to more than a dozen altogether.*

**allusion/delusion/illusion** The nouns *allusion, delusion,* and *illusion* are distinct in meaning but are sometimes confused. *Allusion* means "passing reference":

*There were repeated allusions to her mysterious past.*

*Delusion* means "something mistaken or misleading":

*He labored under a delusion of greatness.*

*Illusion* means "false appearance" or "deceptive impression":

*This effect created an illusion of reality.*

**aloud/allowed** *See* ALLOWED/ALOUD.

**already/all ready** *See* ALL READY/ALREADY.

**alright/all right** *See* ALL RIGHT/ALRIGHT.

**alternate/alternative** The adjectives *alternate* and *alternative* are frequently used to mean the same thing, with *alternate* (originally an adjective meaning "every other" and a verb meaning "occur by turns") being used as an adjective equivalent to *alternative,* meaning "another" (*an alternate way of doing things, an alternate route*).

**alternative/alternate** *See* ALTERNATE/ALTERNATIVE.

**although/though** These conjunctions meaning "despite the fact that" are regarded as synonymous in many contexts, often used interchangeably as replacements for "but" or "yet." *Though,* however, is considered less formal than *although* and can also be used after an adjective (*tasty though low-calorie*) or as a substitute for *however:*

*This situation is different, though.*

**altogether/all together** *See* ALL TOGETHER/ALTOGETHER.

**ambiguous/ambivalent** There is a subtle difference in meaning between these two adjectives, which are often confused. *Ambiguous* means "unclear" or "having more than one possible interpretation or meaning":

*The message was ambiguous.*

*Ambivalent* means "having opposed or conflicting attitudes or emotions":

*He seemed ambivalent about her staying.*

**ambivalent/ambiguous** *See* AMBIGUOUS/AMBIVALENT.

**amend/emend** These two verbs both mean "correct" or "alter" and are both pronounced in similar fashion. *Amend,* however, is the more common usage:

*The government's advice will have to be amended.*

*Emend* is restricted exclusively to discussion of alterations to written text:

> *The inscription has been emended.*

**amiable/amicable** These two adjectives have distinct meanings, though closely related. *Amiable* means "friendly" or "congenial" (*an amiable young journalist*), whereas *amicable* means "characterized by friendliness" (*the restoration of amicable relations*).

**amicable/amiable** *See* AMIABLE/AMICABLE.

**amoral/immoral** These two adjectives have slightly different meanings and should not be confused. *Amoral* means "nonmoral" (*an amoral attitude*), whereas *immoral* means "transgressing accepted moral rules" (*immoral acts*) and suggests a more deliberate flouting of conventional morality.

**an/a** *See* A/AN.

**ante-/anti-** These two prefixes sound similar but have different origins and meanings. *Ante-* means "before" and comes from Latin (*antecedent*), whereas *anti-* means "against" and comes from Greek (*antinuclear*).

**anti-/ante-** *See* ANTE-/ANTI-.

**antisocial/asocial/nonsocial/unsociable/unsocial** These five adjectives are closely related in meaning and are often confused. *Antisocial* means "avoiding the company of others" or "harmful to society" (*an antisocial person, an antisocial act*). *Asocial* means "hostile to society" (*an asocial recluse*). *Nonsocial* means "not socially oriented" (*a nonsocial species*). *Unsociable* means "unfriendly" or "averse to social relationships" (*an unsociable character*). *Unsocial* means "unsuited to participating in society" (*a job that requires working unsocial hours*).

**appraise/apprise** These two verbs resemble each other but have different meanings. *Appraise* means "assess":

> *The committee is appraising the performance of the department.*

*Apprise* means "inform":

> *The president has been apprised of events.*

**apprise/appraise** *See* APPRAISE/APPRISE.

**apt/liable/likely/prone** These four adjectives mean much the same thing, but there are subtle differences between them. *Apt* means "having a tendency":

> *He is apt to lose his temper.*

*Apt* is largely synonymous with *liable* (*liable to leave without warning*) and with *prone* (*a system prone to failure*) but distinct from *likely*, which means "liable in this particular instance":

*The team looks likely to lose.*

**Arab/Arabian/Arabic** These three adjectives all refer to Arabia and Arabs but are used in different contexts. *Arab* is the usual choice when discussing the people or politics of the region (*Arab diplomats, Arab states*), while *Arabian* relates to the geographical area of Arabia (*Arabian desert*), and *Arabic* is usually reserved for the language of the Arabs (*he learned Arabic as a child). All three words may also be employed as nouns.*

**Arabian/Arab/Arabic** *See* ARAB/ARABIAN/ARABIC.

**Arabic/Arab/Arabian** *See* ARAB/ARABIAN/ARABIC.

**arrogate/abrogate** *See* ABROGATE/ARROGATE.

**ascent/assent** These two nouns are pronounced the same but have different meanings. *Ascent* means "climb" or "upward progress":

*They completed the first ascent of the peak.*
*His ascent to power was swift.*

*Assent* means "agreement":

*He nodded to indicate his assent.*

**asocial/antisocial/nonsocial/unsociable/unsocial** *See* ANTISOCIAL/ASOCIAL/NONSOCIAL/UNSOCIABLE/UNSOCIAL.

**assent/ascent** *See* ASCENT/ASSENT.

**assent/consent** These two words, as nouns or verbs, both mean *agree* but can have slightly different overtones. *Assent* suggests a readiness to agree:

*She eagerly gave her assent to the match.*

*Consent* sometimes implies a more reserved attitude:

*Her father eventually consented to the marriage.*

**assume/presume** These two verbs can both mean "take for granted" or "suppose" and are usually considered to be synonymous. The choice between the two words depends chiefly on the context. *Assume* suggests something without having any particular evidence for it:

*I assume you would like to come.*

*Presume* implies some grounds for the case being put forward:

*I presume you planned this moment from the beginning.*

Note that both words have a number of other meanings, in which cases they are not interchangeable:

*The major assumed command.*
*A pupil should not presume to question his teacher.*

**assure/ensure/insure** The verbs *assure, ensure,* and *insure* overlap in meaning. *Assure* can mean "state with conviction" or "inform positively":

*He assured them of his support.*

Both *assure* and *ensure* can mean "make certain":

*He assured himself that the stranger had gone.*
*Substantial growth in profits is thus ensured.*

*Insure* is usually more specific, meaning "protect financially":

*The car is no longer insured.*

It may also mean "safeguard" or "make certain" and is thus synonymous in some contexts with *assure* and *ensure:*

*The venture is insured through the support of other companies.*

**astrology/astronomy** The disciplines of *astrology* and *astronomy* both concern study of the stars but are otherwise distinct from each other. *Astrology* refers to the deducing from the movements of the stars the future pattern of events on earth and in the lives of its inhabitants:

*The president was severely criticized for relying on astrology in deciding such issues.*

*Astronomy* relates to the scientific study of the universe:

*Physics plays a central role in astronomy.*

**astronomy/astrology** *See* ASTROLOGY/ASTRONOMY.

**aural/oral** The adjectives *aural* and *oral* may both be pronounced the same, but *aural* refers to the ears and hearing in general (*aural equipment*), while *oral* relates to speech and the mouth (*oral hygiene, an oral specialist*). *Oral* may also be pronounced with an initial short o-sound.

**authoritarian/authoritative** These two adjectives are sometimes confused. *Authoritarian* means "dictatorial" or "domineering" (*the teacher's authoritarian manner in the classroom*) and carries derogatory overtones, while *authoritative* is more neutral, meaning simply "having authority" (*an authoritative account of the civil war*).

**authoritative/authoritarian** *See* AUTHORITARIAN/AUTHORITATIVE.

**averse/adverse** *See* ADVERSE/AVERSE.

**awhile/a while** The words *awhile* and *a while* both denote a "brief period of time." Their use depends on the grammatical context. *Awhile* is the adverbial form:

*Let us rest here awhile.*

*A while* is a noun phrase:

*She will be here in a while.*

**backward/backwards** *See* FORWARD/FORWARDS.

**bacteria/bacterium** *Bacteria* is the plural form of the noun *bacterium*, but the former is commonly (and incorrectly) used to refer to a single microorganism. *Bacteria* should be used only as a plural noun and given a plural verb:

*Dangerous bacteria were found in the air supply.*

**bacterium/bacteria** *See* BACTERIA/BACTERIUM.

**bail/bale** The words *bail* and *bale* are pronounced the same but have different meanings. The noun *bail* refers to the deposit of security to guarantee the appearance of an arrested person freed prior to trial (*released on bail*). The verb form *bail out* means "obtain freedom by paying bail" or "remove from a situation." The verb *bale* refers to the making of something into a bale or bundle (*paper baled by machine*) or, as a noun, to such a package (*a bale of straw*).

**bale/bail** *See* BAIL/BALE.

**bare/bear** The words *bare* and *bear* are pronounced identically and are sometimes confused. The adjective *bare* means "naked," "exposed," "unfurnished," or "unadorned" (*a bare child, a bare landscape, a bare room, the bare facts of the case*). It may also be found as a verb meaning "expose." *Bear* as a verb means "carry," "support," "bring forth," etc. (*bear the weight, bear further inspection, bear three offspring*). The noun *bear* refers to the animal (*a brown bear*).

**base/bass** The nouns *base* and *bass* should not be confused because they have different meanings, though pronounced identically. *Base* variously means "support," "foundation," or "center of operations" (*the base of such beliefs, operating from a base in the city*), while *bass* means "voice, instrument, or sound of the lowest range" (*singing bass in the choir, a bass note*). As an adjective, *base* can also mean "ignoble" or "inferior in quality."

**bass/base** *See* BASE/BASS.

**bear/bare** *See* BARE/BEAR.

**biannual/biennial** The adjectives *biannual* and *biennial* have different meanings but are easily confused because of their similarity to each other. *Biannual* means "twice yearly":

*These plants are biannuals.*

*Biennial* means "every two years":

*The authorities conduct a biennial inspection.*

**biennial/biannual** *See* BIANNUAL/BIENNIAL.

**blatant/flagrant** The adjectives *blatant* and *flagrant* convey similar ideas but are subtly different in meaning. *Blatant* means "brazen" or "crassly obvious" (*a blatant lie*) and, unlike *flagrant*, can be applied to a person (*a blatant fool*). *Flagrant* means "conspicuously shocking" (*flagrant disregard for the rules*) and places a greater emphasis upon the outrageousness of the person or subject under discussion.

**blond/blonde** The words *blond* and *blonde* both mean "light" or "fair-haired." Sometimes *blond* is reserved for males and *blonde* for females:

*The captain was a tall Scandinavian blond.*
*Mother and daughter are both blondes.*

**blonde/blond** *See* BLOND/BLONDE.

**board/bored** The noun *board* should not be confused with *bored*, the past participle of the verb *bore*. *Board* has various meanings, including "flat piece of wood," "managerial body," and "notice display" (*boards on the floor, a board decision, put results up on a board*). *Bored* means "uninterested" or "wearied" (*bored with such pastimes*).

**bored/board** *See* BOARD/BORED.

**born/borne** The words *born* and *borne* are forms of different verbs and should not be confused. *Born* is derived from the verb *bear* in the context of "give birth" (*born the following day, Mexican-born*), whereas *borne* is the past participle of the verb *bear* in the context of "carry," "withstand," or "support" (*the burden to be borne, the weight borne by the pillars*). Note, however, that in certain contexts *borne* can also be used in relation to giving birth:

*She has borne him another child.*

**borne/born** *See* BORN/BORNE.

**borrow/lend** The verbs *borrow* and *lend* have opposite meanings but are sometimes confused. *Borrow* means "take temporary possession of" (*borrow money from the bank*), while *lend* means "give temporary possession to" (*lend your coat*). Note that *borrow* should be followed by *from:*

*Borrow an instrument from the teacher.*

**bough/bow** The nouns *bough* and *bow* (in certain contexts) are pronounced the same and are sometimes confused. *Bough* refers to "tree limb" (*balanced on a large bough*), while *bow* variously means "prow" or "gesture of respect" (*waves breaking over the bow, make a deep bow*).

**bought/brought** The words *bought* and *brought* are similar in appearance but have different meanings. *Bought* is the past tense and past participle of the verb *buy* (*we bought fruit and vegetables*), whereas *brought* is the past tense and past participle of the verb *bring* (*he brought a pack of cards with him*).

**bow/bough** *See* BOUGH/BOW.

**brake/break** The words *brake* and *break* are pronounced the same and are sometimes confused. *Brake* means "slow down" or "means of slowing down" (*brake suddenly, apply the brake*), whereas the many meanings of *break* include "separate into parts," "render inoperable," or "pause from doing something" (*break in two, break a plate, break for a few minutes*).

**breach/breech** The words *breach* and *breech* have distinct meanings, though they are pronounced the same. *Breach* variously means "infraction or violation of a rule" or "break in continuity" (*a breach of the law, a breach in the wall*), while *breech* means "rear part" (*the breech of a rifle, breech birth*).

**bread/bred** The words *bread* and *bred* are pronounced the same and are sometimes confused. *Bread* refers to the foodstuff (*a slice of bread*), whereas *bred* is the past participle of the verb *breed* (*bred for showing in competition*).

**break/brake** *See* BRAKE/BREAK.

**bred/bread** *See* BREAD/BRED.

**breech/breach** *See* BREACH/BREECH.

**bridal/bridle** The adjective *bridal* and the noun (and verb) *bridle* are sometimes confused. *Bridal* means "of or relating to brides" (*a bridal gown*), whereas *bridle* (as a noun) means "harness for a horse" (*hold onto the bridle*) or (as a verb) "restrain" or "show hostility" (*bridle your temper, bridle at the suggestion*).

**bridle/bridal** *See* BRIDAL/BRIDLE.

**broach/brooch** The verb *broach* and the noun *brooch* are pronounced the same but have different meanings. *Broach* means "break into" or "open up" (*broach a cask, broach an awkward topic*), while *brooch* means "ornament fixed with a pin or clasp" (*an emerald brooch*).

**brooch/broach** *See* BROACH/BROOCH.

**brought/bought** *See* BOUGHT/BROUGHT.

**buy/by/bye** The words *buy, by,* and *bye* are pronounced identically but have different meanings. *Buy* is a verb meaning "purchase" (*buy food supplies*), while *by* is a preposition meaning "near," "through," "past," etc. (*by the exit, by the tunnel, right by them*), and *bye* variously means "farewell" or "automatic progress" (*bye to you all; a bye to the next round*). In certain contexts the terms *by* and *bye* are interchangeable (as in *bylaw, byelaw*).

**by/buy/bye** *See* BUY/BY/BYE.

**bye/buy/by** *See* BUY/BY/BYE.

**cache/cash** The nouns *cache* and *cash* are pronounced identically but have different meanings. *Cache* variously means "secret stock" or, in computing, "quick-access computer memory" (*a munitions cache, retrieve from the cache memory*), whereas *cash* refers to "ready money" (*30 dollars in cash*).

**calendar/colander** These two nouns are totally unrelated in meaning and should not be confused. A *calendar* refers to a "system for arranging dates" or a "list of forthcoming events" (*the Roman calendar, a full calendar over the next few weeks*), whereas a *colander* is a "kitchen utensil used to drain food" (*drain lettuce in a colander*).

**callous/callus** The words *callous* and *callus* are pronounced the same but have different meanings. *Callous* is an adjective meaning "insensitive" or "hardhearted" (*a callous attitude, callous indifference*), whereas the noun *callus* denotes an "area of hardened skin":

> *His skin was covered with calluses.*

**callus/callous** *See* CALLOUS/CALLUS.

**can/may** Confusion can sometimes arise over the use of these two verbs. The words are interchangeable in the sense "be permitted" (*can we stay? may we stay?*), but *can* has the additional sense "be able":

> *She can juggle with five balls.*

*May* has the additional sense "be likely":

> *Things may work out as planned.*

**cannon/canon** The nouns *cannon* and *canon* are similar in appearance but are unrelated in meaning. *Cannon* means "large heavy gun" (*siege cannon*), whereas *canon* variously means "clergyman in a cathedral," "religious law," or, more generally, a "list of authoritative sources" or a "set of accepted rules or principles" (*a canon regular, a statute of canon law, a new addition to the canon, break every* *rule in the canon*). Note that, unlike *canon, cannon* may also be used as a verb:

*The ball cannoned off the wall.*

**canon/cannon** *See* CANNON/CANON.

**canvas/canvass** The words *canvas* and *canvass* are unrelated in meaning. The noun and adjective *canvas* refers to a "closely woven cloth used for sails, tents, and by artists":

*The canvas sail flapped in the breeze.*
*They spent the night under canvas.*
*Come and view the canvas at the studio.*

*Canvass* is a verb meaning "solicit votes or support":

*We intend to canvass on behalf of the vice president.*

**canvass/canvas** *See* CANVAS/CANVASS.

**capital/capitol** These two words are easily confused but have different meanings. *Capital* variously means "seat of government," "punishable by death," or "stock of goods or assets" (*the capital of the country, a capital offense, set against the capital of the company*), while *capitol* means "state legislature" or "building in which a legislature meets":

*The opposition party now dominates the Capitol.*

**capitol/capital** *See* CAPITAL/CAPITOL.

**cash/cache** *See* CACHE/CASH.

**caster/castor** The words *caster* and *castor* are interchangeable in some contexts but differ in meaning in others. *Caster* and *castor* are both acceptable in the context of a "sprinkler" or "shaker," "swivel wheel," or "fine sugar" (*pour sugar from the caster, a chair on casters, use only castor sugar*), but *castor* is the only correct form in relation to *castor oil.*

**castor/caster** *See* CASTER/CASTOR.

**cede/seed** The verbs *cede* and *seed* are pronounced identically but have different meanings. *Cede* means "yield" or "assign" (*cede victory to an opponent, cede rights to the publisher*), while *seed* variously means "sow," "initiate," or "rank in order" (*seed a crop; seed interest in the project; the athlete seeded sixth for the tournament*).

**censer/censor/censure** The words *censer, censor,* and *censure* are similar in appearance but differ in meaning. *Censer* is a relatively rare term for a "vessel used for burning incense":

*The censer swung above the heads of the congregation.*

*Censor* refers to a "person who examines and edits letters, films, and other material and removes offending parts from them" or, as a verb, to the act of doing so:

*The script has been approved by the official censor.*
*The government routinely censored the news.*

*Censure* is a verb meaning "criticize" or "condemn":

*She was censured by the court for her disrespect.*

**censor/censer/censure** *See* CENSER/CENSOR/CENSURE.

**censure/censer/censor** *See* CENSER/CENSOR/CENSURE.

**cereal/serial** *Cereal* and *serial* are pronounced the same but have different meanings. *Cereal,* which derives from Ceres, the name of the Roman goddess of the harvest, relates to grain and food made from it (*cereal crops, breakfast cereal*), whereas *serial* refers to a television series or anything else that consists of a sequence of parts (*the latest episode in this serial, serial killer*).

**ceremonial/ceremonious** The adjectives *ceremonial* and *ceremonious* both refer to *ceremony* and are easily confused. *Ceremonial* simply denotes something connected with ceremony (*ceremonial robes, a ceremonial occasion*), while *ceremonious* describes the formal and possibly overelaborate way in which something is done (*with a ceremonious wave of her arm*). Note that, unlike *ceremonious, ceremonial* may sometimes appear as a noun (*attend the ceremonial*).

**ceremonious/ceremonial** *See* CEREMONIAL/CEREMONIOUS.

**chute/shoot** These two words share the same pronunciation but are unrelated in meaning. *Chute* is a noun meaning "slide" or "quick descent" (*a water chute*), whereas *shoot* as a verb means "fire off" (*shoot a gun*). As a noun, *shoot* is used to refer to the action of shooting or a shooting trip (*a shoot in the jungle*) or taking a photograph or film (*a video shoot*). *Shoots* are the new parts growing on a plant or tree.

**cite/sight/site** These three words are pronounced the same but have distinct meanings. *Cite* is a verb meaning "quote by way of example":

*He cited several legal precedents.*

*Sight* is a noun and verb referring to "seeing":

*He has regained the power of sight.*
*She sighted smoke.*

*Site* is a noun and verb meaning "place":

*The new house is sited on a hill.*
*The materials have been delivered to the building site.*

**civic/civil/civilian** These three words are closely related but remain subtly different in meaning. *Civic* means "of or relating to a city or community" (*civic affairs, civic duty*), whereas *civil* means "of or relating to citizens" (*civil rights, civil responsibilities*), and *civilian* means "not in the armed forces, police, firefighters, and the like" (*retire from the army into civilian life*). Note that *civil* can also mean "courteous" or "polite."

**civil/civic/civilian** *See* CIVIC/CIVIL/CIVILIAN.

**civilian/civic/civil** *See* CIVIC/CIVIL/CIVILIAN.

**classic/classical** The words *classic* and *classical* have different meanings, although they do overlap in some contexts. *Classic* variously means "excellent," "traditional," or "typical" (*a classic performance, classic style, classic symptoms*), while *classical* may refer to the world of ancient Greece and Rome, to music composed before the modern period, or to anything considered authoritative or traditional (*classical archaeology, classical opera, classical mathematics*).

**classical/classic** *See* CLASSIC/CLASSICAL.

**clean/cleanse** Both *clean* and *cleanse* refer to the business of eliminating dirt, although *cleanse* suggests a more thorough washing or purification. Note that *clean* may be used as a verb, noun, adjective, and adverb (*clean your face, give the house a clean, clean hands, wiped clean*), but *cleanse* may be employed only as a verb (*cleansed of impurities*).

**cleanse/clean** *See* CLEAN/CLEANSE.

**clench/clinch** These two verbs are easily confused because they are close in meaning; both mean "hold fast" or "close tightly." But whereas *clench* can refer to a range of subjects (*clench the rung of the ladder, clench your teeth*), *clinch* is usually reserved for gripping or embracing a person (*clinched in a bearhug*), although it can also be used figuratively (*clinch a deal*).

**client/customer** The nouns *client* and *customer* have slightly different meanings and are used in different contexts. A *client* suggests a professional relationship (*the clients of a law firm*), while *customer* denotes a less formal relationship (*customers in a shop*). *Client* or *clientele* or *patron* may sometimes be preferred to *customer* when emphasizing the exclusivity of the relationship involved (*patrons of this establishment*).

**climactic/climatic** These two words are unrelated in meaning, despite their superficial similarity. *Climactic* is an adjective derived from *climax* (*the climactic scene in the play*), while *climatic* is an adjective derived from *climate* (*extreme climatic conditions*).

**climatic/climactic** *See* CLIMACTIC/CLIMATIC.

**clinch/clench** *See* CLENCH/CLINCH.

**coarse/course** The words *coarse* and *course* are pronounced identically but have different meanings. *Coarse* is an adjective meaning "rough," "vulgar," "crude," or "unrefined" (*coarse texture, coarse language, coarse behavior, coarse sand*), whereas *course* variously means "progression" or "route" (*the course of events; take a new course*). Unlike *coarse, course* is occasionally encountered as a verb meaning "hunt," "traverse," or "pass" (*course with dogs; crowds coursing the piazza; the blood coursed in her veins*).

**coherent/cohesive** The adjectives *coherent* and *cohesive* both come from the verb *cohere* but have slightly different meanings and are used in different ways. *Coherent* means "consistent," "understandable," or "coordinated" (*a coherent policy, a coherent statement, a coherent plan of action*), whereas *cohesive* means "sticking together" and is usually employed figuratively (*a cohesive unit within the larger organization*).

**cohesive/coherent** *See* COHERENT/COHESIVE.

**colander/calendar** *See* CALENDAR/COLANDER.

**collaborate/cooperate** The verbs *collaborate* and *cooperate* both entail "working in coordination with others" and are largely interchangeable, but care should be taken in some circumstances where they have different connotations. *Collaborate* tends to be preferred when discussing joint work on an artistic or intellectual project:

*They are collaborating on a new book.*

It can also more specifically denote assisting an enemy:

*She is accused of collaborating with the invaders.*

*Cooperate* is more neutral in tone:

*We will succeed if we cooperate.*

**comic/comical** The two adjectives *comic* and *comical* both come from *comedy* but vary slightly in meaning. *Comic* means "of or relating to comedy" (*a comic performer, a comic novel*), while *comical* means "causing laughter," whether provoking laughter was the intention or not (*a comical incident, comical incompetence*).

**comical/comic** *See* COMIC/COMICAL.

**commandant/commander/commandeer** The words *commandant, commander,* and *commandeer* all relate to the verb *command* but are used differently. *Commandant* denotes a "person in command of a particular group or installation" (*commandant of a prisoner-of-war camp*), whereas *commander* is a more general term for a "commanding officer" of any kind (*commander of the strike force, division commander*). *Commandeer* is a verb meaning "take possession of by force or for military purposes":

*He commandeered the jeep for his own use.*
*The building has been commandeered by the army.*

**commandeer/commandant/commander** *See* COMMANDANT/COMMANDER/COMMANDEER.

**commander/commandant/commandeer** *See* COMMANDANT/COMMANDER/COMMANDEER.

**common/mutual/reciprocal** The adjectives *common, mutual,* and *reciprocal* are close in meaning but are not always interchangeable. *Common* means "joint" or "shared" (*a common interest*), whereas *mutual* means "shared by two or more people" (*mutual hatred*) and *reciprocal* means "done in return" (*reciprocal feelings*).

**compel/impel** The verbs *compel* and *impel* both basically mean "force" but are subtly different. *Compel* suggests an overwhelming element of obligation:

*He was compelled to complete the work.*

*Impel* suggests the influence of an internal urge instead of external obligation:

*He felt impelled to act.*

Note that *impel* can also be applied to the driving forward of inanimate objects:

*The boat was impelled backward by the wave.*

**competition/contest** The nouns *competition* and *contest* mean much the same thing, but there are subtle differences between them. *Competition* can denote rivalry of virtually any kind, whether organized or not (*win the competition, competition between siblings, competition for food*), whereas *contest* suggests rivalry with a degree of organization (*an archery contest, a contest in three heats*). Note also that *competition* can also refer directly to the opposition:

*We face strong competition this year.*

**complacent/complaisant** These two adjectives sound similar but have different meanings. *Complacent* means "self-satisfied" or "smug":

*The authorities have been complacent in not doing something sooner.*

*Complaisant* means "inclined to please or oblige" (*a complaisant bow*).

**complaisant/complacent** *See* COMPLACENT/COMPLAISANT.

**complementary/complimentary** *See* COMPLEMENT/COMPLIMENT.

**complement/compliment** The similarity between these two words means they are easily confused, although they have very different meanings. *Complement* denotes "something that fills up, completes, or perfects something else" or the act of doing so:

*The wine serves as a complement to the food.*
*Her sweater complements the dress she's wearing.*

*Compliment* describes an "admiring or flattering remark or action" or the act of doing so:

*She accepted the compliment gracefully.*
*Let me compliment you on your choice.*

Note that the same confusion can arise in relation to the adjectival forms of these two words, *complementary* and *complimentary* (*complementary medicine, a complimentary letter*). The adjective *complimentary* also has the additional meaning of "given free" (*a complimentary glass of wine with each meal*).

**complement/supplement** The words *complement* and *supplement* have different meanings. *Complement* means "something that fills up, completes, or makes perfect" (*a full complement of faculties; the ship's complement*), whereas *supplement* means "something that adds to" (*a supplement to the main text; a dietary supplement*).

**complex/complicated** These two words both mean "consisting of intricately connected parts" but are subtly different in the way they are used. *Complex* is a fairly neutral term simply referring to the intricacy of the subject under discussion (*a complex network of wires, a complex equation*), while *complicated* emphasizes the difficulty involved in understanding something because of its complexity:

*The system is very complicated.*
*It is a complicated issue.*

**complicated/complex** *See* COMPLEX/COMPLICATED.

**complimentary/complementary** *See* COMPLEMENT/COMPLIMENT.

**compliment/complement** *See* COMPLEMENT/COMPLIMENT.

**compose/comprise/constitute** These three verbs are closely related but there are subtle differences in the way they are used. *Compose* and *constitute* both mean "form the substance of," but in this sense, *compose* is generally used passively:

*The mixture is composed of fuel and air.*

*Constitute* is used actively:

*These difficulties constitute a major obstacle.*

*Comprise* means "consist of, include":

*The train comprised an engine and three coaches.*

*Comprise* should not, however, be freely used as a replacement for *compose* or *constitute* as it always refers to the whole rather than to its parts:

*The entire complex comprises nine buildings.*

Note also that *comprise* should never be followed by *of.*

**comprehensible/comprehensive** The adjectives *comprehensible* and *comprehensive* both come from the verb *comprehend* but have different meanings. *Comprehensible* means "intelligible" (*comprehensible instructions, comprehensible to ordinary people*), whereas *comprehensive* means "inclusive" or "complete" (*a comprehensive overhaul of the system, a comprehensive account*).

**comprehensive/comprehensible** *See* COMPREHENSIBLE/COMPREHENSIVE.

**comprise/constitute/compose** *See* COMPOSE/COMPRISE/CONSTITUTE.

**compulsive/compulsory** The adjectives *compulsive* and *compulsory* both come from the verb *compel* but have distinct meanings. *Compulsive* refers specifically to psychological compulsion or obsession (*a compulsive need to do something, a compulsive liar*), while *compulsory* means "mandatory" or "enforced" and refers specifically to external pressure to do something:

*Attendance in class is compulsory.*
*The judge ordered a compulsory declaration of assets.*

**compulsory/compulsive** *See* COMPULSIVE/COMPULSORY.

**condition/precondition** There is a significant difference in meaning between *condition* and *precondition,* which both refer to stipulations made in connection with the drawing up of a contract or other agreement. A *condition* may refer to something that may be done before or after the agreement is made:

*His retirement is a condition of the contract.*

A *precondition* refers to something that must be done before the agreement may be completed:

*The treaty will not be signed if these preconditions are not met.*

**confidant/confidante/confident** The nouns *confidant* and *confidante* should not be confused with the adjective *confident. Confidant* describes a "trusted friend" or "someone to whom one entrusts secrets" (*a confidant of the president*); *confidante* is the feminine equivalent (*his wife and confidante*). The adjective *confident* means "certain," "assured," or "self-reliant" (*confident of victory, a confident young woman*).

**confidante/confidant/confident** *See* CONFIDANT/CONFIDANTE/CONFIDENT.

**confident/confidant/confidante** *See* CONFIDANT/CONFIDANTE/CONFIDENT.

**congenial/genial** *Congenial* and *genial* both mean "pleasant" or "sociable," but there are differences in the way they are used. *Congenial* is generally used in referring to abstract nouns (*congenial surroundings*), whereas *genial* usually refers to people (*a genial stranger, our genial host*).

**connote/denote** The verbs *connote* and *denote* are often confused. *Connote* means "imply" or "suggest":

*To many the term rural connotes unsophistication.*

*Denote* means "make known" and is more literal in tone:

*Her smile denoted great joy.*

**conscientious/conscious** *Conscientious* and *conscious* have different meanings. *Conscientious means "scrupulous" or "meticulous"* (conscientious about his duties, a conscientious worker), while *conscious* means "awake" or "aware":

*The patient is conscious again.*
*She was acutely conscious of her mistake.*

**conscious/conscientious** *See* CONSCIENTIOUS/CONSCIOUS.

**consent/assent** *See* ASSENT/CONSENT.

**consequent/consequential** Both *consequent* and *consequential* come from the noun *consequence* but vary in meaning in certain contexts. *Consequent* and *consequential* can both mean "following as a result or effect":

*The consequent investigation was very thorough.*
*The consequential accident ruined him.*

*Consequential* can also mean "important":

*This setback proved highly consequential.*

Another meaning is "self-important":

*He spoke in a lugubrious, consequential tone of voice.*

**consequent/subsequent** The adjectives *consequent* and *subsequent* are similar in meaning but are sometimes confused. *Consequent* means "following as a result or effect":

*This error and the consequent damage destroyed his reputation.*

*Subsequent* simply means "occurring after":

*This discovery shaped the course of subsequent events.*

Note that *consequent* takes the preposition *on* (*a change in policy consequent on this decision*), but *subsequent* is followed by *to* (*subsequent to her arrival*).

**consequential/consequent** *See* CONSEQUENT/CONSEQUENTIAL.

**constitute/compose/comprise** *See* COMPOSE/COMPRISE/CONSTITUTE.

**constrain/restrain** The verbs *constrain* and *restrain* both mean "hold back" or "limit" but are used in different contexts. *Constrain* usually implies an element of mental or abstract repression, often of an undesirable kind (*constrained by his natural timidity; constrained from saying what she really felt*), whereas *restrain* often implies more direct, often physical, pressure (*restrained by handcuffs; restraining a disturbed patient*).

**contagious/contiguous** The words *contagious* and *contiguous* have different meanings. *Contagious* means "communicable by contact" (*a contagious disease*), whereas *contiguous* means "in contact with" or "adjacent" (*contiguous sides*).

**contagious/infectious** There is a subtle difference in meaning between *contagious* and *infectious,* though this distinction is commonly ignored. *Contagious* means "communicable by contact":

> *Athlete's foot is contagious.*

*Infectious* denotes something that is communicable by either physical or nonphysical contact:

> *Infectious diseases include influenza and chicken pox.*

Note that both words can be used figuratively:

> *The panic proved contagious.*
> *He has an infectious sense of humor.*

**contemptible/contemptuous** The adjectives *contemptible* and *contemptuous* are both derived from *contempt* but mean different things. *Contemptible* means "worthy of contempt" (*a contemptible person, a contemptible act of betrayal*), whereas *contemptuous* means "manifesting, feeling, or expressing contempt":

> *She was contemptuous of his ambitions.*
> *He greeted the news with contemptuous disdain.*

**contemptuous/contemptible** *See* CONTEMPTIBLE/CONTEMPTUOUS.

**contest/competition** *See* COMPETITION/CONTEST.

**contiguous/contagious** *See* CONTAGIOUS/CONTIGUOUS.

**continual/continuous** These two words are close in meaning but are not synonymous. *Continual* means "frequently recurring" (*continual interruptions*), whereas *continuous* means "unceasing" (*a continuous noise*). The same applies to the adverbs *continually* and *continuously:*

*He is continually resolving to go back to his wife.*
*The conveyor belt operates continuously.*

**continually/continuously** *See* CONTINUAL/CONTINUOUS.

**continuance/continuation/continuity** These three nouns all relate to the verb *continue* but are slightly different in meaning. *Continuance* denotes the "uninterrupted continuing" of something (*the continuance of payments*), whereas *continuation* may suggest the "continuing of something after an interruption" (*the continuation of the campaign after the winter*), and *continuity* describes the "state of being continuous" (*film continuity*).

**continuation/continuance/continuity** *See* CONTINUANCE/CONTINUATION/CONTINUITY.

**continuity/continuance/continuation** *See* CONTINUANCE/CONTINUATION/CONTINUITY.

**continuous/continual** *See* CONTINUAL/CONTINUOUS.

**continuously/continually** *See* CONTINUAL/CONTINUOUS.

**converse/inverse/obverse/reverse** All four of these words loosely mean "opposite," although they are used in different ways. *Converse* is a noun employed in discussing something reversed in order, relation, or action:

*The converse is also true.*

*Inverse* usually appears as an adjective:

*The benefits are in inverse proportion to the amount eaten.*

The noun *obverse* means "counterpart":

*Death is the obverse of life.*

*Reverse* is the most frequently used of the four words and can be employed as a noun, adjective, or verb (*go into reverse; in reverse order; reverse an opinion*).

**cooperate/collaborate** *See* COLLABORATE/COOPERATE.

**corporal/corporeal** The adjectives *corporal* and *corporeal* are superficially similar but are in fact subtly different in meaning. *Corporal* means "of or relating to the body" (*corporal punishment*), while *corporeal* means "material" or "physical" in a wider sense:

*It seemed that his nightmare had taken corporeal form.*

**corporeal/corporal** *See* CORPORAL/CORPOREAL.

**corps/corpse** The nouns *corps* and *corpse* are similar in appearance but different in meaning and should not be confused. *Corps* means "body of persons" (*corps de ballet, military corps*), whereas *corpse* means "dead body" (*a decaying corpse*).

**corpse/corps** *See* CORPS/CORPSE.

**cost/price** The nouns *cost* and *price* have much the same meaning but are not always synonymous. *Cost* usually refers to the payment made for something:

*She met the cost of the apartment.*

*Price* is usually applied to the amount charged for something:

*The price of these items has risen since last week.*
*He demanded a high price for his loyalty.*

**council/counsel** The nouns *council* and *counsel* are pronounced the same and are sometimes confused. *Council* means "administrative, advisory, or executive body of people":

*The council of the university met to discuss the issue.*

*Counsel* means "advice":

*The old man was universally respected for his wise counsel.*

**councilor/counselor** These two nouns are pronounced almost identically but have different meanings. A *councilor* is a "member of a council" (*she was elected councilor last month*), whereas a *counselor* is "someone who provides counsel or listens to a person's problems" (*she is a bereavement counselor*).

**counsel/council** *See* COUNCIL/COUNSEL.

**counselor/councilor** *See* COUNCILOR/COUNSELOR.

**course/coarse** *See* COARSE/COURSE.

**creak/creek** These two words are pronounced identically and may be mistaken for one another. *Creak* describes a "rasping or grating noise":

*The floorboard creaked under his foot.*
*She heard a creak behind her.*

*Creek* means "small inlet," "bay," or "narrow stream":

*A small vessel was anchored in the creek.*
*They crossed the creek with little difficulty.*

**credible/creditable/credulous** The adjectives *credible, creditable,* and *credulous* are related in meaning and are sometimes confused. *Credible* means "believable":

*His story seemed credible to me.*

*Creditable* means "worthy of praise":

*He remarked upon the creditable behavior of the class.*

*Credulous* means "gullible":

*She was not as credulous as she appeared.*

The same subtleties of meaning apply to the associated nouns *credibility, credit,* and *credulity.*

**creditable/credible/credulous** *See* CREDIBLE/CREDITABLE/CREDULOUS.

**credulous/credible/creditable** *See* CREDIBLE/CREDITABLE/CREDULOUS.

**creek/creak** *See* CREAK/CREEK.

**crevasse/crevice** The nouns *crevasse* and *crevice* both relate to cracks, though of different scales. *Crevasse* is the word used to describe a crack in ice, which may be of vast dimensions:

*They crossed one seemingly bottomless crevasse after another.*

*Crevice* may apply to cracks or folds of a generally smaller size:

*He probed the crevice with a penknife.*
*The bird flew into a narrow crevice in the side of a cliff.*

**crevice/crevasse** *See* CREVASSE/CREVICE.

**criteria/criterion** The noun *criterion,* meaning "standard by which something should be measured," is much better known in its plural form *criteria,* but *criteria* should never be used in place of the singular:

*Candidates must meet or exceed this criterion.*
*Employees are evaluated according to a specific set of criteria.*

**criterion/criteria** *See* CRITERIA/CRITERION.

**critic/critique** The nouns *critic* and *critique* are easily confused. A *critic* is a "person who evaluates or finds fault with someone or something" (*drama critic, a critic of the ruling party*), while a *critique* is a "piece of critical writing," typically one of a serious analytical nature (*a critique of contemporary dance theory*).

**critique/critic** *See* CRITIC/CRITIQUE.

**cue/queue** The words *cue* and *queue* are pronounced the same but are unrelated in meaning. *Cue* means "signal" or "hint":

*The actor heard his cue.*
*This signal was the cue for things to start happening.*

In sport it can also denote a stick used in playing billiards, shuffleboards, and similar games:

*He selected a cue from the stand.*

*Queue* variously means "long braid of hair" or "line of people, messages, tasks, and so on":

*She wore her hair in a queue.*
*They joined the long queue of customers.*
*He was faced with a queue of jobs waiting to be done.*

**currant/current** The nouns *currant* and *current* are pronounced virtually identically and are easily confused. A *currant* is a "small seedless raisin" (jelly made from *currants*), whereas *current* denotes "something that runs or flows" (*a current of water, electric current*). *Current* also has the meaning "present" or "happening now" (*current affairs, his current girlfriend*).

**current/currant** *See* CURRANT/CURRENT.

**customer/client** *See* CLIENT/CUSTOMER.

**cymbal/symbol** The nouns *cymbal* and *symbol* are very different in meaning, though pronounced similarly. A *cymbal* is a percussion instrument (*a crash on the cymbal*), whereas a *symbol* denotes a "sign or design that represents something else" (*a symbol of hope*).

**cynical/skeptical** The adjectives *cynical* and *skeptical* are sometimes confused. *Cynical* means "deeply distrustful," especially with regard to human nature and motives:

*She was surprised by their cynical attitude toward idealism.*
*It was an act of cynical cowardice.*

*Skeptical* means "doubtful" or "incredulous":

*We remain skeptical about such claims.*

**deadly/deathly** The adjectives *deadly* and *deathly* are related but have slightly different meanings. *Deadly* variously means "likely to cause death," "implacable," or "boring" (*a deadly blow to the head, in deadly earnest, a deadly evening*), whereas *deathly* means "of or relating to death" (*deathly pale skin, a deathly silence*).

**dear/deer** The words *dear* and *deer* are pronounced the same but are unrelated in meaning. *Dear* variously means "beloved" or "expensive":

*Come in, my dear friend.*
*The food is very dear in this hotel.*

*Deer* denotes the animal (*a herd of deer*), both in the singular and plural.

**deathly/deadly** *See* DEADLY/DEATHLY.

**debar/disbar** The verbs *debar* and *disbar* are close in meaning but are used differently. *Debar* means "preclude" or "bar from":

> *They were debarred from taking part in the competition.*

*Disbar* refers more specifically to the expulsion of a lawyer from the bar or the legal profession:

> *Following the investigation, both attorneys have been disbarred for life.*

**deceitful/deceptive** Both *deceitful* and *deceptive* mean "deceiving" or "misleading," but there are subtle differences between them. *Deceitful* suggests an intention to deceive (*a deceitful character, a deceitful account of events*), while *deceptive* is more neutral in tone and does not necessarily imply any deliberate dishonesty (*deceptive light conditions, a deceptive bend in the road*).

**decent/decorous** The adjectives *decent* and *decorous* both mean "socially acceptable" (*decent behavior, decorous conduct*) but are not freely interchangeable in other contexts, as *decent* has a number of further meanings that it does not share with *decorous*. Thus, *decorous* should not be used as a replacement for *decent* where the meaning is "adequate," "pleasant," or "morally correct" (*a decent enough performance; a decent fellow; a decent house; do the decent thing*).

**deceptive/deceitful** *See* DECEITFUL/DECEPTIVE.

**decidedly/decisively** In some contexts these two words can be used as synonyms of each other, but in others they should not be confused. Both *decidedly* and *decisively* can mean "firmly" or "resolutely" (*she spoke decidedly; they acted decisively*), but *decidedly* can also mean "definitely" or "unquestionably" (*a decidedly awkward situation*), while *decisively* can mean "unwaveringly" (*moving decisively toward his goal*) or "conclusively":

> *This battle decisively settled the war.*

**decisively/decidedly** *See* DECIDEDLY/DECISIVELY.

**decorous/decent** *See* DECENT/DECOROUS.

**deduce/deduct** The verbs *deduce* and *deduct* have totally different meanings and should not be confused. *Deduce* means "determine by deduction" (*deduce the solution to the problem*), while *deduct* means "subtract" (*deduct the cost of the ingredients from the total*). Note that both verbs, though unconnected in meaning, share identical derived forms as the noun *deduction*.

**deduct/deduce** *See* DEDUCE/DEDUCT.

**deer/dear** *See* DEAR/DEER.

**defective/deficient** The adjectives *defective* and *deficient* have similar meanings but are not exact synonyms. *Defective* means "faulty" or "not working properly":

*The machinery is defective.*
*The vehicle has defective steering.*

*Deficient* means "lacking" or "inadequate":

*The system is deficient in terms of flexibility.*
*The funds are deficient for the purpose.*

**defensible/defensive** The adjectives *defensible* and *defensive* both relate to the noun *defense* but have different meanings. *Defensible* means "capable of being defended" (*a defensible position*), whereas *defensive* means "protective" or "serving to defend" (*a defensive formation, defensive tactics*).

**defensive/defensible** *See* DEFENSIBLE/DEFENSIVE.

**deficient/defective** *See* DEFECTIVE/DEFICIENT.

**definite/definitive** The adjectives *definite* and *definitive* have different meanings but are sometimes confused. *Definite* means "distinct," "certain," or "precise" (*a definite arrangement, a definite outline, a definite figure*), while *definitive* means "authoritative" or "exhaustive" (*a definitive account of the revolutionary war, a definitive work of reference*).

**definitive/definite** *See* DEFINITE/DEFINITIVE.

**defuse/diffuse** Though similar in appearance these two verbs have different meanings. *Defuse* means "remove the fuse" or, more figuratively, "make less harmful or potent":

*They will have to defuse the bomb.*
*The threat of inflation has been largely defused.*

*Diffuse* means "spread around" or "scatter":

*The heat was diffused through the building.*

It can also be used as an adjective meaning "widely spread" (*a diffuse light*).

**deliverance/delivery** The nouns *deliverance* and *delivery* differ slightly in meaning. *Deliverance* denotes "liberation" or the "act or state of being delivered" (*the deliverance of the people; bring about your deliverance*), while *delivery* extends more generally to the delivering of something (*the delivery of a letter, delivery of a better service, the baby's easy delivery*).

**delivery/deliverance** *See* DELIVERANCE/DELIVERY.

**delusion/allusion/illusion** *See* ALLUSION/DELUSION/ILLUSION.

**denote/connote** *See* CONNOTE/DENOTE.

**deny/refute** The verbs *deny* and *refute* are subtly different in meaning. *Deny* means "declare untrue" or "refuse to admit":

*He denied any involvement in the affair.*

*Refute* means "prove wrong by argument or evidence":

*These documents refute the government's claims.*

Note that *refute* is fairly commonly used as a synonym of *deny* in meaning "declare untrue," although this usage is, strictly speaking, incorrect.

**deprecate/depreciate** In many contexts the verbs *deprecate* and *depreciate* have different meanings. *Deprecate* means "express disapproval of":

*The investigating board deprecated the disappearance of the records.*

*Depreciate* means "fall in value" or "lower in estimation":

*Shares in the company have depreciated considerably since last week.*

In some senses the two words overlap. Both *depreciate* and *deprecate* can be used to mean "belittle" (*depreciated by his critics; deprecated by all her former friends*). *Deprecate* can also mean "play down" or "show modesty":

*He was self-deprecating about his achievements.*

**depreciate/deprecate** *See* DEPRECATE/DEPRECIATE.

**derisive/derisory** The words *derisive* and *derisory* both come from the verb *deride* but are used differently. *Derisive* means "expressing or causing derision" (*dismissed with a derisive wave of the hand*), while *derisory* means "worthy of derision" (*a derisory effort*).

**derisory/derisive** *See* DERISIVE/DERISORY.

**desert/dessert** These two nouns are pronounced differently and are unrelated in meaning. *Desert* (which is pronounced with the stress on the first syllable) means "arid wasteland" (*a vast, sandy desert*). Note, however, that when used in the plural to mean "deserved reward" (*get your just deserts*) the stress is placed on the second syllable. *Dessert* (which is pronounced with the stress on the second syllable) denotes the "sweet course of a meal" (*a delicious frozen dessert*).

**desirable/desirous** The adjectives *desirable* and *desirous* are easily confused. *Desirable* means "attractive" or "advisable" (*a desirable property, a desirable move*), whereas *desirous* means "wanting" (*desirous of pleasing her*). Note that *desirous* is always followed by *of*.

**desirous/desirable** *See* DESIRABLE/DESIROUS.

**despair/desperation** The nouns *despair* and *desperation* are closely related in meaning but are not always used identically. Both *despair* and *desperation* can mean "hopelessness" (*despair at this news, an atmosphere of desperation*), but *desperation* can also signify "rashness resulting from despair":

> *In desperation he flung the revolver at his adversary.*

**desperation/despair** *See* DESPAIR/DESPERATION.

**despite/in spite of** *Despite* and *in spite of* mean exactly the same thing and are freely interchangeable, but note that it is incorrect to follow *despite* with *of*:

> *He stayed despite their insults.*
> *He stayed in spite of their insults.*

**dessert/desert** *See* DESERT/DESSERT.

**detract/distract** The verbs *detract* and *distract* have different meanings. *Detract* means "take away from" or "diminish":

> *This damage will detract from the final value.*

*Distract* means "divert attention":

> *Her beauty distracted him.*

**device/devise** The words *device* and *devise* are related in meaning but should not be confused. *Device* is a noun meaning "contrivance," "plan," or "trick":

> *He made his fortune from a clever device for opening bottles.*
> *By this device they planned to storm the fortress.*

*Devise* is a verb meaning "plan":

> *We must devise a way out of this situation.*

**devise/device** *See* DEVICE/DEVISE.

**diagnosis/prognosis** The nouns *diagnosis* and *prognosis* have slightly different meanings and are sometimes confused. *Diagnosis* denotes the identification of a medical ailment or other problem through analysis of symptoms or other signs:

> *He was not happy with the doctor's diagnosis.*

*Prognosis* means "forecast," specifically of the future course of an illness or other problem and the chances of improvement:

*The prognosis for the future is not encouraging.*

Note that in both cases the plural is formed by changing the *-is* ending to *-es: diagnoses, prognoses.*

**difference/differentiation** These two nouns are not identical in meaning. *Difference* means "dissimilarity" (*the difference between the two*), whereas *differentiation* describes the process by which two or more things become dissimilar (*the differentiation of the two systems over the centuries*).

**differentiation/difference** *See* DIFFERENCE/DIFFERENTIATION.

**diffuse/defuse** *See* DEFUSE/DIFFUSE.

**dinghy/dingy** The words *dinghy* and *dingy* are unrelated in meaning. The noun *dinghy* describes a small boat (*an inflatable dinghy*), while the adjective *dingy* means "shabby" or "gloomy" (*a dingy apartment, dingy surroundings*). Note that the two words are pronounced differently, *dinghy* with a hard *g* sound (*dingee*) and *dingy* with a soft *g* sound (*dinjee*).

**dingy/dinghy** *See* DINGHY/DINGY.

**disassemble/dissemble** The verbs *disassemble* and *dissemble* are unrelated in meaning. *Disassemble* means "take apart" or "dismantle":

*The team have disassembled the computer.*
*The mechanics will disassemble the engine.*

The more archaic word *dissemble* means "pretend" or "conceal":

*You must not dissemble when questioned about these facts before the court.*

**disassociate/dissociate** These two verbs mean the same and are interchangeable:

*The president disassociated himself from the senator's remarks.*
*He wished to dissociate himself from his past misdeeds.*

Some people prefer *dissociate* to the more clumsy *disassociate.*

**disbar/debar** *See* DEBAR/DISBAR.

**discomfit/discomfort** These two verbs are close in meaning but are not identical. *Discomfit* means "frustrate" or "thwart":

*This change in tactics discomfited the opposition.*

*Discomfort* means "make uncomfortable" or "make uneasy":

*He was discomforted by this revelation.*

Note that the similarity in pronunciation between the two words may also lead to confusion between them.

**discomfort/discomfit** *See* DISCOMFIT/DISCOMFORT.

**discreet/discrete** The adjectives *discreet* and *discrete* are easily confused. *Discreet* means "careful," "prudent," or "not given to gossip" (*a discreet friend*) but can also mean "unobtrusive" or "modest" (*a discreet little house, a discreet outfit*). *Discrete* means "separate," "distinct," or "unconnected" (*the discrete parts of the machinery*).

**discrepancy/disparity** These two nouns are close in meaning but convey slightly different things. *Discrepancy* refers to a generally minor difference between things that should be the same:

*He remarked on the discrepancy between the plans and the finished product.*

*Disparity* suggests a greater degree of difference and suggests an element of imbalance or inequality:

*The disparity between the way in which the two groups are treated is striking.*

**discrete/discreet** *See* DISCREET/DISCRETE.

**discriminating/discriminatory** The adjectives *discriminating* and *discriminatory* both come from the verb *discriminate* but are used differently. *Discriminating* means "discerning" or "able to distinguish one thing from another" (*a discriminating observer, a discriminating palate*). *Discriminatory* refers almost exclusively to discrimination based on prejudice (*discriminatory racial policies*).

**discriminatory/discriminating** *See* DISCRIMINATING/DISCRIMINATORY.

**disinterested/uninterested** The words *disinterested* and *uninterested* are closely related but not identical in meaning. Both *disinterested* and *uninterested* can mean "not interested," "indifferent," or "bored," but *disinterested* can also mean "unbiased," "impartial," or "free from selfish motive or interest" (*to be decided by a judge or other disinterested party*).

**disorganized/unorganized** These two adjectives both mean "not organized" but convey slightly different messages. *Disorganized* means "thrown into confusion" or "incoherent" (*a disorganized office, a disorganized young man*), whereas *unorganized* simply means "lacking organization" (*an unorganized plan of attack*).

**disparity/discrepancy** *See* DISCREPANCY/DISPARITY.

**dispassionate/impassioned** These two words are sometimes confused but are opposite in meaning. *Dispassionate* means "objective" or "emotionally uninvolved" (*a dispassionate approach to the task*), whereas *impassioned* means "passionate" or "full of passion" (*an impassioned account of the affair*).

**dispel/disperse** The verbs *dispel* and *disperse* have slightly different meanings. *Dispel* means "drive away" or "dissipate" (*dispel a rumor, dispel doubt*), whereas *disperse* means "break up" or "scatter about" (*disperse the mob; dispersed far and wide*).

**disperse/dispel** *See* DISPEL/DISPERSE.

**dissemble/disassemble** *See* DISASSEMBLE/DISSEMBLE.

**dissension/dissent** The nouns *dissension* and *dissent* vary slightly in meaning. *Dissension* means "state of disagreement" or "discord" (*dissension over the issue*), while *dissent* means "difference of opinion" (*sound a note of dissent*).

**dissent/dissension** *See* DISSENSION/DISSENT.

**dissociate/disassociate** *See* DISASSOCIATE/DISSOCIATE.

**distinct/distinctive** These two adjectives are easily confused. *Distinct* means "clear" or "definite" (*a distinct view, a distinct difference*), whereas *distinctive* means "characteristic" or "distinguishing" (*a distinctive feature*).

**distinctive/distinct** *See* DISTINCT/DISTINCTIVE.

**distract/detract** *See* DETRACT/DISTRACT.

**distrust/mistrust** The words *distrust* and *mistrust* are virtually identical in meaning but convey slightly different impressions. Though both words suggest a lack of trust, *distrust* is the more emphatic term:

*He distrusted his brother's intentions after this betrayal.*
*She mistrusted her own abilities.*

**disturb/perturb** The meanings of the verbs *disturb* and *perturb* overlap to some extent. Both *disturb* and *perturb* can mean "upset" or "cause disquiet to" (*disturbed by this development; perturbed by her manner*), but *disturb* can also mean "interrupt" or "throw into disorder" (*disturb the concentration; disturb the arrangements*).

**dominate/domineer** The verbs *dominate* and *domineer* have slightly different meanings. *Dominate* means "exert control over":

*He dominated the meeting with his powerful expressions of anger.*

*Domineer* means "behave in a tyrannical or overbearing manner":

*He rules, in fact, domineers, over us.*

**domineer/dominate** *See* DOMINATE/DOMINEER.

**doubtful/dubious** The words *doubtful* and *dubious* both mean "causing doubt" or "questionable" but convey slightly different impressions. *Doubtful* is the more neutral word, referring simply to the uncertain nature of something (*a doubtful outcome, a doubtful claim*), whereas *dubious* suggests something more negative or even dishonest or unrespectable in character (*a dubious reputation for fairness, dubious surroundings*).

**drunk/drunken** The adjectives *drunk* and *drunken* mean virtually the same thing but have slightly different implications. *Drunk* may refer to a single episode of intoxication (*he quickly became drunk*), whereas *drunken* suggests repeated or habitual drunkenness (*a drunken lifestyle, her cruel and drunken father*). Note that *drunk* is usually employed after a verb (*lets get drunk*), while *drunken* usually appears before a noun (*a drunken evening*).

**drunken/drunk** *See* DRUNK/DRUNKEN.

**dual/duel** These two words are pronounced the same but have different meanings. *Dual* is an adjective meaning "double" (*dual citizenship*), whereas *duel* is a noun meaning "fight between two persons" (*a duel to the death*).

**dubious/doubtful** *See* DOUBTFUL/DUBIOUS.

**duel/dual** *See* DUAL/DUEL.

**due to/owing to** These phrases mean almost the same thing but are employed differently. *Due* is an adjective, and so, strictly speaking, *due to* should be used after a linking verb:

*This change is due to political considerations.*

*Owing* to means "because of" and should be employed as a preposition:

*We left earlier than intended owing to the deteriorating weather conditions.*

In practice the two phrases are used in much the same way, at least when speaking or writing informally.

**each/every** The words *each* and *every* are not always interchangeable. *Each* emphasizes the distinctness of a particular person or thing (*each apple in the basket*), whereas *every* refers to a number of persons or things collectively (*every planet in the universe*). Note also that *each* is the correct word to use after a plural noun:

*The children each received a gift.*

Each may refer to just two persons or things (*watching each twin make a choice*), while *every* refers to three or more (*every day of the year*).

**each other/one another** The phrases *each other* and *one another* mean the same thing but are used in different contexts. *Each other* should be employed in circumstances when two persons or things are involved:

*The two men exchanged details with each other.*

*One another* should be used when more than two persons or things are involved:

*Several members of the team ran into one another in their rush to catch the fly ball.*

Note also that *each other* tends to emphasize the individuality of the persons or things involved, while *one another* refers to them more generally.

**earthly/earthy** The adjectives *earthly* and *earthy* both refer to *earth* but have slightly different meanings and are used differently. *Earthly* refers generally to the Earth in terms of the world as a whole (*this earthly existence*), whereas *earthy* refers directly to the soil (*an earthy taste*) or more abstractly to anything unsophisticated or crude (*food with an earthy appeal, earthy language*).

**earthy/earthly** *See* EARTHLY/EARTHY.

**eatable/edible** The words *eatable* and *edible* both mean "suitable for eating" but convey slightly different things. *Eatable* means that something is "reasonably pleasant to eat" (*eatable cafeteria food*), whereas *edible* simply means "possible to eat" (*these roots are edible*) and often refers to food that is not actually poisonous (*edible fungi*). Note that the same distinctions apply to the antonyms *uneatable* and *inedible*.

**economical/economic** *See* ECONOMIC/ECONOMICAL.

**economic/economical** The adjectives *economic* and *economical* both refer to the noun *economy* but have slightly different meanings. *Economic* means simply "of or relating to economics" (*economic affairs, the country's economic future*) or "reasonably profitable" (*the savings should prove economic*), whereas *economical* refers to the frugal use of resources and the avoidance of waste (*an economical use of energy, economical packaging*).

**edible/eatable** *See* EATABLE/EDIBLE.

**effect/affect** *See* AFFECT/EFFECT.

**effective/effectual/efficacious/efficient** These four words are easily confused, although they have slightly different meanings. *Effective* means "producing a decided or desired effect" (*an effective move toward peace*). *Effectual* and *efficacious* mean "capable of achieving the desired effect" (*an effectual withdrawal from the contest*), although *efficacious* is usually reserved for medicinal contexts (*the treatment was efficacious in bringing about a cure*). *Efficient* means "productive of desired effects" (*an efficient way of distributing funds among the poor*). Note that the same distinctions apply to the related antonyms *ineffective, ineffectual, inefficacious,* and *inefficient.*

**effectual/effective/efficacious/efficient** *See* EFFECTIVE/EFFECTUAL/EFFICACIOUS/EFFICIENT.

**effeminate/effete** The adjectives *effeminate* and *effete* have similar meanings and may be confused. *Effeminate* is applied exclusively to males and means "having overly feminine qualities" (*an effeminate young man with ringlets*), whereas *effete* means "weak" but is similarly associated with males exhibiting distinctly feminine traits (*an effete youth unacquainted with the working world*).

**effete/effeminate** *See* EFFEMINATE/EFFETE.

**efficacious/effective/effectual/efficient** *See* EFFECTIVE/EFFECTUAL/EFFICACIOUS/EFFICIENT.

**efficient/effective/effectual/efficacious** *See* EFFECTIVE/EFFECTUAL/EFFICACIOUS/EFFICIENT.

**e.g./i.e.** These abbreviations are sometimes confused but have different meanings. The abbreviation *e.g.* stands for the Latin *exempli gratia* and means "for example":

> *Bring a selection of basic ingredients, e.g., flour and salt.*

The abbreviation *i.e.* stands for the Latin *id est* and means "that is":

> *These are self-sufficient systems, i.e., capable of running without outside interference.*

**egoism/egotism** The nouns *egoism* and *egotism* are slightly different in meaning. *Egoism* refers to self-interest as an underlying motive for action (*driven by his own egoism*), whereas *egotism* denotes a more overt degree of self-obsession (*her boundless egotism*).

**egotism/egoism** *See* EGOISM/EGOTISM.

**elder/older** The words *elder* and *older* are used in different circumstances. *Elder* should only be applied to people (*her elder sister, the elder of the two brothers*), while *older* is preferred in other contexts (*an older house, the older of the two cars*). Note, however, that *elder* can never be followed by *than* and in such circumstances is replaced by *older* (*her sister is two years older than she*). The same rules apply to *eldest* and *oldest*.

**eldest/oldest** *See* ELDER/OLDER.

**electrical/electric** *See* ELECTRIC/ELECTRICAL.

**electric/electrical** The adjectives *electric* and *electrical* mean the same thing but are used slightly differently. *Electric* is usually employed in reference to specific things that carry or are powered by electricity (*an electric toothbrush*), while *electrical* is applied more generally (*electrical engineering, electrical goods*). *Electric* is the more common choice when speaking figuratively (*an electric atmosphere*).

**elemental/elementary** The adjectives *elemental* and *elementary* have different meanings and should not be confused. *Elemental* variously means "of or relating to the elements" or "fundamental" (*lightning and other elemental forces, an elemental truth*), whereas *elementary* means "simple" or "basic" (*elementary mathematics, elementary steps*).

**elementary/elemental** *See* ELEMENTAL/ELEMENTARY.

**elicit/illicit** These two words look and sound similar but have different meanings. *Elicit* is a verb meaning "draw out" or "evoke" (*elicit the truth*), whereas *illicit* is an adjective meaning "illegal" or "prohibited" (*illicit activity, an illicit relationship*).

**eligible/illegible** These two words are similar in appearance but are unrelated in meaning. *Eligible* means "qualified," "worthy," or "suitable" (*eligible to take part in the competition, an eligible bachelor*), whereas *illegible* means "unreadable" or "impossible to decipher" (*written in an illegible hand*).

**ellipse/ellipsis** These two words look similar but are different in meaning. The noun *ellipse* means "oval" (*cut in the shape of an ellipse*), while *ellipsis* is a grammatical term referring to the omission of one or more words (*a sentence ending in an ellipsis*). Note that both words share the identical adjectival form *elliptical,* which can also mean "obscure" or "ambiguous."

**ellipsis/ellipse** *See* ELLIPSE/ELLIPSIS.

**emend/amend** *See* AMEND/EMEND.

**emigrant/immigrant** *See* EMIGRATE/IMMIGRATE.

**emigrate/immigrate** The verbs *emigrate* and *immigrate* are related but have different meanings. *Emigrate* means "leave one's country for another" and refers specifically to the process of leaving:

*They plan to emigrate from Canada when their house is sold.*

*Immigrate* means "enter another country on a permanent basis" and refers specifically to the process of arriving:

*Thousand of foreigners are expected to immigrate to the United States under this policy.*

Note that a person emigrates *from* one place and immigrates *to* another. The same distinctions apply to the nouns *emigrant* and *immigrant* as well as to *emigration* and *immigration.*

**emigration/immigration** *See* EMIGRATE/IMMIGRATE.

**eminent/imminent** The words *eminent* and *imminent* are similar in appearance but have different meanings. *Eminent* means "outstanding," "conspicuous," or "prominent" (*an eminent figure*), whereas *imminent* means "impending" (*imminent victory*).

**emotional/emotive** The adjectives *emotional* and *emotive* are often used interchangeably but have slightly different meanings. *Emotional* means "expressing emotion" (*an emotional outburst, an emotional character*), whereas *emotive* means "arousing emotion" (*an emotive topic, emotive music*).

**emotive/emotional** *See* EMOTIONAL/EMOTIVE.

**endemic/epidemic** The words *endemic* and *epidemic* are often used in similar contexts but should not be confused since they have different meanings. The adjective *endemic* means "occurring in a particular area":

*Despair is endemic in these parts of the city.*

The noun *epidemic* means "widespread occurrence" and is often applied to contagious disease:

*Millions died in the epidemic of influenza that swept the globe in the years following World War I.*

**ensure/assure/insure** *See* ASSURE/ENSURE/INSURE.

**envelope/envelop** *See* ENVELOP/ENVELOPE.

**envelop/envelope** The words *envelop* and *envelope* have similar meanings but should not be confused. The verb *envelop* means "enclose" or "surround" (*the mist enveloped the mountain; enveloped in cloth*) and can also be used figuratively (*enveloped in sadness*). The noun *envelope* means "wrapper" or something used to envelop something else (*a* *letter in an envelope*). Note that in *envelop* the stress falls on the second syllable, while in *envelope* it falls on the first syllable.

**enviable/envious** The adjectives *enviable* and *envious* are close in meaning but are not identical. *Enviable* means "causing envy" (*an enviable position*), while *envious* means "feeling envy" (*envious of his rival's larger salary*).

**envious/enviable** *See* ENVIABLE/ENVIOUS.

**envy/jealousy** These two nouns convey slightly different meanings. *Envy* relates to the desire to possess something enjoyed by someone else:

*She envied her best friend's success.*

*Jealousy* relates to the fear of losing something one already possesses:

*His wife's behavior filled him with jealousy.*

**epidemic/endemic** *See* ENDEMIC/EPIDEMIC.

**epigram/epigraph/epitaph/epithet** These four nouns are easily confused because of their similarity in appearance. An *epigram* is a terse or witty saying (*a writer celebrated for his epigrams*). An *epigraph* is a quotation appearing at the beginning of a literary work (*a theme hinted at in the epigraph*). An *epitaph* is a commemorative statement about a deceased person (*an epitaph carved on a gravestone*). An *epithet* consists of a characterizing word or phrase, usually applied to a person's name:

*He had earned the epithet of "the Brave."*

**epigraph** *See* EPIGRAM/EPIGRAPH/EPITAPH/EPITHET.

**epitaph** *See* EPIGRAM/EPIGRAPH/EPITAPH/EPITHET.

**epithet** *See* EPIGRAM/EPIGRAPH/EPITAPH/EPITHET.

**equable/equitable** The words *equable* and *equitable* are sometimes confused. *Equable* means "moderate" or "regular" (*an equable climate*), whereas *equitable* means "fair" or "impartial" (*an equitable arrangement*).

**equitable/equable** *See* EQUABLE/EQUITABLE.

**eruption/irruption** *See* ERUPT/IRRUPT.

**erupt/irrupt** These two verbs have different meanings. *Erupt* means "burst out" or, figuratively, "begin suddenly" (*lava is erupting from the fissure; erupt with laughter*), whereas *irrupt* means "burst in" (*her* *parents irrupting into the room*). The same distinction applies to the nouns *eruption* and *irruption.*

**especially/specially** The adverbs *especially* and *specially* are often assumed to be interchangeable but actually mean different things. *Especially* means "more than usual" or "above all":

*The tree was blown down by an especially strong gust of wind.*
*She loves cakes, especially chocolate ones.*

*Specially* means "specifically" or "purposely":

*The film was specially intended to appeal to the young.*
*He handed his girlfriend the specially ordered bouquet.*

**estimate/estimation** The nouns *estimate* and *estimation* are sometimes confused. *Estimate* means "rough or approximate calculation" (*an estimate of the size of the meteorite*), while *estimation* refers to the process by which such estimates are made (*engaged in making a rough estimation of the time required*). Note that *estimation* can also have the additional meaning of "opinion" or "regard":

*What, in your estimation, will come of these changes?*
*She went up in his estimation after this.*

**estimation/estimate** *See* ESTIMATE/ESTIMATION.

**every/each** *See* EACH/EVERY.

**everyday/every day** The different ways in which *everyday* and *every day* are used are reflected in the way they are written. *Everyday* means "ordinary" or "routine" and is used as an adjective (*an everyday occurrence*), while *every day* means "daily" and is used as an adverb (*she works every day of the week*).

**every day/everyday** *See* EVERYDAY/EVERY DAY.

**exaltation/exultation** *See* EXALT/EXULT.

**exalt/exult** The verbs *exalt* and *exult* are sometimes confused but have different meanings. *Exalt* means "raise up" and can be used either literally or figuratively (*exalted to the post of vice president; exalted by his followers*), whereas *exult* means "rejoice" (*exult in victory*). The same distinction applies to the nouns *exaltation* and *exultation.*

**exceed/accede** *See* ACCEDE/EXCEED.

**except/accept** *See* ACCEPT/EXCEPT.

**exceptionable/exceptional** The words *exceptionable* and *exceptional* are unrelated in meaning and should not be confused. *Exceptionable* means "objectionable":

*We found her manner exceptionable.*

*Exceptional* variously means "very unusual" or "above or below average":

*Exceptional weather conditions are forecast for this area.*
*Tests confirmed that he was an exceptional child in need of additional support.*

**exceptional/exceptionable** *See* EXCEPTIONABLE/EXCEPTIONAL.

**excess/access** *See* ACCESS/EXCESS.

**exclude/preclude** The verbs *exclude* and *preclude* have different meanings. *Exclude* means "leave out" or "keep out":

*The optional extras are excluded at this price.*
*They have been excluded from the party.*

*Preclude* means "make impossible" or "rule out in advance":

*This development will effectively preclude any further negotiation.*

**exercise/exorcise** These two verbs are similar in appearance but are unrelated in meaning. *Exercise* variously means "exert oneself physically," "use," or "engage the attention of" (*exercise in the gym; exercise your authority; exercise the imagination*), while *exorcise* means "expel" (*exorcise your fears*).

**exhausting/exhaustive** The words *exhausting* and *exhaustive* both have their origins in the verb *exhaust* but mean different things and are not synonymous. *Exhausting* means "extremely tiring" or "wearying" (*an exhausting run, exhausting work*), whereas *exhaustive* means "thorough" (*an exhaustive investigation*).

**exhaustive/exhausting** *See* EXHAUSTING/EXHAUSTIVE.

**exorcise/exercise** *See* EXERCISE/EXORCISE.

**expedient/expeditious** The adjectives *expedient* and *expeditious* are easily confused but have different meanings. *Expedient* means "suitable in the given circumstances" (*a politically expedient measure*), whereas *expeditious* means "prompt and efficient" (*the expeditious removal of all opposition*).

**expeditious/expedient** *See* EXPEDIENT/EXPEDITIOUS.

**explicit/implicit** The words *explicit* and *implicit* are sometimes confused. *Explicit* means "clear," "unambiguous," or "undisguised" (*leave explicit instructions; sexually explicit*), while *implicit* means "implied" (*an implicit acceptance of the proposal*).

**extant/extinct** Although superficially similar, the words *extant* and *extinct* are virtually opposite in meaning. *Extant* means "still existing" (*an extant species*), whereas *extinct* means "no longer existing" or "no longer active" (*an extinct reptile; an extinct volcano*).

**extempore/impromptu** These two words are closely related in meaning but are not identical. *Extempore* means "delivered with minimal preparation" (*an expression of regret delivered in extempore fashion from the platform*), while *impromptu* suggests a greater degree of improvisation with perhaps no prior notice (*a speech full of impromptu quips and witticisms*).

**extemporize/temporize** These two words are unrelated in meaning and should not be confused. *Extemporize* means "make up without prior preparation":

*He extemporized a brilliant guitar solo.*

*Temporize* means "delay" or "stall":

*Lacking any clear alternative, he temporized until an opportunity to leave presented itself.*

**extended/extensive** The adjectives *extended* and *extensive* are slightly different in meaning. *Extended* means "stretched" or "lengthened" (*an extended building, extended talks*), whereas *extensive* means "large" or "wide ranging" (*an extensive property, extensive knowledge of a subject*).

**extensive/extended** *See* EXTENDED/EXTENSIVE.

**exterior/external/extraneous** These three words are subtly different in meaning. *Exterior* means "on the outside" (*an exterior wall*); *external* means "outwardly visible" (*external appearances*); and *extraneous* means "from the outside" or "not essential" (*extraneous noise, extraneous matters*).

**external** *See* EXTERIOR/EXTERNAL/EXTRANEOUS.

**extinct/extant** *See* EXTANT/EXTINCT.

**extract/extricate** The verbs *extract* and *extricate* are close in meaning but not identical. *Extract* means "draw forth" or "remove" (*extract the truth; extract a tooth*), whereas *extricate* means "withdraw" or "disentangle" (*extricate yourself from an awkward situation; extricate his foot from the barbed wire*).

**extraneous** *See* EXTERIOR/EXTERNAL/EXTRANEOUS.

**extricate/extract** *See* EXTRACT/EXTRICATE.

**extrinsic/intrinsic** The adjectives *extrinsic* and *intrinsic* are opposite in meaning and should not be confused. *Extrinsic* means "extraneous" or "inessential" (*these and other extrinsic factors*), whereas *intrinsic* means "inherent" or "essential" (*intrinsic to the whole enterprise, of intrinsic importance*).

**extrovert/introvert** These two words are opposite in meaning but are sometimes confused. *Extrovert* (sometimes also spelled *extravert*) describes a person who is outgoing or confident:

> *Her father was an ebullient, even overbearing extrovert.*

*Introvert* denotes a person who is inward-looking or withdrawn:

> *The boy is an introvert with a quiet sense of humor.*

**exult/exalt** *See* EXALT/EXULT.

**facility/faculty** These two nouns resemble each other and in certain circumstances overlap in meaning. *Facility* means "aptitude" or "ease" and usually refers to an acquired skill (*facility with a paintbrush*), whereas *faculty* denotes a "natural skill" or "gift" (*a faculty for languages*). Both words have a number of other meanings, in which circumstances they should not be considered interchangeable. *Facility,* for example, can also mean the equipment, services, or buildings provided for a particular purpose (*sports facilities*) or an additional service (*an overdraft facility*). Faculty can also refer to the whole teaching staff at a university, college, or school (*the faculty supports the changes in curriculum*).

**factious/fractious** The adjectives *factious* and fractious are easily confused but are different in meaning. *Factious* means "showing dissension" or "full of dissent" as between different factions (*a factious response, a factious political party*), whereas *fractious* means "unruly" or "quarrelsome" (*fractious children*).

**faculty/facility** *See* FACILITY/FACULTY.

**faint/feint** These two words are pronounced in the same way but have different meanings and should not be confused. The verb *faint* means "lose consciousness" (*the loss of blood caused him to faint*), whereas the noun *feint* describes a movement intended to mislead an opponent (*make a feint to one side; a diversionary feint on the flank*).

**fair/fare** These two nouns have identical pronunciations but different meanings. A *fair* is a form of public entertainment with amusements, sideshows, and the like or else a commercial exhibition (*all the fun of the fair, trade fair*), whereas *fare* variously means "price charged for transport," "passenger in a taxi," or "choice of food or entertainment" (*pay your fare to the driver; pick up a fare; wholesome fare*).

**fallacious/fallible** These two adjectives do not mean the same thing and should not be confused. *Fallible* means "liable to make a mistake":

*This failure only goes to prove that we are all fallible.*

*Fallacious* means "containing a mistake":

*She argued that he had based his thesis on fallacious research.*

**fallible/fallacious** *See* FALLACIOUS/FALLIBLE.

**fare/fair** *See* FAIR/FARE.

**farther/further** In many contexts *farther* and *further* are interchangeable, but there are circumstances in which one is more correct than the other. When discussing physical distance, either word may be used, although *farther* is preferred:

*The ocean is farther away to the west.*
*India is farther from New York than Ireland is.*
*The town is located in that direction further than you can see.*

In abstract and figurative contexts *further* is generally preferred:

*He found himself agreeing to go further than he had originally intended.*
*Nothing could be further from my mind.*
*Further details will follow shortly.*

Note that the same distinctions apply to *farthest* and *furthest*. As a verb, only *further* is used (*to further their goals, they undertook an advertising campaign*).

**farthest/furthest** *See* FARTHER/FURTHER.

**fatal/fateful** The words *fatal* and *fateful* have different meanings and should not be confused. *Fatal* means "causing death" or "bringing ruin or failure" (*a fatal dose of poison, fatal to their enterprise*), whereas *fateful* means "having momentous consequences" (*a fateful decision*).

**fateful/fatal** *See* FATAL/FATEFUL.

**faze/phase** The words *faze* and *phase* share the same pronunciation but have different meanings. The verb *faze* means "disconcert" or "daunt" (*we were not fazed by her indifference*), whereas the noun *phase* means "stage" or "step" (*move on to the next phase; go through a troublesome phase*). Note that *faze* is a relatively recent coinage and is best restricted to informal use.

**feint/faint** *See* FAINT/FEINT.

**female/feminine** The adjectives *female* and *feminine* mean much the same thing but are used slightly differently. *Female* is applied widely to living things, including people, animals, and plants (*the female spider monkey*), whereas *feminine* has only to do with women (female human beings) or words (*her feminine side; the feminine form of the noun; the policies benefited from a feminine perspective*).

**feminine/female** *See* FEMALE/FEMININE.

**ferment/foment** These two verbs are interchangeable in some contexts but not in others. In the sense "stir up" either *ferment* or *foment* can be used (*ferment trouble; foment rebellion*). *Foment* cannot, however, be used as an alternative to *ferment* in the sense of "undergo fermentation" (*fermenting beer*), while *ferment* cannot be substituted for *foment* in its literal sense of "apply warmth to" (*foment the skin*).

**fewer/less** These two words mean almost the same thing and are easily confused. *Fewer* means "a smaller number of" (*fewer people*), whereas *less* means "a smaller amount of" (*less water in the mixture*). Note that *fewer* is used when discussing countable nouns (*fewer cars*), while *less* is employed in relation to uncountable nouns (*less traffic*). The same distinction extends to the phrases *fewer than* and *less than* (*fewer than a thousand, less than that*).

**fictional/fictitious** The adjectives *fictional* and *fictitious* are subtly different in meaning. *Fictional* means "not factual" or "something invented" (*a fictional story*), whereas *fictitious* means "false" or "imaginary" (*a fictitious identity*). In practice the two words are often treated as interchangeable in the senses of "imaginary" or "invented," although *fictional* is the term most closely related to literary fiction.

**fictitious/fictional** *See* FICTIONAL/FICTITIOUS.

**flagrant/blatant** *See* BLATANT/FLAGRANT.

**flair/flare** These two nouns have identical pronunciations but mean different things. *Flair* means "natural aptitude" or "stylishness" (*a flair for music; dress with flair*), whereas *flare* means "blaze of light" (*an orange flare, the flare of a searchlight*).

**flare/flair** *See* FLAIR/FLARE.

**flaunt/flout** The verbs *flaunt* and *flout* should not be confused as they have different meanings. *Flaunt* means "show off" (*flaunt your credentials*), whereas *flout* means "treat with contempt" (*flout convention*).

**flounder/founder** The verbs *flounder* and *founder* are sometimes confused. *Flounder* means "struggle" or "act clumsily":

*He floundered helplessly in the surf.*

*Founder* means "collapse," "sink," or "fail":

> *The project seems likely to founder.*

**flout/flaunt** *See* FLAUNT/FLOUT.

**foment/ferment** *See* FERMENT/FOMENT.

**forbear/forebear** These two words are easily confused but are unrelated in meaning. The verb *forbear* is used in formal contexts to mean "refrain" (*forbear from swearing*), whereas the noun *forebear* means "ancestor" (*an illustrious forebear*). Note that *forbear* is also acceptable as an alternative spelling of the noun *forebear*. The two words are pronounced differently, the stress falling on the second syllable of *forbear* and on the first syllable of *forebear*.

**forbid/prohibit** The verbs *forbid* and *prohibit* mean the same thing but are used slightly differently. *Forbid* means simply "refuse to allow" (*forbid permission*), whereas *prohibit* means "forbid with authority" and carries with it additional force (*prohibit by order*). Note that *forbid* is followed by *to* (*forbid you to leave*), while *prohibit* is followed by *from* (*prohibit from taking part*).

**forceful/forcible** The adjectives *forceful* and *forcible* are interchangeable in many contexts but are subtly different in meaning. *Forceful* means "having great force" or "effective" (*a forceful blow, a forceful argument*), whereas *forcible* means "using force" (*forcible entry*). *Forcible* cannot be replaced by "forceful" when physical force is referred to (*forcible expulsion*).

**forcible/forceful** *See* FORCEFUL/FORCIBLE.

**forebear/forbear** *See* FORBEAR/FOREBEAR.

**forego/forgo** These two verbs are sometimes confused. *Forgo* means "do without" or "give up" (*forgo the opportunity*). Forego, means "go before" and is more usually encountered in the adjectival forms *foregoing* and *foregone* (*a foregone conclusion*).

**foreword/forward** These two words are pronounced in the same way but have different meanings. *Foreword* refers to a passage inserted in a book or other publication prior to the main text (*a foreword by the professor*), whereas *forward* means "in an onward direction" (*keep going forward*).

**forgo/forego** *See* FOREGO/FORGO.

**formally/formerly** The words *formally* and *formerly* are similar in pronunciation and are sometimes confused. *Formally* means "in a formal manner":

*The queen greeted her guests formally.*

*Formerly* means "previously":

*He was formerly mayor of the city.*

**former/latter** The terms *former* and *latter* are sometimes confused although they have opposite meanings. *Former* denotes "the first of two previously mentioned things," whereas *latter* refers to "the second of two previously mentioned things":

*The classic baby colors are blue and pink, the former being reserved for boys and the latter for girls.*

**formerly/formally** *See* FORMALLY/FORMERLY.

**forth/fourth** The words *forth* and *fourth* are pronounced identically but are not related in meaning. *Forth* means "forward" (*go forth*), while *fourth* refers to the number (*fourth in line*).

**fortuitous/fortunate** These two adjectives have different meanings. *Fortuitous* means "occurring by chance" (*a fortuitous result*), whereas *fortunate* means "lucky" or "auspicious" (*a fortunate turn of events*). Note that *fortuitous* is never applied to people (*a fortunate young man*).

**fortunate/fortuitous** *See* FORTUITOUS/FORTUNATE.

**forward/foreword** *See* FOREWORD/FORWARD.

**forward/forwards** *Forward* and *forwards* are both acceptable as adverbs (*he walked forward; she moved forwards*), although *forward* is preferred. Note that only *forward* is correct as an adjective (*a forward remark*). The exact same is true regarding *backward* and/or *backwards* as an adverb and an adjective.

**forwards/forward** *See* FORWARD/FORWARDS.

**foul/fowl** The nouns *foul* and *fowl* are unrelated in meaning and should not be confused. *Foul* means "illegal act" (*commit a foul*), whereas *fowl* means "bird(s)" (*hunt wild fowl*).

**founder/flounder** *See* FLOUNDER/FOUNDER.

**fourth/forth** *See* FORTH/FOURTH.

**fowl/foul** *See* FOUL/FOWL.

**fractious/factious** *See* FACTIOUS/FRACTIOUS.

**funeral/funereal** These two words are related in meaning but are employed differently. The noun *funeral* is fairly narrow in meaning, denoting the ceremony surrounding a burial or cremation (*a quiet funeral*) or, figuratively, the destruction of something (*the funeral of her hopes*), whereas the adjective *funereal* has the wider sense of "gloomy" or "mournful" (*funereal surroundings*).

**funereal/funeral** *See* FUNERAL/FUNEREAL.

**further/farther** *See* FARTHER/FURTHER.

**furthest/farthest** *See* FARTHER/FURTHER.

**gait/gate** The nouns *gait* and *gate* are pronounced identically but are unrelated in meaning. *Gait* means "manner of walking":

*She recognized him by his unusual gait, arms swinging out of time with his legs.*

*Gate* means "opening in wall or fence":

*The visitors entered by the garden gate.*

**gamble/gambol** The verbs *gamble* and *gambol* share the same pronunciation but have different meanings. *Gamble* means "stake something on an uncertain outcome":

*He gambled everything he had on reaching town before dawn.*

*Gambol* means "frisk," "frolic," or "skip about in play":

*He gamboled like a newborn lamb on the lawn.*

**gambol/gamble** *See* GAMBLE/GAMBOL.

**gate/gait** *See* GAIT/GATE.

**general/generic** These two adjectives are related in meanings but are not synonymous. *General* includes among its meanings "overall," "as a whole," and "widespread" (*a general armistice, in general, a general effect*), whereas *generic* is more specific, meaning "of or relating to a group or class" (*a generic term*). *Generic* also has the secondary meaning of "nonproprietary" (*a generic drug*).

**generic/general** *See* GENERAL/GENERIC.

**genes/jeans** These two words are unrelated in meaning and should not be confused in spelling. *Genes* are the units of inheritance responsible for transferring certain traits from one generation to another (*inherit genes from your parents*), whereas *jeans* are trousers made from hard-wearing cotton twill cloth or denim (*a pair of blue jeans*).

**genial/congenial** *See* CONGENIAL/GENIAL.

**gibe/gybe/jibe** These three words are pronounced identically but have different meanings. *Gibe,* or *jibe,* is a verb meaning "jeer" or "taunt," whereas *jibe,* and its variant *gybe,* is a nautical verb or noun referring to a shifting movement made by a ship when under sail.

**gild/guild** The words *gild* and *guild* are pronounced in the same way but are unrelated in meaning. The verb *gild* means "overlay with gold" or "make more attractive" (*gild the legs of the chair; gild the truth*), whereas the noun *guild* means "association of people with similar interests" (*a trade guild, a guild of leading citizens*). Note that *gild* may very occasionally be encountered as an alternative spelling of *guild.*

**gilt/guilt** These two nouns are unrelated in meaning, though pronounced identically. *Gilt* means "gold" or "golden covering" (*a gilt candlestick; scratch the gilt*), whereas *guilt* means "culpability" (*admit your guilt; where the guilt lies*).

**gorilla/guerrilla** These two words are unrelated in meaning and should not be confused. A *gorilla* is one of the great apes of equatorial Africa (*an extinct species of gorilla*), whereas a *guerrilla* is an irregular soldier, a fighter belonging to an independent armed force (*an attack by guerrillas, guerrilla tactics*). Note that both the spellings *guerrilla* and *guerilla* are acceptable, although some people consider the original Spanish *guerrilla* the more correct.

**gourmand/gourmet** These two words are sometimes confused although they have significantly different meanings. A *gourmand* is someone who loves eating and drinking to excess (*the insatiable appetite of a gourmand*), whereas a *gourmet* is someone who is more interested in the quality of the food and drink they consume (*in the opinion of a respected gourmet*).

**gourmet/gourmand** *See* GOURMAND/GOURMET.

**graceful/gracious** The adjectives *graceful* and *gracious* both refer to the noun *grace* but are subtly different in meaning. *Graceful* refers to grace or elegance in form or movement (*a graceful outline; a graceful wave*). *Gracious* means "courteous" or "benevolent" and is applied in descriptions of character or personal behavior (*a gracious old lady, a gracious act of kindness*), although it can also have the senses of "condescending" (*a gracious smile*) or "luxurious" (*a gracious interior*).

**gracious/graceful** *See* GRACEFUL/GRACIOUS.

**Grecian/Greek** These two adjectives are sometimes mistakenly assumed to be freely interchangeable. *Greek* means "of or relating to Greece" (*the Greek language, a Greek resort*), whereas *Grecian* means "of or relating to classical Greece" and should not be applied to contemporary Greece (*Grecian elegance, Grecian myth*). Note, however, that *Greek* can refer to both modern and classical Greece.

**Greek/Grecian** *See* GRECIAN/GREEK.

**grille/grill** *See* GRILL/GRILLE.

**grill/grille** These two words overlap in meaning but are not always synonymous. Both words refer to a framework of metal bars, but *grill* refers specifically to such a frame when used in cooking food (*burgers on a grill; put food under the grill*) and is sometimes extended generically to a place where such food is served (*eat at the grill on the corner*). A *grille* is a framework of metal bars set in a door or other opening (*speak through the grille, radiator grille*), in which sense it can also be spelled *grill.*

**grisly/grizzly** These two words are easily confused being pronounced identically. The adjective *grisly* means "gruesome" (*a grisly tale*). *Grizzly* is an alternative for *grizzled* and means "streaked or sprinkled with gray" (*a grizzly beard*), although it can also mean "grumbling" or "whining" (*grizzly children*). As a noun, *grizzly* refers to the large brown *grizzly bear* of northern North America (*mauled by a grizzly*).

**grizzly/grisly** *See* GRISLY/GRIZZLY.

**guerrilla/gorilla** *See* GORILLA/GUERRILLA.

**guild/gild** *See* GILD/GUILD.

**guilt/gilt** *See* GILT/GUILT.

**gybe/gibe/jibe** *See* GIBE/GYBE/JIBE.

**hail/hale** The words *hail* and *hale* have different meanings and should not be confused. The noun *hail* means "freezing rain" (*a shower of hail*), while the verb means "call" or "come from" (*hail a cab; hail from Los Angeles*). *Hale* is a relatively rarely encountered adjective meaning "healthy" or "sound" (*hale and hearty*).

**hair/hare** The nouns *hair* and *hare* are pronounced identically but are unrelated in meaning. *Hair* refers to the pigmented filaments that grow on the skin of humans and other animals (*comb your hair*), whereas *hare* refers to the long-eared mammal (*a hare's foot*).

**hale/hail** *See* HAIL/HALE.

**hangar/hanger** The nouns *hangar* and *hanger* are sometimes confused but are unrelated in meaning. A *hangar* is a "covered area for storing aircraft" (*the plane is in the hangar*), whereas a *hanger* is a wire, plastic, or wooden device upon which coats and other articles of clothing may be hung (*coat hanger*).

**hanged/hung** Both *hanged* and *hung* are correct forms of the verb *hang*, but they are used in different contexts. *Hanged* is only used in connection with the hanging of a person or animal from a rope as a means of execution or suicide (*hanged by the neck until dead; found hanged in an empty warehouse*), while *hung* is employed in all other circumstances (*a jacket hung on a hook; hung from the ceiling*).

**hanger/hangar** *See* HANGAR/HANGER.

**hare/hair** *See* HAIR/HARE.

**heal/heel** These two verbs are pronounced identically but have different meanings. *Heal* means "restore to health" or "mend":

*The wound should heal within a few days.*

*Heel* means "lean to one side":

*The boat heeled to port as the wave struck.*

Note that *heel* is also the correct spelling for the noun referring to the back part of a foot or shoe (*the heel of his sneaker*).

**healthful/healthy** The adjectives *healthful* and *healthy* overlap in meaning but are used in slightly different ways. Strictly speaking, both words can mean "having good health" or "promoting good health," but in practice it is more common for *healthful* to be used to mean "promoting good health" (*a healthful lifestyle*) and for *healthy* to mean "having good health" (*a healthy individual*).

**healthy/healthful** *See* HEALTHFUL/HEALTHY.

**heard/herd** The words *heard* and *herd* are pronounced identically but mean different things. *Heard* is the past participle of the verb *hear* (*heard by all present*), whereas *herd* is a noun meaning "group of cattle or other animals" (*a herd of cows*).

**heel/heal** *See* HEAL/HEEL.

**herd/heard** *See* HEARD/HERD.

**hesitance/hesitancy/hesitation** These three nouns are all derived from the verb *hesitate* but have subtly different meanings. Both *hesitance* and *hesitancy* describe the "state of being hesitant" (*show some hesitance at the suggestion; a note of hesitancy*), whereas *hesitation* refers to an "act or instance of hesitating" (*without hesitation, after a momentary hesitation*).

**hesitancy** *See* HESITANCE/HESITANCY/HESITATION.

**hesitation** *See* HESITANCE/HESITANCY/HESITATION.

**hew/hue** These two words are pronounced in the same way and are sometimes confused. *Hew* is a verb meaning "cut" or "carve" (*hew down the undergrowth*), whereas *hue* is a noun meaning "shade of color" (*paint the walls and woodwork in contrasting hues*).

**Hindi/Hindu** The words *Hindi* and *Hindu* are not interchangeable. *Hindi* refers to the Indo-Aryan language spoken by millions in northern India (*translated into Hindi*), while *Hindu* refers to the religion of Hinduism or to its followers (*a Hindu festival, crowds of Hindus*).

**Hindu/Hindi** *See* HINDI/HINDU.

**historic/historical** These two adjectives are closely related in meaning but are not identical. *Historic* means "important in terms of history" (*a historic decision, a historic discovery*), whereas *historical* can mean, in its broadest sense, "of or relating to history or the past" (*historical accounts of the invasion, historical analysis*) or more precisely, can refer to something or someone with a basis in historical fact rather than in fiction or in the imagination (*a proven historical event, based on a historical ruler of Egypt*).

**historical/historic** *See* HISTORIC/HISTORICAL.

**histrionic/hysterical** The adjectives *histrionic* and *hysterical* both relate to emotional outbursts but have quite different meanings. *Histrionic* means "deliberately affected" or "theatrical" (*outrageous histrionic behavior*), while *hysterical* describes "involuntary behavior resulting from hysteria" (*hysterical screaming, a hysterical laugh*). The same distinction applies to the nouns *histrionics* and *hysterics*.

**hoard/horde** The words *hoard* and *horde* have identical pronunciations and are sometimes confused. The noun *hoard* describes "something stored away for possible future use" (*a hoard of gold*), whereas *horde* means "throng" or "swarm" (*a horde of schoolchildren*).

**hoarse/horse** The pronunciation of these two words is the same and can lead to confusion between them. *Hoarse* is an adjective meaning "harsh" or "grating" (*a hoarse whisper*), while the noun *horse* refers to the equine quadruped (*a horse with a black mane*).

**holey/holy/wholly** The similarity between these three words can lead to their being confused, although they are unrelated in meaning. The adjective *holey* means "full of holes" (*a holey sock*), whereas the adjective *holy* means "sacred" or "divine" (*a holy man, holy Scripture*), and the adverb *wholly* means "completely" (*a wholly unsubstantiated accusation*).

**holy/holey/wholly** *See* HOLEY/HOLY WHOLLY.

**honorable/honorary** These two adjectives both relate to the noun *honor* but have subtly different meanings. *Honorable* means "worthy of honor" (*an honorable enterprise*), whereas *honorary* means "given as an honor" (*an honorary award*) or "unpaid" (*honorary secretary, an honorary member*).

**honorary/honorable** *See* HONORABLE/HONORARY.

**horde/hoard** *See* HOARD/HORDE.

**horse/hoarse** *See* HOARSE/HORSE.

**hour/our** These two words are identical in pronunciation but are unrelated in meaning. *Hour* is a noun meaning "60 minutes" (*the longest hour of his life*), whereas *our* is an adjective meaning "belonging to us" (*that is our house*).

**hue/hew** *See* HEW/HUE.

**humane/human** *See* HUMAN/HUMANE.

**human/humane** The adjectives *human* and *humane* are similar in appearance but do not mean the same thing. *Human* means "of or relating to human beings" (*human society*), whereas *humane* means "compassionate" or "kind" (*the humane treatment of prisoners of war*). The same distinction applies to the antonyms *inhuman* and *inhumane*.

**humanist/humanitarian** These two words have slightly different meanings and should not be confused. *Humanist* means "of or relating to the philosophy of humanism" (*a humanist writer*), whereas *humanitarian* describes a person inclined to defend the welfare of fellow human beings (*a humanitarian attitude toward condemned prisoners*).

**humanitarian/humanist** *See* HUMANIST/HUMANITARIAN.

**humiliation/humility** These two nouns are related but not identical in meaning. *Humiliation* means "embarrassment" or "mortification" (*the humiliation of having to beg in public*), whereas *humility* means "the quality or state of being humble" (*a brilliant and successful man known for his humility*).

**humility/humiliation** *See* HUMILIATION/HUMILITY.

**hung/hanged** *See* HANGED/HUNG.

**hyper-/hypo-** These two prefixes are similar in appearance and can be confused. *Hyper-* means "above" or "excessively" (*hypersensitive*), whereas *hypo-* means "under" or "beneath" (*hypodermic*).

**hypo-/hyper-** *See* HYPER-/HYPO-.

**hysterical/histrionic** *See* HISTRIONIC/HYSTERICAL.

**idle/idol/idyll** These three words look similar but are unrelated in meaning. *Idle* is an adjective meaning "lazy" or "inactive" (*an idle workforce*); *idol* is a noun meaning "object of worship" (*a pagan idol*); and *idyll* is a noun describing a pleasant situation of peace and contentment (*a romantic idyll*) or a piece of writing depicting such a scene.

**idol/idle/idyll** *See* IDLE/IDOL/IDYLL.

**idyll/idle/idol** *See* IDLE/IDOL/IDYLL.

**i.e./e.g.** *See* E.G./I.E.

**illegal/illegitimate** These two adjectives are close in meaning but are not always interchangeable. *Illegal* and *illegitimate* can both mean "unlawful" (*an illegal act, the illegitimate installation of a new government*), but *illegitimate* has the additional meanings of "born outside marriage" (*an illegitimate baby*) or "illogical" (*an illegitimate conclusion*).

**illegible/eligible** *See* ELIGIBLE/ILLEGIBLE.

**illegible/unreadable** *See* LEGIBLE/READABLE.

**illegitimate/illegal** *See* ILLEGAL/ILLEGITIMATE.

**illicit/elicit** *See* ELICIT/ILLICIT.

**illusion/allusion/delusion** *See* ALLUSION/DELUSION/ILLUSION.

**imaginary/imaginative** The adjectives *imaginary* and *imaginative* are related but have different meanings and should not be confused. *Imaginary* means "existing only in the imagination" (*an imaginary city*), whereas *imaginative* means "having or indicating a lively imagination" (*an imaginative writer, imaginative thinking, an imaginative version of a well-known story*).

**imaginative/imaginary** *See* IMAGINARY/IMAGINATIVE.

**immigrant/emigrant** *See* EMIGRATE/IMMIGRATE.

**immigrate/emigrate** *See* EMIGRATE/IMMIGRATE.

**immigration/emigration** *See* EMIGRATE/IMMIGRATE.

**imminent/eminent** *See* EMINENT/IMMINENT.

**immoral/amoral** *See* AMORAL/IMMORAL.

**immunity/impunity** The nouns *immunity* and *impunity* mean slightly different things. *Immunity* means "protection against or exemption from something" (*grant immunity from prosecution, immunity from disease*), whereas *impunity* means "exemption from punishment or retribution" (*defy the law with apparent impunity*).

**impassioned/dispassionate** *See* DISPASSIONATE/IMPASSIONED.

**impel/compel** *See* COMPEL/IMPEL.

**imperial/imperious** The adjectives *imperial* and *imperious* have different meanings and are not interchangeable. *Imperial* means "of or relating to empire" (*by imperial decree*), whereas *imperious* means "overbearing" or "domineering" (*an imperious manner*).

**imperious/imperial** *See* IMPERIAL/IMPERIOUS.

**impinge/infringe** The verbs *impinge* and *infringe* are similar in appearance and can overlap in meaning. Both *impinge* and *infringe* can mean "encroach" (*impinge upon your authority; infringe on a person's rights*), but *impinge* is more commonly used in the more abstract sense "affect" (*experiences that impinge on our consciousness*). Note that both verbs are followed by *on* or *upon,* except where *infringe* has the sense "violate" (*infringe the regulations*).

**implication/inference** *See* IMPLY/INFER.

**implicit/explicit** *See* EXPLICIT/IMPLICIT.

**imply/infer** These two verbs have very similar meanings and are frequently confused. *Imply* means "suggest" or "hint at":

> *The general implied that an attack on the enemy position was imminent.*

*Infer* means "deduce" or "conclude":

> *She inferred from his message that her services were no longer required.*

The same distinction applies to the nouns *implication* and *inference.*

**impracticable/impractical** *See* PRACTICABLE/PRACTICAL.

**impromptu/extempore** *See* EXTEMPORE/IMPROMPTU.

**impugn/impute** These two verbs have different meanings but are sometimes confused. *Impugn* means "question the integrity of":

> *He did not expect the press to impugn his intentions.*

*Impute* means "attribute":

> *Her subsequent actions have been imputed to grief or the effect of drugs.*

**impunity/immunity** *See* IMMUNITY/IMPUNITY.

**impute/impugn** *See* IMPUGN/IMPUTE.

**inapt/inept** These two adjectives are closely related but are subtly different in meaning. *Inapt* means "not suitable" (*an inapt suggestion*), whereas *inept* is usually employed to mean "incompetent" (*an inept commander of troops*).

**incredible/incredulous** The adjectives *incredible* and *incredulous* are related in meaning but are not synonymous. *Incredible* means "unbelievable" (*an incredible story*), while *incredulous* means "disbelieving" (*an incredulous response*).

**incredulous/incredible** *See* INCREDIBLE/INCREDULOUS.

**indexes/indices** These are both acceptable plural forms of the noun *index*. *Indexes* is the more common of the two (*a book with full indexes*), *indices* being confined largely to mathematical or technical contexts (*economic indices*).

**indices/indexes** *See* INDEXES/INDICES.

**indiscriminate/undiscriminating** The adjectives *indiscriminate* and *undiscriminating* have slightly different meanings. *Indiscriminate* means "random" or "haphazard" (*an indiscriminate choice of victim*), while *undiscriminating* means "lacking in discrimination" (*undiscriminating in his choice of business partner*).

**industrial/industrious** The adjectives *industrial* and *industrious* are sometimes confused. *Industrial* means "of or relating to industry" (*an industrial region*), whereas *industrious* means "diligent" or "hard-working" (*an industrious nature*).

**industrious/industrial** *See* INDUSTRIAL/INDUSTRIOUS.

**inedible/uneatable** *See* EATABLE/EDIBLE.

**ineffective/ineffectual/inefficacious/inefficient** *See* EFFECTIVE/EFFECTUAL/EFFICACIOUS/EFFICIENT.

**inept/inapt** *See* INAPT/INEPT.

**infectious/contagious** *See* CONTAGIOUS/INFECTIOUS.

**inference/implication** *See* IMPLY/INFER.

**infer/imply** *See* IMPLY/INFER.

**infinite/infinitesimal** The words *infinite* and *infinitesimal* are easily confused but are virtually opposite in meaning. *Infinite* means "unending" or "limitless" (*an infinite number of possibilities, the infinite universe*), whereas *infinitesimal* means "extremely small" (*an infinitesimal chance of things going wrong, an infinitesimal flaw*).

**infinitesimal/infinite** *See* INFINITE/INFINITESIMAL.

**inflammable/inflammatory** The adjectives *inflammable* and *inflammatory* appear similar but have different meanings and should not be confused. *Inflammable* means "capable of burning" (*inflammable material*) but can also be used figuratively to mean "excitable" or "easily angered" (*a person with a dangerously inflammable temper*). *Inflammatory* means "tending to arouse strong feelings" (*an inflammatory topic of conversation*).

**inflammatory/inflammable** *See* INFLAMMABLE/INFLAMMATORY.

**informant/informer** The nouns *informant* and *informer* do not mean exactly the same thing. An *informant* gives information:

*Our informant tells us a strike is imminent.*

An *informer* is someone who gives information to the police or other authorities:

*The police offered an amnesty to any informer who might come forward.*

**informer/informant** *See* INFORMANT/INFORMER.

**infringe/impinge** *See* IMPINGE/INFRINGE.

**ingenious/ingenuous** Despite their superficial similarity, the adjectives *ingenious* and *ingenuous* are unrelated in meaning. *Ingenious* means "clever," "resourceful," or "inventive" (*an ingenious solution, an ingenious device*), whereas *ingenuous* means "naive" or "innocent" (*an ingenuous look*).

**ingenuous/ingenious** *See* INGENIOUS/INGENUOUS.

**inhumane/inhuman** *See* INHUMAN/INHUMANE.

**inhuman/inhumane** *See* HUMAN/HUMANE.

**in spite of/despite** *See* DESPITE/IN SPITE OF.

**instantaneously/instantly** These two adverbs both mean "immediately" and are interchangeable in most circumstances. Note, however, that they are not interchangeable when *instantaneously* has the meaning "almost simultaneously":

> *The picture appeared instantaneously on the screen when the button was pressed.*

**instantly/instantaneously** *See* INSTANTANEOUSLY/INSTANTLY.

**institute/institution** These two nouns can both mean "association" or "organization," typically one of a professional, academic, or charitable nature, but are not always interchangeable. Note that *institution* can also mean "act of establishment" or "accepted social custom or practice" (*the institution of new laws, the institution of the monarchy*), in which cases it is not synonymous with *institute.*

**institution/institute** *See* INSTITUTE/INSTITUTION.

**instructional/instructive** Though similar in appearance these two adjectives do not mean the same thing. *Instructional* means "providing instruction" (*an instructional video on carpentry*), whereas *instructive* means "enlightening" or "informative" (*an instructive series of lectures*).

**instructive/instructional** *See* INSTRUCTIONAL/INSTRUCTIVE.

**insure/assure/ensure** *See* ASSURE/ENSURE/INSURE.

**intense/intensive** These two adjectives have slightly different meanings and should not be considered freely interchangeable. *Intense* means "extreme," "very strong," or "earnest" (*intense pressure, intense colors, an intense young man*), while *intensive* means "concentrated" or "thorough" (*intensive effort, intensive examination*). Note that *intensive* also has more specialized meanings in such fields as grammar and agriculture (*the use of intensives in ordinary speech, intensive farming*) and is sometimes combined with other words to form new compounds:

> *The company aims to introduce less labor-intensive systems in the near future.*

**intensive/intense** *See* INTENSE/INTENSIVE.

**inter-/intra-/intro-** These three prefixes are easily confused. *Inter-* means "between" or "reciprocally" (*intermediary, intercourse*), while *intra-* means "within" (*intravenous*), and *intro-* means "inward" (*introvert*).

**interment/internment** These two nouns have different meanings and should not be confused. *Interment* means "burial" (*prepare the body for interment*), whereas *internment* means "imprisonment" and is usually applied to the detention of suspects who are considered dangerous to a state even though they might not have actually committed an actual crime (*the internment of opposition leaders*).

**internment/interment** *See* INTERMENT/INTERNMENT.

**into/in to** Confusion sometimes arises over the use of *in to* and *into*. *In to* often represents *in* as an adverb and *to* as part of an infinitive and in such cases should always be written as two words (*come in to shelter from the rain; go in to get your things*). *In to* can also function as an adverb plus a preposition (*go in to class*). *Into,* meanwhile, is a preposition (*come into range; saunter into the house*).

**intra-/inter-/intro-** *See* INTER-/INTRA-/INTRO-.

**intrinsic/extrinsic** *See* EXTRINSIC/INTRINSIC.

**intro-/inter-/intra-** *See* INTER-/INTRA-/INTRO-.

**introvert/extrovert** *See* EXTROVERT/INTROVERT.

**inveigh/inveigle** These two verbs are unrelated in meaning and should not be confused. *Inveigh* means "condemn" or "criticize" (*inveigh against foreign exporters*), whereas *inveigle* means "use cunning or deceit to persuade" (*inveigled into agreeing the concession*). Note that *inveigh* is always followed by *against,* while *inveigle* is usually used with *into.*

**inveigle/inveigh** *See* INVEIGH/INVEIGLE.

**inverse/converse/obverse/reverse** *See* CONVERSE/INVERSE/OBVERSE/REVERSE.

**irrupt/erupt** *See* ERUPT/IRRUPT.

**irruption/eruption** *See* ERUPT/IRRUPT.

**its/it's** The insertion or omission of an apostrophe in *it's* or *its* is a source of confusion for many people. *It's* is a contraction of *it is* or *it has* (*it's easy; it's been ages*), while *its* is the possessive form of *it* (*the house and its owners*).

**jealousy/envy** *See* ENVY/JEALOUSLY.

**jeans/genes** *See* GENES/JEANS.

**jibe/gibe/gybe** *See* GIBE/GYBE/JIBE.

**join/joint** The nouns *join* and *joint* both refer to the point where things meet but do not share exactly the same meaning. *Join* is preferred in relation to visual joinings of a two-dimensional nature (*attempt to hide the join in the carpet*), whereas *joint* usually refers to the joining of three-dimensional parts (*carpentry joints*).

**joint/join** *See* JOIN/JOINT.

**judicial/judicious** The meanings of these two adjectives sometimes overlap, but they should not be confused since they are not interchangeable. *Judicial* means "of or relating to a court of law" (*the judicial system, a judicial ruling*), whereas *judicious* means "characterized by sound judgment" (*a judicious withdrawal of troops*).

**judicious/judicial** *See* JUDICIAL/JUDICIOUS.

**junction/juncture** These two nouns are distantly related in meaning but are not synonymous. *Junction* means "joint" or "place where two things meet" (*the junction between two roads*), whereas *juncture* means "point" or "point in time":

*We cannot predict what will happen at this juncture.*

Note that many people dislike the overuse of the phrase *at this juncture* as a replacement for *now.*

**juncture/junction** *See* JUNCTION/JUNCTURE.

**knight/night** These two nouns share the same pronunciation but are unrelated in meaning. A *knight* is a medieval warrior in armor (*knights of old*), whereas a *night* is the period of darkness between dusk and dawn (*a cold, dark night*).

**knot/not** These two words sound the same and are sometimes confused. A *knot* is a noun meaning "tangled thread" or "convoluted mass" (*a knot in a shoelace, a knot of bindweed*), whereas *not* is an adverb indicating a negative (*not a good day*).

**laden/loaded** These two words are close in meaning but convey slightly different things. *Laden* is an adjective meaning "burdened" or "weighed down" (*a table laden with piles of food*) and is generally understood to mean "overloaded." *Loaded* is the past tense and past participle of the verb *load* (*loaded with barrels; loaded with shopping*). Note that *loaded* is sometimes employed in a figurative sense to mean "misleading" or "with hidden implications" (*a loaded question*).

**larva/lava** These two nouns are unrelated in meaning. *Larva* describes the form taken by some insects after hatching from an egg (*mosquito larva*), whereas *lava* refers to the molten rock released in volcanic eruptions (*a flow of lava*).

**lath/lathe** These two nouns have different meanings and should not be confused. A *lath* is a thin, narrow strip of wood (*nail the laths in position*), whereas a *lathe* is a machine used to shape wood or metal (*an electric lathe*).

**lathe/lath** *See* LATH/LATHE.

**latter/former** *See* FORMER/LATTER.

**lava/larva** *See* LARVA/LAVA.

**lawful/legal/legitimate** The three adjectives all mean "authorized by law," but are used slightly differently. *Lawful* means "rightful" or "conforming with the law" (*go about your lawful business*). *Legal* can also mean "of or relating to the law" (*a legal career*), and *legitimate* can also mean "valid," "reasonable," "genuine," or "born within marriage" (*a legitimate excuse, a legitimate argument, a legitimate claim, a legitimate child*).

**lay/lie** These two verbs are frequently confused, largely because *lay* is the past tense of *lie* as well as a verb in its own right. *Lay* means "put down" (*lay a carpet, lay a body on the floor*) and, as a transitive verb, always has an object (*hens lay eggs*). *Lie* means "rest" (*lie on the bed; lie down on the grass*) and, as an intransitive verb, does not have an object. Further confusion can arise with *lie* because it also has the meaning "tell an untruth," although its past tense is not the same (*I lay on the couch; he lied through his teeth*).

**leach/leech** These two words are unrelated in meaning and should not be confused. *Leach* is a verb meaning "draw out" or "drain away" (*a project that leaches money*), whereas *leech* is a noun referring to a blood-sucking freshwater worm (*a leech placed on the arm*).

**lead/led** These two words are sometimes confused, although they have different meanings. *Lead* is a noun referring to the heavy metallic element (*an ingot of lead, as heavy as lead*) and is pronounced the same as *led,* the past tense of the verb *lead* (pronounced *leed*), which means "take the front" (*the tour guide led the way; lead through the dark*).

**leak/leek** These two words are pronounced identically but are unrelated in meaning. *Leak* is a verb meaning "seep away" or "become known" (*water leaking from a hose; leak a story to the press*), whereas *leek* is a noun referring to an edible vegetable with a thick cylindrical stalk (*a dish of leeks in cheese sauce*).

**learn/teach** The verbs *learn* and *teach* are almost opposite in meaning but are occasionally confused. *Learn* means "acquire knowledge" (*learn the rules*), whereas *teach* means "impart knowledge" (*teach a class*).

**leave/let** In many contexts the verbs *leave* and *let* are freely interchangeable, but there are circumstances in which they cannot be used as replacements for each other. They are synonymous in the sense of "refrain from interfering with" (*leave it alone; let it alone*), but *let* cannot replace *leave* in the sense of "allow or cause to be alone":

*Don't leave the child alone for too long.*

Note also that only *let alone* is acceptable as a set phrase meaning "not to mention":

*The car won't go two miles, let alone twenty.*

**led/lead** *See* LEAD/LED.

**leech/leach** *See* LEACH/LEECH.

**leek/leak** *See* LEAK/LEEK.

**legal/lawful/legitimate** *See* LAWFUL/LEGAL/LEGITIMATE.

**legible/readable** The adjectives *legible* and *readable* are synonymous in the sense of "decipherable" or "capable of being read" but are not always interchangeable. *Readable* can also mean "capable of being read with ease or enjoyment" (*a readable story*), in which sense it cannot be replaced by *legible*. The same distinction applies to the words *illegible* and *unreadable*.

**legitimate/lawful/legal** *See* LAWFUL/LEGAL/LEGITIMATE.

**lend/borrow** *See* BORROW/LEND.

**less/fewer** *See* FEWER/LESS.

**let/leave** *See* LEAVE/LET.

**liable/apt/likely/prone** *See* APT/LIABLE/LIKELY/PRONE.

**libel/slander** The nouns *libel* and *slander* are often confused, although they have different meanings in law. *Libel* describes defamatory statements that are written or recorded in some form:

*The letter formed the basis of a suit of libel.*

*Slander* relates to defamation by word of mouth or gesture:

*She was the object of slander every time she went into the street.*

**lie/lay** *See* LAY/LIE.

**lifelong/livelong** The adjectives *lifelong* and *livelong* have different meanings and should not be confused. *Lifelong* means "lasting a lifetime" (*a lifelong guarantee*), whereas the less commonly encountered *livelong* means "whole" or "entire" (*the livelong day*).

**lightening/lightning** These two words are unrelated in meaning and should not be confused. *Lightening* is the present participle of the verb *lighten* (*lightening the load*). *Lightning* is a noun describing the flashes of light from atmospheric electricity (*thunder and lightning*). By extension, *lightning* may be used adjectivally to describe anything that happens unexpectedly and very quickly (*a lightning strike against the enemy positions*).

**lightning/lightening** *See* LIGHTENING/LIGHTNING.

**likely/apt/liable/prone** *See* APT/LIABLE/LIKELY/PRONE.

**liqueur/liquor** The nouns *liqueur* and *liquor* both refer to alcoholic drinks but are not synonymous. *Liqueur* refers to a category of strong, sweet alcoholic drinks, such as Cointreau and crème de menthe (*an after-dinner liqueur*). *Liquor* applies generally to alcoholic drink of any kind (*a taste for strong liquor*).

**liquidate/liquidize** The verbs *liquidate* and *liquidize* are sometimes confused but have different meanings. *Liquidate* variously means "convert into cash" and, informally, "kill" (*liquidate the assets of the company; liquidate your rivals*), whereas *liquidize* means "turn into liquid" (*liquidize in a blender*).

**liquidize/liquidate** *See* LIQUIDATE/LIQUIDIZE.

**liquor/liqueur** *See* LIQUEUR/LIQUOR.

**literal/literary/literate** These three adjectives differ in meaning and should not be confused. *Literal* means "actual" or "exact" (*the literal meaning of the passage*), while *literary* means "of or relating to literature" (*a literary tome*). *Literate* means "well-read" or "well-educated" (*a literate young woman, written in a literate hand*).

**literary/literate/literal** *See* LITERAL/LITERARY/LITERATE.

**literate/literal/literary** *See* LITERAL/LITERARY/LITERATE.

**livelong/lifelong** *See* LIFELONG/LIVELONG.

**loaded/laden** *See* LADEN/LOADED.

**loath/loathe/loth** These three words are related in meaning and are commonly confused. *Loth* is a variant of the adjective *loath,* meaning "unwilling" or "disinclined" (*loath to give in; loth to concede defeat*). *Loathe,* however, is a verb meaning "detest":

*She loathes her sister.*

**loathe/loath/loth** *See* LOATH/LOATHE/LOTH.

**locale/locality/location** These three nouns all mean "place" but with subtle differences. They are therefore not interchangeable. *Locale* means "setting for an event or series of events" (*the locale for the campaign*); whereas *locality* means "area" (*the spreading of the news through the locality*); and "location" denotes "a particular place" (*point out the location on the map*).

**locality/locale/location** *See* LOCALE/LOCALITY/LOCATION.

**location/locale/locality** *See* LOCALE/LOCALITY/LOCATION.

**loose/loosen/lose** These three verbs are sometimes confused, although they vary in meaning. *Loose* means "undo" or "set free" (*loose the knot; loose the dog*), whereas *loosen* means "make less tight" (*loosen the fastening*). *Lose* variously means "fail to win," "suffer the loss of," or "fail to keep" (*lose the battle; lose your shoes; lose your way*). Note that *loose* and *loosen* are pronounced with a soft *s* (as in *noose*), unlike *lose,* which is pronounced with a hard *z* sound (as in *ooze*).

**loosen/loose/lose** *See* LOOSE/LOOSEN/LOSE.

**lose/loose/loosen** *See* LOOSE/LOOSEN/LOSE.

**loth/loath/loathe** *See* LOATH/LOATHE/LOTH.

**lour/lower** *Lour* is a variant of the verb *lower* in the sense of "look threatening" or "frown" (*the thick mist lowered over the valley*), and both spellings are pronounced to rhyme with *power.* They may also appear in adjectival form (*a louring look*). *Lower,* however, can also appear as an adjective meaning "less high" (*lower on the list*) or as a verb meaning "move down" (*lower the flag*). In these cases *lour* is not an acceptable form. Note that *lower* in these latter contexts is pronounced differently, to rhyme with *grower.*

**lower/lour** *See* LOUR/LOWER.

**low/lowly** The adjectives *low* and *lowly* are related but have significantly different meanings. *Low* means "reduced in elevation, quantity, quality, etc." (*a low roof, low supplies, a low voice*), whereas *lowly* means "humble" or "meek" (*a lowly position, a lowly servant, of lowly origins*).

**lowly/low** *See* LOW/LOWLY.

**lumbar/lumber** The words *lumbar* and *lumber* share the same pronunciation and are sometimes confused. *Lumbar* is an adjective meaning "of or relating to the lower back" and is largely confined to medical contexts (*the lumbar region*), whereas *lumber* is a noun or verb meaning "timber" or "move ponderously," respectively (*a pile of lumber; lumber along the road with arms swinging*).

**lumber/lumbar** *See* LUMBAR/LUMBER.

**luxuriant/luxurious** The adjectives *luxuriant* and *luxurious* have different meanings and are not interchangeable. *Luxuriant* means "lush," "prolific," or "profuse" (*luxuriant vegetation, a luxuriant head of hair*), whereas *luxurious* means "characterized by luxury" or "sumptuous" (*luxurious surroundings, a luxurious home*).

**luxurious/luxuriant** *See* LUXURIANT/LUXURIOUS.

**magnate/magnet** These two nouns are unrelated in meaning but are sometimes confused because of their similar appearance and pronunciation. A *magnate* is a "person of power or influence" (*a business magnate*), whereas a *magnet* denotes a "magnetic body" (*held in place by a magnet*), sometimes used figuratively to describe "something that attracts":

*The bar is a magnet for tourists.*

**magnet/magnate** *See* MAGNATE/MAGNET.

**mail/male** These two nouns are pronounced identically and are sometimes confused. *Mail* means "communication by post or other means" (*receive a letter in the mail*), whereas *male* means "person, animal, or plant of the male gender" (*the male of the species*).

**male/masculine** Both *male* and *masculine* apply to the gender opposite to *female,* but they are used differently. *Male* may refer to a human being, animal, or plant of the male gender (*a male lion*), whereas *masculine* is an adjective reserved exclusively for men (male human beings) or alternatively words (*a masculine approach, the masculine form of the noun*).

**malevolent/malicious/malignant** These three adjectives are similar in meaning but are not identical. *Malevolent* means "ill-willed" or "spiteful" (*a malevolent rogue, a malevolent glare*). *Malicious* means "motivated by malice" and is sometimes interchangeable with *malevolent* (*a malicious rumor*). *Malignant* means "relentlessly malicious" and is the strongest of the three terms (*a malignant nature*). Note that *malignant* also has an additional role as a medical term meaning "harmful" (*a malignant growth*).

**malicious/malevolent/malignant** *See* MALEVOLENT/MALICIOUS/MALIGNANT.

**malignant/malevolent/malicious** *See* MALEVOLENT/MALICIOUS/MALIGNANT.

**mantel/mantle** The nouns *mantel* and *mantle* are pronounced in the same way but are unrelated in meaning. *Mantel* means "lintel above a fireplace" (*lean on the mantel*), whereas *mantle* means "cloak" or "something that covers or shrouds" (*a long blue mantle, a mantle of secrecy*).

**mantle/mantel** *See* MANTEL/MANTLE.

**marital/martial** These two adjectives are similar in appearance but are unrelated in meaning. *Marital* means "of or relating to marriage" (*the marital home*), whereas *martial* means "of or relating to war or the military" (*martial law*).

**marshal/martial** Despite their different spelling these two words are pronounced identically and may be confused. *Marshal* may be employed as a noun meaning "officer" or "official" (*a marshal in the fire department*) or as a verb meaning "organize" or "assemble" (*marshal the volunteers; marshaled in the yard*). *Martial* is an adjective meaning "of or relating to war or the military" (*martial music*).

**martial/marital** *See* MARITAL/MARTIAL.

**martial/marshal** *See* MARSHAL/MARTIAL.

**masculine/male** *See* MALE/MASCULINE.

**masterful/masterly** These two adjectives are sometimes confused though they have somewhat different meanings. *Masterful* means "domineering" or "imperious" (*a masterful manner as team captain*), whereas *masterly* means "highly skilled":

*The general was respected for his masterly grasp of tactics.*

**masterly/masterful** *See* MASTERFUL/MASTERLY.

**may/can** *See* CAN/MAY.

**maybe/may be** The phrase *may be* is sometimes confused with the word *maybe,* though the two have different meanings. *May be* means "may happen that":

*It may be that the weather will change.*

*Maybe* means "perhaps":

*Maybe something will break.*

**may/might** Confusion often arises over the use of the verb *may* and its past tense *might.* In many circumstances the two words are interchangeable in the present tense, although *might* is generally more tentative than *may:*

*May I come in?*
*Might I come in?*

In some circumstances, however, *might* cannot be substituted by *may,* primarily where it refers to the past:

*He might have let us stay for a minute at least.*
*It might have turned out all right if she hadn't panicked.*

**meantime/meanwhile** These two phrases mean much the same thing, but there is a subtle difference in the way they are generally used. *Meantime* is usually employed as a noun in the phrases *in the meantime* and *for the meantime,* in the sense "for the time being":

*Do nothing in the meantime without checking with me.*

*Meanwhile* is used chiefly as an adverb, meaning "in the intervening time" or "at the same time":

*Meanwhile, news of the invasion had reached the capital.*

**meanwhile/meantime** *See* MEANTIME/MEANWHILE.

**medal/meddle** The words *medal* and *meddle* share the same pronunciation but mean different things. *Medal* is a noun meaning "award or decoration" (*a medal for bravery*), whereas *meddle* is a verb meaning "interfere" (*meddle with things that don't concern you*).

**meddle/medal** *See* MEDAL/MEDDLE.

**melted/molten** These two words are close in meaning, but they are not identical. *Melted* is the past tense and past participle of the verb *melt* (*ice melted in the sun*) and is also employed as an adjective (*melted candle wax*). *Molten* is an adjective that also means "melted" but usually conveys the suggestion that the material in question is still in a melting (and probably hot) state:

*She expertly handled the molten glass with metal rods.*

**meretricious/meritorious** These two adjectives have different meanings and should not be confused. *Meretricious* means "falsely attractive," "insincere," or "pretentious" (*a meretricious speech*), whereas *meritorious* means "deserving merit" (*meritorious conduct*).

**meritorious/meretricious** *See* MERETRICIOUS/MERITORIOUS.

**metal/mettle** These two nouns are sometimes confused as they share the same pronunciation. *Metal* describes the material (*made of metal*), whereas *mettle* means "strength of character" (*test your mettle*). In fact, *mettle* was itself originally derived from the word *metal.*

**mettle/metal** *See* METAL/METTLE.

**might/may** *See* MAY/MIGHT.

**militate/mitigate** These two verbs are similar in appearance but are unrelated in meaning. *Militate* means "exert a strong influence" and is usually followed by *against:*

*Such a move militates against the restoration of peaceful industrial relations.*

*Mitigate* means "moderate" or "alleviate":

*This setback was mitigated by the discovery of a new way forward.*

**miner/minor** These two words are pronounced in the same way but are unrelated in meaning. *Miner* is a noun meaning "worker in a mine" (*a miner like his father*), whereas *minor* is a noun meaning "person below the age of majority" (*in charge of a minor*) and an adjective meaning "less important" (*a minor issue*).

**minor/miner** *See* MINER/MINOR.

**mistrust/distrust** *See* DISTRUST/MISTRUST.

**misuse/abuse** *See* ABUSE/MISUSE.

**mitigate/militate** *See* MILITATE/MITIGATE.

**modern/modernistic** These two adjectives are subtly different in meaning. *Modern* means "contemporary" or "up-to-date" (*a modern building, the modern world*), whereas *modernistic* means "of or relating to modern trends" and is sometimes used in a negative way (*modernistic music*).

**modernistic/modern** *See* MODERN/MODERNISTIC.

**molten/melted** *See* MELTED/MOLTEN.

**momentary/momentous** The adjectives *momentary* and *momentous* are superficially similar, both being derived from the noun *moment,* but are unrelated in meaning. *Momentary* means "brief" (*a momentary lapse of concentration*), whereas *momentous* means "hugely significant" (*a momentous decision*).

**momentous/momentary** *See* MOMENTARY/MOMENTOUS.

**monogram/monograph** These two nouns may resemble each other in appearance but they are unrelated in meaning. A *monogram* is a "design made from the initials of a person's name" (*a monogram on a shirt cuff*), whereas a *monograph* is a "learned treatise on a particular subject" (*author of a respected monograph on the history of porcelain*).

**monograph/monogram** *See* MONOGRAM/MONOGRAPH.

**moral/morale** These two words have similar spellings but are pronounced differently and mean different things. *Moral* is an adjective meaning "ethical" or "conforming to the principles of right and wrong" (*a moral foreign policy, falling moral standards*), whereas *morale* is a noun meaning "psychological or emotional condition":

*Morale in the armed forces is high.*

Note that *moral* is pronounced with the stress on the first syllable and *morale* with the stress on the second syllable.

**morale/moral** *See* MORAL/MORALE.

**mortgagee/mortgagor** These two nouns concerning the holding of mortgages are sometimes confused. A *mortgagee* is a "person or company offering to lend money in exchange for a mortgage" (*under pressure from the mortgagee to settle the claim*), while a *mortgagor* is a "person who takes out a mortgage in exchange for a loan" (*a mortgagor with one of the big companies*).

**mortgagor/mortgagee** *See* MORTGAGEE/MORTGAGOR.

**motif/motive** The nouns *motif* and *motive* are different in meaning and should not be confused. A *motif* is a "recurrent theme in a piece of music, written work, and the like" (*return to the central motif*), whereas a *motive* is a "reason for doing something" (*a motive for committing murder*).

**motive/motif** *See* MOTIF/MOTIVE.

**muscle/mussel** The nouns *muscle* and *mussel* sound the same but have different meanings. A *muscle* may be defined as "fibrous tissue" but can also be used figuratively to mean "strength" or "power" (*show your muscles; have a lot of muscle in city hall*), whereas a *mussel* is a variety of shellfish (*gather mussels on the shore*).

**mussel/muscle** *See* MUSCLE/MUSSEL.

**mutual/common/reciprocal** *See* COMMON/MUTUAL/RECIPROCAL.

**mythical/mythological** The adjectives *mythical* and *mythological* are subtly different in meaning. *Mythical* means "imaginary" (*a mythical beast*), whereas *mythological* means "of or relating to mythology" (*a mythological tradition*). Note that while *mythological* cannot be used as a substitute for *mythical, mythical* is often employed as an alternative for *mythological* (*a mythical king*).

**mythological/mythical** *See* MYTHICAL/MYTHOLOGICAL.

**naked/nude** These two adjectives both mean "undressed," but they are not synonymous in all contexts. *Naked* has a wide range of figurative senses, among them "unvarnished," "bare," and "uncovered" (*the naked truth, a naked landscape, naked flames*). *Nude* is generally restricted to the context of undressed bodies (*a nude portrait*).

**naturalist/naturist** The nouns *naturalist* and *naturist* mean different things. A *naturalist* is a "person who studies nature" (*the world-famous naturalist*), whereas a *naturist* is a "nudist" (*an area reserved for naturists*).

**naturist/naturalist** *See* NATURALIST/NATURIST.

**naval/navel** These two adjectives are pronounced the same but are unrelated in meaning. *Naval* is an adjective meaning "of or relating to naval matters" (*a naval force*), while *navel* is a noun meaning "belly button" (*a stud in your navel*) or, figuratively, the "central point" (*the navel of the world*).

**navel/naval** *See* NAVAL/NAVEL.

**neglectful/negligent/negligible** These three words resemble each other but are not synonymous. *Neglectful* and *negligent* both share the meaning "careless" or "forgetful," although *negligent* is the slightly stronger term (*neglectful parents, a negligent motorist*), whereas *negligible* means "trifling" or "insignificant" (*a negligible contribution, of negligible importance*).

**negligible/neglectful/negligent** *See* NEGLECTFUL/NEGLIGENT/NEGLIGIBLE.

**negligent/neglectful/negligible** *See* NEGLECTFUL/NEGLIGENT/NEGLIGIBLE.

**niceness/nicety** These two nouns are both derived from *nice* but mean different things and are not interchangeable. *Niceness* describes the "quality of being nice" (*the niceness of her family*), whereas a *nicety* is a "detail" or "subtlety" (*a nicety of manners*). Note, however, that *nice* has long been considered both overused and a lazy substitute for more precise words and should be avoided in formal contexts.

**nicety/niceness** *See* NICENESS/NICETY.

**night/knight** *See* KNIGHT/NIGHT.

**nonsocial/asocial/antisocial/unsociable/unsocial** *See* ANTISOCIAL/ASOCIAL/NONSOCIAL/UNSOCIABLE/UNSOCIAL.

**notable/noted/noteworthy** These three adjectives have slightly different meanings and are used in different contexts. *Notable* and *noteworthy* both mean "remarkable" or "worthy of note," although *noteworthy* is usually restricted to facts or events (*a notable writer, a* *noteworthy discovery*). *Noted* means "famous" or "well-known" (*a noted philosopher*).

**notable/noticeable** These two adjectives are not identical in meaning and should not be confused. *Notable* means "remarkable" or "worthy of note" (*a notable day*), whereas *noticeable* means "visible" or "perceptible" (*a noticeable effect, a noticeable lump in the carpet*).

**noted/notable/noteworthy** *See* NOTABLE/NOTED/NOTEWORTHY.

**noteworthy/notable/noted** *See* NOTABLE/NOTED/NOTEWORTHY.

**noticeable/notable** *See* NOTABLE/NOTICEABLE.

**not/knot** *See* KNOT/NOT.

**noxious/obnoxious** The adjectives *noxious* and *obnoxious* both mean "very unpleasant" but are used in different contexts. *Noxious* usually refers to something that is actually harmful as well as unpleasant (*noxious gas, noxious waste*), while *obnoxious* is usually applied to people (*an obnoxious salesclerk*).

**nude/naked** *See* NAKED/NUDE.

**nutritional/nutritious/nutritive** These two adjectives both relate to *nutrition* but have slightly different meanings. *Nutritional* means "of or relating to nutrition" (*nutritional information*), whereas *nutritious* means "nourishing" (*a nutritious diet*). *Nutritive* is a relatively rare adjective sometimes used as a formal substitute for *nutritional,* though also occasionally encountered as a replacement for *nutritious* (*the nutritive content of food*).

**nutritious/nutritional** *See* NUTRITIONAL/NUTRITIOUS/NUTRITIVE.

**nutritive/nutritional/nutritious** *See* NUTRITIONAL/NUTRITIOUS/NUTRITIVE.

**oar/or/ore** These three words, which are all pronounced in the same way, are unrelated in meaning and should not be confused. *Oar* is a noun meaning "paddle" or "pole for propelling a boat" (*pull on the oars*), whereas *or* is a conjunction indicating an alternative (*black or white*) and *ore* is a noun meaning "metal-producing mineral" (*iron ore*).

**objective/subjective** These two adjectives have opposite meanings but are sometimes confused. *Objective* means "free of personal feeling or prejudice" (*an objective view of the matter*), whereas *subjective* means "influenced by personal feeling or prejudice" (*accused of being partial and subjective*). Note that *objective* may also be encountered as a noun with the meaning "aim" or "target":

*The airport is the next objective of this mission.*

**obligated/obliged** These two adjectives are synonymous in some contexts but are not interchangeable in others. In the sense "morally or legally bound," the two words can be used as substitutes for each other, although *obligated* is the more formal term (*feel obliged to say something; feel obligated to agree*). *Obliged* can, however, also have the additional meaning of "physically constrained," in which case it cannot be replaced by *obligated:*

> *They were obliged by the pressure of the crowd around them to go with the flow.*

**obliged/obligated** *See* OBLIGATED/OBLIGED.

**obnoxious/noxious** *See* NOXIOUS/OBNOXIOUS.

**observance/observation** These two nouns are similar in appearance but have different meanings. *Observance* denotes the "observing of a customary practice, ritual, or ceremony" (*observance of the Sabbath*), while *observation* refers to the "act of noticing or watching" or else to a "remark or statement" (*observation of the stars, a pertinent observation*).

**observation/observance** *See* OBSERVANCE/OBSERVATION.

**obverse/converse/inverse/reverse** *See* CONVERSE/INVERSE/OBVERSE/REVERSE.

**occupied/preoccupied** The adjectives *occupied* and *preoccupied* have slightly different meanings. *Occupied* means "busy" or "taken" (*occupied with her studies; all seats already occupied*), whereas *preoccupied* means "absorbed" or "lost in thought" (*preoccupied with his own worries*).

**odious/odorous** These two adjectives resemble each other but mean different things. *Odious* means "vile" or "unpleasant" (*an odious person, an odious job*), whereas *odorous* means "fragrant" or "strong-smelling" (*an odorous cheese*). Note that *odorous* may be applied to either foul- or sweet-smelling things.

**odorous/odious** *See* ODIOUS/ODOROUS.

**offer/proffer** These two verbs both mean "present" but are not always synonymous. *Offer* is the more common usage (*offer a handkerchief; offer a helping hand*), with *proffer* being confined largely to more formal contexts (*proffer apologies*). Note that *proffer* cannot be used as a replacement for *offer* in more complex constructions (*offer the court an explanation*) or in the sense "propose" or "suggest" (*offer to take someone home*).

**official/officious** These two adjectives have slightly different meanings and are not interchangeable. *Official* means "authorized" or "of or relating to an office" (*in an official capacity, official duties*), whereas *officious* means "meddlesome" or "self-important" (*an officious government agent, officious behavior*).

**officious/official** *See* OFFICIAL/OFFICIOUS.

**older/elder** *See* ELDER/OLDER.

**one another/each other** *See* EACH OTHER/ONE ANOTHER.

**onto/on to** Confusion sometimes arises over the use of *on to* and *onto*. *On to* often represents *on* as an adverb and *to* as part of an infinitive and in such cases should always be written as two words (*go on to enjoy great success*). *On to* can also function as an adverb plus a preposition (*run on to the next page; move on to the next task*). *Onto*, meanwhile, is a preposition (*put one brick onto another; walk onto the aircraft*).

**oppress/repress/suppress** These three verbs are related in meaning but are used in different ways. *Oppress* means "weigh down," "burden," or "subdue" (*oppressed by doubt; the dictator oppresses his people*). *Repress* can also mean "subjugate" but has the additional meanings of "conceal or control your feelings" (*repress your desire*). *Suppress* means "restrain" or "control" (*suppress the urge to giggle*) but can also mean "check" or "subdue" (*suppress a rumor, suppress dissenting opinion*).

**oral/aural** *See* AURAL/ORAL.

**ordinance/ordnance** These two nouns are similar in appearance but have different meanings. *Ordinance* means "decree" or "official order" (*issue a new ordinance*), whereas *ordnance* denotes "military supplies" or, more specifically, "artillery" (*army ordnance; siege ordnance*).

**ordnance/ordinance** *See* ORDINANCE/ORDNANCE.

**ore/oar/or** *See* OAR/OR/ORE.

**or/ore/oar** *See* OAR/OR/ORE.

**ostensible/ostentatious** These two adjectives are slightly different in meaning. *Ostensible* means "apparent" (*the ostensible cause of the accident*), whereas *ostentatious* means "showy" or "pretentiously vulgar" (*an ostentatious demonstration of loyalty*). Both words have negative or derogatory connotations.

**ostentatious/ostensible** *See* OSTENSIBLE/OSTENTATIOUS.

**our/hour** *See* HOUR/OUR.

**overlay/overlie** The verbs *overlay* and *overlie* overlap in meaning but are not always synonymous. *Overlay* means "cover" or "place on top of" (*concrete overlaid with pebbles*), whereas the rarer *overlie* means "lie over" or "lie upon" (*the visible layer overlies another*). Note that *overlay* may also be encountered as the past tense of *overlie.*

**overlie/overlay** *See* OVERLAY/OVERLIE.

**overtone/undertone** These two nouns are closely related in meaning but are not exactly synonymous. *Overtone* means "additional quality or meaning" (*a message with political overtones*), while *undertone* means "underlying effect" (*an undertone of resentment*). Note that the two words are not synonymous in their various other meanings, namely *overtone* as "harmonic," and *undertone* as "lowered voice."

**owing to/due to** *See* DUE TO/OWING TO.

**pain/pane** These two nouns share the same pronunciation but mean different things. *Pain* denotes "acute physical or mental discomfort" (*wince with pain, pain at her indifference*), whereas *pane* means "sheet of glass or other material" (*break a pane of glass*).

**palate/palette/pallet** These three nouns are similar in appearance but have different meanings. *Palate* variously means "roof of the mouth" or "sense of taste" (*a cleft palate, a refined palate*). *Palette* means "board or tablet used to mix paints" or "selection of colors" (*an artist's palette*). *Pallet* means "wooden platform for stacking goods" (*a heap of pallets*).

**palette/palate/pallet** *See* PALATE/PALETTE/PALLET.

**pallet/palate/palette** *See* PALATE/PALETTE/PALLET.

**pane/pain** *See* PAIN/PANE.

**paradigm/paragon** These two nouns are unrelated in meaning. *Paradigm* means "example" or "pattern" (*a paradigm of achievement, a paradigm shift*), whereas *paragon* means "model of excellence" (*a paragon of environmentally sound technology*).

**paragon/paradigm** *See* PARADIGM/PARAGON.

**partially/partly** These two adverbs are synonymous in some contexts but are not interchangeable in others. Both words can mean "to a limited extent" or "not completely" (*partially won over, partially sighted, partly finished, partly covered*), but *partly* also has a number of other meanings, such as "concerning one part" (*partly one thing, partly another*).

**partly/partially** *See* PARTIALLY/PARTLY.

**passed/past** These two words are easily confused as their pronunciations are identical. *Passed* is the past participle of the verb *pass:*

*The couple passed the window.*

*Past* is the correct form when used as a noun, adjective, preposition, and adverb (*lost in the past, past deeds, past caring, walk past*).

**past/passed** *See* PASSED/PAST.

**peaceable/peaceful** The adjectives *peaceable* and *peaceful* have similar meanings but are not always interchangeable. Both words can mean "disposed to peace" or "tranquil" (*a peaceable scene, a peaceful view*), but *peaceable* is usually applied in relation to peace-loving people (*a peaceable disposition*), while *peaceful* is the more common term when used to mean "calm" or "undisturbed" (*a peaceful existence*).

**peaceful/peaceable** *See* PEACEABLE/PEACEFUL.

**peace/piece** These two nouns are pronounced in the same way but have different meanings. *Peace* means "state of tranquility or peaceful relations" (*peace and order*), while *piece* means "part," "fragment," or "section" (*a piece of wood, bits and pieces*).

**peak/peek/pique** The nouns *peak, peek,* and *pique* share the same pronunciation but mean different things. *Peak* means "summit" or "high point" (*the peak of the mountain, a peak in profits*); *peek* means "glimpse" or "look" (*a peek at the present, a peek inside*); and *pique* means "resentment" or "wounded vanity" (*in a fit of pique*).

**peal/peel** These two nouns are pronounced identically but mean different things. *Peal* denotes the "ringing of bells" or any "loud sound" (*a peal of the cathedral bells, a peal of thunder*), while *peel* refers to the "outer layer, or skin, of fruit" (*apple peel*).

**pedal/peddle** These two words are pronounced in the same way and are sometimes confused. A *pedal* describes a "lever operated by the foot" (*pedal bin, bicycle pedal*) or the action of pushing on such a pedal (*pedal furiously up the hill*), whereas *peddle* is a verb meaning "deal in" and may imply a degree of illegality in so doing (*peddle illegal narcotics*).

**peddle/pedal** *See* PEDAL/PEDDLE.

**peek/peak/pique** *See* PEAK/PEEK/PIQUE.

**peel/peal** *See* PEAL/PEEL.

**peer/pier** The words *peer* and *pier* have different meanings but are sometimes confused. *Peer* as a noun means "equal" (*respected among his peers*) and as a verb "look closely" (*peer at the menu*), whereas *pier* is a noun denoting a "jetty" or "vertical structural support":

*There were two fishing vessels moored alongside the pier.*
*They have designed an arched roof supported by a double row of metal piers.*

**peninsula/peninsular** Confusion sometimes arises over the use of these two words. *Peninsula* is a noun denoting a "strip of land extending into a body of water" (*a peninsula connected to the mainland by a narrow isthmus*), while *peninsular* is the adjectival form of this noun (*the peninsular character of the coast*).

**peninsular/peninsula** *See* PENINSULA/PENINSULAR.

**people/persons** These two nouns are both plural forms of *person* but are used slightly differently. *People* is the usual preferred form (*hundreds of people*), while *persons* is a more formal term, as used in legal contexts (*person or persons unknown*).

**perceptible/perceptive** These two adjectives are related in meaning but should not be confused. *Perceptible* means "noticeable" or "capable of being perceived" (*a perceptible shift in opinion, a barely perceptible crack*), whereas *perceptive* means "observant" or "discerning" (*a perceptive comment, a perceptive young woman*). Equal care should be taken not to confuse the adverbs *perceptibly* and *perceptively.*

**perceptive/perceptible** *See* PERCEPTIBLE/PERCEPTIVE.

**peremptory/perfunctory** The adjectives *peremptory* and *perfunctory* are easily confused, although they have different meanings. *Peremptory* means "dogmatic," "masterful," or "ignoring contradiction" (*a peremptory tone, a peremptory decision*), while *perfunctory* means "mechanical" or "cursory" (*a perfunctory smile, a perfunctory inspection*).

**perfunctory/peremptory** *See* PEREMPTORY/PERFUNCTORY.

**permissible/permissive** The adjectives *permissible* and *permissive* are sometimes confused. *Permissible* means "permitted" (*permissible to enter*), whereas *permissive* means "tolerant" (*the permissive society*).

**permissive/permissible** *See* PERMISSIBLE/PERMISSIVE.

**perpetrate/perpetuate** These two verbs are similar in appearance but are unrelated in meaning. *Perpetrate* means "commit" or "perform" (*perpetrate an outrage*), while *perpetuate* means "carry on" or "continue" (*perpetuate a long-standing custom*).

**perpetuate/perpetrate** *See* PERPETRATE/PERPETUATE.

**perquisite/prerequisite** The nouns *perquisite* and *prerequisite* are unrelated in meaning and should not be confused. *Perquisite* means "benefit" or "privilege" (*a perquisite of the job*) and is often abbreviated to *perk*. *Prerequisite* denotes a "precondition":

*An understanding manner is a prerequisite for this kind of social work.*

**persecute/prosecute** These two verbs are sometimes confused because of their superficial similarity. *Persecute* means "harass" or "pester" (*persecuted with questions; persecuted by their critics*), whereas *prosecute* means "perform" or "bring a legal action against" (*prosecute the campaign with determination; decide to prosecute on a charge of tax evasion*).

**personage/personality** These two nouns both mean "famous person" but are used slightly differently. *Personage* tends to be reserved for a "person of rank or distinction" (*an important personage*), while *personality* is usually applied to a person who has achieved popular fame in the arts, business, sports, and so on (*a television personality*).

**personality/personage** *See* PERSONAGE/PERSONALITY.

**persons/people** *See* PEOPLE/PERSONS.

**perspective/prospective** These two words are unrelated in meaning and should not be confused. *Perspective* is a noun meaning "aspect" or "view" (*the perspective from the terrace*), whereas *prospective* is an adjective meaning "expected" or "likely" (*my prospective income, a prospective buyer*). Note that *perspective* also has a more specialized meaning in art, denoting the arrangement and sizing of objects in a picture to create a realistic sense of depth and distance, and that in this sense it may also be used figuratively to mean "point of view" or "sense of relative importance" (*an artist's control of perspective; maintain your perspective*).

**perturb/disturb** *See* DISTURB/PERTURB.

**perverse/perverted** These two adjectives are easily confused but have distinctly different meanings. *Perverse* is the more general term, meaning "corrupt," "improper," or "obstinate" (*a perverse decision; take a perverse pleasure in upsetting others; perverse in his stubbornness*), whereas *perverted* means "of or relating to abnormal sexual behavior" (*a perverted interest in women's shoes*).

**perverted/perverse** *See* PERVERSE/PERVERTED.

**phase/faze** *See* FAZE/PHASE.

**phenomena/phenomenon** Confusion can arise over the use of these two words. *Phenomena* is the plural form of the noun *phenomenon*, which means "exceptional person, event, or thing" (*an unexplained phenomenon; unusual phenomena*).

**phenomenon/phenomena** *See* PHENOMENA/PHENOMENON.

**physician/physicist** The nouns *physician* and *physicist* mean different things and should not be confused. A *physician* is a "doctor of medicine":

> *The patient has been ordered to rest by his physician.*

A *physicist* is a "scientist working in the field of physics":

> *A combined theory has so far eluded the world's top physicists.*

**physicist/physician** *See* PHYSICIAN/PHYSICIST.

**piece/peace** *See* PEACE/PIECE.

**pier/peer** *See* PEER/PIER.

**pique/peak/peek** *See* PEAK/PEEK/PIQUE.

**piteous/pitiable/pitiful** These three adjectives all mean much the same thing but are not always synonymous. In the sense "arousing or deserving pity," all three words are interchangeable (*a piteous condition, a pitiable sight, a pitiful example*), but *pitiable* and *pitiful* can also have the additional sense "arousing or deserving contempt," in which case they cannot be substituted by *piteous:*

> *The government offered the victims a pitiable amount of compensation.*
> *His attempts to apologize were universally condemned as pitiful.*

**pitiable/piteous/pitiful** *See* PITEOUS/PITIABLE/PITIFUL.

**pitiful/piteous/pitiable** *See* PITEOUS/PITIABLE/PITIFUL.

**place/plaice** These two nouns share the same pronunciation but mean different things. The various meanings of *place* include "location," "position," or "space" (*a beautiful place, a place at the table, no place for more*), whereas *plaice* is the name of an edible flat fish (*plaice cooked in butter*).

**plaice/place** *See* PLACE/PLAICE.

**plain/plane** The nouns *plain* and *plane* are sometimes confused because of their identical pronunciation. *Plain* denotes a "level, treeless expanse" (*a windswept plain*), whereas *plane* variously means "surface," "leveling tool," or "airplane" (*where two planes overlap;*

*remove flaws with a plane; transport plane*). As adjectives, *plain* and *plane* have slightly different but still distinct meanings, *plain* meaning "clear," "undecorated," or "straightforward" (*the plain truth, a plain design, plain facts*), while *plane* means "flat" (*a plane surface*).

**plaintiff/plaintive** The words *plaintiff* and *plaintive* are unrelated in meaning and should not be confused. *Plaintiff* is a legal term meaning "person bringing an action to court" (*a plaintiff seeking compensation*), whereas *plaintive* is an adjective meaning "melancholy" (*a plaintive cry*).

**plaintive/plaintiff** *See* PLAINTIFF/PLAINTIVE.

**plane/plain** *See* PLAIN/PLANE.

**plumb/plum** *See* PLUM/PLUMB.

**plum/plumb** The words *plum* and *plumb* mean different things but are sometimes confused because of their superficial similarity. *Plum* is a noun meaning "edible fruit of a plum tree" (*a juicy plum*), whereas *plumb* is a verb meaning "install plumbing" and, figuratively, "probe" (*plumb in a metal bath; plumb the underlying meaning*). *Plumb* may also be encountered as an adverb meaning "vertically" or "absolutely" (*it is aligned plumb to the bottom of the shaft, plumb loco*) or as an adjective meaning "vertical" (*a plumb drop*). A *plumb line* is used to check that a line is vertical.

**political/politic** *See* POLITIC/POLITICAL.

**politic/political** The adjectives *politic* and *political* are different in meaning and are not interchangeable. *Politic* means "shrewd" or "advantageous in the circumstances" (*a politic move*), while *political* means "of or relating to politics" (*the latest political news*). Note that the two words are pronounced differently, with the stress on the first syllable in *politic* and on the second syllable in *political.*

**populace/populous** These two words are related in meaning and share the same pronunciation but are not interchangeable and should not be confused. *Populace* is a noun meaning "inhabitants" (*the populace of the town, the general populace*), whereas *populous* is an adjective meaning "densely populated" (*a populous area*).

**populous/populace** *See* POPULACE/POPULOUS.

**pore/pour** These two verbs are pronounced identically but are unrelated in meaning. *Pore* means "study intently" and is always followed by *over* (*pore over the details*), whereas *pour* means "cause to flow" or "dispense freely" (*pour drinks from a jug; pour money into a company*). Note that *pore* may also be encountered as a noun denoting a "minute opening in the skin" (*sweat produced by the pores*).

**pour/pore** *See* PORE/POUR.

**practicable/practical** These two adjectives are slightly different in meaning and are not interchangeable. *Practicable* means "capable of being done" (*a practicable suggestion*), whereas *practical* variously means "realistic," "sensible," "useful," "suitable," "virtual," or "capable of doing or making things" (*a practical way forward, for practical purposes, a practical tool, a practical coat, practical loss of all mobility, practical skills*). The same distinction applies to *impracticable* and *impractical.*

**practical/practicable** *See* PRACTICABLE/PRACTICAL.

**pray/prey** These two words are pronounced identically but have different meanings. *Pray* is a verb meaning "address God in prayer" or, more generally, "entreat" or "implore" (*pray for deliverance*), whereas *prey* is a verb meaning "hunt an animal or other victim" or a noun referring to the victim of such a hunt (*prey on small mammals; go after other prey*). *Prey* may also mean "obsess" (*a memory that preyed upon her for months*). Note that the verb *prey* is always followed by *on* or *upon.*

**precedence/precedent** These two nouns are both derived from the verb *precede* and are similar in appearance but are not interchangeable as they vary in meaning. *Precedence* means "priority in importance":

> *This regulation takes precedence over all previous rules.*

*Precedent* means "previous example" or "model":

> *This decision establishes a legal precedent for similar cases in the future.*

**precedent/precedence** *See* PRECEDENCE/PRECEDENT.

**precede/proceed** The verbs *precede* and *proceed* are easily mistaken for each other. *Precede* means "come before":

> *The ceremony will be preceded by a procession of all those taking part.*

*Proceed* means "go on" or "continue":

> *The car proceeded down the street.*
> *The police are proceeding with the investigation.*

**precipitate/precipitous** These two adjectives are sometimes considered synonymous but are in fact slightly different in meaning. *Precipitate* means "hasty," "rash," or "headlong" (*a precipitate decision, a precipitate flight*), whereas *precipitous* means "very steep" (*a precipitous drop*). Note that *precipitate* may also be encountered as a verb and noun.

**precipitous/precipitate** *See* PRECIPITATE/PRECIPITOUS.

**preclude/exclude** *See* EXCLUDE/PRECLUDE.

**precondition/condition** *See* CONDITION/PRECONDITION.

**predicate/predict** The verbs *predicate* and *predict* have slightly different meanings. *Predicate* means "affirm," "declare," or "base" (*predicate your faith; a belief predicated upon personal conviction*), whereas *predict* means "foretell" (*predict a change in the weather*). Note that *predicate* may also be encountered as a noun with relevance in grammar and logic.

**predict/predicate** *See* PREDICATE/PREDICT.

**preface/prefix** The meanings of two words overlap in some contexts, but they are not always synonymous. Both *preface* and *prefix* may be encountered as nouns meaning "foreword" or "introductory remarks" (*a short preface, a prefix to the document*), but as verbs it is often considered more correct in most contexts to use *preface* instead of *prefix:*

*I would like to preface my statement with a few brief observations.*

*Prefix* is thus usually restricted to its literal sense of "add as a prefix":

*Either word may be prefixed with ante- or anti-.*

**prefix/preface** *See* PREFACE/PREFIX.

**premier/premiere** The words *premier* and *premiere* are related in meaning but are not interchangeable. As a noun *premier* is the "prime minister" (*the UK premier Tony Blair*), and as an adjective *premier* means "foremost" or "best" (*the premier figure in this field, a premier product*). *Premiere* is a noun meaning "first performance" (*film premiere*). *Premiere* is also sometimes used as a verb (*another film to premiere next summer*), but this use is disliked by some people.

**premiere/premier** *See* PREMIER/PREMIERE.

**preoccupied/occupied** *See* OCCUPIED/PREOCCUPIED.

**prerequisite/perquisite** *See* PERQUISITE/PREREQUISITE.

**prerequisite/requisite** These two words are sometimes confused, though they have slightly different meanings. A *prerequisite* is a noun meaning "something required in advance":

*A substantial fund to draw upon is a prerequisite for getting involved in this particular market.*

A *requisite* is a noun meaning "something considered essential":

*A requisite for any successful political party is dynamic leadership.*

Both words may also be encountered as adjectives.

**prescribe/proscribe** The verbs *prescribe* and *proscribe* are similar in appearance but mean different things. *Prescribe* means "recommend" or "authorize a medical prescription" (*prescribe a course of treatment; prescribe drugs*), whereas *proscribe* means "condemn" or "prohibit" (*the school proscribed such behavior; proscribed by law*).

**presume/assume** *See* ASSUME/PRESUME.

**presumptive/presumptuous** These two adjectives are similar in appearance but unrelated in meaning. *Presumptive* means "based on presumption or probability" (*the presumptive father*), whereas *presumptuous* means "impudent" or "bold" (*a presumptuous act, a presumptuous attempt to score*).

**presumptuous/presumptive** *See* PRESUMPTIVE/PRESUMPTUOUS.

**pretense/pretension/pretentiousness** These three nouns are related in meaning but are not always interchangeable. *Pretense* denotes an "act of pretending" (*a pretense of ignorance*), whereas *pretension* means "claim" (*harbor a pretension to greatness*) and *pretentiousness* means "affectation" or "ostentation" (*the pretentiousness of the decor*). Note that in certain limited contexts *pretense* may be substituted for *pretension,* notably in the sense of "false claim," while both *pretense* and *pretension* may sometimes be used as replacements for *pretentiousness.*

**pretension/pretense/pretentiousness** *See* PRETENSE/PRETENSION/PRETENTIOUSNESS.

**pretentiousness/pretense/pretension** *See* PRETENSE/PRETENSION/PRETENTIOUSNESS.

**prevaricate/procrastinate** The verbs *prevaricate* and *procrastinate* have different meanings and should not be confused. *Prevaricate* means "evade," "mislead," or "equivocate" (*to prevaricate when questioned by the police*), whereas *procrastinate* means "delay" or "put off":

*He sought to procrastinate until the return of his parents.*

**prey/pray** *See* PRAY/PREY.

**price/cost** *See* COST/PRICE.

**principal/principle** These two words share the same pronunciation but are unrelated in meaning. *Principal* is an adjective meaning "of chief importance" (*the principal consideration*) but may also be encountered as a noun meaning "head of an organization" (*principal of the local school*). *Principle* is a noun meaning "fundamental truth" or "guiding ideal" (*compromise your principles; run in accordance with high-minded principles*). Note that *principle* is also the correct form in the phrases *in principle,* which means "in theory," and *on principle,* which means "as a matter of principle":

*In principle such a method of procedure would seem reasonable.*
*He refused the bribe on principle.*

**principle/principal** *See* PRINCIPAL/PRINCIPLE.

**procedure/proceeding** The nouns *procedure* and *proceeding* mean different things and should not be confused. *Procedure* means "way of doing something" (*introduce a new procedure in the factory*), while *proceeding* means "legal action" or "transaction" (*court proceedings, an interruption in proceedings*).

**proceeding/procedure** *See* PROCEDURE/PROCEEDING.

**proceed/precede** *See* PRECEDE/PROCEED.

**procrastinate/prevaricate** *See* PREVARICATE/PROCRASTINATE.

**prodigy/protégé** These two nouns are similar in meaning and are sometimes confused. A *prodigy* is an "unusually talented child or youth" or, more generally, "something extraordinary or inexplicable" (*a child prodigy, a prodigy of the imagination*). A *protégé* is a "pupil under the tutelage of someone else":

*She numbered some of the world's greatest ballet dancers among her many protégés.*

**produce/product** These two nouns are close in meaning but are not identical. *Produce* denotes "something that is produced" or "yield" and tends to be associated principally with things that are grown or farmed (*agricultural produce*), while *product* generally refers to a particular "commodity" and includes things manufactured by industrial processes (*our company's latest product*). Unlike *produce, product* is sometimes used in an abstract sense (*the product of a troubled childhood*). Note that *produce* may also be encountered as a verb meaning "make" or "manufacture," in which case the stress falls on the second syllable (in contrast to the noun, where the stress falls on the first syllable).

**product/produce** *See* PRODUCE/PRODUCT.

**proffer/offer** *See* OFFER/PROFFER.

**prognosis/diagnosis** *See* DIAGNOSIS/PROGNOSIS.

**prohibit/forbid** *See* FORBID/PROHIBIT.

**prone/apt/liable/likely** *See* APT/LIABLE/LIKELY/PRONE.

**prone/prostrate/supine** These three adjectives are similar in meaning and are sometimes confused. *Prone* and *prostrate* both mean "lying face down" (*prone on the floor, lying prostrate on the ground*), whereas *supine* means "lying face up":

*The body lay supine on the table.*

Note that *prostrate* may also be encountered in the sense "lying flat," "exhausted," or "overwhelmed" (*prostrate after their exertions, prostrate with fear*).

**prophecy/prophesy** Confusion often arises over the spelling of *prophecy* and *prophesy,* which are forms of the same word. *Prophecy* is a noun meaning "prediction" (*a biblical prophecy*), while *prophesy* is a verb meaning "foretell" (*prophesy the future*).

**prophesy/prophecy** *See* PROPHECY/PROPHESY.

**proportional/proportionate** These two adjectives both mean "in proportion" but are not always interchangeable. *Proportional* and *proportionate* can be substituted for each other in most contexts (*a proportional change in inflation, a proportionate decrease in employment*), but in the phrase *proportional representation, proportional* cannot be replaced by *proportionate.*

**proportionate/proportional** *See* PROPORTIONAL/PROPORTIONATE.

**proposal/proposition** The nouns *proposal* and *proposition* mean virtually the same thing but are not always used in the same way. *Proposal* and *proposition* both mean broadly "something put forward" or "suggestion" (*an unwelcome proposal, a business proposition*) but both words have other meanings in which they are not interchangeable. *Proposal* cannot be replaced by *proposition* when it means "offer of marriage" (*a marriage proposal*), while *proposition* cannot be substituted by *proposal* in the sense a "sexual advance" (*he made a lewd proposition to his female colleagues*). In this last sense *proposition* can also be a verb.

**proposition/proposal** *See* PROPOSAL/PROPOSITION.

**proscribe/prescribe** *See* PRESCRIBE/PROSCRIBE.

**prosecute/persecute** *See* PERSECUTE/PROSECUTE.

**prospective/perspective** *See* PERSPECTIVE/PROSPECTIVE.

**prostate/prostrate** These two words are similar in appearance but are unrelated in meaning and should not be confused. *Prostate* is a noun referring to a "gland associated with the bladder in males" (*examine the prostate for cancer*), while *prostrate* is an adjective meaning "lying face down" (*prostrate upon the floor*).

**prostrate/prone/supine** *See* PRONE/PROSTRATE/SUPINE.

**prostrate/prostate** *See* PROSTATE/PROSTRATE.

**protégé/prodigy** *See* PRODIGY/PROTÉGÉ.

**providential/provident** *See* PROVIDENT/PROVIDENTIAL.

**provident/providential** These two ostensibly similar adjectives have different meanings and are not interchangeable. *Provident* means "prudent" or "frugal" (*a provident measure, a provident housekeeper*), whereas *providential* means "fortunate" (*a providential relaxation in official regulation*).

**psychiatrist/psychologist** *See* PSYCHIATRY/PSYCHOLOGY.

**psychiatry/psychology** The disciplines of *psychiatry* and *psychology* are distinct, and the terms should not be confused. *Psychiatry* describes the "study of emotional, mental, and behavioral disorders" (*psychiatry as a branch of medicine*), whereas *psychology* denotes the "study of the mind" (*Freudian psychology*). The same distinction applies to the related words *psychiatrist* and *psychologist.*

**psychologist/psychiatrist** *See* PSYCHIATRY/PSYCHOLOGY.

**psychology/psychiatry** *See* PSYCHIATRY/PSYCHOLOGY.

**punctilious/punctual** These two adjectives are unrelated in meaning and should not be confused. *Punctilious* means "careful" or "with scrupulous attention to detail" (*a punctilious inspection of equipment*), whereas *punctual* means "prompt" or "on time" (*expected to be punctual; a punctual arrival*).

**punctual/punctilious** *See* PUNCTILIOUS/PUNCTUAL.

**pupil/student** These two nouns are close in meaning but are not always interchangeable. *Pupil* refers to a "schoolchild" or, more generally, to a "person being taught by a teacher or expert" (*a hundred pupils in the school, a pupil of the great master*). *Student* means "person engaged in study" and, while also used of schoolchildren, is generally applied to those who attend college or university or are otherwise pursuing studies at a more senior level (*a student of classical music, students at Harvard, an adult student*).

**purposefully/purposely** These two adverbs are similar in appearance and are sometimes confused. *Purposefully* means "with determination" or "in pursuit of a particular end" (*stride forward purposefully, a purposefully arranged photograph*), whereas *purposely* means "with a deliberate purpose" (*a purposely provocative statement*).

**purposely/purposefully** *See* PURPOSEFULLY/PURPOSELY.

**queue/cue** *See* CUE/QUEUE.

**rack/wrack** These two words share the same pronunciation but are unrelated in meaning. *Rack* is a noun variously denoting a "framework, stand, or grating" or an "instrument of torture" (*a rack for luggage; stretched on the rack*). It is also used as a verb meaning "cause to suffer" (*racked with pain*). *Wrack* is a noun meaning "seaweed" (*wrack on the seashore*). Note that *rack* as encountered in the phrase *rack* and *ruin,* meaning "collapse" or "state of destruction" (*all in rack and ruin*), or in *nerve-racking,* meaning "causing anguish or tension" (*a nerve-racking prospect*), may also be spelled *wrack* (*wrack and ruin, nerve-wracking*).

**racket/racquet** These two words are synonymous in the sense of "bat used in sport" (*sports racket, tennis racquet*) but are not interchangeable in other contexts. *Racket* cannot be replaced by *racquet* in such senses as "cacophony" or "illegal enterprise" (*the racket from the street, the numbers racket*).

**racquet/racket** *See* RACKET/RACQUET.

**rain/reign/rein** These three nouns are pronounced identically but are unrelated in meaning. *Rain* is a noun meaning "fall of water from clouds" (*a sky full of rain*); *reign* means "rule of a monarch or other leader" (*during the reign of the present queen*); and *rein* is a "leather strap used to control a horse" (*pull on the rein*). All three words are also used as verbs.

**raise/raze** These two verbs are pronounced identically but have different meanings. *Raise* variously means "lift up," "incite," "invigorate," "grow," or "bring up" (*raise your head; raise a rebellion; raise the spirits; raise a crop; raise a family*), whereas *raze* means "destroy" or "obliterate" (*raze to the ground*).

**raise/rise** The verbs *raise* and *rise* have virtually the same meaning of "lift up" but are used in different contexts. The essential difference between the two words lies in the fact that *raise* is used transitively and thus it has an object (*raise a hand; raise the alarm*), while *rise* is used intransitively and therefore appears without an object:

*The cost is expected to rise.*

**rang/ringed/rung** These three words are all forms of the verb *ring* and are easily confused. *Rang* is the past tense of *ring* in the sense "make a ringing sound" (*when the bell rang*), while *rung* is the past participle:

*No one has rung.*

*Ringed* is that past tense and past participle of *ring* in the sense "surround with a ring":

*The campsite was ringed with trees.*

**rapt/wrapped** These two words share the same pronunciation but should not be confused since they are unrelated in meaning. *Rapt* is an adjective meaning "absorbed" or "fascinated" (*rapt in thought, rapt by the performance*), while *wrapped* is the past tense of the verb *wrap* (*a gift wrapped in paper*). Note, however, that the two words sometimes overlap in the sense of "engrossed" (*rapt in reading a story; wrapped up in a book*).

**ravage/ravish** The verbs *ravage* and *ravish* are slightly different in meaning and should not be confused. *Ravage* means "devastate" or "lay waste" (*ravaged by invaders*), while *ravish* means "seize by force" or "rape" (*ravished by bandits; ravish the women*). Note that *ravish* can also have the meaning of "delight" or "enrapture" (*ravished by the stupendous view*), in which sense it is usually encountered in its adjectival form *ravishing* (*a ravishing panorama; a ravishing young woman*).

**ravish/ravage** *See* RAVAGE/RAVISH.

**raze/raise** *See* RAISE/RAZE.

**readable/legible** *See* LEGIBLE/READABLE.

**realism/reality** The nouns *realism* and *reality* are related in meaning but are not interchangeable. *Realism* refers to "acceptance of the realities of life" (*a new sense of realism*), while *reality* denotes the "state of being real" (*the reality of such phenomena*).

**reality/realism** *See* REALISM/REALITY.

**real/reel** These words are pronounced the same but are unrelated in meaning. *Real* is an adjective meaning "actual" or "existent" (*a real threat; a real character*), whereas *reel* as a verb means "stagger or waver" and is sometimes used figuratively (*reel from a blow; reel at the news*). As a noun, *reel* is a cylinder on which something is wound and also a dance.

**rebound/redound** These two verbs have different meanings but are sometimes confused. *Rebound* means "spring back":

*The stone rebounded and hit the window.*
*The accusations made by the senator appear set to rebound upon him.*

*Redound* means "contribute to" or "accrue":

*This achievement redounds to the president's growing reputation as an international negotiator.*

Note that *rebound* may also be encountered as a noun, usually referring to "recovery" (*meet someone on the rebound; a rebound in prices*) or a ball that bounces back (*the opposing team stole the rebound*).

**reciprocal/mutual/common** *See* COMMON/MUTUAL/RECIPROCAL.

**recourse/resort/resource** These three words are similar in appearance and are sometimes confused, although they mean slightly different things. *Recourse* and *resort* are interchangeable in the sense "source of help" (*have recourse to; resort to*). *Resort* and *resource* are interchangeable in the same sense of "source of help" in the phrases *as a last resort* and *as a last resource,* although the former is usually the preferred alternative.

**recover/re-cover** The presence or absence of a hyphen in what is otherwise a pair of identical words decides their meaning. *Re-cover* is a verb meaning "cover again" (*re-cover the body with the sheet*), while *recover* is a verb variously means "get well again" or "retrieve" (*she should recover in a couple of days; recover the dinghy from the sea*).

**redouble/reduplicate** These two verbs are not synonymous and should not be confused. *Redouble* means "intensify" or "strengthen" (*redouble your efforts*), whereas *reduplicate* means "double" or "copy" (*a call reduplicated in several states*).

**redound/rebound** *See* REBOUND/REDOUND.

**reduplicate/redouble** *See* REDOUBLE/REDUPLICATE.

**reek/wreak** The verbs *reek* and *wreak* share the same pronunciation but are unrelated in meaning. *Reek* means "stink" (*reek of perfume*), whereas *wreak* means "cause" or "bring about" (*wreak havoc*).

**reel/real** *See* REAL/REEL.

**reflective/reflexive** The adjectives *reflective* and *reflexive* are similar in appearance but have different meanings. *Reflective* means "reflecting light" or, in a figurative context, "thoughtful" (*a reflective surface, a reflective look*), whereas *reflexive* refers to a "pronoun referring to the subject of a sentence or clause" (*reflexive pronouns such as* oneself *and* ourselves).

**reflexive/reflective** *See* REFLECTIVE/REFLEXIVE.

**refute/deny** *See* DENY/REFUTE.

**regretfully/regrettably** *See* REGRETFUL/REGRETTABLE.

**regretful/regrettable** The adjectives *regretful* and *regrettable* have slightly different meanings and are not interchangeable. *Regretful* means "feeling regret" (*a regretful apology*), while *regrettable* means "causing regret" (*a regrettable state of affairs*). The same distinction applies to the adverbs *regretfully* and *regrettably*.

**regrettable/regretful** *See* REGRETFUL/REGRETTABLE.

**regrettably/regretfully** *See* REGRETFUL/REGRETTABLE.

**reign/rain/rein** *See* RAIN/REIGN/REIN.

**rein/rain/reign** *See* RAIN/REIGN/REIN.

**relation/relationship** These two nouns are closely related in meaning but are not always interchangeable. *Relation* and *relationship* can be substituted for each other in the sense of "connection" (*the relation between good and evil, the relationship between the two sides*), although *relationship* is generally reserved for human relationships. Note that the plural form *relations* usually refers to "dealings," typically of a business or sexual nature (*industrial relations, marital relations*).

**relationship/relation** *See* RELATION/RELATIONSHIP.

**reliable/reliant** The adjectives *reliable* and *reliant* have slightly different meanings and should not be confused. *Reliable* means "dependable" (*a reliable witness*), while *reliant* means "dependent" and usually appears in the phrase *be reliant on:*

*We are reliant on our car getting us there.*

**reliant/reliable** *See* RELIABLE/RELIANT.

**remediable/remedial** The adjectives *remedial* and *remediable* are subtly different in meaning and should not be considered interchangeable. *Remedial* means "intended as a remedy" (*a remedial course*), whereas *remediable* means "capable of being remedied" (*a remediable mistake*).

**remedial/remediable** *See* REMEDIABLE/REMEDIAL.

**remission/remittance** The nouns *remission* and *remittance* vary slightly in meaning. *Remission* has a number of meanings, including "discharge," "release," or "period in which something is remitted" (*remission of sin, remission from prison, a disease in remission*). *Remittance* is largely confined in meaning to "payment" (*remittance of the bill*).

**remittance/remission** *See* REMISSION/REMITTANCE.

**repairable/reparable** These two adjectives are slightly different in meaning. Both words mean "capable of being repaired" (*repairable damage, a reparable error of judgment*), but *repairable* is generally preferred when discussing actual physical damage, with *reparable* being used in more abstract contexts. Note that in *repairable* the stress is placed on the second syllable, while in *reparable* it falls on the first syllable.

**reparable/repairable** *See* REPAIRABLE/REPARABLE.

**repellent/repulsive** The adjectives *repellent* and *repulsive* both mean "arousing disgust" (*a repellent idea, a repulsive creature*) but are not interchangeable in all contexts. *Repulsive* is the stronger term but cannot be used as a substitute for *repellent* in its additional sense "resistant" (*water-repellent sunblock*).

**repetitious/repetitive** The adjectives *repetitious* and *repetitive* are subtly different in meaning. *Repetitious* means "tediously repeating" (*a repetitious chant*), while *repetitive* means "characterized by repetition" (*the repetitive rhythm of the machine*).

**repetitive/repetitious** *See* REPETITIOUS/REPETITIVE.

**replace/substitute** These two verbs mean virtually the same thing but are used slightly differently. *Replace* is usually followed by the preposition *with* or *by* and the thing replacing what was there before (*despair replaced by hope*), whereas *substitute* is used with *for* followed immediately by the thing being substituted by something else (*substitute an actor for the president*).

**repress/suppress/oppress** *See* OPPRESS/REPRESS/SUPPRESS.

**repulsive/repellent** *See* REPELLENT/REPULSIVE.

**requisite/prerequisite** *See* PREREQUISITE/REQUISITE.

**resign/re-sign** These two verbs differ only in the presence or absence of a hyphen but have different meanings. *Re-sign* means "sign again" (*re-sign the agreement*), whereas *resign* means "give up" (*resign your position*).

**resin/rosin** These two nouns refer to slightly different things and should not be confused. *Resin* denotes the "natural sticky secretions of trees and plants" or similar synthetic substances (*resin oozing from the splintered bark*), whereas *rosin* is a particular type of "pine tree resin" that is best known for its use as a varnish and as a means to improve the frictional qualities of the bow of a stringed instrument (*violin rosin*).

**resister/resistor** The nouns *resister* and *resistor* refer to different things and are not interchangeable. A *resister* is "someone who resists" (*a resister against the government*), whereas a *resistor* is "device used to reduce the flow of an electric current" (*a series of resistors*).

**resistor/resister** *See* RESISTER/RESISTOR.

**resort/recourse/resource** *See* RECOURSE/RESORT/RESOURCE.

**resource/recourse/resort** *See* RECOURSE/RESORT/RESOURCE.

**respectable/respectful/respective** These three adjectives are easily confused, although they do not all mean the same thing. *Respectable* means "deserving respect" (*a respectable occupation*), while *respectful* means "showing respect" (*make a respectful bow*). *Respective* is unrelated to the two other words, meaning "particular" or "separate" (*the two sisters and their respective homes*).

**respectful/respectable/respective** *See* RESPECTABLE/RESPECTFUL/RESPECTIVE.

**respective/respectable/respectful** *See* RESPECTABLE/RESPECTFUL/RESPECTIVE.

**restive/restless** The adjectives *restive* and *restless* are not synonymous and should not be confused. *Restive* means "resisting control" (*a restive population*), whereas *restless* means "fidgety" or "disturbed" (*a restless audience*).

**restless/restive** *See* RESTIVE/RESTLESS.

**restrain/constrain** *See* CONSTRAIN/RESTRAIN.

**retch/wretch** These two words share the same pronunciation but are unrelated in meaning. *Retch* is a verb meaning "make an effort to vomit" (*retch at the sight*), whereas *wretch* is a noun meaning "wretched person" (*a half-starved wretch*).

**reversal/reversion** These two nouns have different meanings and should not be confused. *Reversal* denotes the "act of reversing" (*reversal of opinion*), whereas *reversion* refers to an "act of reverting" (*a reversion to your former way of life*).

**reverse/converse/inverse/obverse** *See* CONVERSE/INVERSE/OBVERSE/REVERSE.

**reversion/reversal** *See* REVERSAL/REVERSION.

**review/revue** These two nouns are pronounced the same way but are unrelated in meaning. *Review* variously means "inspection," "reassessment," or "critical evaluation" (*a review of the army, a review of the proposal, theater review*), whereas *revue* denotes a "theatrical production comprising songs and comic sketches" (*a Broadway revue*).

**revue/review** *See* REVIEW/REVUE.

**right/write** These two words share the same pronunciation and are sometimes confused. *Right* has a number of meanings, including "the opposite of left," "good," "correct," and "appropriate" (*turn to the right; right and wrong; the right thing to do; the right costume*), whereas *write* is a verb meaning "inscribe" or "form letters or characters" (*write a poem*).

**ringed/rang/rung** *See* RANG/RINGED/RUNG.

**ring/wring** The verbs *ring* and *wring* are pronounced identically but mean different things. *Ring* variously means "make a ringing sound" and "surround" (*ring the bell; ring with flowers*), while *wring* means "squeeze" or "twist" (*wring the cloth dry; wring the last drops of juice from a lemon*). Note that the past tense and past participle of *wring* is *wrung,* which is pronounced in the same way as *rung,* the past tense of *ring.*

**rise/raise** *See* RAISE/RISE.

**rosin/resin** *See* RESIN/ROSIN.

**route/rout** *See* ROUT/ROUTE.

**rout/route** These two nouns share the same pronunciation but should not be confused since they are unrelated in meaning. *Rout* means "total defeat" or "panicked flight" (*the rout of an enemy; a parade that became a rout*), while *route* means "line of travel" or "course" (*the quickest route home*). Note that the same distinction applies to the same words when used as verbs.

**rung/rang/ringed** *See* RANG/RINGED/RUNG.

**rung/wrung** *See* RING/WRING.

**rural/rustic** The adjectives *rural* and *rustic* both refer to life in the country but are subtly different in meaning. *Rural* means "of or relating to the country" (*rural surroundings*), whereas *rustic* means "unsophisticated or quaint, as typical of life in the countryside" (*rustic charm, a rustic gate*).

**rustic/rural** *See* RURAL/RUSTIC.

**sack/sac** *See* SAC/SACK.

**sac/sack** These two words have a similar meaning but are applied in different contexts. *Sac* denotes a "baglike part" of an animal or plant (*egg sac*), while *sack* describes a "large bag" of virtually any other kind (*a sack of apples*).

**sail/sale** These two words share the same pronunciation but have entirely different meanings. *Sail* is a noun meaning "expanse of fabric used to propel a ship" (*a ship with white sails*) and is also used as a verb describing propulsion achieved through such means. *Sale* is a noun denoting the "selling of something" (*book sale, house for sale*).

**sale/sail** *See* SAIL/SALE.

**salubrious/salutary** The adjectives *salubrious* and *salutary* are fairly close in meaning and are sometimes confused. *Salubrious* means "healthful" or "health-promoting" (*move to more salubrious surroundings*), whereas *salutary* means "remedial" or "beneficial" in a more general sense (*a salutary lesson*).

**salutary/salubrious** *See* SALUBRIOUS/SALUTARY.

**sank/sunk/sunken** These three words are closely related in meaning and liable to be confused. *Sank* and *sunk* are past forms of the verb *sink:*

> *The ship sank in deep water.*
> *By the time rescue arrived the boat had sunk.*

*Sunken* is usually encountered as an adjective:

> *We spent several weeks searching for sunken galleons.*

**sate/satiate/satisfy** These three verbs overlap in meaning, although there are subtle differences. While *satisfy* means "meet a need" or "fulfill" (*satisfy a hunger; satisfy your curiosity*), *sate* and *satiate* are usually understood to mean "satisfy to excess" or "indulge to the full":

> *The king's greed for gold was finally sated.*
> *After more than a dozen courses her green face suggested her appetite was satiated.*

**satiate/sate/satisfy** *See* SATE/SATIATE/SATISFY.

**satisfy/sate/satiate** *See* SATE/SATIATE/SATISFY.

**sea/see** The words *sea* and *see* have the same pronunciation but mean different things. *Sea* is a noun meaning "ocean" or "oceanlike expanse" (*sail on the sea; a sea of faces*), whereas *see* is a verb meaning "perceive" or "catch sight of" (*see a light on the horizon; see what happens*).

**seasonable/seasonal** The adjectives *seasonable* and *seasonal* have slightly different meanings and are not interchangeable. *Seasonal* means "of or relating to a particular season" (*a seasonal crop*), while *seasonable* means "suited to the season," "timely," or "opportune" (*seasonable weather, a seasonable intervention*).

**seasonal/seasonable** *See* SEASONABLE/SEASONAL.

**seed/cede** *See* CEDE/SEED.

**see/sea** *See* SEA/SEE.

**sensibility/sensitivity** *See* SENSIBLE/SENSITIVE.

**sensible/sensitive** These two adjectives are unrelated in meaning and should not be confused. *Sensible* means "not foolish," "levelheaded," or "practical" (*a sensible move, a sensible outfit*), whereas *sensitive* means "emotional," "receptive," or "delicate" (*a sensitive nature, sensitive equipment, a sensitive topic*). The same distinction applies to the nouns *sensibility* and *sensitivity.*

**sensitive/sensible** *See* SENSIBLE/SENSITIVE.

**sensitivity/sensibility** *See* SENSIBLE/SENSITIVE.

**sensual/sensuous** The adjectives *sensual* and *sensuous* both relate to the noun *sense* but are not interchangeable. *Sensual* means "fleshly" or "voluptuous" and refers to gratification of physical appetites, usually those of a sexual character (*sensual pleasure, sensual movements*), whereas *sensuous* means "appealing to the senses" and usually concerns aesthetic or spiritual pleasure (*sensuous poetry*).

**sensuous/sensual** *See* SENSUAL/SENSUOUS.

**sentimentality/sentiment** *See* SENTIMENT/SENTIMENTALITY.

**sentiment/sentimentality** These two nouns are sometimes used incorrectly through confusion with each other. *Sentiment* means "emotion," "opinion," or "nostalgic or romantic feeling" and is fairly neutral in tone (*a noble sentiment, prevailing political sentiment*). *Sentimentality* refers to the "quality or state of being sentimental" and is often employed in a derogatory sense (*a novel flawed by sentimentality*).

**septic/skeptic** The words *septic* and *skeptic* are unrelated in meaning and should not be confused. *Septic* is an adjective meaning "putrefied," "causing putrefaction," or "used in the treatment of sewage" (*a septic wound, a septic tank*), whereas *skeptic* is a noun meaning "person disposed to skepticism" (*a skeptic in matters of religion*).

**serf/surf** These two nouns share the same pronunciation but have different meanings. A *serf* describes a medieval peasant (*serfs toiling on the land*), while *surf* relates to "waves breaking on a shore" (*a shark swimming in the surf*). Note that *surf* may also be encountered as a verb meaning "ride the surf" or "skim" and has enjoyed increased usage since being applied to browsing on the Internet.

**serial/cereal** *See* CEREAL/SERIAL.

**shear/sheer** These two words are sometimes confused, although they have different meanings. *Shear* means "cut off," "break," or "remove" (*shear a sheep; shear off at the joint; shear hundreds of jobs*), whereas *sheer* means "vertical" or "unqualified" (*a sheer drop, sheer brilliance*).

**sheer/shear** *See* SHEAR/SHEER.

**shoot/chute** *See* CHUTE/SHOOT.

**shrank/shrunk/shrunken** These three words are all derived from the verb *shrink* but are not always synonymous. *Shrank* is the past tense of the verb:

*She shrank from his touch.*

*Shrunk* is the past participle:

*He found his coat had shrunk.*

*Shrunken* is usually encountered as an adjective:

*Her uncle had a whiskery, shrunken face.*

**shrunken/shrank/shrunk** *See* SHRANK/SHRUNK/SHRUNKEN.

**shrunk/shrank/shrunken** *See* SHRANK/SHRUNK/SHRUNKEN.

**sight/site/cite** *See* CITE/SIGHT/SITE.

**simulate/stimulate** The verbs *simulate* and *stimulate* are similar in appearance but should not be confused. *Simulate* means "copy," "imitate," or "feign" (*simulate desert conditions in a laboratory*), whereas *stimulate* means "arouse" or "animate" (*stimulate interest in something*).

**site/cite/sight** *See* CITE/SIGHT/SITE.

**skeptical/cynical** *See* CYNICAL/SKEPTICAL.

**skeptic/septic** *See* SEPTIC/SKEPTIC.

**slander/libel** *See* LIBEL/SLANDER.

**soar/sore** These words share the same pronunciation but have different meanings. *Soar* is a verb meaning "glide" or "sail through the air" (*the bird soared above*), while *sore* is an adjective meaning "painful" or "tender" (*a sore hand, a sore head*).

**sociable/social** These two adjectives are related in meaning but are not interchangeable. *Sociable* means "friendly" or "convivial" (*a sociable character, a sociable gathering*), whereas *social* means "of or relating to society" or "promoting friendship" (*social issues, a social club*). The words overlap in the additional sense "gregarious," *sociable* being interpreted as "enjoying the company of others" (*a sociable young woman*) and *social* meaning "living in company" (*a social species*).

**social/sociable** *See* SOCIABLE/SOCIAL.

**sole/soul** These two words share the same pronunciation but are unrelated in meaning. *Sole* may be encountered as an adjective meaning "single" or "solitary" (*a sole figure, the sole entrant in the race*) or as a noun variously meaning "flatfish of the family Soleidae" or "undersurface of a foot or shoe" (*a fine catch of sole, a shoe with a worn sole*). *Soul* is a noun meaning "spirit" (*gain the earth and lose your soul; play with some soul*).

**soluble/solvable** These two adjectives overlap in meaning but are not always interchangeable. Both words can mean "capable of being solved" (*a soluble problem, a solvable riddle*), but *soluble* cannot be replaced by *solvable* in the sense "dissolvable in water" (*soluble paint*).

**solvable/soluble** *See* SOLUBLE/SOLVABLE.

**sometime/some time** Confusion sometimes arises over the choice between these two spellings. *Some time* means "period of time" (*some time after this event*), whereas *sometime* is an adverb meaning "at some point in time":

> *We must meet up sometime.*

Note that *sometime* may also be encountered occasionally as an adjective meaning "former" (*the sometime world champion*).

**sore/soar** *See* SOAR/SORE.

**soul/sole** *See* SOLE/SOUL.

**specially/especially** *See* ESPECIALLY/SPECIALLY.

**sped/speeded** These two words are both valid past forms of the verb *speed* but are applied slightly differently. *Sped* is the past tense and past participle of the verb and is interpreted as meaning "go quickly" (*sped downhill*), whereas *speeded* means "go too quickly" (*fined after he speeded on the highway*) or is employed as the past form of the phrasal verb *speed up:*

*The runner speeded up as she approached the finish line.*

**stair/stare** These two words are pronounced identically but have different meanings. *Stair* is a noun meaning "one of a series of steps" (*trip on the stair*), while *stare* is a noun and verb meaning "look hard" (*stare in amazement; give a distant stare*).

**stank/stunk** These two words are both legitimate past tenses of the verb *stink* but are not always interchangeable. *Stank* and *stunk* may be replaced by each other as past tenses of the verb:

*The water stank.*
*The house stunk of gas.*

*Stunk,* however, cannot be replaced by *stank* as the past participle of *stink:*

*The drains have stunk since the pipe was installed.*

**stare/stair** *See* STAIR/STARE.

**stationary/stationery** The words *stationary* and *stationery* are similar in appearance but unrelated in meaning. *Stationary* is an adjective meaning "motionless" or "standing" (*a stationary vehicle*), whereas *stationery* is a noun referring to "writing materials" (*a note written on monogrammed stationery*).

**stationery/stationary** *See* STATIONARY/STATIONERY.

**steal/steel** These two words share the same pronunciation but mean different things. *Steal* is a verb meaning "take illegally" or "move unobtrusively" (*steal money from your employer; steal through the undergrowth*), whereas *steel* is a noun meaning "iron alloy" (*a girder made of steel*).

**steel/steal** *See* STEAL/STEEL.

**steppe/step** *See* STEP/STEPPE.

**step/steppe** These two nouns mean different things. *Step* has a number of meanings, including "footstep," "tread," "stride," or "stage in an undertaking" (*hear a step outside, a flight of steps, a halting step, the next step in the project*). *Steppe* is a more specialized noun referring to a "vast treeless plain," typical of those of southeastern Europe and Asia (*the snow-covered steppe*).

**stimulant/stimulus** The nouns *stimulant* and *stimulus* are related in meaning but are not identical. A *stimulant* is "something that stimulates" and usually refers to alcohol, drugs, or other physical agents (*artificial stimulants*), whereas *stimulus* refers more widely to an "incentive" (*a stimulus for economic development of a region*).

**stimulate/simulate** *See* SIMULATE/STIMULATE.

**stimulus/stimulant** *See* STIMULANT/STIMULUS.

**straight/strait** These two words share the same pronunciation but mean different things. *Straight* means "free from curves, bends, or angles" and may be encountered as an adjective, adverb, or noun (*a straight line; give it to me straight; overtake on the straight*), whereas *strait* is usually encountered as a noun meaning "narrow seaway" (*a yacht entering the strait*). Note that *strait* may also be encountered in the phrase *dire straits,* meaning "difficult circumstances" (*find yourself in dire straits*). As part of certain longer words, however, *strait* or *straight* may be used (*straitjacket, straightjacket; straitlaced, straightlaced*). The phrase *straight and narrow,* meaning "the honest or moral path," derives from the Bible: "Because strait is the gate, and narrow is the way, which leadeth unto life" (Matthew 7:14, King James Version).

**strait/straight** *See* STRAIGHT/STRAIT.

**stratagem/strategy** These two nouns are close in meaning but not identical. A *stratagem* is a "scheme" or "ruse" (*win by a clever stratagem*), while *strategy* denotes "a plan or policy" or "planning to gain an advantage or achieve success" (*adopt a defensive strategy; the campaign has little sense of strategy*).

**strategy/stratagem** *See* STRATAGEM/STRATEGY.

**student/pupil** *See* PUPIL/STUDENT.

**stunk/stank** *See* STANK/STUNK.

**subconscious/unconscious** These two adjectives are slightly different in meaning. *Subconscious* means "based on instinct or automatic reflex" (*a subconscious terror of cats*), whereas *unconscious* means "totally unaware" or "unintentional" (*an unconscious patient, unconscious of having caused offense, an unconscious act*).

**subjective/objective** *See* OBJECTIVE/SUBJECTIVE.

**subsequent/consequent** *See* CONSEQUENT/SUBSEQUENT.

**substantial/substantive** The adjectives *substantial* and *substantive* can overlap in meaning but are not generally considered interchangeable.

*Substantial* means "considerable in size, quantity, or importance" (*a substantial weight, a substantial amount of money, a substantial factor*), whereas *substantive* means "real," "firm," or "essential" (*substantive proof of guilt*).

**substantive/substantial** *See* SUBSTANTIAL/SUBSTANTIVE.

**substitute/replace** *See* REPLACE/SUBSTITUTE.

**successfully/successively** These two adverbs are similar in appearance and are easily confused. *Successfully* means "with success" (*apply successfully*), whereas *successively* means "in succession" (*deal with each problem successively*).

**successively/successfully** *See* SUCCESSFULLY/SUCCESSIVELY.

**suite/suit** *See* SUIT/SUITE.

**suite/sweet** These two words are pronounced in the same way but are unrelated in meaning. *Suite* is a noun meaning "set of furniture or rooms," or a "sequence of musical pieces" (*a three-piece suite, a suite of rooms, a piano suite*), whereas *sweet* is an adjective meaning "pleasing," "kind," "cute," or "sugary" (*a sweet smile, a sweet demeanor, a sweet gesture, a sweet taste*) or a noun meaning "dessert" (*a restaurant famous for its sweets*).

**suit/suite** The nouns suit and suite both refer to "sets" of things but are not synonymous. A *suit* variously denotes a "set of clothes," a "set of playing cards," or a "court action" (*a smart Italian suit, the suit of diamonds, a lawsuit*), whereas *suite* may refer to a "set of furniture or rooms," or a "sequence of musical pieces" (*a three-piece suite, a suite of rooms, a piano suite*). Note the contrasting pronunciations of the two words, *suit* rhyming with *toot* and *suite* being pronounced *sweet.*

**sunken/sank/sunk** *See* SANK/SUNK/SUNKEN.

**sunk/sank/sunken** *See* SANK/SUNK/SUNKEN.

**supine/prone/prostrate** *See* PRONE/PROSTRATE/SUPINE.

**supplement/complement** *See* COMPLEMENT/SUPPLEMENT.

**suppress/oppress/repress** *See* OPPRESS/REPRESS/SUPPRESS.

**surf/serf** *See* SERF/SURF.

**suspect/suspicious** The words *suspect* and *suspicious* are synonymous in some contexts but are not always interchangeable. The adjectives *suspect* and *suspicious* both mean "causing suspicion" (*a suspect package, a suspicious turn of events.*) *Suspect,* however, may also be employed as a noun or verb (*arrest a suspect; suspect his motive*). Both words have additional meanings in which they cannot be substituted for each other. *Suspicious,* for instance, can mean "feeling or showing suspicion" (*suspicious of your opponent's intentions*), while *suspect* can mean "doubtful" or "possibly unreliable" (*a suspect safety system*).

**suspense/suspension** The nouns *suspense* and *suspension* have different meanings and should not be confused. *Suspense* denotes a "state of anxiety or nervous anticipation" (*unbearable suspense*), whereas *suspension* refers to the "suspending of something" (*suspension from the ceiling*), although it is more often encountered in a figurative sense meaning "interruption," "postponement," or "temporary expulsion" (*the suspension of negotiations, suspension of the match, suspension from the team*).

**suspension/suspense** *See* SUSPENSE/SUSPENSION.

**suspicious/suspect** *See* SUSPECT/SUSPICIOUS.

**sweet/suite** *See* SUITE/SWEET.

**symbol/cymbal** *See* CYMBAL/SYMBOL.

**systematic/systemic** These two adjectives overlap in meaning but are not usually interchangeable. *Systematic* means "methodical" or "orderly" (*a systematic check of equipment*), while *systemic* means "of or relating to a system" and is often applied to the circulation of blood in the body (*a systemic disease*).

**systemic/systematic** *See* SYSTEMATIC/SYSTEMIC.

**tail/tale** Care should be taken to distinguish between these two nouns, which share the same pronunciation but are unrelated in meaning. *Tail* means "extension of the spine" or "rear part" (*a dog's tail, the tail of an aircraft*), whereas *tale* means "story" (*a tale told by someone who is mad*).

**tale/tail** *See* TAIL/TALE.

**tasteful/tasty** These two adjectives both refer to *taste* but have slightly different meanings. *Tasteful* means "having good taste" (*tasteful decoration, a tasteful outfit*), whereas tasty usually refers to "good-tasting food" (*a tasty dish*).

**tasty/tasteful** *See* TASTEFUL/TASTY.

**taught/taut** These two words share the same pronunciation but have different meanings. *Taught* is the past tense and past participle of the verb *teach* (*taught by the master*), whereas *taut* is an adjective meaning "tightened" or "under tension" (*a taut wire*). Note that *taut* may also be encountered in a figurative sense, meaning "anxious" or "high-strung" (*taut nerves; whisper in a taut voice*).

**taut/taught** *See* TAUGHT/TAUT.

**teach/learn** *See* LEARN/TEACH.

**team/teem** These two words are pronounced identically and are sometimes confused. *Team* is a noun meaning "group of colleagues" (*a team of players, a team of fellow workers*) and may also be encountered as a verb (*team up on a project*). *Teem* is a verb meaning "pour" or "abound" (*teeming rain; the area is teeming with ants*).

**technical/technological** These two adjectives are closely related in meaning but are not interchangeable. *Technical* means "scientific" or "mechanical" (*technical qualifications, a technical failure*), whereas *technological* means "of or relating to technology" or "relating to the practical use of science" (*a technological revolution*). Note that *technical* may also be used in the sense "strictly speaking" (*a technical foul*).

**technological/technical** *See* TECHNICAL/TECHNOLOGICAL.

**teem/team** *See* TEAM/TEEM.

**temerity/timidity** These two nouns are similar in appearance and are sometimes confused, although their meanings are virtually opposite. *Temerity* means "audacity" or "rashness" (*have the temerity to disagree*), whereas *timidity* means "lack of courage" or "fearfulness" (*the timidity of a child*).

**temporal/temporary** The adjectives *temporal* and *temporary* have different meanings and should not be confused. *Temporal* means "of or relating to earthly matters" or "of or relating to time" (*temporal concerns*), whereas *temporary* means "for a limited time" or "not permanent" (*a temporary arrangement, temporary madness*).

**temporary/temporal** *See* TEMPORAL/TEMPORARY.

**temporize/extemporize** *See* EXTEMPORIZE/TEMPORIZE.

**their/there/they're** These three words are easily confused because they share the same pronunciation. *Their* is a possessive pronoun meaning "of them or belonging to them" (*their clothes, their share of the money*), while *there* means "in or at that place" (*in there*) and may be employed as an adverb, pronoun, adjective, or noun. *They're* is an abbreviated form of *they are:*

*They're coming tomorrow.*

**there/their/they're** *See* THEIR/THERE/THEY'RE.

**they're/their/there** *See* THEIR/THERE/THEY'RE.

**though/although** *See* ALTHOUGH/THOUGH.

**threw/through** These two words are pronounced the same but are unrelated in meaning. *Threw* is the past participle of the verb *throw* (*threw the stick*), whereas *through* means "among," "by way of," or "past" (*go through the hotel*).

**through/threw** *See* THREW/THROUGH.

**tide/tied** The words *tide* and *tied* are sometimes confused. *Tide* is a noun meaning "ebb and flow" and is variously employed with reference to the sea and in figurative contexts (*the incoming tide, a tide in the affairs of men*). *Tied* is the past tense and past participle of the verb *tie* (*tied the ribbon in a bow; tied to your job*).

**tied/tide** *See* TIDE/TIED.

**timidity/temerity** *See* TEMERITY/TIMIDITY.

**titillate/titivate** These two verbs are similar in appearance but are unrelated in meaning. *Titillate* means "stimulate" or "tease sexually" (*titillate with a glimpse of stocking*), whereas *titivate* means "smarten up" (*titivate yourself; titivate a room*). Note that *titillate* usually conveys a derogatory suggestion of superficiality or indecency (*a titillating story*).

**titivate/titillate** *See* TITILLATE/TITIVATE.

**tolerance/toleration** The words *tolerance* and *toleration* are close in meaning, but there is a subtle difference between them. *Tolerance* means "capacity to tolerate" (*an attitude of tolerance*), while *toleration* means "act of tolerating":

> *She decided to act with toleration toward her children's bad behavior.*

Note that *tolerance* also has a range of technical meanings referring to the behavior of materials or bodies (*tolerance of pressure*).

**toleration/tolerance** *See* TOLERANCE/TOLERATION.

**too/to/two** *See* TO/TOO/TWO.

**tortuous/torturous** These two adjectives both have their roots in *torture* but mean different things. *Tortuous* means "winding," "circuitous," or "involved" (*a tortuous route, a tortuous knot*) but may also be encountered with the figurative sense of "crooked" or "tricky" (*a tortuous plan*). *Torturous* means "applying torture" or "very painful or unpleasant" (*torturous interrogation, torturous progress*).

**torturous/tortuous** *See* TORTUOUS/TORTUROUS.

**to/too/two** These three words are easily confused. *To* is generally encountered as a preposition or as part of the infinitive form of a verb (*to the city; to please her*); *too* is an adverb meaning "as well" or "excessively" (*come too; too fast*); and *two* refers to the number between one and three (*two bananas*).

**transient/transitory** These two adjectives both mean "short-lived," but there are subtle differences between them. *Transient* suggests an element of "passing by quickly" (*transient visitors*), whereas *transitory* conveys a sense of regret at the temporary nature of something (*the transitory cycle of life*).

**transitory/transient** *See* TRANSIENT/TRANSITORY.

**transverse/traverse** These two words are related in meaning but are not synonymous. *Transverse* is an adjective meaning "set crosswise" or "at right angles" (*a transverse section*), whereas *traverse* is a verb used in formal contexts to mean "go across" (*traverse a mountain gorge*). Note that *traverse* is occasionally encountered as a noun meaning "way across."

**traverse/transverse** *See* TRANSVERSE/TRAVERSE.

**treble/triple** The words *treble* and *triple* both mean "threefold" and are interchangeable in many contexts, although there are subtle differences between them. *Treble* tends to be preferred in the sense "three times as great" (*treble the amount*), while *triple* is preferred in the sense "comprising three parts" (*a triple explosion*). Only *treble* is used to refer to a high-pitched sound or voice (*treble and bass sound controls*).

**triple/treble** *See* TREBLE/TRIPLE.

**triumphal/triumphant** These two adjectives have somewhat different meanings. *Triumphal* means "of or relating to victory" (*a triumphal parade*), whereas *triumphant* means "victorious" (*a triumphant cheer*).

**triumphant/triumphal** *See* TRIUMPHAL/TRIUMPHANT.

**troop/troupe** These two nouns both describe "groups of people" but are used in different contexts. *Troop* is usually applied to a "group of soldiers," although it is also sometimes used more generally (*a troop of marines, a troop of Girl Scouts*), whereas *troupe* is usually reserved for a "group of performers" of some kind (*a troupe of actors, a troupe of dancers*).

**troupe/troop** *See* TROOP/TROUPE.

**turbid/turbulent/turgid** These three adjectives are sometimes confused, although they have different meanings. *Turbid* means "thick," "opaque," or "muddy" (*turbid waters*); *turbulent* means "agitated" or "restless" (*a turbulent crowd*); and *turgid* means "swollen" but is more often encountered in its figurative sense of "bombastic" (*a turgid speech*).

**turbulent/turbid/turgid** *See* TURBID/TURBULENT/TURGID.

**turgid/turbid/turbulent** *See* TURBID/TURBULENT/TURGID.

**two/to/too** *See* TO/TOO/TWO.

**unaware/unawares** These two words are not synonymous despite their superficial similarity. *Unaware* is an adjective meaning "not aware" (*unaware of this development*), whereas *unawares* is an adverb meaning "unexpectedly" or "without warning" (*caught unawares*).

**unconscious/subconscious** *See* SUBCONSCIOUS/UNCONSCIOUS.

**underlay/underlie** These two verbs are slightly different in meaning and are easily confused. *Underlay* means "lay something beneath something else" (*underlay with plastic*) and is equally familiar as a noun referring to a layer of material placed under a carpet, whereas *underlie* means "form the basis of" and is usually employed figuratively (*no mistaking the tension underlying the statement*). Note that further confusion can arise from the fact that *underlay* is also the past tense and past participle of *underlie*.

**underlie/underlay** *See* UNDERLAY/UNDERLIE.

**undertone/overtone** *See* OVERTONE/UNDERTONE.

**undiscriminating/indiscriminate** *See* INDISCRIMINATE/UNDISCRIMINATING.

**uneatable/inedible** *See* EATABLE/EDIBLE.

**unexceptionable/unexceptional** These two adjectives have different meanings but are sometimes confused because of their superficial similarity. *Unexceptionable* means "inoffensive" or "unobjectionable" (*make a few unexceptionable remarks*), whereas *unexceptional* means "unremarkable" or "usual" (*an unexceptional novel, unexceptional conditions*).

**unexceptional/unexceptionable** *See* UNEXCEPTIONABLE/UNEXCEPTIONAL.

**uninterested/disinterested** *See* DISINTERESTED/UNINTERESTED.

**unorganized/disorganized** *See* DISORGANIZED/UNORGANIZED.

**unreadable/illegible** *See* LEGIBLE/READABLE.

**unsociable/asocial/antisocial/nonsocial/unsocial** *See* ANTISOCIAL/ASOCIAL/NONSOCIAL/UNSOCIABLE/UNSOCIAL.

**unsocial/asocial/antisocial/nonsocial/unsociable** *See* ANTISOCIAL/ASOCIAL/NONSOCIAL/UNSOCIABLE/UNSOCIAL.

**urbane/urban** *See* URBAN/URBANE.

**urban/urbane** These two adjectives are similar in appearance but different in meaning. *Urban* means "of or relating to a town or city" (*an urban development, urban society*), whereas *urbane* means "sophisticated" or "socially refined" (*an urbane gentleman*).

**usage/use** Confusion sometimes arises over the correct employment of these two nouns, which are close in meaning. *Usage* refers to the "way in which something is used" (*correct usage of the apparatus*), whereas *use* denotes the "act of using" (*the use of language in communication*).

**use/usage** *See* USAGE/USE.

**vacuous/vacant** The adjectives *vacant* and *vacuous* differ in meaning and are not usually interchangeable. *Vacant* means "empty," "not occupied," or "expressionless" (*a vacant seat, a vacant job, a vacant look*), whereas *vacuous* means "empty-headed" or "inane" and is more derogatory in tone (*a vacuous mind, a vacuous comment*).

**vacant/vacuous** *See* VACUOUS/VACANT.

**vain/vane/vein** These three words share the same pronunciation but are unrelated in meaning and should not be confused. *Vain* is an adjective meaning "conceited" or "futile" (*a vain movie star, a vain effort*), whereas *vane* is a noun meaning "blade operated by wind or water" (*a weather vane*), and *vein* is a noun denoting a "blood vessel" or "thin layer or course" of something (*feel the blood flowing through your veins; a vein of gold; a vein of humor*).

**vale/veil** These two nouns share the same pronunciation but are unrelated in meaning. *Vale* means "valley" or "dale" (*a pleasant vale*), whereas *veil* denotes a "thin layer of material masking a face" or anything that serves to conceal something (*a bridal veil, a veil of secrecy*).

**vane/vain/vein** *See* VAIN/VANE/VEIN.

**veil/vale** *See* VALE/VEIL.

**vein/vane/vain** *See* VAIN/VANE/VEIN.

**venal/venial** The adjectives *venal* and *venial* are similar in appearance and can be confused. *Venal* means "purchasable" or "corruptible" (*a venal politician*), whereas *venial* means "forgivable" or "excusable" (*venial sin*).

**venial/venal** *See* VENAL/VENIAL.

**vicious/viscous** The adjectives *vicious* and *viscous* are similar in appearance and may be confused. *Vicious* means "cruel," "savage," or "malicious" (*a vicious bandit, a vicious dog, a vicious rumor*), whereas *viscous* means "fluid or semifluid" (*a viscous liquid*).

**viscous/vicious** *See* VICIOUS/VISCOUS.

**visitation/visit** *See* VISIT/VISITATION.

**visit/visitation** These two nouns have slightly different meanings and are not always interchangeable. *Visit* means "call" or "short stay" (*a visit to the city, a visit lasting several days*) and is also encountered as a verb (*visit the country; visit our Web site*), whereas *visitation* means "official visit" and is often used ironically (*a visitation from the ambassador, a visitation from your mother-in-law*).

**waist/waste** These two nouns share the same pronunciation but are unrelated in meaning. *Waist* refers to that "portion of the body between the chest and the hips" (*a slim waist*), whereas *waste* means "rubbish," "trash," or "something squandered" (*a heap of waste, a waste of material*). Note that *waste* also functions as a verb (*waste time*).

**wait/weight** Confusion can sometimes arise between these two nouns because they have the same pronunciation. *Wait* means "period of waiting" (*a short wait*), whereas *weight* means "heaviness" (*increase in weight, a weight of material*). Note that both words also function as verbs (*wait outside; weight with rocks*).

**waiver/waver** These two words sound the same but are unrelated in meaning. *Waiver* is a noun denoting the "relinquishment of a right or option" (*a formal waiver of all rights in the matter*), whereas *waver* is a verb meaning "fluctuate" or "hesitate" (*waver in your convictions*).

**waive/wave** The verbs *waive* and *wave* have different meanings and should not be confused. *Waive* means "relinquish" or "set aside" (*waive the option; waive the fee*), whereas *wave* means "undulate" or "move to and fro" (*wave in the breeze; wave your hand*).

**wander/wonder** Confusion can sometimes arise over the spelling of these two words, which look similar but are unrelated in meaning.

*Wander* means "ramble" or "meander" (*wander about the countryside; wander dreamily*), whereas *wonder* means "think" or "feel curiosity" (*wonder about the future*). Both words also function as nouns (*have a wander around the grounds, a sense of wonder*). Note that the pronunciation of the two words is not the same: *wander* rhymes with *ponder,* and *wonder* rhymes with *plunder.*

**ware/wear/where** These three words are unrelated in meaning. *Ware* is a noun meaning "goods" or "products" (*peddle your wares*). *Wear* is a verb meaning "bear" or "have on the person" (*wear a coat*). *Where* is an adverb or conjunction meaning "at what place" or "in what situation":

*This point is where we must part company.*

**warn/worn** These two words are identical in pronunciation and are easily confused. *Warn* is a verb meaning "caution" (*warn against going too far*), whereas *worn* is the past participle of the verb *wear* (*she has worn the dress many time; worn at the knee*).

**wastage/waste** These two nouns are related in meaning but are not exactly synonymous. *Wastage* refers to "loss through leakage, decay, or erosion" (*wastage of water in times of drought*), while *waste* can denote any "act of squandering" (*a waste of money, a waste of his talent*).

**waste/waist** *See* WAIST/WASTE.

**waste/wastage** *See* WASTAGE/WASTE.

**waver/waiver** *See* WAIVER/WAVER.

**wave/waive** *See* WAIVE/WAVE.

**weal/wheal/wheel** These three nouns are sometimes confused. *Weal* and *wheal* both refer to a "raised mark on the skin" and are usually applied to the marks left by blows from whips and similar weapons:

*Her back was covered with red wheals.*

A *wheel* is a "circular frame used in the operation of a wide variety of machines" (*the wheels of a car*).

**wear/ware/where** *See* WARE/WEAR/WHERE.

**weather/whether** The words *weather* and *whether* are unrelated in meaning. *Weather* is a noun referring to "climatic conditions" (*uncomfortably hot weather*), while *whether* is a conjunction meaning "if," commonly used to introduce two alternatives:

*She wondered whether she should say something.*

**weight/wait** *See* WAIT/WEIGHT.

**wet/whet** These two words mean different things. *Wet* is an adjective meaning "soaking," "moist," or "rainy" (*wet clothes, a wet towel, wet weather*), whereas *whet* is a verb meaning "sharpen" or "stimulate" (*a whetted knife; whet your appetite*).

**wheal/weal/wheel** *See* WEAL/WHEAL/WHEEL.

**wheel/weal/wheal** *See* WEAL/WHEAL/WHEEL

**where/ware/wear** *See* WARE/WEAR/WHERE.

**whether/weather** *See* WEATHER/WHETHER.

**whet/wet** *See* WET/WHET.

**wholly/holy/holey** *See* HOLEY/HOLY/WHOLLY.

**whom/who** *See* WHO/WHOM.

**whose/who's** *See* WHO'S/WHOSE.

**who's/whose** Owing to their identical pronunciation, *who's* and *whose* can be the source of confusion. *Whose* means "of whom" or "of which" (*the men whose families were lost in the storm, the newspapers whose ideals are being questioned*). *Who's* is an abbreviated form of *who is* or *who has:*

*Who's taking the children swimming next week?*

**who/whom** Confusion often arises over the correct use of the pronouns *who* and *whom.* The basic rule is that *who* is employed when it is the subject of a verb (*the man who called yesterday, the woman who wrote that book*), while *whom* is the correct word to use where it is the object of a verb or preposition (*the boy whom you met last week, the person to whom the letter was addressed*). Note that a particular source of confusion is the choice between the two words in questions, in which cases *whom* is the more strictly correct word, although in practice it is commonly replaced by *who,* especially in informal and almost always in spoken contexts.

*Whom did you see this morning?*
*Who left the door open?*

**wonder/wander** *See* WANDER/WONDER.

**wood/would** The words *wood* and *would* share the same pronunciation but are unrelated in meaning. *Wood* is a noun meaning "timber" or "large group of trees" (*a table made of wood; lost in the wood*), while *would* is the past tense of the verb *will* (*he would not go*).

**worn/warn** *See* WARN/WORN.

**would/wood** *See* WOOD/WOULD.

**wrack/rack** *See* RACK/WRACK.

**wrapped/rapt** *See* RAPT/WRAPPED.

**wreak/reek** *See* REEK/WREAK.

**wreak/reek** *See* REEK/WREAK.

**wreathe/wreath** *See* WREATH/WREATHE.

**wreath/wreathe** The words *wreath* and *wreathe* are closely related in meaning but are not synonymous. *Wreath* is a noun meaning "garland of flowers or foliage" (*a funeral wreath*), while *wreathe* is a verb meaning "interweave" or "encircle":

*Smoke wreathed around the chimneys.*

Note that the two words are pronounced differently, *wreath* being pronounced to rhyme with *teeth* and *wreathe* to rhyme with *seethe.*

**wretch/retch** *See* RETCH/WRETCH.

**wring/ring** *See* RING/WRING.

**write/right** *See* RIGHT/WRITE.

**wrung/rung** *See* RING/WRING.

**you're/your** *See* YOUR/YOU'RE.

**your/you're** Confusion sometimes arises over the use of these two words. *Your* means "belonging to you" (*your keys*), while *you're* is a contracted form of *you are:*

*You're in the wrong place.*

# 7

# Punctuation

## INTRODUCTION

The purpose of punctuation is to make clear the meaning of sentences and texts. This is achieved by controlling the shape of sentences through the use of periods, commas, semicolons, and so on, thereby breaking up texts into manageable pieces. Punctuation enables important phrases to be emphasized and connections to be made between clauses and sentences so that they combine to form an intelligible narrative.

Punctuation in writing plays the role that is fulfilled in spoken English by pauses and changes in intonation. As such punctuation is as essential as grammar and vocabulary. A proper understanding of punctuation is important because inadequate or incorrect punctuation can result in ambiguity and misunderstanding.

The following example illustrates how simple changes in punctuation can completely change the way in which the same set of words may be interpreted:

> *The foreign ambassador who arrived today said the president is to be trusted.*

Without any punctuation beyond the initial capital letter and the final period, this sentence appears to suggest that the foreign ambassador was one of several ambassadors arriving on different days and that it is he or she who said the president was to be trusted. The same sentence has a different meaning, however, when two commas are inserted:

> *The foreign ambassador, who arrived today, said the president is to be trusted.*

Here it is clear only one foreign ambassador, the one who just arrived, is under discussion and, as before, that he or she is the person who believed the president was to be trusted. Yet another interpretation is possible when quotation marks are inserted:

> *"The foreign ambassador, who arrived today," said the president, "is to be trusted."*

Here, it is the president who speaks and declares that the foreign ambassador who just arrived is to be trusted. Note that with the exception of the punctuation marks, all three examples are identically worded.

Punctuation is governed by various rules and conventions, but there is considerable scope for personal preference and the dictates of house style. It should be noted, however, that it is possible to use too much punctuation. Overloading a passage with punctuation can render it very difficult to read. The modern style is to keep punctuation to a minimum, especially in informal and nontechnical writing. Caution still needs to be exercised, however, since using too few punctuation marks may lead to ambiguity and confusion of meaning.

## PUNCTUATION MARKS

| | |
|---|---|
| ' | apostrophe |
| ( ) | parentheses |
| [ ] | brackets |
| : | colon |
| , | comma |
| — | dash |
| ... | ellipsis |
| ! | exclamation point |
| - | hyphen |
| . | period |
| ? | question mark |
| " " or ' ' | quotation marks |
| ; | semicolon |
| / | slash |

(*See also* SYMBOLS, page 216.)

## APOSTROPHE

An apostrophe (') denotes possession of something or a possessive relationship with another person (*mother's room, my brother's house, the book's cover, my friend's sister*). Note that the apostrophe should never be used to form the plurals of ordinary nouns.

Mistakes in the use of apostrophes are common: The apostrophe is often omitted where it should be used (*one year's guarantee, two days' stay*) or inserted where it should not be (*all day breakfasts; my pen has lost its top*). Sometimes the apostrophe is purposely omitted to "clean up" the look of a word, a practice that is especially common in brand or trade names.

Confusion sometimes arises over the possessive use of the apostrophe, specifically whether an apostrophe should be placed before or after the final *s* when attached to a noun. The general rule is that possessive nouns are formed by adding *'s* to a singular noun (*the girl's dog, the people's choice*). In the case of plural nouns that end in *s* the possessive noun is formed by adding a final apostrophe (*a bees' nest; the soldiers' barracks; five years' experience*).

In the case of names or singular nouns ending in *s, x,* or *z,* the apostrophe may or may not be followed by *s.* The *s* following the apostrophe is often omitted in the case of names that end in a *z* sound, especially when they have more than one syllable (*James' home, Socrates' theories*). In the case of names or other words of just one syllable, the convention is to use *'s* (*Baz's cat, the box's lid, a bass's voice*). In other cases where words end in a *z* sound, the presence or absence of a final *s* is variously governed by common practice, convention, or pronunciation (*an ox's head, a princess's dress*).

Apostrophes are never used with possessive personal pronouns (*her friends, his shoes, its appearance*) but are used in the case of indefinite pronouns (*go in anyone's car, someone's idea*). Note the exceptional case of *else* in such phrases as *anyone else* or *someone else: Else* is neither a noun nor a pronoun but nonetheless takes *'s* (*anyone else's parents, someone else's book*).

The possessive forms *its* and *whose* are a particular source of confusion, because of the risk of confusion with *it's* and *who's* (the abbreviated forms of *it is* or *it has* and *who is* or *who has*). Neither the possessive *its* nor *whose* should ever take an apostrophe:

*The idea has lost its appeal.*
*The children whose parents have arrived may leave.*
*Whose house is this?*

Apostrophes are not generally employed to make singular nouns plural, but there are a very few circumstances in which they may fulfill this function, specifically where the noun refers to individual letters and numbers:

*She cannot pronounce her r's.*
*This pack of cards has no 5's.*

In everyday usage apostrophes are often used to make abbreviations plural (*GI's, CD's*), but in reality no apostrophe is required (*GIs, CDs*).

Note that the placing of the apostrophe is particularly important in contexts where the possessive noun may be singular or plural: *The boy's toys*, which refers to the toys of just one boy, is not the same as *the boys' toys*, which refers to the toys of more than one boy, even though *boy's* and *boys'* are pronounced identically. It should also be noted that when a plural noun lacks the usual *-s* ending, the possessive is formed the same as for a singular noun (*children's clothing, men's health, women's rights*).

Apostrophes can also be used to indicate where a letter has been omitted in a contraction. Examples of words that are commonly contracted in such a manner include the word *not* when used next to a verb (*can't, don't, haven't, isn't, shan't, won't, wouldn't*), personal pronouns when run together with a verb (*I'm, he'll, she'll, it'll, it's, they're, they've, we're, you're, you've*), and the conjunction *and* (*rock 'n' roll*). In informal contexts, some other words are also written with apostrophes in the place of individual letters in order to replicate their pronunciation in everyday speech (*'fraid so; s'pose so*).

In former times the word *of* was often reduced to *o'*, but this and other abbreviated forms is now largely of historical interest only (*e'er, ne'er, o'er, 'tis, 'twere*). Note, however, that it remains current in the phrase *o'clock* (*three o'clock*).

# CAPITAL LETTERS

Initial capital letters are always used to mark the start of new sentences, but they have many other uses as well. They are used to draw attention to particular words, to signal the start of direct quotations, or sometimes to begin the first word of a complete sentence following a colon or the first word of a new line of poetry. Initial capital letters are also used to mark names, titles of artistic works, and proper nouns and adjectives derived from them. Note, though, that in some cases the adjective has become divorced from its parent noun to the extent that it may not necessarily take a capital letter (*french windows*).

Capital letters are not generally used for verbs derived from nouns (*anglicize*). Some words take capitals when part of a proper name but not when used alone (*Dr. Jones/give it the doctor; Aunt Sally/her aunt*). In the case of institutions, capitals are usually employed where an institution is identified specifically but not when spoken of in more general terms (*President Jimmy Carter, former presidents; the Catholic Church/go to church*). It will be gathered from such examples that there is some scope for personal choice and the influence of house style.

The pronoun *I* is always rendered as a capital letter, although capitals are not usually used with other personal pronouns (*he, she, they,* etc.). Rare exceptions include references to God (*He, Him, His*) or to royalty and other senior ranks (*Her Majesty, Her Royal Highness, His Excellency*).

Initial capital letters are also used for days of the week (*Sunday, Friday*), months (*January, December*), holidays (*Labor Day, Thanksgiving*) and religious feasts (*Easter, Hanukkah*). Note, however, that capitals are not used for the names of the seasons (*spring, winter*). Initial capitals are conventionally used for the names of historical, cultural, and geological periods (*War of Independence, Renaissance, Bronze Age*) and also for such miscellaneous categories as personal titles preceding a name (*District Attorney Jennifer Jones, Professor Hawkins*).

The use of capitals for emphasis is generally disapproved of in formal writing and is rarely found except in very informal writing and children's stories. One alternative is to use italics instead.

The rules regarding capitals have relaxed increasingly since the introduction of the e-mail and of text messaging by cell phone. The difference between upper and lower case is often ignored, for instance, in e-mail or Web site addresses or when searching the Internet. This convention has the advantage of making searches quicker to execute. The lower case is used almost exclusively in electronic addresses, even for names. The rules are also often deliberately broken when devising brand names and company names in order to convey a sense of modernity or informality.

# COLON

The colon (:) introduces a word or clause that explains, interprets, or adds to what precedes it:

> *The battle could have gone either way: The outcome depended on the weather.*

It can also be used to introduce lists:

*You will need four ingredients for this recipe: cream, fruit, raisins, and sugar.*
*They have three reservations about the house: It is too expensive, it lacks character, and it is in the wrong location.*

In contrast to semicolons, it is not essential that the subsequent phrase be a complete sentence. It is important, though, that the clause before the colon is capable of standing independently of whatever is tacked on after the colon.

An initial capital should be used after a colon when the first word that follows is a proper noun or is part of a quotation in which it is capitalized and when the colon follows a formal greeting or instruction:

*In this now-famous speech Franklin Delano Roosevelt stated: "The only thing we have to fear is fear itself."*
*To whom it may concern: This building will be closed from dusk.*
*Warning: Safety helmets must be worn.*

An initial capital letter may also be used where the material following the colon constitutes a complete sentence or sentences:

*This is the crucial question: Are we ready to strike out independently?*

The colon can also be used to introduce direct speech or quotations (a device commonly employed in newspaper articles):

*In the words of the chairman: "There will be a significant announcement some time next week."*

Sometimes the passages prefaced by an introductory phrase and a colon may be substantial in length:

*Abraham Lincoln's address at Gettysburg: "In a larger sense we cannot dedicate, we cannot consecrate, we cannot hallow this ground. The brave men, living and dead, who struggled here, have consecrated it far above our power to add or detract. The world will little note, nor long remember, what we say here, but it can never forget what they did here. It is for us, the living, rather to be dedicated here to the unfinished work which they who fought here have thus far so nobly advanced. It is rather for us to be here dedicated to the great task remaining before us . . . that we here highly resolve that the dead shall not have died in vain, that this nation, under God, shall have a new birth of freedom; and that government of the people, by the people, and for the people, shall not perish from the earth."*

A colon is also convenient where it is necessary to identify the speaker of each line of dialogue, as in play scripts:

*Polonius: I hear him coming; let's withdraw, my lord.*
*Hamlet: To be, or not to be: that is the question. . . .*

Colons are commonly used before subtitles of written works of various kinds (*Night and Day: A Study of New York*). They are also widely used in letters (*Dear Mrs. Bloomingdale:*) and in business correspondence (*Ref.: 287361*), as well as in biblical references (*Genesis 1:1*), in references to the time of day (*2:10*), and to indicate a relationship between numbers, such as in ratios (*2:1*).

When a colon immediately follows material placed in quotation marks, it should be noted that the colon is placed outside the closing quotation mark:

*She called him her "reason to live": Without him, she would have died years ago.*

# COMMA

The comma (,) is used more frequently than most other punctuation marks. Useful though it undoubtedly is, it is often the cause of confusion since inappropriate use of a comma can change the whole meaning of a sentence and totally mislead the reader. The rules relating to commas have been relaxed in recent years, and their use is now often largely governed by personal preference. It is important to be consistent, however, whatever approach is adopted by the writer.

The comma is used both to separate and to link words and clauses within a sentence. Nowadays, it is often used as an alternative to semicolons or colons, and it is preferred because it does not interrupt the flow of a sentence in quite so abrupt a manner. Commas may be used more than once in the same sentence, but if too many appear in a single sentence, it may be better to reword the sentence.

The comma is often used to separate items in a list of three or more in order to avoid multiple repetitions of *and* or *or:*

*The bag contains documents, photographs, and maps.*
*We shall enjoy the game, whether we win, lose, or draw.*

Called a **serial comma** in this particular case, it is usually placed before the final *and* or *or.* Use of the serial comma is optional, however, as its presence or absence is often a matter of personal taste or house style (*red, white, and blue*/*red, white and blue*). The same rule applies when separating items in lists that consists of phrases or clauses rather than single words:

*She opened the bottle, poured out a glass, and sat down at the table.*
*He shook his head, shrugged his shoulders and left the room.*

Regarding the serial comma, purists argue that for precision of meaning a comma should always be inserted before each and every item in a list. The reasoning is to avoid confusion that may otherwise arise over such constructions as the following:

*The shirts come in yellow, blue and white, and green.*

Without the serial comma in this example the reader might be misled into thinking the shirts are available in yellow, blue, white, and green.

Commas are sometimes used where more than one adjective precedes a noun (*a bright, dazzling light; a tall, dark, handsome stranger*), but such constructions other times do not require commas (*a dark green suit; a big red apple*). If the last adjective in a series has a closer relationship with the noun than those preceding, then no comma should be placed before it (*a famous German spa; an intelligent, charming little girl*). It should also be noted that whereas commas may be placed between two adjectives (*hard, grey concrete*), they should not be placed between adverbs and adjectives (*bright green curtains*). Similarly, commas should not be placed before nouns that are being used adjectivally in front of other nouns (*an old gas engine*).

Commas may also be used to separate nonrestrictive clauses and phrases within a sentence, acting in much the same way as parentheses:

*His mother, who is a nurse, tended the victims.*
*My car, which runs on unleaded gasoline, is very cost-effective.*
*I wrote a complaint to the store's manager, F. Johnson.*

Care should be taken to ensure that the nonrestrictive clause or phrase is enclosed by two commas (unless it comes at the end of the sentence and is ended with a period, exclamation mark, or question mark). Note that the nonrestrictive clause or phrase should be capable of being omitted without disrupting the sense of the surrounding sentence. Careful writers avoid placing single commas between the subject and its verb, although such constructions are increasingly being found in informal contexts:

*The snake, with distinctive yellow markings and a red zigzag pattern, is of a species hitherto unknown to science.*

For further explanation of nonrestrictive clauses, see page 155.

A comma should be used when a person (or persons) is being addressed directly by name, as the name is not considered essential to the meaning of the sentence:

*Thank you, Mrs. Simpson, but I already have everything I need.*
*Ladies and gentlemen, let me introduce tonight's speaker.*

Commas are not placed around restrictive clauses or phrases, which are judged essential to the structure of the surrounding sentence:

*The CD player that I gave my brother has stopped working.*
*The former world champion boxer Mike Tyson has lost his latest bout.*
*The physician who is on-call today is Dr. Williams.*

In the above examples the clauses or phrases at issue effectively define or identify rather than merely describe the person or object in question. For further explanation of restrictive clauses, see page 155.

Care should be taken over the placing of commas where their presence or omission may alter the meaning of the sentence. In the following sentence, for instance, the presence of the commas suggests that the writer has only one cat, called Mittens:

*Our cat, Mittens, has white paws.*

If the commas in this example are omitted, however, the implication is that Mittens may well be one of many cats owned by the writer and therefore requires specification:

*Our cat Mittens has white paws.*

Commas are also commonly used around such transitional adverbs as *for example, however, nevertheless, of course,* and *therefore:*

*This conclusion, however, is based on untested evidence.*
*These paintings, for example, show the influence of Orientalism.*
*We shall, of course, offer the usual guarantees.*

Note, though, that in such cases commas are optional, especially when they do not interrupt the flow of the sentence:

*We shall indeed study all aspects of the Civil War, including the political and social causes.*
*The committee could therefore cancel the event altogether.*

Commas are always inserted to separate interjections, terms of address, and tags used to construct questions:

*Ah, I see you have already eaten.*
*Please follow me, sir, and I will show you the way.*
*This is a pretty pattern, don't you think?*

Commas may also be used to separate subordinate clauses from the main clause of a sentence when they begin or end the sentence:

*Bearing in mind what happened last time, the coach decided not to say very much before the game.*
*Admired for his versatility as an actor, he was also a talented singer.*

Again, the comma here is optional and may sometimes be omitted:

*Before opening the door the stranger looked nervously up and down the road.*
*When the others come back we will go straight to the beach.*

There is some danger of confusion, however, if the subordinate clause ends with a verb and the next clause begins with a noun. In these cases a comma is necessary:

*If you refuse to run, another candidate must be found.*
*After we ran outside, the house exploded.*

In order to avoid similar confusion, commas should also be employed when sentences begin with an adverb:

*Nevertheless, we shall proceed with the plan.*
*However, there is still hope.*

The same applies when a sentence begins with an adverbial phrase or an adverbial clause:

*Funnily enough, there was a coffee shop round the very next corner.*
*If nothing goes wrong, the shipment should arrive tonight.*

It is also usual to insert a comma where a sentence begins with a phrase based on the infinitive form of a verb or a participle:

*To tell the truth, the outlook is not encouraging.*
*Thinking about it again, we may have acted hastily.*
*Having seen the state of the place, demolition seems the only solution.*

When a sentence ends with a subordinate clause, it is conventional to insert a comma after the main clause:

*I have made up my mind, although I still have my doubts.*
*There is plenty of food in the house, if you get hungry later.*

A comma should not be used before a subordinate clause that begins with *that:*

*He heard that he was to be dismissed the following day.*
*It is likely that the whole operation will be closed down shortly.*

Note, though, that the serial comma is used for lists in which each item begins with *that:*

*They complained that they had been kept waiting, that they had been offered nothing to eat or drink, and that they had no idea how long it would be before a decision was reached.*

When two or more main (or independent) clauses are linked by a coordinating conjunction such as *and* or *or,* a comma should be placed before the conjunction:

*The apartment was bright and airy, and the kitchen was well equipped.*
*She shot him a dazzling smile, but he was not to be won over that easily.*

Note, however, that when the independent clauses are short the comma is often dispensed with:

*The meal arrived but he was not hungry.*
*It was a good deal and they made money.*

There is no need for a comma before the coordinating conjunction if it links phrases that share the same subject or object:

*The water spilled out of the bucket and formed a pool on the floor.*
*She kissed and hugged the child.*

Main clauses that are not linked by a coordinating conjunction but form part of a single sentence are separated by a semicolon (*see* SEMICOLON, page 358). For further explanation of main clauses, page 151.

Commas may be employed in elliptical constructions so as to avoid repeating the same verb or verb phrase in related clauses:

*He enjoys French and Italian food; his wife, Tex-Mex and Creole.*
*She decided to go on holiday to Greece; we, to Acapulco.*

Commas have an important role in punctuating direct speech. The convention is to place a comma between the last word that is spoken and any associated reporting clause (*I said, replied the woman,* etc.). Note that the comma is inserted inside the closing quotation mark:

*"Go and tell the others to come in," he ordered.*

If the reporting clause is inserted in the middle of the direct speech, another comma should be placed before speech is resumed:

*"Go and tell the others to come in," he ordered, "but take any weapons off them first."*

Note that no comma should be used with indirect speech:

*He replied that he would be back soon.*

For further explanation of direct and indirect speech, see REPORTING SPEECH (page 167).

The comma also has a role in the rendering of large numbers in numerical form, generally being used to split digits into groups of three (*1,000; 10,000; 100,000; 1,000,000*). Alternatively, albeit rarely, some writers insert a space in the place of a comma in such numbers or omit the commas for numbers of just four digits in length.

Commas are never used in year dates (*1776, 1944*) except where they are more than four digits in length (*12,000* B.C.). They are, however, used in dates to separate the month and day from the year (*September 11, 2001*).

Other miscellaneous uses of commas include the insertion of a comma between a person's name followed by their job title, rank, honorific title, educational qualification, or the like (*George Washington, president of the United States; Bill Jones, head of personnel*). They are also used to separate lines in addresses, though not zip codes (*The White House, 1600 Pennsylvania Avenue NW, Washington, D.C. 20500*).

# DASH

The dash (–) is a versatile punctuation mark that is used both singly (technically referred to as the **en dash**) and doubly (forming what is technically known as the **em dash**), sometimes as an alternative to other punctuation marks such as commas, hyphens, and parentheses. It often behaves as an informal version of a colon. Overuse of dashes is to be avoided in formal writing. Note that there are no spaces on either side of the dash.

The single (en) dash is used principally to represent a range, as in dates and with other numbers (*1939–45, July 12–14, 98–99 percent, pages 401–435*). It is also used in place of a hyphen to link elements in which one of them is an open compound (*Washington–New York shuttle, post–World War I Europe*).

Note that when a dash connects numbers there is no need to use *from* and *to* or *between* and *and:*

*It is estimated that 300–400 people died in the disaster.*

Double (em) dashes commonly represent sudden or abrupt changes, often explanatory or digressive in nature. This includes linking statements that may be summaries of what has gone before or afterthoughts:

*Good health and independence—these are what people value most in old age.*
*This is disappointing news—but perhaps we should have expected it.*

On other occasions they are used to introduce lists:

*These are the things we will need—a harness, rope, and safety hats.*
*Take three of the girls with you—Emma, Laura, and Charmain.*

Double dashes may also be used to tack on a word, phrase, or clause at the end of a sentence, usually expressed in an emphatic or contrasting manner:

*Let's get out of here—fast!*
*This is the end—or is it?*

They may indicate a change in subject or continuity:

*They never gave us the key—can you pick locks?*
*That is a beautiful dress—but it doesn't suit her.*

A double dash may be employed to indicate that a word or sentence has been suddenly broken off:

*They'll never hit me from that dist—*

Similarly, it can also convey hesitation in speech:

*She's er—not available at present. She's um—busy right now.*

A double dash is used in attributing quotations:

*"There is a tide in the affairs of men." —Shakespeare*

Double dashes are used in pairs to indicate breaks within a sentence, acting in a similar way to parentheses:

*I will expect the best room—supposing I come at all—and the use of a car.*
*This is an unexpected development—not altogether unwelcome—that will require some thought.*

In many instances, this use of double dashes is in place of commas, in order to avoid the presence of too many commas or a cluttering of punctuation in general:

*The latest range of vehicles—which includes sedans, all-purpose terrain vehicles, and trucks—looks set to be a big hit with consumers.*
*My new girlfriend—how is it that none of my girlfriends last more than a week or two?—doesn't speak a word of English.*

In these cases it should always be possible to remove the material enclosed by dashes and leave the surrounding sentence grammatically intact.

## ELLIPSIS

The word *ellipsis* has two meanings in grammar. The first refers to the omission of words in a sentence in order to avoid repetition or the use of other words deemed unnecessary:

*I can dance as well as you [can dance].*
*[I shall] See you tomorrow.*

Caution should be exercised in the use of such ellipses, since there is some danger that the omitted words may not harmonize with the words repeated:

*She has not and never will agree to the proposal.*

In the above example the omitted word is *agreed,* not *agree,* as the elliptical construction dictates it should be. The one exception where the omitted word does not have to match precisely the actual word given is the verb *be:*

*We're flying out tonight, and the rest, on Monday.*

The other meaning of the word *ellipsis* refers to its use as a punctuation mark (. . .), which similarly indicates that material has been omitted. It is commonly employed at the beginning or end of quoted passages to indicate that these are extracts of longer pieces of writing that follow or precede the quote:

*Friends, Romans, countrymen, lend me your ears. . . .*
*. . . the rest is silence.*
*The tour guide reminded us, When in Rome . . .*

In cases where a complete sentence ends with an ellipsis it is conventional to add the ellipsis after the closing period. Where a whole sentence is omitted it is customary to insert a period before the ellipsis:

*"We look forward to a world founded upon four essential human freedoms. . . . The fourth is freedom from fear . . . anywhere in the world."*

Ellipses may also be employed in much the same way as dashes, variously representing breaks in speech or an unfinished word or sentence. Note, though, that whereas a dash suggests a sudden interruption in speech, an ellipsis implies a more gradual trailing off:

*She was in shock from the news. She sputtered, "But he was just here. . . . He said . . . We were . . ." She began to sob.*

# EXCLAMATION POINT

An exclamation point (!) is used at the end of a sentence to indicate surprise, anger, or another expression of emotion or urgency (*Yes! Stop! Fire! Get out!*). It replaces the period and if part of a quotation is placed within the quotation marks:

*Heaven help us!*
*"Come here!" he ordered.*

Exclamation points are commonly used after interjections and oaths (*Damn! Hell! Ow!*), words expressing loud noises (*Bang! Crash!*), warnings (*Careful! Watch out!*), commands (*Be quiet! Run!*), and insults or other verbal assaults (*You pig! Screw you!*). They may also be used with such words as *how* or *what* in expressions of delight, disgust, outrage, pleasure, etc. (*How lovely! What cheek!*), sometimes having the effect of turning what would otherwise be a question into a statement (*Isn't she a scream! Aren't we lucky!*). They may also be used at the end of longer sentences as an indication of strong emotion:

*We're fed up with being taken for granted around here!*
*This is the most wonderful thing that's ever happened to me or my family!*

Note that the presence of an exclamation point can determine the way in which the sentence concerned is interpreted or spoken:

*The old lady is dying.*
*The old lady is dying?*
*The old lady is dying!*

The period at the end of the first example makes the sentence a simple statement of fact. The question mark at the end of the second example makes it a query, with a suggestion of an emotional interest in the answer. The exclamation point at the end of the third example transforms it into an expression of surprise, delight, horror, or dismay, as dictated by the context.

Exclamation points are occasionally employed within the body of sentences, usually in subordinate phrases enclosed by parentheses or dashes:

*The great lady did not (thank heavens!) want to see the kitchen.*
*The ball left the bat—the same one he had previously refused!—like the proverbial rocket.*

Restraint should always be used with regard to exclamation points, since their overuse blunts their impact and may convey the impression that the writer is being insincere or overexcitable. They should rarely, if ever, be employed in formal writing, in which the tone should always be moderate rather than excitable, and they should never be doubled or tripled except in very informal contexts.

# HYPHEN

The hyphen (-) has a number of uses, chief of which is the linking of two or more existing words to create new word compounds (*all-encompassing, non-English-speaking, off-air*). Note that in many cases involving the adjoining of standard prefixes with words, the hyphen in the resulting compound is omitted (*intermix, prearrange, unmanned*). When a hyphen links words of which at least one is an open compound it is replaced by a dash (*a New York–based company*). (*See* DASH, page 347.)

In some circumstances the insertion of a hyphen helps to avoid ambiguity and confusion as regards meaning or pronunciation (*re-form/reform*). (*See* RECOVER/RE-COVER and RESIGN/RE-SIGN, pages 315 and 317). In many others, however, the presence or omission of a hyphen is a matter of choice. Where the addition of a prefix results in two vowels being joined, for instance, many writers choose to insert a hyphen (*pre-empt, re-establish*), but just as many leave out the hyphen. Note that prefixes added to proper nouns should generally have a hyphen (*pro-American, anti-Semitic*). Other than this particular instance, however, the tendency in modern times is increasingly to omit the hyphen in favor of a single word.

The one case in which a hyphen is always inserted, even today, is where the prefix ends in a letter *i* and the next word begins with the same letter (*anti-imperialist, semi-illiterate*). Hyphens are also usually employed in the case of the prefixes *ex-*, where it means "former," and *self-* (*ex-employee, self-denial*).

Hyphens are generally inserted in the case of compounds of two or more words that are being used adjectivally before a noun (*a half-finished model, a boarded-up window*). The presence of a hyphen in such cases may have an influence on how the meaning of the phrase is interpreted: *a bright-red face* describes a face that is bright red in color, whereas *a bright red face* could be referring to a face that is both bright in aspect and red in color. *A red-wine bottle,* meanwhile, refers specifically to a bottle for holding red wine, whereas a *red wine bottle* could refer to a red bottle used to contain wine of any color.

Hyphens are usually employed in two-word compound adjectives ending in *-ed* (*half-hearted, wished-for*). They are also generally kept in place in the case of compounds comprising three or more words (*father-in-law, down-at-the-heels, run-of-the-mill*). Some compounds based on phrasal verbs keep their hyphen (*falling-outs, psyched-up, walk-up*), while others are always rendered as a single word (*breakthrough, runaway*). Again, in many cases both the hyphenated and unhyphenated forms are commonly encountered (*die-hard/diehard, babysit/baby-sit*). Most compounds of this type continue to be used in their original unhyphenated phrasal verb form as well as in their hyphenated noun form (*drive through* [verb]/*drive-through* [noun]; *sit in* [verb]/*sit-in* [noun]).

Compounds containing adverbs are usually hyphenated when employed adjectivally before a noun (*a half-forgotten episode; an ill-used child*), often to clarify meaning: *His best-known work* describes a work that is better known than all his others, whereas *his best known work* refers to a work that is the best of his known to exist, although there may be (or have been) other better ones now unknown. Note that there is an exception in the case of compounds in which the adverb ends in *-ly,* which do not require a hyphen (*a closely observed experiment, a newly minted coin*).

Sometimes it is unnecessary to repeat a word that is common to two or more hyphenated compounds, but the hyphen must still be included:

*We can offer both long- and short-term contracts.*

The same applies to single-word compounds that share common elements:

*Let us celebrate the achievements of our sportsmen and -women.*

Note, though, that this convention is disapproved of by some readers, who would prefer to see both compounds written in full.

Often the use of hyphens is governed by a range of factors besides personal preference, among them the frequency of the word compound concerned (the more often it is used, the more likely it is that the hyphen will be dropped) and the house style of the publication a writer might be writing for. In many cases compound nouns are likely to be encountered with a hyphen just as often as they appear without one (*living room/living-room; decision-making/decision making*).

Hyphens are used frequently when numerals between 21 and 99 are written out in full (*twenty-two, seventy-seven, ninety-nine*). They are also employed when writing out fractions in full (*one-fifth, four-tenths, two-twelfths*) and to indicate numbers that do not represent a range (*have a 50-50 chance*), including scorelines (*our team won 4-3*) or votes (*a 5-4 decision in the Supreme Court*).

Hyphens are also commonly used in printed material to indicate where a word has been split at the end of one line and continued on to the next due to lack of space. Where the hyphen should be placed in such circumstances is not always obvious. Traditionally, the break should come at a place dictated by a word's etymology (that is, dividing the constituent elements of a word from a historical point of view), but increasingly the hyphen today tends to be placed where it feels phonetically comfortable (that is, where it sounds most natural). One should consult the dictionary for proper division of a word.

Broadly speaking, a hyphen should be placed between syllables, after any prefix, before any suffix, or where there is an existing hyphen. Note that words of one syllable should never be split and also that a word should never be split so as to leave the first or last letter of the word alone on a separate line. Caution should also be exercised to avoid splitting words where the resulting elements spell misleadingly different words in their own right (thus, *man-slaughter,* not *mans-laughter,* and *le-gend,* not *leg-end*). Care should also be taken not to split a word where the result might be confused with another word with a fixed hyphen (thus, *rec-reation,* not *re-creation*).

# ITALICS

A sloping, or *italic,* typeface has a number of uses in printed material. Italics are by convention applied to titles of books, paintings, pieces of music, and other works of art, as well as to the names of newspapers and other publications, films, and plays (*Far from the Madding Crowd; Sergeant Pepper's Lonely Hearts Club Band, The Lord of the Rings, New York Times*). They are also widely used for the names of specific spacecraft, ships, and aircraft (*Challenger* space shuttle, *Titanic* ocean liner, Lindbergh's *Spirit of St. Louis*). It is also accepted practice to put words or phrases from foreign languages in italics (*dulce et decorum est; sans pareil; weltenschauung*), although words and phrases from foreign languages that have become thoroughly absorbed into the English language (siesta; ad nauseum; je ne sais quois) are more likely rendered in ordinary (roman) type.

In other circumstances, italics are used to highlight a particular word or phrase or to add emphasis. Care should be taken not to employ italics in this manner too frequently, because overuse tends to blunt the impact. Italics may also be used to denote quotations or (as in this book) examples.

Note that when writing by hand it is possible to indicate passages that are intended to be printed in italic by *underlining* them.

# PARAGRAPH

The paragraph is a means of punctuating a longer piece of writing by subdividing it into smaller sections. As noted in chapter 2 (page 63), a paragraph is the basic unit of a written document. Generally, a paragraph is made up of two or more sentences. A paragraph deals with one particular issue or idea. It links with the larger text of which it is part but is also, to some extent, capable of existing independently.

In terms of length, a paragraph can vary from just one sentence to a passage having many sentences with a total of several hundred words. Care should be taken over the use of large numbers of short paragraphs, as used in newspaper articles, since these can serve to break up the text to the extent that it becomes disjointed. Conversely, very long paragraphs can result in the text seeming dense and difficult to read.

A new paragraph always begins on a new line and the first line is usually indented, although style can vary from one piece of writing to another. Note that the usual style for dialogue is to start a new paragraph with each change in speaker. In the case of a long speech by a single speaker, one alternative is to break it up into a series of paragraphs, each beginning with fresh opening quotation marks, and only inserting closing quotation marks at the very end of the speech, marking where the speaker finishes speaking (*see* QUOTATION MARKS, page 356).

# PARENTHESES AND BRACKETS

Parentheses, ( ), are used in pairs and are placed around additional or explanatory words or phrases within longer sentences:

*The young man (newly appointed as spokesperson for the organization) gave a report to the press.*
*The lion (once anesthetized by a marksman) turned out to have an infected paw.*

Parentheses can also enclose complete sentences or even paragraphs. The only material that should be placed within parentheses, however, is the kind of additional detail that could be omitted without changing the meaning or destroying the grammatical structure of the surrounding sentence or text.

Material placed within parentheses typically includes items of explanatory or interpretative information, such as birth and death dates or the full version of an abbreviation:

*Abraham Lincoln (1809–65) was elected president in the year 1861.*
*1100 hours EST (eastern standard time).*

Parentheses are preferred to commas or dashes when the material concerned needs to be made distinct from the rest of the sentence. These cases include asides to the reader:

*The company's profit (with luck) should exceed $10 million.*

Note that material placed within parentheses does not usually start with a capital letter, and punctuation such as periods is not usually employed, though these rules do not hold true when the parentheses enclose a complete sentence. No change needs to be made to the punctuation of the surrounding sentence when parentheses material is interposed. Where parentheses clauses need to be inserted next to any existing punctuation, the material in parentheses should precede the punctuation already in use:

*This was bad news (though not unexpected), and worse was to come.*

There are a number of other uses to which parentheses may also be put: confirming a number in a contract—*within 7 (seven) days*—enclosing letters or numbers in a series—*(1)* or *(a)*—and encompassing possible alternatives—*please return the enclosed form(s).*

Brackets, [ ], are placed around words or phrases furnishing additional explanatory information or editorial comments, often within other parenthetical material:

*The decisions to be made later that year (at the "Yalta meeting" [between Roosevelt, Stalin, and Churchill]) would affect the whole course of the war.*
*I first met Henry James when the author was about 50 years old [the author stayed at the house of James's neighbor for three weeks].*

Brackets are also used for corrections to mistakes in an original text, either containing the correct version of what is given or else the word *sic* to indicate that the mistake exists in the original and that the writer is aware of it:

*He say [sic] trouble is bound to result from this betrayal by the colonial power.*

# PERIOD

A period (.) is a punctuation mark used principally to indicate the end of any sentence that does not otherwise finish with a question mark or exclamation point:

*The water is hot.*
*These birds are wild.*
*That is my pen.*

The fact that no sentence should have more than one period is relevant when rendering direct speech, specifically sentences that would normally end with a period. In such instances, the period may be replaced by a comma, as below:

*"Here is the money," I said, handing over the bag.*

Periods are also traditionally placed after or between each letter of abbreviations (*U.S.*), although the modern tendency is increasingly to omit periods in abbreviations altogether. Periods are sometimes employed in dates (*9.11.01*) and are customary when reducing personal names to initials (*D. H. Lawrence*) and in decimal fractions (*1.3 centimeters*).

The period has enjoyed a new lease on life recently as the dot commonly used in e-mail and Web site addresses (*www.factsonfile.com*).

# QUESTION MARK

A question mark (?) is a punctuation mark used in place of a period at the end of a sentence to indicate that it is a direct question:

*What do you mean?*
*When will you leave?*

In some circumstances, such as quoted questions, the question mark does not necessarily appear at the end of the sentence but is placed inside the closing quotation marks:

*"Are you staying?" she asked anxiously.*
*"Is this the quickest way home?" he inquired.*

Other rare exceptions to the placement of question marks anywhere but at the end of a sentence are in parentheses or when used to question a particular fact, such as an uncertain statistic or a speculative birth or death date (*St. Gereon* [*d. 304?*]). Here the question mark is usually placed immediately after the dubious fact being given.

Question marks should not be used in the case of indirect questions:

*They asked if that was all that was left.*
*We were just wondering what you intend to do.*
*She is curious to know how it happened.*

They are necessary, however, in the case of rhetorical questions, even though no answer is expected:

*How can he be so stupid?*
*Why do people do things like that?*

Question marks can follow single words, as well as longer sentences:

*Are you coming? Yes? No?*

In some contexts the presence of a question mark can turn what is ostensibly a statement into a question:

*You're going to eat that?*
*They can't be serious?*

Question marks are frequently used in requests:

*May I sit down?*
*Could I open the window?*

Longer requests, however, tend to end in a period not a question mark, especially where they are closer to an order:

*Would all customers please check their change before leaving.*

A special case deserving attention is that of direct questions containing such "thinking" verbs as *wonder,* which generally require a question mark:

*How will this story end, we wonder?*

Note, however, that if the verb is in the past, then the question should be treated as reported speech and therefore does not require a question mark:

*How would the story end, we wondered.*

As with exclamation points, question marks should not be doubled or tripled for emphasis, except in very informal contexts, such as personal diaries or notes to friends. The same applies to the combination of a question mark and an exclamation mark at the end of a sentence.

## QUOTATION MARKS

Quotation marks (" " or ' '), or **inverted commas,** are inserted at the start and end of direct quotations to indicate that what they enclose represents actual spoken words:

*"Stand to attention!" the Major barked.*
*"Come in," she whispered, "but don't make a noise."*

The quotation marks surround only the actual words spoken and include any punctuation that forms part of the quotation (as shown in the first example above). Note that in the case of commas and periods the comma or period comes before the closing quotation marks (as in the second example).

Quotation marks are not used in reference to reported speech, although they might be used for specific phrases that the writer wishes to highlight as having been actually spoken:

*He called the whole business "a regrettable misunderstanding."*

Alternatively, they may be used to convey to the reader that a particular word or phrase is not one the writer would normally choose to use:

*The spokesman said the secretary of state was "chilling" after a busy day.*

In American English, double quotation marks are preferred; in British English single quotation marks are used. Whichever is used, the other form is kept in reserve for any quoted material that falls within a quotation:

*"I remember that his last words were 'I shall return.'" [American English]*
*'His mother always said "Life is for living."' [British English]*

Quotation marks are used to render titles of short works such as poems or individual song titles and unpublished works. They are also sometimes used for title of works in general, as is customary in newspapers.

Quotation marks may also be employed to indicate words that are slang or are otherwise out of context:

*The jazz they play is of the "hot" variety.*

When quotation marks are used in this manner they can sometimes convey an ironic or even sarcastic attitude:

*Calling graffiti "art" is stretching a point.*
*His "talent" is no more than a gift for attracting a great deal of attention without actually doing anything.*

On other occasions quotation marks are employed around definitions or interpretations:

*Halcyon means "peaceful, calm, prosperous, idyllic."*

It is incorrect to add a period after a quotation that already has a period, question mark, or exclamation mark before the closing quotation mark:

*"This could be the biggest shock in the history of the game!"*

Also note that if the material enclosed by the quotation marks constitutes a complete sentence, it should always begin with a capital letter:

*She murmured, "Pay up, and this will be the last time you will ever see me."*
*The detective lit a cigarette and asked, "Where were you last night around eleven?"*

Whereas periods and commas following quotations should be placed in front of the closing quotation marks, semicolons and colons should be placed afterward:

*This is not what I call "playing the game," unless you can explain your action.*

*This is not what I call "playing the game"; that is, the same rules must apply to all.*

Exclamation points, question marks, and dashes that do not punctuate the quoted material should appear outside the quotation marks:

*Are you sure she said "I killed him"?*
*It is simply impossible for you just to wash your hands of it and say "it has nothing to do with me"!*

Sometimes quotations are of considerable length and extend beyond a single paragraph. In such circumstances, opening quotation marks are placed at the beginning of each new paragraph, but closing quotation marks are put in place only when the quotation finally ends:

*The detective addressed the group of suspects: "My theory that the murder was committed by one of the people in this room still stands. Nothing the major has told us alters the fact that when Mrs. Clitheroe went out onto the veranda, someone must have been waiting for her. That someone is here now. That someone not only knows who killed the doctor, but also where the diamonds are.*

*"Let us cast our minds back to what the young policeman said when he first discovered the body. He remarked that it was strange that the grass under the corpse was wet, when according to the version of events suggested by the inspector it only started raining after the murder must have already happened. The grass under the body, therefore, should have been dry."*

## SEMICOLON

A semicolon (;) is used to link clauses that are related in sense but not otherwise connected by a conjunction. Unlike other punctuation marks, semicolons may be replaced in all cases by other punctuation marks or through rewording of the sentence, and their use in modern writing has diminished in favor of commas and dashes.

A semicolon should be used only where the phrases on either side of it are capable of standing alone as independent sentences but have greater impact when combined in this way:

*The tree is in need of attention; there are plans to have it felled.*
*The new engine looks promising; we hope to break the speed record soon.*

In both of these examples the use of the semicolon adds a dynamism to the sentence that would be lacking if a period was used instead. It also improves the narrative flow.

A semicolon can also serve to highlight any contrast between the two associated clauses:

*She wanted a new house in the suburbs; he wanted to keep things as they were.*

There is no rule preventing the use of more than one semicolon in a single sentence:

*The meeting was unruly; one side had rebellion on its mind; the other side wanted only peace.*

Semicolons should not be used with such conjunctions as *and* or *but* but are frequently used before such words as *however, nevertheless,* or *nonetheless:*

*The army is in retreat; however, this is not the end of the campaign.*
*His family is in a state of shock; nonetheless, life must go on.*

Note that in most cases a semicolon should be replaced by a comma only when there is no comma already in the sentence. In the case of creating a list, however, semicolons can be used alongside commas as a means of splitting the list into manageable parts, which are then subdivided, as appropriate, by commas:

*The book covers the author's childhood, youth, and early career; his most important novels, short stories, and articles; and his last works, declining health, and premature death.*

It should be noted that in this instance it is not essential that the phrases that appear on either side of the semicolon be complete sentences in themselves.

Where a semicolon appears after a phrase in quotation marks, it should always appear after the closing quotation mark, not before:

*It was what my father would have called "a proper do"; no expense was spared.*

# SLASH

A slash (/) is used to separate alternatives (*and/or, his/her, men/women*). Otherwise called a **solidus, slant, virgule,** or **oblique,** it can imply that both alternatives are equally appropriate in a given context (*missing/stolen; damaged/wornout*). Slashes are also used in the numerical form of fractions (*1/5, 3/16*), as a symbol representing the word *per* (*beats/minute, feet/second*), and in expressions of dates (*2005/06; 9/11/01*). Slashes are also used to indicate the beginnings of new lines in passages of poetry, when not laid out separately as in the original: *Shall I compare thee to a summer's day? / Thou art more lovely and more temperate.*

Note that with the rapid development of electronic communications in recent years, the slash has been integrated into the rendering of Web site addresses (*http://www.factsonfile.com/*).

8

# Reference Resources

## INTRODUCTION

There are many places where the budding writer may obtain help with the correct use of grammar and vocabulary. These include books from bookstores and libraries as well as electronic resources.

Resources available in book form can be subdivided into three broad categories: dictionaries, thesaurusis, and other reference works. Details of these are given below.

## DICTIONARIES

The first and in many respects most comprehensive resort for most writers is a good dictionary.

Entries in a dictionary are arranged alphabetically. Different dictionaries provide varying levels of information about each word, depending largely on the space available.

Each entry begins with a **headword** consisting of the word or compound words in question, printed in bold, and often indicating its syllables. Writers seeking to check spelling need read no further than the headword. Depending on the scope of the dictionary consulted, the headword may be followed by a **pronunciation guide,** which indicates how a word should be spoken. Some dictionaries make use of special symbols to represent particular sounds (with a key to these usually included at the beginning or end of the book and even sometimes at the foot of the page); others represent the words phonetically (that is, spelling words out exactly as they are pronounced using ordinary letters). The special symbols sometimes used in pronunciation guides may seem unfamiliar at first sight and be somewhat off-putting—for example, ə, the "schwa," to represent the unstressed vowel sound, as in the final vowel of *China*—but with a little practice most readers can soon master these. Vertical marks or other symbols may also be inserted to indicate where the stress falls in a particular word, showing which part or parts of the word should be emphasized when spoken. When choosing a dictionary, it is worth checking that the text includes pronunciation guides, as even quite substantial dictionaries may omit them. They are particularly useful for broadcasters of various kinds and more generally for anyone whose daily conversation is likely to include many multisyllabic (possibly technical) words or words of foreign origin.

The order of what follows in a particular entry varies from book to book, but a likely next feature is an indication of the part of speech appropriate to a particular word (noun, verb, adjective, etc.). This may be followed, again depending on style and the quality of the dictionary, by information about a word's etymology (its origins and development), including the language from which it might have come into English and even the word in the language from which it is ultimately descended.

The main part of each entry is an explanation of a word's meaning. Often a word has more than one meaning and each of these is described in turn, perhaps numbered and lettered separately.

Entries in smaller dictionaries often end at this point. More comprehensive books may also state approximately when each sense of a word first came into use in English and offer examples of the word's usage. There may also be a note indicating in what contexts a word may be used, for example, informally or colloquially, or as slang. The entry may close with details of variations of a headword as different parts of speech (as a noun, adjective, adverb, etc.).

Depending on the size of a dictionary, the text may also include boxed information on usage of a particular word, or even relevant illustrations. As well as ordinary vocabulary words, larger dictionaries may also contain entries for abbreviations, famous people, geographical locations, jargon, and slang.

It should be remembered, when consulting even the best dictionaries, that there is no single overall authority on what is correct and what is incorrect. Writers of dictionaries follow trends and changes in language and do not dictate them. What a good dictionary represents is merely the prevailing state of the language at a particular time, reflecting what is currently happening throughout the English-speaking world.

Some leading English dictionaries include

*Merriam-Webster's Collegiate Dictionary*
*American Heritage Dictionary*
*Webster's New World College Dictionary*
*Random House Webster's College Dictionary*
*New Oxford Dictionary of English*
*New Oxford American Dictionary*
*Collins English Dictionary*
*Cambridge Dictionary of American English*
*Collins Cobuild English Language Dictionary*
*Longman Dictionary of American English*
*Longman Dictionary of the English Language*
*Webster's New Universal Unabridged Dictionary*
*Encarta World English Dictionary*

## THESAURI

Another useful reference source is a thesaurus, a word book that operates differently from a dictionary. Instead of defining words and what they mean, thesauri create links between related words so that the reader may choose from various alternatives. This makes the thesaurus an invaluable tool for writers seeking to avoid repetition of the same word or looking for a more accurate or evocative alternative to a word they have already considered. For example, you may have used the word *important* already. A thesaurus would list *significant, critical, vital,* and *crucial* as possible synonyms (words that mean much the same thing). It might also include antonyms (words that have an opposite meaning).

Some thesauri are arranged alphabetically, while others adopt a thematic approach, with an index at the end guiding the reader to entries relevant to a particular word.

Some leading English thesauri include

*Roget's International Thesaurus*
*Merriam-Webster's Collegiate Thesaurus*
*Webster's New World Thesaurus*
*The Bloomsbury Thesaurus*
*The New Penguin Thesaurus*
*The Cassell Thesaurus*
*The Oxford Thesaurus*
*Collins English Thesaurus*
*Chambers Thesaurus*

## OTHER REFERENCE BOOKS

As well as dictionaries and thesauri, there are several other specialized types of reference source of use to writers.

**Dictionaries of English usage** provide help with the correct usage of grammar and vocabulary and offer much information that is not included in the average language dictionary.

Fowler, H. W., and R. Burchfield, eds. *New Fowler's Modern English Usage.* Oxford and New York: Oxford University Press, 1998.
Manser, Martin H. *Good Word Guide.* 5th ed. London: Bloomsbury, 2003.
*Merriam-Webster's Dictionary of English Usage.* Springfield, Mass.: Merriam-Webster, 1993.
Peters, Pam. *The Cambridge Guide to English Usage.* New York and Cambridge: Cambridge University Press, 2004.

**Manuals of style** offer detailed advice on writing styles, including punctuation, spelling, grammar, citations, bibliographies, indexes, writing and book-making procedures, and more.

*The Chicago Manual of Style.* 15th ed. Chicago: University of Chicago Press, 2003.
*MLA Style Manual.* 2d ed. New York: Modern Language Association, 1998.
*The Gregg Reference Manual.* New York: McGraw-Hill/Irwina, 2004.
*Words into Type.* 3d ed. New York: Prentice Hall, 1974.

Some **style guides** offer more general advice on how to improve writing style. *The Elements of Style* (often known more familiarly as "Strunk and White") has long been considered a classic in this genre. *The Facts On File Guide to Style,* the companion to this volume, builds on the material presented here and looks in more detail at the aesthetic aspects of writing and the practical problems of adapting the way you write to suit your readership and expressing yourself clearly for a particular occasion.

Manser, Martin H., and Stephen Curtis. *The Facts On File Guide to Style.* New York: Facts On File, 2006.
Strunk, William, and E. B. White. *The Elements of Style, Fourth Edition.* New York: Longman, 2000.

**Dictionaries of idioms** provide helpful information about idioms and idiomatic usages and make for diverting reading. They can be useful aids in enlivening your own writing. **Dictionaries of proverbs** are also useful in a similar way.

Manser, Martin H. *Dictionary of Everyday Idioms.* 2nd ed. London: Prentice Hall, 1997.
———. *The Facts On File Dictionary of Proverbs.* New York: Facts On File, 2002.
Speake, Jennifer. *Oxford Dictionary of Idioms.* Oxford and New York: Oxford University Press, 2000.

**Dictionaries of quotations** are an invaluable and fascinating source for writers seeking famous or thought-provoking quotations to illustrate their own writing. They may be organized in one of many different ways, for instance, thematically, chronologically, or alphabetically by the names of the people who originated them. Some dictionaries are general in scope, while others are dedicated to particular subjects.

*Bartlett's Familiar Quotations.* 17th ed. New York: Little, Brown, 2002.
Knowles, Elizabeth. *Oxford Dictionary of Quotations.* Oxford and New York: Oxford University Press, 2004.

Other useful sources that arguably merit a place on any writer's bookshelf include **dictionaries of clichés, dictionaries of slang, dictionaries of catchphrases, English grammars,** and **dictionaries of phrase and fable.**

## ELECTRONIC REFERENCE SOURCES

Writers working on personal computers have a range of additional resources available to them electronically.

Word-processing packages routinely include an electronic thesaurus and spell-checking facilities. There are limits to what a computer can check, but it can at least highlight (or automatically correct) incorrect spellings and provide alternative words where requested. A spell-checker compares what has been keyed with what the program holds in its electronic word banks: If it does not recognize a word, it highlights or underlines the word or otherwise suggests that it should be changed. Computer users can choose what kind of English they would like their text to be checked in (for instance, American English or British English). It should be noted, though, that electronic spell-checkers and thesaurusis vary in extent, and few can make claims to be seriously comprehensive in the way that good printed equivalents can be. Computer users do, however, have the option of adding extra words to their electronic spell-checker so that its performance should in theory steadily improve. Stand-alone spell-checkers generally offer more choices than those included in standard computer packages.

One less avoidable and more significant drawback to electronic spell-checkers is that they will not correct a word that has been misspelled if it happens to be identical in form with another word that they hold in their word bank, for example, *there* for *their, fro* for *for, who's* for *whose,* and *your* for *your're.*

It is possible to install computer programs designed to check grammar and readability. These will query grammatical and stylistic errors such as repetitions of the same word, overlong sentences, and the suitability of certain words in a particular context. It is possible, for instance, to set the computer to check the appropriateness of the vocabulary in a business document or in a piece of informal writing. Such programs tend to lack flexibility, however, and rarely work as well as might be hoped: Care should be taken not to rely too heavily on them.

For discussion on use of electronic resources, including the Internet, when undertaking research, see under COLLECTING MATERIAL (page 13).

# 9

# Glossary of Grammatical Terms

The following list includes the more commonly encountered grammatical terms, together with brief explanations of their meaning. Many of the terms included are discussed in greater depth elsewhere in the book.

**abbreviation** A shortened form of a word or phrase used as a convenient alternative to the fuller term (*CIA, d.o.a., Mr.*).

**abstract noun** A noun that refers to something that lacks an actual physical existence (*dream, sound*).

**accent** A symbol placed above or below a letter to indicate how it should be pronounced, restricted to words borrowed from certain foreign languages (*café, fräulein, soupçon*).

**acronym** A type of abbreviation formed from the initial letter or letters of the major parts of the full name of an organization or other entity and pronounced as a word in its own right (*NATO, radar*).

**active** Used to describe a verb in which the action is performed by the subject of the sentence (*she **kissed** her mother*).

**adjectival noun** A noun that is used as an adjective (*the **summer** holidays, **leisure** facilities*).

**adjective** A word that describes an accompanying noun (*a **black** coat; a **rough** surface; the explosion was **loud***).

**adjective phrase** An adjective accompanied by other words providing further information about it (*a **very cold** day, a **deep enough** hole, a **wilder-than-ever** party*).

**adjunct** A form of adverb that is attached to the verb of a clause or sentence but is not itself the main structural element in the sentence (*wait **impatiently; climb onto the top***).

**adverb** A word that modifies a verb, adjective, or other part of speech, providing further information about that word or phrase (*arrive* ***early;*** *rain* ***heavily;*** ***very*** *hot; walk* ***unsteadily***).

**adverbial** The part of a sentence that has the function of an adverb, providing further information about the nature of what is taking place (*enter the building* ***cautiously***).

**adverbial clause** A subordinate clause within a sentence beginning with because, if, or a similar word:

*She gasped* ***when she saw what had happened.***

**adverbial phrase** A phrase containing one or more adverbs (*rather slowly, very deeply*).

**agent** The source of action in a passive sentence:

*The race was won by* ***Alice.***

**agreement (concord)** The coordination of gender or number, involving two or more words in the same sentence, as dictated by the rules of grammar:

*Please leave the* ***books*** *in* ***their*** *covers.*
*The* ***soldiers*** *in question* ***have*** *all been arrested.*

**alternative question** A question that cannot be answered by a simple affirmative or negative reply and typically necessarily requires repetition of one or more of the words of the question in the answer:

*Would you like pasta or potatoes with your meal?*

**animate noun** A noun referring to a person or other living creature (*boy, lamb, seagull, visitor*).

**apostrophe** A symbol (') variously denoting the omission of a letter, the possessive case, or the plural of a letter (*isn't, Bill's car, dot the i's and cross the t's*).

**apposition** The linking of two nouns or noun phrases that refer to the same thing:

*George Washington, the first president of the United States.*

**appositive clause** A clause providing further information about an abstract noun (*the fact* ***that his mother was dead;*** *the truth* ***that nothing will be changed by this decision***).

**article** *See* DEFINITE ARTICLE; INDEFINITE ARTICLE.

**aspect** The action of a verb in relation to whether it is complete or still to be completed.

**attributive adjective** An adjective that appears before the noun it describes (*a **cold** day, a **slight** advantage*).

**auxiliary verb** A verb that precedes the main verb in a sentence:

> *We just **had** to come.*
> ***Could** you pass me that box.*
> ***Did** you ask for a discount?*

**back formation** The formation of a new word by removing a real (or supposed) prefix or suffix from an existing longer word (e.g., *sightsee* from *sightseeing*).

**base form** The basic infinitive form of a verb, without any additional endings (*go; fly; whisper*).

**blend** *See* PORTMANTEAU WORD.

**brackets** A pair of symbols, [ ], placed around words or phrases that provide additional explanatory information or editorial comments, especially in quoted material or parenthetical material:

> *He replied, "Hasta mañana [until tomorrow]," and rode off on his stallion, never to be seen again.*
> *The decisions to be made later that year (at the "Yalta meeting" [between Roosevelt, Stalin, and Churchill]) would affect the whole course of the war.*

**capital letter** An uppercase letter, as used at the start of sentences and for the initial letter of a proper noun.

**cardinal numeral** The grammatical term for a number (*one, ninety-nine*). *See also* ORDINAL NUMERAL.

**case** The form of a noun or pronoun, as dictated by its grammatical role within a sentence.

**clause** A group of words within a sentence, usually including a subject and a finite verb:

> *She knows **she has little chance.***

**cliché** A word or phrase that is so overused it may be considered stale or unoriginal (*at the end of the day, never say die*).

**collective noun** A noun used to describe a group of people or objects (*gang, government, herd, people, tribe*).

**colloquial** Used to describe language of an informal, everyday character. The frequent use of casual colloquialisms in formal contexts is generally best avoided.

**colon** A punctuation mark (:) that introduces a clause or word, used to expand upon something already mentioned or to introduce a list, quotation, or other material.

**comma** A punctuation mark (,) that is commonly used to separate clauses within a sentence or to delineate separate items in a list.

**comment clause** A clause within a sentence in which the writer communicates his or her views on what is being discussed:

*To be honest, this was never a good idea.*

**common noun** Any noun that cannot otherwise be classed as a proper noun.

**comparative** A class of adjective used to compare two people or things (*paler, stronger, more interesting*).

**comparative clause** A clause in which two people or things are compared:

*That ball is **bouncier than the other one.***

**complement** A word, usually an adjective or noun, or phrase that follows a linking verb such as *be, feel,* or *seem:*

*He is **a genius.***
*She seems **distracted** today.*

**complex preposition** A preposition that consists of more than one word (*as well as, because of, in addition to*).

**complex sentence** A sentence that includes a main clause and one or more subordinate clauses (typically introduced by *because, if, while,* etc.):

*It won't work because the wires are incorrectly connected.*

**compound adjective** An adjective created through the combination of two or more words, at least one of which is usually an adjective (*hard-won, work-shy*).

**compound adverb** An adverb created through the combination of two or more words (*anywhere, thereby*).

**compound noun** A noun created through the combination of two or more words, at least one of which is a noun (*showstopper, strike force*).

**compound sentence** A sentence that includes two or more main clauses, typically linked by such words as *and, but,* or *or:*

*The door opened, and a tall stranger walked in.*

**concord** *See* AGREEMENT.

**concrete noun** A noun that describes something that has an actual physical existence of some kind (*plastic, mountain, pencil*).

**conjunct** A category of adverbs that provide links between clauses, sentences, or paragraphs (*for example, therefore*).

**conjunction** A word or phrase that serves to link two clauses or parts of a sentence (*and, but, if*). Conjunctions can be subdivided into coordinating conjunctions and subordinating conjunctions.

**consonant** The sound represented by certain letters of the alphabet whose pronunciation is characterized by constriction of the breath. The term is commonly extended to the letters of the alphabet themselves, with the exception of the vowels *a, e, i, o,* and *u.*

**continuous tense** A form of the present tense that describes actions that are continuing to be performed at the time in question, constructed through the combination of *be* with the *-ing* form of the verb (*I am working; you are annoying me*).

**contraction** The shortening of a word achieved through the omission of one or more letters and the attachment of the abbreviated word to the preceding word (*isn't, he'd, you're*). Another form of contraction involves the omission of all the intervening letters of a word between the first and last letters (*Dr., Mr.*).

**conversion** The reinvention of words through the absorption of existing words into new word classes (for example, treating an existing noun as a verb):

*We need to action this immediately.*

**coordinating conjunction (coordinator)** A conjunction that serves to link words or clauses of equal status (*rise* ***and*** *fall, cruel* ***but*** *fair; black* ***or*** *white*).

**coordination** The linking together parts of a sentence that have equal status, typically through the use of a coordinating conjunction:

*The weather that morning was* ***wet and windy.***

**coordinator** *See* COORDINATING CONJUNCTION.

**copular verb** *See* LINKING VERB.

**correlatives** Conjunctions that are used in pairs to link parts of a sentence (*either . . . or, both . . . and*).

**countable noun (count noun)** A noun that is capable of being made plural (*hill/hills, man/men*).

**count noun** *See* COUNTABLE NOUN.

**dangling participle (hanging participle, unattached participle)** A participle that is incorrectly placed within a sentence and therefore risks misleading the reader into linking it with the wrong subject:

> ***Driving round the corner,*** *the hotel comes into sight.*

**dash** A punctuation mark (–) that when used in its double form (—) indicates a break in the meaning or structure of a sentence:

> *He turned to go—but then he heard a noise.*
> *She was known for her short dresses—this was back in the sixties—and was much imitated.*

**defining clause** *See* RESTRICTIVE CLAUSE.

**definite article** The word *the*. *See also* INDEFINITE ARTICLE.

**demonstrative pronoun** A pronoun such as *this, that, these,* or *those* used to distinguish between things being referred to:

> *This is my hat; that is yours.*

**dependent clause** *See* SUBORDINATE CLAUSE.

**derivation** The process through which new words are created by the addition of prefixes, suffixes, and combining forms (*reliable/unreliable, help/helpful*).

**determiner** A word such as *a/an, the, my, this,* or *whose* that precedes a noun and variously specifies the particular person or object or its number (*a dog, the house, my car, this switch, whose keys*).

**dialect** A regional variety of language, as variously distinguished by characteristics of vocabulary, grammar, pronunciation, etc.

**diphthong** The combination of two vowel sounds as one sound, as found in such words as *boat* or *toy*.

**directive** A clause or sentence that communicates an order or instruction:

> *Stop talking!*

**direct object** A word (usually a noun or pronoun) or phrase that is directly affected by the action of the verb:

> *The arrow pierced* ***the target.***

**direct speech** The writing down of the actual words that were spoken, in contrast to reported, or indirect, speech in which they are reworded or otherwise not rendered verbatim:

*"**Hand me the gun,**" said the police officer.*

**disjunct** A category of adverbs in which the writer comments on the content or style of a clause or sentence:

***Personally,** I could not see the difference.*

**double negative** The presence of two negatives in a single sentence, as a result of which they cancel out each other:

*She didn't see nothing.*

**ellipsis** The omission of part of a sentence in order to avoid repetition:

*We expected her to come, but she didn't [**come**].*

Also, the punctuation mark (. . .), which indicates that material has been omitted, and is used in quoted passages to indicate that the extract has been shortened by omission of words:

*The tour guide reminded us, when in Rome . . .*
*In the letter she wrote, "Although not well, . . . I will travel tomorrow."*

**emphatic pronoun** A reflexive pronoun that is positioned within a sentence in order to add emphasis:

*I **myself** have seen the ghost on a number of occasions.*

**equivalence** The comparison of two people or things that are judged to be equal, employing the structure *as . . . as:*

*This bag is **as heavy as** that one.*

**exclamation** A word, clause, or sentence expressing surprise, anger, approval, delight, etc.:

*Heavens! What a beautiful baby!*

**exclamation point** A symbol (!) denoting surprise, anger, approval, delight, etc.

**expletive** An exclamatory word or phrase, typically of an obscene or profane nature. The term may also be used to refer to a syllable, word, or phrase that is inserted in a sentence without adding to the sense:

*We need to make **it** clear that bad behavior will not be tolerated.*

**etymology** The study of words and their historical origins.

**euphemism** A word used as a substitution for a more offensive or insensitive term.

**feminine** *See* GENDER.

**finite clause** A clause that includes a finite verb:

*He stopped the car.*

**finite verb** A verb that has a subject and is used in the present, past, or future tense, as appropriate (*he* ***closes*** *the door; they* ***lifted*** *the lid*), in contrast to the basic infinitive form.

**first person** The pronouns *I* (singular) and *we* (plural), or the form of a verb used with these pronouns.

**fronting** The practice of positioning a word at the start of a sentence in order to give it greater prominence:

*Over the hills came the storm.*

**future tense** The tense used in referring to events yet to happen, usually constructed using the auxiliary verbs *will* or *shall.*

**gender** The classification of nouns and pronouns into masculine and feminine genders, as appropriate. Most nouns in English have no gender and take the pronoun *it.*

**genitive case** *See* POSSESSIVE CASE.

**gerund** The *-ing* form of a verb when used as a noun (*no diving; elegant dancing*).

**gradable** Describing an adjective that indicates a particular level or degree (*an* ***old*** *man; a* ***high*** *risk, a very* ***cheap*** *option*).

**hanging participle** *See* DANGLING PARTICIPLE.

**hyphen** A symbol (-) that is used to link, create, or divide compound nouns, word elements, numbers, etc.

**imperative mood** The form of a verb when used in commands or instructions (*sit down! take care*).

**indefinite article** The word ***a*** or ***an***. ***See also*** DEFINITE ARTICLE.

**indefinite pronoun** A pronoun that refers to a group of people or objects in general terms (*anybody, everybody, everyone, everything, no one, something*), or a pronoun expressing quantity (*all, some*).

**independent clause** *See* MAIN CLAUSE.

**indicative mood** The ordinary form of a verb used in making statements or asking questions:

*Have you received my letter?*
*These* ***are*** *my things.*

**indirect object** A word, typically a noun or pronoun, or phrase that is indirectly affected by the action of the verb, in contrast to a direct object:

*She bought* ***the child*** *a toy.*

**indirect speech** *See* REPORTED SPEECH.

**infinitive** The base form of a verb, typically preceded by *to* (*to give, to sell, to yield*).

**inflection** The changing of the base form of a word in order to express person, gender, number, or tense (*talk/talked, train/trains, be/is, I/me*).

**intensifier** An adverb that serves to render a word greater or less in intensity, strength, amount, etc. (*quite, slightly, very, too*).

**interjection** An expression of anger, approval, pain, surprise, etc. (*ah! oh! ouch! ugh!*).

**interrogative** A pronoun or adverb used to introduce a question, in most cases one beginning *wh-* (*how, what, when, where, which, who, whom, whose, why*):

*What are you planning to do?*

**intonation** The variation in the pitch of a speaker's voice when asking a question, making a statement, and so on.

**intransitive verb** A verb that lacks a direct object (*the flames rose; the bottle leaked*), in contrast to a transitive verb.

**invariable noun** A noun that is either always singular or always plural (*athletics; cattle; news; scissors; shears*).

**inversion** Reversing the usual order of a subject and noun for the purposes of asking a question, increasing emphasis, etc.:

*Have you change?*
*Dark is the night.*

**inverted commas** *See* QUOTATION MARKS.

**irregular** Used to describe a word that does not follow the standard pattern for words of a particular class. Irregular words include verbs that have an irregular form for the past tense and past participle (*see/saw/seen, take/took/taken*) and nouns that vary from the standard pattern in their plural forms (*pony/ponies, half/halves*).

**linking verb (copular verb)** A verb such as *be, feel,* or *seem* that serves to link a subject and a complement (*the sea* ***is*** *blue; she* ***seems*** *friendly*).

**main clause (independent clause)** The principal clause in a sentence, which is capable of standing alone independently of any subordinate clauses:

*The cat yawned* then entered the house.

**main verb** The chief verb in a verb phrase, in contrast to any secondary or auxiliary verb (*must have* ***started;*** *might have* ***known***).

**major sentence** A complete sentence (one that includes a finite verb together with any necessary subject, object, etc.), in contrast to a minor sentence:

*We stayed up all night.*

**masculine** *See* GENDER.

**mass noun** *See* UNCOUNTABLE NOUN.

**minor sentence** A sentence that lacks a finite verb (*Ridiculous! What a scream!*), in contrast to a major sentence.

**modal verb** A verb that is capable of being used as an auxiliary verb only (*can, could, may, must, shall, should, would*), in contrast to a primary verb.

**modifier** A word that provides further information about another word or phrase (***house****coat,* ***water****-ski;* ***temperature*** *gauge*).

**mood** A form of a verb expressing the imperative, indicative, subjunctive, and so on.

**morphology** The study and description of word formation.

**multiple sentence** A sentence that consists of more than one clause, typically one that contains a main clause and one or more subordinate clauses:

*Times were hard, but we were happy.*

**multiword verb** *See* PHRASAL VERB.

**negation** The process of transforming a sentence from the positive to the negative, for instance, through the use of the word *not:*

*They are* ***not*** *coming after all.*

**negative** A word expressing the negative (*never, not*).

**nominal adjective** An adjective that is employed as a noun:

> *When all else has been discounted, the* ***unlikely*** *is the only solution left.*

**noncount noun** *See* UNCOUNTABLE NOUN.

**nondefining clause** *See* NONRESTRICTIVE CLAUSE.

**nonequivalence** The comparison of two people, or things, that are judged to be unequal, employing such structure *less . . . than, more . . . than:*

> *He earns more money than his father ever did.*

**nonfinite clause** A clause that includes a nonfinite verb phrase, in contrast to a finite clause.

**nonfinite verb** A verb in its infinitive form (*to fly*) or otherwise in use as a present participle (*flying*) or as a past participle (*flown*).

**nonfinite verb phrase** A verb phrase that includes one or more nonfinite verbs but lacks a finite verb (*having lost the game*).

**nongradable** Term describing an adjective that cannot be used with words such as *very* or *too* to indicate a particular level or degree (*impossible, perfect*).

**nonrestrictive clause (nondefining clause)** A clause that includes incidental information that could be omitted from the sentence:

> *This hospital,* ***which is among the best in the country,*** *is chronically short of funds.*

**noun** A word that refers to a person, thing, place, feeling, notion, etc. (*cat, desk, glass, physics, sadness, teacher, Hugh, New York*).

**noun phrase** A phrase that contains a noun or pronoun and typically forms the subject or object of a clause or sentence (*a venomous snake, a boat with red sails*).

**number** The subject of a sentence as expressed in terms of singular or plural. The verb must agree with the number of the noun or pronoun that makes up its subject.

**numeral** The expression of a number in the form of a word. Numerals may be subdivided into cardinal numerals and ordinal numerals.

**object** A noun or pronoun that is affected by the action of the verb, usually placed within a sentence after the verb:

*The child threw **the stick.***

*See also* DIRECT OBJECT; INDIRECT OBJECT.

**object case** The form of a pronoun when it serves as the object of a sentence or when it succeeds a preposition (*me, him, them, us*).

**objective** Used to describe the case or form of a pronoun when it serves as the object of a verb or after a preposition (*me, him, them, whom,* etc.).

**ordinal numeral** A number expressed in terms of its place within an ordered sequence (*first, second, third*). *See also* CARDINAL NUMERAL.

**paragraph** A block of writing within a larger work, typically comprising two or more sentences and beginning on a new (often indented) line.

**parentheses** A pair of symbols, ( ), used to enclose a subsidiary clause or piece of additional information, commentary, and the like within a sentence:

> *The police **(who arrived soon afterward)** were hopeful that all would be well.*

**parsing** Distinguishing the constituent parts of a sentence in grammatical terms by describing parts of speech, inflections, and so on.

**participial adjective** An adjective that shares the same form as the present or past participle of a verb (*confusing, interesting*).

**participle** *See* PAST PARTICIPLE; PRESENT PARTICIPLE.

**particle** An adverb or preposition that forms part of a phrasal verb.

**part of speech** The identity of a word as belonging to a particular class (nouns, verbs, adjectives, etc.) depending on the word's function within a sentence.

**passive** Used to describe a sentence in which the subject is affected by the action of the verb (*the window **was opened***).

**past participle** The form of a verb used to express something in the past, typically through the addition of an *-ed* ending (*halted, tried, weeded*) and often in combination with *have* or *be* (*it had closed; she was heartbroken*).

**past tense** Verb tense used to refer to things that happened in the past, in the case of regular verbs expressed through the addition of an *-ed* ending (*hesitated, whispered*).

**perfect tense** The past tense of a verb as formed by the auxiliary verb *have* and (in the case of regular verbs) an *-ed* ending (*I have asked; he has resigned; they have disappeared*).

**period** A punctuation mark (.) used to indicate the end of a sentence or to indicate an abbreviation (*Mr.*).

**person** *See* FIRST PERSON; SECOND PERSON; THIRD PERSON.

**personal pronoun** A pronoun (*I, you, he, she, it, we, they* and their related possessive and reflexive forms) delineating a specific person or thing.

**phonetics** The study and classification of speech sounds.

**phrasal verb (multiword verb)** A verb consisting of a verb in combination with an adverb or preposition or both (*die away, die down*).

**plural** The form of a word that refers to more than one person or thing, typically indicated in the case of regular nouns by the simple addition of an *-s* ending.

**portmanteau word (blend)** A new word created through the combination of two existing words (*shopaholic, triggerhappy*).

**possessive case (genitive case)** The case of a noun or pronoun that indicates possession (***Bob's** house; **my** keys; that ball is **theirs***).

**possessive pronoun** A personal pronoun that indicates possession (*mine, his, hers, its, ours, theirs*).

**postmodifier** A word or phrase that makes specific the meaning of a word or phrase that precedes it.

**postpositive adjective** An adjective that appears immediately after a noun or pronoun (*something **odd**, things **unsaid***).

**pragmatics** The study of the practical applications of language in particular situations.

**predicate** That part of a sentence or clause that describes the subject, usually comprising a verb and any associated objects, complements, or adverbial modifiers.

**predicative adjective** An adjective that follows a linking verb such as *be, become,* or *seem:*

> *That man is **untrustworthy**.*

**prefix** An affix attached to the beginning of an existing word to create a new word with a distinct meaning (***anti**nuclear, **re**open, **un**biased*).

**premodifier** A word or phrase that makes specific the meaning of a word or phrase that follows it.

**preposition** A word or phrase that serves to link two parts of a clause or sentence and typically creates some sort of relationship between them (*after, behind, for, in, of, out,* etc.):

*The tiger backed* **into** *the cage.*

**present participle** The form of a verb used to express something in the continuous present, future, or past, typically through the addition of an *-ing* ending (*sleeping, holding, smiling*) and often in combination with *be* (*she is cleaning; it was ripping*).

**present tense** The form of a verb used to express events happening at the present time (*aim, runs, turns*).

**primary verb** A verb that is capable of being used both as a main verb and as an auxiliary verb (*be, do, have*).

**pronoun** A word that can be used in the place of a noun or noun phrase (*I, he, she, it, both, mine, herself, themselves, these, who, you,* etc.).

**pronunciation** The manner in which a particular word, clause, or sentence is spoken.

**proper noun** A noun referring to a particular person, place, or thing, by convention always written with an initial capital letter (*Abraham, District of Columbia, Buddhism, Peace Corps, Monday*).

**punctuation** The use of special standardized symbols (punctuation marks) to clarify meaning and to indicate the ends of sentences and other breaks in structure.

**question** An interrogative clause or sentence, conventionally indicated by the insertion of a question mark at the end:

*Are you coming with us?*

**question mark** Punctuation mark (?) inserted at the end of a sentence to indicate a direct question.

**quotation marks (inverted commas)** Punctuation marks (" " or ' ') inserted around clauses or sentences to indicate variously that they represent spoken words or a quotation from elsewhere:

*This was not "haute cuisine" territory.*
*"Say nothing, if you value your life," the general warned.*

**reciprocal pronoun** A pronoun (such as *each other*) used when the subjects share the same relationship with one another:

*The siblings had little love for* ***one another.***

**reflexive pronoun** A pronoun that refers to the subject of the clause or sentence within which it is placed, typically formed by adding *-self* or *-selves* to the object or the possessive form of the personal pronoun (*myself, yourself, himself, herself, itself, oneself, ourselves, yourselves, themselves*):

*He had expected better of* ***himself.***

**reflexive verb** A verb that has a reflexive pronoun as its direct object:

*She* ***embarrassed herself*** *at the mall.*

**regular** Used to describe words that conform to a standard pattern.

**relative adverb** Either of the adverbs *when* or *where* when used to introduce a relative clause.

**relative clause** A clause that provides further information about the noun that follows. A relative clause is typically introduced by *that, when, where, which, who,* or *whose:*

*These are the shoes* ***that I told you about.***

**relative pronoun** A pronoun such as *that, which, who, whom,* or *whose* that introduces a relative clause.

**reported speech (indirect speech)** A clause in which the gist of what has been said is communicated without repeating the actual spoken words and thus without resorting to the use of quotation marks:

*The minister replied that he would be absent the following week.*

**reporting clause** A clause comprising a verb of speaking and its subject, as in sentences containing direct or indirect speech:

*"Get yourselves into a straight line,"* ***ordered Lieutenant Johnson.***

**restrictive clause (defining clause)** A clause that contains essential information identifying a particular person or object and which cannot therefore be removed from a sentence without disrupting its meaning:

*The boy* ***applying for the job*** *is waiting outside.*

**rhetorical question** A question that is asked merely for effect and to which a reply is not expected.

**second person** The pronouns *you, yourself, yourselves,* etc., or the form of a verb used with these pronouns.

**semantics** The study of meanings of words and of linguistic development.

**semicolon** A punctuation mark (;) used to indicate a break in the structure or meaning of a sentence, stronger than a comma but not as strong as a colon.

**sentence** A group of clauses or phrases that form a meaningful syntactical unit, conventionally beginning with an initial capital letter and ending with a period, exclamation point, or question mark.

**sentential relative clause** A relative clause that refers to the preceding clause as a whole:

*The decision was greeted with derision,* ***which was predictable.***

**simile** A figure of speech in which two dissimilar things are compared, typically introduced by *like* or *as:*

*She had skin like marble.*

**simple sentence** A sentence that consists of a single clause.

**singular** Referring to only one person, one object, etc., in contrast to plural.

**split infinitive** An infinitive in which an adverb or other word is placed between the *to* and the base part of the verb (*to sometimes break, to gently persuade*).

**standard English** The form of English that is generally considered universally acceptable and formally correct in terms of spelling, grammar, pronunciation, and vocabulary.

**statement** A sentence in which a fact (or facts) is declared, without a response being necessarily expected.

**stress** The emphasizing of a word or part of a word when speaking aloud.

**subject** A word or phrase (usually a noun or pronoun) that precedes the verb in most sentences and is the prime mover behind the action of the verb:

***The child*** *ran into the garden.*

**subject case** The form of a pronoun when it serves as the subject of a sentence (*I, you, he, she, it, we,* etc.).

**subjective** Used to describe the case or form of a pronoun when it serves as the subject of a verb (*I, he, they, who,* etc.).

**subjunct** An adverb that plays a subordinate role in a clause or sentence:

*I thought she seemed* ***rather*** *pleased with herself.*

**subjunctive mood** The form of a verb used in expressing demands, wishes, possibilities, etc.:

*I insist you **return** to the office at once.*

**subordinate clause (dependent clause)** A clause that plays a subordinate role in a sentence and cannot stand alone independently of the rest of the sentence:

*The plan was never likely to work **because of flaws in the preparations.***

**subordinating conjunction (subordinator)** A conjunction that links parts of a sentence that are unequal in status:

*They stopped **when** they reached the roadblock.*

**subordination** The linking of parts of a sentence that are unequal in status, usually through the use of a subordinating conjunction.

**subordinator** *See* SUBORDINATING CONJUNCTION.

**suffix** An affix attached to the end of an existing word to create a new word with a distinct meaning (*breakable, lively, weakness*).

**superlative** An adjective or adverb when used to compare three or more people or things (*wisest, most impressive, most important*).

**syntax** The study of grammar relating to sentence structure.

**tag question** A statement followed by a phrase (such as *is it?* or *aren't you?*) that turns it into a question:

*That's your responsibility, **isn't it?***

**tense** The form of a verb that indicates whether it refers to time present, time past, or some time in the future.

**third person** The pronouns *he, him, himself, she, her, herself, it, itself, they, them, themselves* or the form of a verb used with these pronouns.

**transitive verb** A verb that has a direct object (*I love you; she cooks eggs*), in contrast to an intransitive verb.

**unattached participle** *See* DANGLING PARTICIPLE.

**uncount noun** *See* UNCOUNTABLE NOUN.

**uncountable noun (mass noun, noncount noun, uncount noun)** A noun that cannot normally be made plural and is thus never preceded by ***a*** or ***an*** (*blood, joy, sadness*), in contrast to a countable noun.

**variable noun** A noun that varies in form when changed from singular to plural (*woman/women, chair/chairs*), in contrast to an invariable noun.

**verb** A word expressing action, being, change, or having (*be, fight, love, want*).

**verbless clause** A clause that lacks a verb (*as soon as possible, out of action*).

**verb phrase** A verb that comprises more than one word (*go in, run out*).

**vocative** A word or phrase that serves to address what is being said to a particular person:

> ***Children,*** *stop making such a noise.*

**voice** *See* ACTIVE; PASSIVE.

**vowel** Those letters of the alphabet not otherwise categorized as consonants (*a, e, i, o, u,* and, sometimes, *y*).

**zero plural** A noun that remains the same in its singular and plural forms (*deer, sheep*).

# INDEX

**Boldfaced** page numbers indicate major treatment of a topic. *Italicized* terms indicate a reference to the usage of that word, phrase, prefix, or suffix.

## A

## B

## D

## E

## G



## H

## J



## K



## L

## M

## S